Learning and Teaching Early Math

Most everyone agrees that effective mathematics teaching involves "meeting the students where they are" and helping them build on what they know. But that is often easier said than done. In this important new book for pre- and in-service teachers, early math experts Douglas Clements and Julie Sarama show how "learning trajectories" help diagnose what mathematics a child knows. By opening up new windows to seeing young children and the inherent delight and curiosity behind their mathematical reasoning, learning trajectories ultimately make teaching more joyous. They help teachers understand the varying level of knowledge and thinking of their classes and the individuals within them as key in serving the needs of all children. In straightforward, no-nonsense language, this book summarizes what is known about how children learn mathematics, and how to build on what they know to realize more effective teaching practice. It will help teachers understand the learning trajectories of early mathematics and become quintessential professionals.

Douglas H. Clements is SUNY Distinguished Professor of Early Childhood, Mathematics, and Computer Education at the University at Buffalo, State University of New York.

Julie Sarama is an Associate Professor of Mathematics Education at the University at Buffalo, State University of New York.

Studies in Mathematical Thinking and Learning
Alan H. Schoenfeld, Series Editor

Learning and Teaching Early Math

The Learning Trajectories Approach

Douglas H. Clements and Julie Sarama

University at Buffalo, State University of New York

Routledge
Taylor & Francis Group

NEW YORK AND LONDON

First published 2009
by Routledge
270 Madison Ave, New York, NY 10016

Simultaneously published in the UK
by Routledge
2 Park Square, Milton Park, Abingdon, Oxon OX14 4RN

Routledge is an imprint of the Taylor & Francis Group, an informa business

© 2009 Taylor & Francis

Typeset in Minion by
RefineCatch Limited, Bungay, Suffolk
Printed and bound in the United States of America on acid-free paper by
Edwards Brothers, Inc.

Library of Congress Cataloging-in-Publication Data
Clements, Douglas H.
  Learning and teaching early math : the learning trajectories approach / Douglas H. Clements & Julie Sarama.
     p. cm.—(Studies in mathematical thinking and learning)
  1. Mathematics—Study and teaching (Early childhood)   2. Educational psychology.   3. Child development.
  4. Curriculum planning.   I. Sarama, Julie A.   II. Title.
  QA135.6.C58 2009
  372.7—dc22

                                                                                    2008033304

ISBN10: 0–415–99591–4 (hbk)
ISBN10: 0–415–99592–2 (pbk)
ISBN10: 0–203–88338–1 (ebk)

ISBN13: 978–0–415–99591–7 (hbk)
ISBN13: 978–0–415–99592–4 (pbk)
ISBN13: 978–0–203–88338–9 (ebk)

Contents

Preface

Who dares to teach must never cease to learn.

(John Cotton Dana)

Everyone knows that effective teaching calls for "meeting the students where they are" and helping them build on what they know. But that's easier said than done. Which aspects of the mathematics are important, which less so? How do we diagnose what a child knows? How do we build on that knowledge—in what directions, and in what ways?

*We believe that **learning trajectories** answer these questions and help teachers become more effective professionals.* Just as important, they *open up windows to seeing young children and math in new ways, making teaching more joyous,* because the mathematical reasoning of children is impressive and delightful.

Learning trajectories have three parts: a specific mathematical goal, a developmental path along which children develop to reach that goal, and a set of instructional activities that help children move along that path. So, teachers who understand learning trajectories understand the math, the way children think and learn about math, and how to help children learn it better.

Learning trajectories connect research and practice. They connect children to math. They connect teachers to children. They help teachers understand the level of knowledge and thinking of their classes *and* the individuals in their classes as key in serving the needs of all children. (Equity issues are important to us and to the nation. The entire book is designed to help you teach all children, but equity concerns are discussed at length in Chapters 14, 15, and 16.) This book will help you understand the learning trajectories of early mathematics and become a quintessential professional.

Learning and teaching, of course, take place in a context. For the last decade we have had the honor and advantage of working with several hundred early childhood teachers who have worked with us creating new ideas for teaching and invited us into their classrooms to test these ideas with the children in their charge. Next we wish to share with you a bit about this collaborative work.

Background

In 1998, we began a four-year project funded by the National Science Foundation. The purpose of *Building Blocks—Foundations for Mathematical Thinking, Pre-Kindergarten to Grade 2: Research-based Materials Development* was to create and evaluate mathematics curricula for young children based on a theoretically sound research and development framework. Based on theory and research on early childhood learning and teaching, we determined that *Building Blocks'* basic approach would be *finding the mathematics in, and developing mathematics from, children's activity*. To do so, all aspects of the Building Blocks project are based on learning trajectories. Teachers have found the combination of that basic approach and learning trajectories to be powerful teaching tools.

More than a decade later, we are still finding new opportunities for exciting research and development in early mathematics. Funding from the U.S. Department of Education's Institute of Education Sciences (IES) has allowed us to work closely with hundreds of teachers and thousands of children over the past ten years. All these agencies and individuals have contributed ideas to these books. In addition, these projects have increased our confidence that our approach, based on learning trajectories and rigorous empirical testing at every step, can in turn make a contribution to all educators in the field of early mathematics. The model for working with educators in all positions, from teachers to administrators to trainers to researchers, has been developed with IES funding to our TRIAD project, an acronym for Technology-enhanced, Research-based, Instruction, Assessment, and professional Development.[1]

The "Companion" Books

We believe that our successes are due to the people who have contributed to our projects and to our commitment to grounding everything we have done in research. Because the work has been so drenched in research, we decided to publish two companion books. The companion to the present book reviews the research underlying our *learning trajectories,* emphasizing the research that describes the paths of learning—children's natural progressions in developing the concepts and skills within a certain domain of mathematics. *This* book describes and illustrates how these learning trajectories can be implemented in the classroom.

Reading *this* Book

In straightforward, no-nonsense language, we summarize what is known about how children learn, and how to build on what they know. In Chapter 1, we introduce the topic of mathematics education for very young children. We discuss why people are particularly interested in engaging young children with mathematics and what President Bush's National Math Advisory Panel recommended. Next we describe the idea of learning trajectories in detail. We end with an introduction to the *Building Blocks* project and how learning trajectories are at its core.

Most of the following chapters address one mathematics topic. We describe how children understand and learn about that topic. These descriptions are brief summaries of the more elaborate reviews of the research that can be found in the companion book, *Early Childhood Mathematics Education Research: Learning Trajectories for Young Children* (Sarama & Clements, 2009). Next we describe how experiences—from the beginning of life—and classroom-based education affect children's learning of the topic. Each of these chapters (2 to 12) then culminates in a detailed description of learning trajectories for the chapter's topic.

Read more than the topic chapters, even if you just want to teach a topic! In the last three chapters we discuss issues that are important for putting these ideas into practice. In Chapter 14 we describe how children think about mathematics and how their feelings are involved. Equity concerns complete that chapter. In Chapter 15 we discuss the contexts in which early childhood education occurs, and the curricula that are used. In Chapter 16 we review what we know about specific instructional practices. The topics of these three chapters are unique to this book. Because there is no corresponding chapters in the companion book, there is more research reviewed. We have made the implications for practitioners clear.

To teach children with different needs, and to teach effectively, make sure you read Chapters 14, 15, and especially 16. Some readers may wish to read those chapters immediately following chapter 1! Whichever way you choose, please know that the learning trajectories that describe children's learning and effective teaching for each topic are only *part* of the story—the other critical part is found in those three chapters.

Across all the chapters, this is not a typical book of "cute teaching ideas." We believe, however, that it may be the most practical book you, as a teacher of early mathematics, could read. The many teachers we have worked with claim that, once they understood the learning trajectories and ways to implement them in their classrooms, they—and the children they teach—were changed forever.

Acknowledgments

Appreciation to the Funding Agencies

We wish to express our appreciation for the funding agencies that have not only provided financial support but intellectual support in the form of guidance from program officers (most notably and recently Caroline Ebanks), opportunities to collaborate with other projects, and attend conferences to exchange ideas with colleagues. The ideas and research reported here have been supported by all of the following grants. Any opinions, findings, and conclusions or recommendations expressed in this material are those of the authors and do not necessarily reflect the views of the funding agencies.

1. Clements, D. H. & Sarama, J. *Scaling Up TRIAD: Teaching Early Mathematics for Understanding with Trajectories and Technologies—Supplement.* Awarded by the U.S. Department of Education, IES (Institute of Education Sciences; as part of the Interagency Educational Research Initiative, or IERI program, a combination of IES, NSF, and NIH).
2. Clements, D. H., Sarama, J., & Lee, J. *Scaling Up TRIAD: Teaching Early Mathematics for Understanding with Trajectories and Technologies.* Awarded by the U.S. Department of Education, IES (Institute of Education Sciences; as part of the Interagency Educational Research Initiative, or IERI program, a combination of IES, NSF, and NIH).
3. Clements, D. H., Sarama, J., Klein, A., & Starkey, Prentice. *Scaling Up the Implementation of a Pre-Kindergarten Mathematics Curricula: Teaching for Understanding with Trajectories and Technologies.* Awarded by the National Science Foundation (NSF, as part of the Interagency Educational Research Initiative, or IERI program, a combination of NSF, U.S. Dept. of Education IES, and NIH).
4. Starkey, Prentice, Sarama, J., Clements, D. H., & Klein, A. *A Longitudinal Study of the Effects of a Pre-Kindergarten Mathematics Curriculum on Low-Income Children's Mathematical Knowledge.* Awarded by OERI, Department of Education as Preschool Curriculum Evaluation Research (PCER) project.
5. Clements, D. H. *Conference on Standards for Preschool and Kindergarten Mathematics Education.* Awarded by the ExxonMobil Foundation.
6. Clements, D. H., Watt, Daniel, Bjork, Elizabeth, & Lehrer, Richard. *Technology-Enhanced Learning of Geometry in Elementary Schools.* Awarded by the National Science Foundation, Elementary, Secondary, and Informal Science Education, Research on Educational Policy and Practice.
7. Clements, D. H. *Conference on Standards for Preschool and Kindergarten Mathematics*

Education. Awarded by the National Science Foundation, Elementary, Secondary, and Informal Science Education, grant number ESI-9817540.

8. Clements, D. H. & Sarama, J. *Building Blocks—Foundations for Mathematical Thinking, Pre-Kindergarten to Grade 2: Research-based Materials Development.* Awarded by the National Science Foundation, Instructional Materials Development, grant number ESI-9730804.

9. Sarama, J. & Clements, D. H. *Planning for Professional Development in Pre-School Mathematics: Meeting the Challenge of Standards 2000.* Awarded by the National Science Foundation, Teacher Enhancement Program, grant number ESI-9814218.

Appreciation to SRA/McGraw-Hill

The author and Publisher wish to express appreciation to SRA/McGraw-Hill for kindly giving permission for the many screen shots provided by them for use throughout this title.

1

Young Children and Mathematics Learning

The snow was falling in Boston and preschool teacher Sarah Gardner's children were coming in slowly, one bus at a time. She had been doing high-quality mathematics all year, but was still amazed at her children's keeping track of the situation: The children kept saying, "Now 11 are here and 7 absent. Now 13 are here and 5 absent. Now. . . ."

Why are so many people interested in mathematics for very young children?[1] According to a recent report from the U.S. President's National Math Panel, mathematics is increasingly important in a modern global economy, but mathematics achievement in the U.S. has been declining. Also, U.S. math achievement is far lower than that of most other countries, as early as first grade, kindergarten . . . and even preschool! U.S. children do not even get the *chance* to learn the more advanced mathematics taught in many other countries.

An even larger and more damaging gap lies between children growing up in higher- and lower-resource communities. For these children especially, the long-term success of their learning and development requires high-quality experience during their early "years of promise" (Carnegie Corporation, 1998). These early years have been found to be *especially important for mathematics*

During most of the 20th century, the United States possessed peerless mathematical prowess—not just as measured by the depth and number of the mathematical specialists who practiced here but also by the scale and quality of its engineering, science, and financial leadership, and even by the extent of mathematical education in its broad population. But without substantial and sustained changes to its educational system, the United States will relinquish its leadership in the 21st century.

The National Math Panel[2] (NMP, 2008, p. xi)

development. From the first years of life children have an ability to learn math and develop their interest in math. What they know when they enter kindergarten and first grade predicts their mathematics achievement for years to come—even throughout their school career. Moreover, what they know in math predicts their *reading* achievement later. Their early knowledge of literacy also predicts their later reading ability ... but that's all. Because math predicts later math and later reading, mathematics appears to be a core component of cognition.

If children have limited knowledge initially and achieve less later in school, especially compared to other countries, can there possibly be a bright spot? Yes. In high quality early childhood education programs, young children can engage in surprisingly deep investigations of mathematics ideas. They can learn skills, problem-solving, and concepts in ways that are natural and motivating to them. *This brings us to the main reason to engage young children in mathematics.*

Young children love to think mathematically. They become exhilarated by their own ideas and the ideas of others. To develop the whole child, we must develop the mathematical child. Further, teachers enjoy the reasoning and learning that high-quality mathematics education brings forth from their children. High-quality mathematics throughout early childhood does not involving pushing elementary arithmetic onto younger children. Instead, good education allows children to experience mathematics as they play in and explore their world. A higher proportion of children are in early care and education programs every year. We teachers are responsible for bringing the knowledge and intellectual delight of mathematics to all children, especially those who have not yet had many high-quality educational experiences. Good teachers can meet this challenge with research-based "tools."

Research and expert opinion provide guidance on how to help children learn in ways that are both appropriate and effective. In this book, we pull all that knowledge together to provide *learning trajectories* for each major topic in early mathematics.

> *Most children acquire considerable knowledge of numbers and other aspects of mathematics before they enter kindergarten. This is important, because the mathematical knowledge that kindergartners bring to school is related to their mathematics learning for years thereafter—in elementary school, middle school, and even high school. Unfortunately, most children from low-income backgrounds enter school with far less knowledge than peers from middle-income backgrounds, and the achievement gap in mathematical knowledge progressively widens throughout their PreK—12 years.*
>
> The National Math Panel (NMP, 2008, p. xvii)

> *Fortunately, encouraging results have been obtained for a variety of instructional programs developed to improve the mathematical knowledge of preschoolers and kindergartners, especially those from low-income backgrounds. There are effective techniques—derived from scientific research on learning—that could be put to work in the classroom today to improve children's mathematical knowledge.*
>
> The National Math Panel (NMP, 2008, p. xvii)

What are Learning Trajectories?

Children follow natural developmental progressions in learning and development. As a simple example, they learn to crawl, then walk, then run, skip, and jump with increasing speed and dexterity. They follow natural developmental progressions in learning math, too, learning mathematical ideas and skills in their own way. When teachers understand these developmental progressions, and sequence activities based on them, they build mathematics learning environments that are particularly developmentally appropriate and effective. These developmental paths are the

Figure 1.1 Carmen Brown encourages a preschooler to *mathematize*.

basis for this book's *learning trajectories*. Learning trajectories help us answer several questions. What objectives should we establish? Where do we start? How do we know where to go next? How do we get there?

Learning trajectories have three parts: a mathematical goal, a developmental path along which children develop to reach that goal, and a set of instructional activities, or tasks, matched to each of the levels of thinking in that path that help children develop ever higher levels of thinking. Let's examine each of these three parts.

Goals: The Big Ideas of Mathematics

The first part of a learning trajectory is a *mathematical goal*. Our goals are the *big ideas of mathematics*—clusters of concepts and skills that are mathematically central and coherent, consistent with children's thinking, and generative of future learning. These big ideas come from several large projects, including those from the National Council of Teachers of Mathematics and the National Math Panel (Clements & Conference Working Group, 2004; NCTM, 2006; NMP, 2008). For example, one big idea is *counting can be used to find out how many in a collection*.

Development Progressions: The Paths of Learning

The second part of a learning trajectory consists of levels of thinking, each more sophisticated than the last, that lead to achieving the mathematical goal. That is, the developmental progression describes a typical path children follow in developing understanding and skill about that mathematical topic. Development of mathematics

> *Humans are born with a fundamental sense of quantity.*
>
> (Geary, 1994, p. 1)

abilities begins when life begins. As we will see, young children have certain mathematical-like competencies in number, spatial sense, and patterns from birth. However, young children's ideas and their interpretations of situations are uniquely different from those of adults. For this reason, good early childhood teachers are careful not to assume that children "see" situations, problems, or solutions as adults do. Instead, good teachers interpret what the child is doing and thinking and attempt to see the situation from the child's point of view. Similarly, when they interact with the child, these teachers also consider the instructional tasks and their own actions from the child's point of view. This makes early childhood teaching both demanding and rewarding.

Our learning trajectories provide simple labels and examples for each level of each developmental progression. The "Developmental Progression" column in Table 1.1 describes three main levels of thinking in the counting learning trajectory (this is just a sample of levels that actually have other levels in between them—the full learning trajectory is described in Chapter 3). Under each description is an example of children's thinking and behavior for each level.

Instructional Tasks: The Paths of Teaching

The third part of a learning trajectory consists of a set of instructional tasks matched to each of the levels of thinking in the developmental progression. These tasks are designed to help children learn

Table 1.1 Samples from the Learning Trajectory for Counting.

Age (years)	Developmental Progression	Instructional Tasks
1–2	**Chanter** *Verbal* Chants "sing-song" or sometimes indistinguishable number words. Count for me. "one, two-twee, four, sev-, en, ten"	Repeated experience with the counting sequence in varied contexts.
3	**Corresp>Corresponder** Keeps one-to-one correspondence between counting words and objects (one word for each object), at least for small groups of objects laid in a line. Counts: □ □ □ □ "1, 2, 3, 4" But may answer the question, "How many?" by re-counting the objects or naming any number word.	*Kitchen Counter* Students click on objects one at a time while the numbers from one to ten are counted aloud. For example, they click on pieces of food and a bite is taken out of each as it is counted.
	Counter (10) Counts arrangements of objects to 10. May be able to write numerals to represent 1–10. May be able to tell the number just after or just before another number, but only by counting up from 1. Accurately counts a line of 9 blocks and says there are 9. What comes after 4? "1, 2, 3, 4, 5. 5!"	*Counting Towers (Up to 10)* A day before read Shape Space. Ask what shapes work well in which part of a tower (e.g., would the "tip on the triangle" make it a good base?). Set up stations with different objects to stack. Encourage children to stack as many as they can, and count them to see how many they stacked.

the ideas and skills needed to achieve that level of thinking. That is, as teachers, we can use these tasks to promote children's growth from one level to the next. The last column of Table 1.1 provides example tasks. (Again, the complete learning trajectory in Chapter 3 includes not only all the developmental levels but several instructional tasks for each level.)

In summary, learning trajectories describe the goals of learning, the thinking and learning processes of children at various levels, and the learning activities in which they might engage. People often have several questions about learning trajectories. You may wish to read our responses to those questions that interest you now and return to this section after you read more about specific learning trajectories in the chapters that follow.

Frequently Asked Questions (FAQ) about Learning Trajectories

Why use learning trajectories? Learning trajectories allow teachers to build the *mathematics of children—the thinking of children as it develops naturally.* So, we know that all the goals and activities are within the developmental capacities of children. We know that each level provides a natural *developmental building block* to the next level. Finally, we know that the activities provide the *mathematical building blocks* for school success, because the research on which they are based typically involves more children who have had the educational advantages that allow them to do well at school.

When are children "at" a level? Children are identified to be "at" a certain level when most of their behaviors reflect the thinking—ideas and skills—of that level. Often, they show a few behaviors from the next (and previous) levels as they learn.

Can children work at more than one level at the same time? Yes, although most children work mainly at one level or in transition between two levels (naturally, if they are tired or distracted, they may operate at a much lower level). Levels are not "absolute stages." They are "benchmarks" of complex growth that represent distinct ways of thinking. So, another way to think of them is as a sequence of different *patterns* of thinking and reasoning. Children are continually learning, within levels and moving between them.

Can children jump ahead? Yes, especially if there are separate "subtopics." For example, we have combined many counting competencies into one "Counting" sequence with subtopics, such as verbal counting skills. Some children learn to count to 100 at age 6 after learning to count objects to 10 or more; some may learn that verbal skill earlier. The subtopic of verbal counting skills would still be followed. Children also may learn deeply and jump ahead several "levels" in some cases.

Are all levels similar in nature? Most levels are *levels of thinking*—a distinct period of time of qualitatively distinct ways of thinking. However, some are merely "levels of attainment," similar to a mark on a wall to show a child's height, that is, a couple signify simply that a child has gained more knowledge. For example, children must learn to name or write more numerals, but knowing more does not require deeper or more complex thinking. Thus, some trajectories are more tightly constrained by natural cognitive development than others. Often a critical component of such constraints is the mathematical development in a domain; that is, mathematics is a highly sequential, hierarchical domain in which certain ideas and skills must be learned before others.

How are learning trajectories different from just a scope and sequence? They are related, of course. But they are *not* lists of everything children need to learn, because they don't cover every single "fact" and they emphasize the "big ideas." Further, they are about children's levels of thinking, not just about the answer to a mathematics question. So, for example, a single mathematical problem may be solved *differently* by students at *different* (separable) levels of thinking.

Does every trajectory represent just "one path"? In broad terms, there is one main developmental path; however, for some topics, there are "subtrajectories"—strands within the topic. For example, as previously stated, the counting learning trajectory in Chapter 3 includes both verbal and object counting—they are related, but can develop somewhat independently. In some cases, the names make this clear. For example, in Comparing and Ordering, some levels are about the "Comparer" levels, and others about building a "mental number line." Similarly, the related subtrajectories of "Composition" and "Decomposition" are easy to distinguish. Sometimes, for clarification, subtrajectories are indicated with a note in italics after the title. For example, in Shapes, "Parts" and "Representing" are subtrajectories within the Shapes trajectory.

Other questions address *how to use* the learning trajectories.

How do these developmental levels support teaching and learning? The levels help teachers, as well as curriculum developers, assess, teach, and sequence activities. *Teachers who understand learning trajectories (especially the developmental levels that are at their foundation) are more effective and efficient.* Through planned teaching and also by encouraging informal, incidental mathematics, teachers help children learn *at an appropriate and deep level.*

There are ages in the charts. Should I plan to help children develop just the levels that correspond to my children's ages? No! The ages in the table are typical ages children develop these ideas. *But these are rough guides only*—children differ widely. Furthermore, the ages are often lower bounds on what children achieve without high-quality instruction. So, these are *"starting levels" not goals.* We have found that children who are provided high-quality mathematics experiences are capable of developing to levels one or more years beyond their peers.

Are the instructional tasks the only way to teach children to achieve higher levels of thinking? No, there are many ways. In some cases, however, there is some research evidence that these are especially effective ways. In other cases, they are simply illustrations of the *kind* of activity that would be appropriate to reach that level of thinking. Further, teachers need to use a variety of pedagogical strategies in teaching the content, presenting the tasks, guiding children in completing them, and so forth.

Other Critical Goals: Strategies, Reasoning, Creativity, and a Productive Disposition

Learning trajectories are organized around topics, but they include far more than facts and ideas. *Processes* and *attitudes* are important in every one. Chapter 13 focuses on general processes, such as problem-solving and reasoning. But these general processes are also an integral part of every learning trajectory. Also, specific processes are involved in every learning trajectory. For example, the process of composition—putting together and taking apart—is fundamental to both number and arithmetic (e.g., adding and subtracting) and geometry (shape composition).

Finally, other general educational goals must never be neglected. The "habits of mind" mentioned in the box include curiosity, imagination, inventiveness, risk-taking, creativity, and persistence. These are some of the components of the

As important as mathematical content are general mathematical processes such as problem-solving, reasoning and proof, communication, connections, and representation; specific mathematical processes such as organizing information, patterning, and composing, and habits of mind such as curiosity, imagination, inventiveness, persistence, willingness to experiment, and sensitivity to patterns. All should be involved in a high-quality early childhood mathematics program.

(Clements & Conference Working Group, 2004, p. 57)

essential goal of *productive disposition*. Children need to view mathematics as sensible, useful, and worthwhile and view themselves as capable of thinking mathematically. Children should also come to appreciate the beauty and creativity that is at the heart of mathematics.

All these should be involved in a high-quality early childhood mathematics program. These goals are included in the suggestions for teaching throughout this book. Further, Chapters 14, 15, and 16 discuss how to achieve these goals. These chapters discuss different learning and teaching contexts, including early childhood school settings and education, equity issues, affect, and instructional strategies.

Learning Trajectories and the *Building Blocks* Project

The *Building Blocks* project was funded by the National Science Foundation (NSF)[3] to develop Pre-K to grade 2, software-enhanced, mathematics curricula. *Building Blocks* was designed to enable all young children to build mathematics concepts, skills, and processes. The name *Building Blocks* has three meanings (see Figure 1.1). First, our goals are to help children develop the main *mathematical building blocks*—that is, the *big ideas* described previously. Second is the related

> *The overriding premise of our work is that throughout the grades from pre-K through 8 all students can and should be mathematically proficient. [p. 10]*
>
> *Mathematical proficiency . . . has five strands:*
>
> - *conceptual understanding— comprehension of mathematical concepts, operations, and relations*
> - *procedural fluency—skill in carrying out procedures flexibly, accurately, efficiently, and appropriately*
> - *strategic competence—ability to formulate, represent, and solve mathematical problems*
> - *adaptive reasoning—capacity for logical thought, reflection, explanation, and justification*
> - *productive disposition—habitual inclination to see mathematics as sensible, useful, and worthwhile, coupled with a belief in diligence and one's own efficacy.*
>
> (Kilpatrick, Swafford, & Findell, 2001, p. 5)

goal to develop *cognitive building blocks:* general cognitive and metacognitive (higher-order) processes such as moving or combining shapes to higher-order thinking processes such as self regulation. The third is the most straightforward—children should be using building blocks for many purposes, but one of them is for learning mathematics.

Based on theory and research on early childhood learning and teaching (Bowman, Donovan, & Burns, 2001; Clements, 2001), we determined that *Building Blocks'* basic approach would be *finding the mathematics in, and developing mathematics from, children's activity. To do so, all aspects of the* Building Blocks *project are based on learning trajectories.* Therefore, most of the examples of learning trajectories stemmed from our work developing, field-testing, and evaluating curricula from that project.

Manipulative Building Blocks

Mathematical Building Blocks

Cognitive Building Blocks

Number

Geometry

Copying, creating, and combining numbers and shapes.

Figure 1.1 The Building Blocks project was named because we wanted to use manipulatives like children's building blocks (on and off the computer) to help children develop mathematical and cognitive building blocks—the foundations for later learning (see http://www.gse.buffalo.edu/org/buildingblocks/).

Final Words

Against this background, let us explore the learning trajectories in Chapters 2 through 12. Chapter 2 begins with the critical topic of *number*. When do children first understand number? *How* do they do it? How can we help children's initial ideas develop?

2
Quantity, Number, and Subitizing

> Three pictures hang in front of a six-month-old child. The first shows
> two dots, the others one dot and three dots. The infant hears three
> drumbeats. Her eyes move to the picture with three dots.

Before you read farther, what do you *make* of this startling research finding? *How* in the world could such a young child *do* this? At some intuitive level, this infant has recognized number, and a change in number. When developed, and connected to verbal number names, this ability is called *subitizing*—recognizing the numerosity of a group quickly, from the Latin "to arrive suddenly." In other words, people can see a small collection and almost instantly tell how many objects are in it. Research shows that this is *one of the main abilities very young children should develop*. Children from low-resource communities and those with special needs often lag in subitizing ability, harming their mathematical development. This is why the first learning trajectory we discuss involves subitizing.

Types of Subitizing

When you "just see" how many objects in a very small collection, you are using *perceptual subitizing* (Clements, 1999b). For example, you might see three dots on a die and say "three." You perceive the three dots intuitively and simultaneously.

How is it you can see an eight-dot domino and "just know" the total number, when evidence indicates that this lies above the limits of perceptual subitizing? You are using *conceptual subitizing*—seeing the parts and putting together the whole. That is, you might see each side of the domino as composed of four individual dots and as "one four." You see the domino as composed of two groups of four and as "one eight." All of this can happen quickly—it is still subitizing—and often is not conscious.

Another categorization involves the different types of things people can subitize. Spatial patterns such as those on dominoes are just one type. Other patterns are temporal and kinesthetic, including finger patterns, rhythmic patterns, and spatial-auditory patterns. Creating and using these patterns through conceptual subitizing helps children develop abstract number and arithmetic strategies. For example, children use temporal patterns when counting on. "I knew there were three more so

I just said, nine . . . *ten, eleven, twelve*" (rhythmically gesturing three times, one "beat" with each count). They use finger patterns to figure out addition problems. Children who cannot subitize conceptually are handicapped in learning such arithmetic processes. Children who can may only subitize small numbers at first. Such actions, however, can be "stepping stones" to the construction of more sophisticated procedures with larger numbers.

Subitizing and Mathematics

The ideas and skills of subitizing start developing very early, but they, as every other area of mathematics, are not just "simple, basic skills." Subitizing introduces basic ideas of cardinality— "how many," ideas of "more" and "less," ideas of parts and wholes and their relationships, beginning arithmetic, and, in general, ideas of quantity. Developed well, these are related, forming webs of connected ideas that are the building blocks of mathematics through elementary, middle, and high school and beyond.

As we discuss the details of children's initial learning of subitizing, let's not lose the whole—the big picture—of children's mathematical future. Let's not lose the wonderment that children so young can think, profoundly, about mathematics.

Moving from Easy to More Challenging Subitizing Tasks

An important, even if obvious, factor in determining the difficulty of subitizing tasks is the size of the collection. At 3 years of age or earlier, children can distinguish between collections with one and more than one objects. In the next year, they also distinguish two, then three. Four-year-olds recognize collections up to up to four, and then subitizing and counting become connected, a point to which we return in Chapter 3. Another factor is the spatial arrangement of objects. For young children, objects in a line are easiest, then rectangular arrangements (pairs of objects in rows) and "dice" or "domino" arrangements, then scrambled arrangements.

Experience and Education

Two preschoolers are watching a parade. "Look! There's clowns!" yells Paul. "And three horses!" exclaims his friend Nathan. Both friends are having a great experience. But only Nathan is having a mathematical experience at the same time. Other children see, perhaps, a brown, a black, and a dappled horse. Nathan sees the same colors, but also sees a quantity—*three* horses. The difference is probably this: At school and at home, Nathan's teachers and family notice and talk about numbers.

Parents, teachers, and other caregivers should begin naming very small collections with numbers after children have established names and categories for some physical properties such as shape and color (Sandhofer & Smith, 1999). Numerous experiences naming such collections help children build connections between quantity terms (number, how many) and number words, then build word-cardinality connections (• • is "two") and finally build connections among the representations of a given number. Nonexamples are important, too, to clarify the boundaries of the number (Baroody, Lai, & Mix, 2006).

In contrast to this research-based practice, mis-educative experiences (Dewey, 1938/1997) may lead children to perceive collections as figural arrangements that are not exact. Richardson (2004) reported that for years she thought her children understood perceptual patterns, such as those on dice. However, when she finally asked them to *reproduce* the patterns, she was amazed that they did not use the same number of counters. For example, some drew an "X" with nine dots and called it "five." Thus, without appropriate tasks and close observations, she had not seen that her children did not even accurately imagine patterns, and their patterns were certainly not numerical. Such insights are important in understanding and promoting children's mathematical thinking.

Textbooks often present sets that discourage subitizing. Their pictures combine many inhibiting factors, including complex embedding, different units with poor form (e.g., birds that are not compact as opposed to squares), lack of symmetry, and irregular arrangements (Carper, 1942; Dawson, 1953). Such complexity hinders conceptual subitizing, increases errors, and encourages simple one-by-one counting.

Due to their curriculum, or perhaps their lack of knowledge of subitizing, teachers do not do sufficient subitizing work. One study showed that children *regressed* in subitizing from the beginning to the end of kindergarten (Wright, Stanger, Cowper, & Dyson, 1994).

Research provides guidelines for developmentally generative subitizing. Naming small groups with numbers, before counting, helps children understand number words and their cardinal meaning without having to shift between ordinal (counting items in order) and cardinal uses of number words inherent in counting (cf. Fuson, 1992a). Briefly, such naming of small, subitized groups can more quickly, simply, and directly provide a wide variety of examples and contrasting counterexamples for number words and concepts (Baroody, Lai, & Mix, 2005). These can be used to help infuse early counting with meaning (see Chapter 3 on counting).

Another benefit of number recognition and subitizing activities is that different arrangements suggest different views of that number (Figure 2.1).

Many number activities can promote conceptual subitizing. Perhaps the most direct activity is known as "Quickdraw" (Wheatley, 1996) or "Snapshots" (Clements & Sarama, 2003a). As an example, tell children they have to quickly take a "snapshot" of how many they see—their minds have to take a "fast picture." Show them a collection of children for 2 seconds, and then cover it. Then, ask children to construct a collection with the same number or say the number. At first, use lines of objects, then rectangular shapes, and then dice arrangements with small numbers. As children learn, use different arrangements and larger numbers.

There are many worthwhile variations of the "Snapshots" activity.

- Have students construct a quick image arrangement with manipulatives.
- Play Snapshots on the computer (see Figure 2.2).
- Play a matching game. Show several cards, all but one of which have the same number. Ask children which does not belong.
- Play concentration games with cards that have different arrangements for each number and a rule that you can only "peek" for 2 seconds.
- Give each child cards with 0 to 10 dots in different arrangements. Have students spread the cards in front of them. Then announce a number. Students find the matching card as fast as possible and hold it up. Have them use different sets of cards, with different arrangements, on different days. Later, hold up a written numeral as their cue. Adapt other card games for use with these card sets (see Clements & Callahan, 1986).

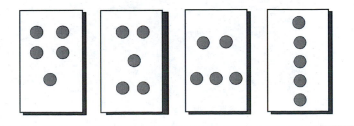

Figure 2.1 Arrangements for conceptual subitizing that may suggest 5 as 4 + 1, 2 + 1 + 2, 2 + 3 or 5.

- Place various arrangements of dots on a large sheet of poster board. With students gathered around you, point to one of the groups as students say its number as fast as possible. Rotate the poster board on different sessions.
- Challenge students to say the number that is one (later, two) more than the number on the quick image. They might also respond by showing a numeral card or writing the numeral. Or, they can find the arrangement that matches the numeral you show.
- Encourage students to play any of these games as a free-time or station activity.
- Remember that patterns can also be temporal and kinesthetic, including rhythmic and spatial-auditory patterns. A motivating subitizing and numeral writing activity involves auditory rhythms. Scatter children around the room on the floor with individual chalkboards. Walk around the room, then stop and make a number of sounds, such as ringing a bell three times. Children should write the numeral 3 (or hold up three fingers) on their chalkboards and hold it up.

Across many types of activities, from class discussions to textbooks, show children pictures of numbers that encourage conceptual subitizing. Follow these guidelines to make groups to be subitized: (a) groups should not be embedded in pictorial context; (b) simple forms such as homogeneous groups of circles or squares (rather than pictures of animals or mixtures or any shapes) should be used for the units; (c) regular arrangements should be emphasized (most including symmetry, with linear arrangements for preschoolers and rectangular arrangements for older students being easiest); and (d) good figure-ground contrast should be provided.

Encourage conceptual subitizing to help students advance to more sophisticated addition and subtraction (see also Chapters 5 and 6). For example, a student may add by counting on one or two, solving 4 + 2 by saying "4, 5, 6," but be unable to count on five or more, as would be required to solve 4 + 5 by counting "4, 5, 6, 7, 8, 9." Counting on two, however, gives them a way to figure out how counting on works. Later they can learn to count on with larger numbers, by developing their conceptual subitizing or by learning different ways of "keeping track." Eventually, students come to recognize number patterns as both a whole (as a unit itself) and a composite of parts (individual

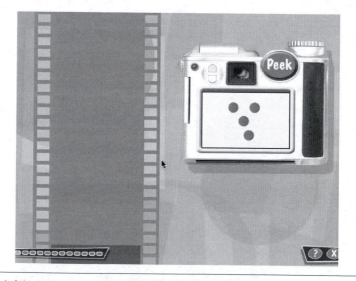

Figure 2.2 An early level of the activity "Snapshots" from *Building Blocks*. (a) Children are shown an arrangement of dots for 2 seconds; (b) They are then asked to click on the corresponding numeral. They can "peek" for 2 more seconds if necessary; (c) They are given feedback verbally and by seeing the dots again.

Figure 2.2b

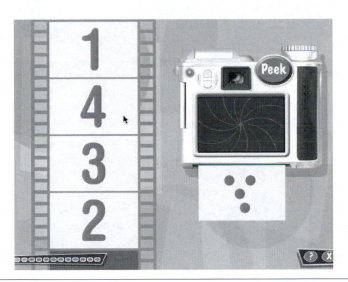

Figure 2.2c

units). At this stage, a student is capable of viewing number and number patterns as units of units (Steffe & Cobb, 1988). For example, students can repeatedly answer what number is "10 more" than another number. "What is ten more than 23." "33!" "Ten more?" "43!"

Learning Trajectory for Recognition of Number and Subitizing

Due to the nature of subitizing, this learning trajectory is straightforward. The goal is increasing children's ability to subitize numbers, as described in the Curriculum Focal Points in Figure 2.3. To meet that goal, Table 2.1 provides the two additional components of the learning trajectory, the developmental progression and the instructional tasks. (Note that the ages in all the learning trajectory tables are only approximate, especially because the age of acquisition usually depends

Pre-K

Number and Operations: Developing an understanding of whole numbers, including concepts of correspondence, counting, cardinality, and comparison

Children develop an understanding of the meanings of whole numbers and recognize the number of objects in small groups without counting . . .

Kindergarten

Number and Operations: Representing, comparing, and ordering whole numbers and joining and separating sets

Children choose, combine, and apply effective strategies for answering quantitative questions, including quickly recognizing the number in a small set . . .

Figure 2.3 Curriculum focal points (NCTM, 2006) emphasizing subitizing in the early years.[1]

heavily on experience. Children who receive high-quality education progress one or more years beyond the "typical" ages in these learning trajectories.) Using the "Snapshots" activity described above as one basic instructional task, the learning trajectory shows different number and arrangements of dots that illustrate instructional tasks designed to promote that level thinking. *Although the activities in the learning trajectories presented in this book constitute a research-based core of an early childhood curriculum, a complete curriculum includes more* (e.g., relationships between trajectories and many other considerations; for example, see Chapter 15).

As an extension, later primary grade students can improve numerical *estimation* with modifications of "Snapshots." For example, show students arrangements that are too large to subitize exactly. Encourage them to use subitizing in their estimation strategies. Emphasize that using good strategies and being "close" is the goal, not getting the exact number. Begin with organized geometric patterns, but include scrambled arrangements eventually. Encourage students, especially those in higher grades, to build more sophisticated strategies: from guessing to counting as much as possible and then guessing to comparing ("It was more than the previous one") to grouping ("They are spread about four in each place. I circled groups of four in my head and then counted six groups. So, 24!"). Students do perform better, using more sophisticated strategies and frames of reference, after engaging in such activities (Markovits & Hershkowitz, 1997). For these and for all subitizing activities, stop frequently to allow students to share their strategies. *If students do not quickly develop more sophisticated strategies based on place value and arithmetic operations, estimation activities may not be a good use of instructional time.* "Guessing" is not mathematical thinking. (See Ch. 4.)

Meeting special needs. Special populations deserve special attention to subitizing. Because conceptual subitizing often depends on accurate enumeration skill, teachers should remedy deficiencies in counting early (Baroody, 1986). Teachers should cultivate familiarity of regular patterns by playing games that use number cubes or dominoes and avoid taking basic number competencies such as subitizing for granted in special populations.

Pattern recognition of fives and tens frames, such as illustrated in Figure 2.4, can assist students with mental handicaps and learning disabilities as they learn to recognize the five- and ten-frame configuration for each number. "These arrangements . . . help a student first to recognize the number and use the model in calculating sums. It is this image of the number that stays with the student and becomes significant" (Flexer, 1989). Visual-kinesthetic finger patterns can similarly help, especially with the critical number combinations that sum to ten.

Table 2.1 A Learning Trajectory for Recognition of Number and Subitizing.

Age (years)	Developmental Progression	Instructional Tasks
0–1	**Pre-Explicit Number** Within the first year, dishabituates to number, but does not have explicit, intentional knowledge of number. For infants, this is first collections of rigid objects one.	Besides providing a rich sensory, manipulative environment, use of words such as "more" and actions of adding objects directs attention to comparisons.
1–2	**Small Collection Namer** Names groups of 1 to 2, sometimes 3. Shown a pair of shoes, says, "Two shoes."	Gesture to a small group of objects (1 or 2, later 3 when the children capable). Say, "There are two balls. Two!" When the children are able, ask them how many there are. This should be a natural part of interaction *throughout* the day. Name collections as "two." Also include nonexamples as well as examples, saying, for instance, "That's not two. That's three!" Or, put out three groups of two and one group of three and have the child find out "the one that is not like the others." Discuss why. Make your own groups in canonically structured arrangements, such as the following for 3, and see how fast children can name them.
3	**Maker of Small Collections** Nonverbally makes a small collection (no more than 4, usually 1–3) with the same number another collection (via mental model; i.e., not necessarily by matching—for that process, see Compare Number). Might also be verbal. When shown a collection of 3, makes another collection of 3.	Ask children to get the right number of crackers (etc.) for a small number of children. Lay out a small collection, say two blocks. Hide them. Ask children to make a group that has the same number of blocks as your group has. After they have finished, show them your group and ask them if they got the same number. Name the number. Play "Snapshots" on or off the computer with matching items.
4	**Perceptual Subitizer to 4** Instantly recognizes collections up to 4 briefly shown and verbally names the number of items. When shown 4 objects briefly, says "four."	Play "Snapshots" with collections of 1 to 4 objects, arranged in line or other simple arrangement, asking children to respond verbally with the number name. Use any of the bulleted modifications on pp. 11–12. Start with the smaller numbers and easier arrangements, moving to those of moderate difficulty only as children are fully competent and confident.

Continued Overleaf

Age (years)	Developmental Progression	Instructional Tasks
5	**Perceptual Subitizer to 5** Instantly recognizes briefly shown collections up to 5 and verbally names the number of items. Shown 5 objects briefly, says "five."	Play "Snapshots" on or off the computer with matching dots to numerals with groups up to and including 5. 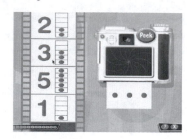 Play "Snapshots" with dot cards, starting with easy arrangements, moving to more difficult arrangements as children are able. 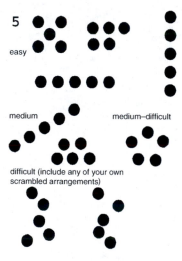
	Conceptual Subitizer to 5 Verbally labels all arrangements to about 5, when shown only briefly. "5! Why? I saw 3 and 2 and so I said five."	Use different arrangements of the various modifications of "Snapshots" to develop conceptual subitizing and ideas about addition and subtraction. The goal is to encourage students to "see the addends and the sum as in 'two olives and two olives make four olives' " (Fuson, 1992b, p. 248). 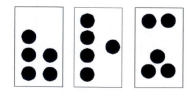

Age (years)	Developmental Progression	Instructional Tasks
	Conceptual Subitizer to 10 Verbally labels most briefly shown arrangements to 6, then up to 10, using groups. "In my mind, I made two groups of 3 and one more, so 7."	Play "Snapshots" on or off the computer with matching dots to numerals. The computer version's feedback emphasizes that "three and four make seven." 
6	**Conceptual Subitizer to 20** Verbally labels structured arrangements up to 20, shown only briefly, using groups. "I saw three fives, so 5, 10, 15."	Use fives and tens frame to help children visualize addition combinations, but also move to mental arithmetic. 
7	**Conceptual Subitizer with Place Value and Skip Counting** Verbally labels structured arrangements, shown only briefly, using groups, skip counting, and place value. "I saw groups of tens and twos, so 10, 20, 30, 40, 42, 44, 46 . . . 46!"	Play "Snapshots" on or off the computer with matching dots to numerals. 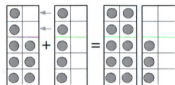
8	**Conceptual Subitizer with Place Value and Multiplication** Verbally labels structured arrangements shown only briefly, using groups, multiplication, and place value. "I saw groups of tens and threes, so I thought, 5 tens is 50 and 4 threes is 12, so 62 in all."	Play "Snapshots" with structured groups that support the use of increasingly sophisticated mental strategies and operations, such as asking children how many dots in the following picture. 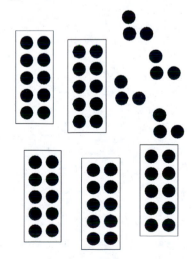

Figure 2.4

Final Words

"Subitizing is a fundamental skill in the development of students' understanding of number" (Baroody, 1987, p. 115) and must be developed. However, it is not the only way to quantify groups. Counting is ultimately a more general and powerful method, and we turn to this topic in Chapter 3.

3
Verbal and Object Counting

Before her fourth birthday, Abby was given five train engines. She walked in one day with three of them. Her father said, "Where's the other ones?" "I lost them," she admitted. "How many are missing?" he asked. "I have 1, 2, 3. So [pointing in the air] foooour, fiiiive . . . two are missing, four and five. [pause] No! I want these to be [pointing at the three engines] one, three, and five. So, two and four are missing. Still two missing, but they're numbers two and four."

Abby thought about counting and numbers—at least small numbers—abstractly. She could assign 1, 2, and 3 to the three engines, or 1, 3, and 5! Moreover, she could count the numbers. That is, she applied counting . . . to counting numbers! What *are* the ideas and skills that develop in such sophisticated counting? What do most young children know about counting? What more could they learn?

Changing Views of Counting

In the middle of the 20th century, Piaget's research on number strongly influenced views of early mathematics. Among the many positive influences were an appreciation for children's active role in learning, and the depth of the mathematical ideas they constructed. One unfortunate influence was that Piaget believed that, until children can *conserve* number, counting is meaningless.

For example, asked to give herself the same number of "candies" as an interviewer's, a 4-year-old might use matching as in Figure 3.1. But when the interviewer spreads his objects out as in Figure 3.2, the child may claim that the interviewer now has more. Even asking the child to count the two collections may not help her determine the correct answer.

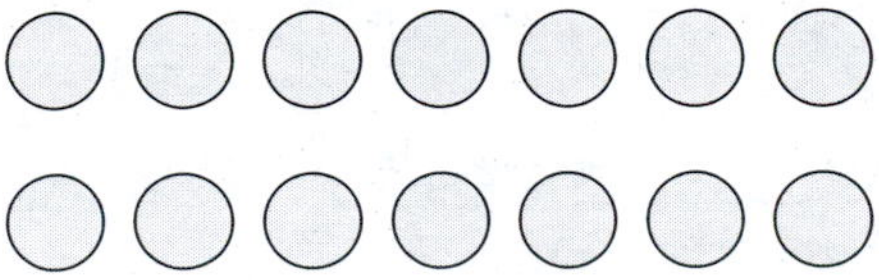

Figure 3.1 After an adult makes the bottom row of "candies," and asks the child to give herself the same number, the child uses 1-to-1 correspondence.

Figure 3.2 The adult spreads his "candies" out and the child now states he has more.

The Piagetians believed that children needed to develop the "logic" that underlies conservation of number before counting was meaningful. This logic consists of two types of knowledge. First was hierarchical classification, such as knowing that, if there are 12 wooden beads, 8 blue and 4 red, there are more wooden beads than blue beads. What does that have to do with *number* and counting? To understand counting, Piagetians argued, children must understand that each number *includes* those that came before such as in Figure 3.3.

The second type of logical knowledge is sequencing. Children have to both properly produce number words in sequence and sequence the objects they count so that they count each object exactly once (no easy task for young children faced with an unorganized group). Also, children have to understand that each counting number is *quantitatively* one more than the one before as in Figure 3.4.

Both these notions have much truth in them. Children must learn these ideas to understand number well. However, *children learn much about counting and number before they have mastered these ideas.* And, in fact, rather than requiring these ideas before counting is meaningful, counting may help children make sense of the logical ideas. That is, *counting can help **develop** knowledge of classification and seriation* (Clements, 1984).

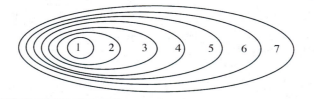

Figure 3.3 The hierarchical inclusion of numbers (cardinality, or "how many" property).

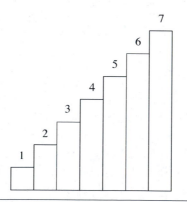

Figure 3.4 The ordinal, or sequencing, property of numbers.

Verbal Counting

The Mathematics of Verbal Counting

Although counting to small numbers is universal in human cultures, counting to large numbers requires a *system* to keep track. Our Hindu-Arabic numeral system is based on two ideas (Wu, 2007). First, there are only ten symbols called *digits* (0, 1, 2, 3, 4, 5, 6, 7, 8, 9). Second, all possible counting numbers are created by using those ten digits in different places—the concept of place value. Any number, then is the product of the "face" (digit) and the "place"; for example, 1,926 is 1 *thousand*, 9 *hundred*, 2 *tens*, and 6 *ones*. When we count, we get up to 9, and then signify the next number with the digit 1 in the tens place and the digit 0 as a "placeholder" in the ones place: 10. Then we work through ten digits in the ones place, 10 to 19, at which point we run out again, so we put 2 in the tens place: 20. So, 21 means we cycled through 0 to 9 twice, so we knew we counted 20 times plus one more time.

Children's Development of Verbal Counting

This brief mathematical description suggests why we use the term "verbal counting" rather than "rote counting." There are other reasons. Without verbal counting, *quantitative* thinking does not develop. As an example, children who can continue counting starting at any number are better on *all* number tasks. Children learn that numbers derive order and meaning from their embeddedness in a system, and they learn a set of relationships and rules that allows the generation, not recall, of the appropriate sequence.

This learning occurs over years. At first, children can only say some numbers in words, but not necessarily in sequence. Then, they learn to count verbally by starting at the beginning and saying a *string* of words, but they do not even "hear" counting words as separate words. Then, they do separate each counting word and they learn to count up to 10, then 20, then higher. Only later can children start counting from any number, what we call the "Counter from N (N+1, N−1)" level. Even later, they learn to skip count and count to 100 and beyond. Finally, children learn to count the number words themselves (e.g., to "count on"; see Chapter 4).

Object Counting

As shown in Chapter 2, naming how many items are in small configurations of items requires experiences in which the configurations are labeled with a number word by adults or older children ("Here are two blocks"), which enable children to build meaning for number words such as telling how many. The capstone of early numerical knowledge is connecting the counting of objects in a collection to the number of objects in that collection. Initially, children may not know how many objects there are in a collection after counting them. If asked how many are there, they typically count again, as if the "how many?" question is a directive to count rather than a request for how many items are in the collection. Children must learn that the last number word they say when counting refers to how many items have been counted.

Thus, to count a set of objects, children must not only know verbal counting but also learn (a) to coordinate verbal counting with objects by pointing to or moving the objects and (b) that the last counting word names the cardinality of ("how many objects in") the set. This process is illustrated in Figure 3.5.

Such counting is basic in many ways. It is the method for quantifying groups larger than small subitizable collections. It is the necessary building block for all further work with number.

"one… two… three… four… five… six… seven… Seven in all!"

Figure 3.5 Object counting including 1-to-1 correspondence and cardinality ("how many uses").

Also, *counting is the first and most basic and important algorithm.* That is, most everything else in number, algebra, and beyond depend in some way on counting. Why is it an algorithm—a word usually used for ways to represent and process arithmetic with multidigit numbers (e.g., "column addition")? Because an algorithm is a step-by-step procedure that is guaranteed to solve a specific category of problems. Counting is the first step-by-step procedure that children learn that solves certain problems—determining how many elements are in a finite set.

The easiest type of collection for 3-year-olds to count has only a few objects arranged in a straight line that can be touched as children proceed with their counting. Between 3 and 5 years of age, children acquire more skill as they practice counting, and most become able to cope with numerically larger collections.

There are many additional counting skills children need to learn. They need to produce a collection of a given number, that is, "count out" a group. To adults, that may seem to be no more difficult than counting a collection. However, to produce 4, children have to keep track of the number word they are on, and keep one-to-one correspondence, *and* compare the number word they said to the 4 with each count. Before they reach that level of competence, they often just keep going!

Next, children learn to count objects in different arrangements, keeping track of which they have and have not yet counted. Eventually they learn to count collections without needing to touch or move objects during the act of counting. Children also learn to quickly tell how many there are in a collection if one is added or removed by counting up or down. Finally, children learn sophisticated counting strategies, such as counting on or counting backward to solve arithmetic problems, which we will describe in more detail in Chapter 4.

Zero

Five-year-old Dawn was changing the speed of moving objects on the computer screen by entering commands. SETSPEED 100 made them go fast. SETSPEED 10 made them go slower. She tried speed limits such as 55 and very slow speeds like 5 and 1. Suddenly, she excitedly called her friend and then her teacher. Visitor Seymour Papert and the teacher were confused. What was exciting? Nothing was happening.

They found out that *"Nothing"* was happening. Zero! She had entered SETSPEED 0 and the object stopped. Dawn talked about that it was "moving," but the speed was zero. Zero was a number! Not "none" or "nothing" but a real number. Papert concluded that such discoveries lie at the heart of learning mathematics. This story also reveals that zero is *not* an obvious concept. It was invented by people far later than were the counting numbers. However, even children as young as 3 or 4 years of age can learn to use zero to represent the absence of objects.

Children think about zero in different ways and build special rules to account for this exceptional number. The same attributes that make zero difficult may also make it serve children's mathematical development. Zero may play a special role in children's increasingly algebraic knowledge of number. Because they have to be conscious of the rules for zero, such experiences may build a foundation for the creation of generalized rules in the structures of arithmetic.

During dinner, a father asked his second grader what he had learned in school.

Son: I learned that if you multiply or divide by zero, the answer is always zero.

Dad: What would be the answer if you multiplied two by zero?

Son: Zero.

Dad: What if you divided two by zero?

Son: Zero.

Dad: What is two divided by two?

Son: One.

Dad: What is two divided by one? How many ones are there in two?

Son: Two.

Dad: What is two divided by one-half? How many halves are there in two?

Son: Four.

Dad: What is two divided by one-quarter?

Son: Eight.

Dad: What seems to be happening as we divide by numbers closer to zero?

Son: The answer is getting bigger.

Dad: What do you think about the idea that two divided by zero is zero?

Son: It's not right. What is the answer?

Dad: It doesn't look like there is an answer. What do you think?

Son: Daddy, wouldn't the answer be infinity?

Dad: Where did you learn about infinity?

Son: From Buzz Lightyear.

(adapted from Gadanidis, Hoogland, Jarvis, & Scheffel, 2003)

Summary

Early numerical knowledge includes four *interrelated* aspects (as well as others): recognizing and naming how many items of a small configuration (small number recognition and, when done quickly, subitizing), learning the names and eventually ordered list of number words to ten and beyond, enumerating objects (i.e., saying number words in correspondence with objects), and understanding that the last number word said when counting refers to how many items have been counted. Children learn these aspects, often separately through different kinds of experiences, but gradually connect them during the preschool years (cf. Linnell & Fluck, 2001). For example, very young children may learn to focus on the number in small groups and, separately, learn verbal counting, while enumerating these and other groups (initially without accurate correspondence) as a verbal string. As these abilities grow, they motivate the use of each, and become increasingly interrelated, with recognition motivating verbal counting, as well as building subitizing ability that supports object counting skills of correspondence and cardinality (Eimeren, MacMillan, & Ansari, 2007). Skilled object counting then motivates and supports more advanced perceptual and conceptual subitizing abilities. Each of the aspects begins with the smallest numbers and gradually includes larger numbers. In addition, each includes significant developmental levels. For example, small number recognition moves from nonverbal recognition of one or two objects, to quick recognition and discrimination of one to four objects, to conceptual subitizing of larger (composed) groups. As children's ability to subitize grows from perceptual to conceptual patterns, so too does their ability to count and operate on collections grow from perceptual to conceptual.

Experience and Education

Many early childhood teachers, working with the youngest children through first grade students and beyond, underestimate children's ability to do, and to learn more about, counting. Too often, children learn little or nothing about counting from preschool to first grade. Textbooks "introduce" counting skills that children already possess and spend considerable time on one number, such as 3, eventually moving to 4, then 5 . . . usually neglecting numbers above 10. Research suggests several positive alternatives.

Verbal counting. Initial verbal counting involves learning the list of number words, which to ten, and usually twenty, is an arbitrary list for English speakers with few salient patterns (Fuson, 1992a)—initially, a "song to sing" (Ginsburg, 1977). Children learn at least some of this list as they do general language or the ABCs. Thus, rhythms and songs can play a role, although attention should be given to separating the words from each other and under-standing each as a counting word (e.g., some children initially tag two items with the two syllables of "se-ven"). Beyond these, the patterns and structure of verbal counting should be emphasized by making the base-ten, place value, and structure of number names more accessible to young children (Miller, Smith, Zhu, & Zhang, 1995). Familiarizing U.S. children with Arabic numerals at an earlier age than at present might help compensate. Further, anecdotal reports of counting with English words and English translations of East Asian structures ("ten-one, ten-two . . . two-tens, two-tens-one, two-tens-two . . .") are suggestive. The goal is to help children map the single-digit to decade terms, both to facilitate the counting sequencing and to mitigate potential harmful effects on children's belief systems if they experience this early mathematics task as being confusing and arbitrary, demanding mostly memorization (Fuson, 1992a).

If children make mistakes, emphasize the importance of accuracy and encourage students to count slowly and carefully (Baroody, 1996). Invite children to count with you. Then ask them to do it (the same task again) alone. If necessary, have the child mirror you, number by number. "Say each number after I say it. 'One'" (pause). If they do no respond, repeat "one" and then tell the children to say "one." If children say "two," then say "three" and continue, allow them to mirror you or continue your counting. If children still make the mistake when counting on their own, mark this as a special "warm-up" exercise for the child every day.

Finally, replace the misnomer "rote counting" with the phrase "verbal counting." Verbal count-ing should be meaningful and part of a *system* of number, even for young children (Pollio & Whitacre, 1970).

Language before object counting. Number words play a role in naming very small collections (recall subitizing in Chapter 2) and also orienting children to attend to numerical aspects of situations. They bring number to conscious awareness. For example, a girl was sitting with her dog when another wandered into the yard. She says, "Two doggie!" She then asked her mother to give her "two treats" and gave one to each. As another example, noted researcher Grayson Wheatley was interacting with a 4-year-old with dominoes. The child would build and make shapes with them but did not attend to the number of dots. Wheatley began to talk as he put pieces together, saying, "These two go together because there are three dots on each. After doing this for a while as he was still building, he began to attend to the dots and put together pieces that had the same number of dots. He had made a start at abstracting three. Research suggests provision of multiple experiences such as these before any major focus on object counting.

Subitizing and counting. When trying to develop subitizing concepts, consciously try to connect experiences with counting and subitizing. Young children may use perceptual subitizing to make units for counting and to build their initial ideas of cardinality. For example, their first cardinal meanings for number words may be labels for small sets of subitized objects, even if they counted the sets first (Fuson, 1992b; Steffe, Thompson, & Richards, 1982).

Use many ways to link counting objects to children's recognition of the numbers in small collections. One effective demonstration strategy emphasizes that counting tells "how many" (from Clements & Sarama, 2007a): With four counters out of sight in your hand, ask children to help you count to find out how many counters you have hidden in your hand. Remove one with the other hand, placing it in front of the children so they see and focus on this one. Emphasize that the counting number, one, tells how many there are. Repeat until you have counted out all four objects. Display your now-empty hands. Ask children how many there were in all. Agree there are four; we counted and there are four. Repeat with new objects and a new number; also, have the children do the verbal counting with you. Notice that children hear each (ordinal) counting word as it is spoken in enumeration while observing the corresponding collection containing that number of objects. Another technique would be to ask children to count a collection they can subitize. Then add or subtract an object and have the children count again.

Children can use perceptual subitizing, counting, and patterning abilities to develop conceptual subitizing. This more advanced ability to quickly group and quantify sets in turn supports their development of number sense and arithmetic abilities. A first grader explains the process for us. Seeing a 3 by 3 pattern of dots, she says "nine" immediately. Asked how she did it, she replies, "When I was about four years old, I was in nursery school. All I had to do was count. And so, I just go like 1, 2, 3, 4, 5, 6, 7, 8, 9, and I just knew it by heart and I kept on doing it when I was five too. And then I kept knowing 9, you know. Exactly like this [she pointed to the array of nine dots]" (Ginsburg, 1977, p. 16).

Object counting. Of course, children also need substantial experience counting along with others and counting by themselves. Counting objects takes considerable practice to coordinate and can be facilitated by having children touch objects as they count and by counting objects organized into a row. However, children are also well prepared for such coordination, especially if rhythm is introduced, although they must concentrate and try hard to achieve continuous coordination throughout the whole counting effort. Such effort increases their accuracy substantially (Fuson, 1988), and asking children to "slow down" and "try very hard to count just right" might be the first intervention to use when you observe an error in counting. Parents and some teachers may discourage pointing at objects, or assume that when children use correspondence in simple tasks, they do not need help using it in more complex tasks (Linnell & Fluck, 2001). However, errors increase when the indicating act is eye fixations and such errors may be internalized. Therefore, allow—and encourage parents to allow—children to point to objects, and encourage it as another early intervention when counting errors are observed (Fuson, 1988, 1992a; Linnell & Fluck, 2001). Encourage children with special difficulties, such as learning disabilities, to work slowly and carefully and to move objects to a new location (Baroody, 1996).

Cardinality is one of the most frequently neglected aspects of counting instruction, and its role may not be appreciated explicitly by teachers or parents (Linnell & Fluck, 2001). Use the demonstration strategy above, which was designed to emphasize the ordinal–cardinal connection in several ways. In addition, when observing children, teachers are often satisfied by accurate enumeration and do not ask children "how many?" following enumeration. Use this question for assessment and to help prompt children to make the count to cardinal transition. Seek to understand your children's conceptualizations and the benefits of discussing counting and its purposes and creating opportunities for both adult- and child-generated situations that require counting.

To develop these concepts and skills, children need extensive experience in contexts where they have to know "how many." Parents may ask, "How many?", but only as a request to enumerate, *not* to address the count-to-cardinal transition (Fluck, 1995; Fluck & Henderson, 1996). Instead, activities such as those in Table 3.1 emphasize the cardinal value of the counted collection. The activities demand that the cardinality be known, and some of them hide the objects so the request to tell "how many" cannot be misinterpreted as a request to recount the collection.

Ask children to get 3 crackers, get as many straws as children at their table, and so forth. These situations emphasize awareness of plurality, a particular cardinal goal, and the activity of counting. In this way, most counting tasks should emphasize the situation and goal and the cardinal result of counting, not just the activity of counting (Steffe & Cobb, 1988, personal communication).

One study indicated that collaborative counting, in which pairs of kindergartners counted 1 set of materials, contributed to individual cognitive progress by allowing an expansion of the range and sophistication of the children's strategies, such as a heightened explicit awareness of the need to keep track of one's counting acts when counting items of a hidden collection (Wiegel, 1998). An important feature of the tasks was that they were designed on research-based developmental progressions of counting (Steffe & Cobb, 1988).

Sophian evaluated a curriculum, informed by her earlier research, designed to facilitate children's awareness of the units they are counting, because a sound understanding of units is a conceptual basis for much later mathematics learning. Derived from a measurement perspective (Davydov, 1975), the activities emphasized that the numerical result we obtain from counting or other measurement operations will depend on our choice of a unit and that units of one kind can be combined to form higher-order units or taken apart to form lower-order ones. Results were statistically significant, but modest (Sophian, 2004b).

Research from the field (Baroody, 1996) and from the *Building Blocks* curriculum project suggests the following teaching strategies are useful when children make errors. See Box 1.

Teaching zero. Education can make a difference in children's learning of zero. For example, one university preschool, compared to others, increased children's development of idea about zero by one full year (Wellman & Miller, 1986). Because situations and problems involving zero are often solved differently by young children (Evans, 1983), specific use of the term "zero" and the symbol "0," connected to the development of the concept—discuss real-world knowledge of "nothing"—should begin early. Activities might include counting backward to zero, naming collections with zero (a time for the motivation of silliness, such as the number of elephants in the room), subtracting concrete objects to produce such collections, and discussing zero as the smallest whole number (non-negative integer). Eventually, such activities can lead to a simple generalized rule, such as adding zero does not change the value, and an integration of their knowledge of zero with knowledge of other numbers.

Language, numbers, and object counting. Subitizing and counting rely on careful and sustained application of number words. Seeing multiple examples of the same number that differ in all aspects except numerosity, and nonexamples, is particularly helpful (Baroody et al., 2006).

Similarly, using *numerals* ("1" or "4") meaningfully helps children develop number concepts. Children may begin to use written representations for number as early as 3 years of age or as late as 6 years, depending on the home and preschool environments (Baroody et al., 2005). Number and numeral games such as "Tins" are motivating for children and emphasize representations of number. A different number of objects is placed in each of 4 covered tins, which are scrambled. The child has to find the tin with the number of objects the teacher states. Soon after introducing the game, the teacher introduces a new feature: Children can write on sticky notes to help themselves find the correct tin (Hughes, 1986). Children can use iconic representations or, better, numerals.

Indeed, several curricula use games of various types to develop counting abilities in young children (see Chapter 15). Children as young as 3 years of age can successfully play such games

Box 1: Teaching Strategies for Specific Counting Errors

- One-to-One Errors (includes keeping-track-of-what's-been-counted errors):
  - Emphasize the importance of accuracy and encourage the children to count slowly and carefully to "count each item exactly once."
  - When relevant, explain a keeping-track strategy. If moving objects is possible and desirable in the activity, suggest the strategy of moving items to a different pile or location. Otherwise, explain making a verbal plan, such as "Go from top to bottom. Start from the top and count every one."—then carry out the plan together.
  - If the children return and re-count objects (e.g., in a circular arrangement): (a) Stop and tell them they counted that item already. Suggest that they start on one they can remember (e.g., one at the "top" or "the corner" or "the blue one"—whatever makes sense in the activity; if there is no identifier, highlight an item in some way). (b) Ask the children to click on items as they count in the computer activity "Kitchen Counter" (see Table 3.1, p. 30), providing highlighting to the object, marking it. If they click on a highlighted item, the character immediately says they counted that item already.
- Cardinality ("The How Many Rule") Errors:
  - Ask the children to re-count.
  - Demonstrate the cardinality rule on the collection. That is, count the collection, pointing to each item in turn, then gesture at them all, saying, "Five in all!"
  - Demonstrate the cardinality rule on a small (subitizable) collection in an easily recognizable arrangement (see the Snapshots activities in Chapter 2).
- Cardinality Errors (Production tasks—Knowing when to stop):
  - Remind the children of the goal number and ask to re-count.
  - Count the collection, say that is not the requested number, and ask the children to try again.
  - If there were too few, count the existing collection quickly and ask the children to put on another object, saying when that has been done, "And that makes—." Allow the children to add more than one as long as this does not exceed a total.
  - If there were too many, ask the children to remove one or more items, and then re-count. So, count the existing collection quickly and say, "There are too many. Take some away so that we have—."
  - Demonstrate.
- Guided Counting Sequence (when the above are not sufficient):
  - Ask the children to count out loud as they point to each object. Suggest a keeping-track strategy if necessary.
  - If there are still errors after this remediation, say, "Count with me," and name the keeping-track strategy you will model. Have the children point to each item and says the correct counting word, thus walking the children through the counting.
  - Demonstrate the cardinality rule—repeat the last counting number, gesture in a circular motion to all the items, and say, "That's how many there are in all." For "Counter to" activities, emphasize the goal number, saying, "[Five!] That's what we wanted!"
- Skip Counting
  - Say, "Try again," and remind them of the goal number.
  - Say, "Count with me. Count by [tens]." [if you are counting items, move the appropriate amount with each count]
  - Say, "Count by [tens] like this: [demonstrate]. Now count with me."

with peers after they have been introduced by an adult (Curtis, 2005). Instruction in counting and numeral-naming can help children transfer their knowledge to other areas, such as addition and subtraction, but may not transfer to other skills such as comparison (Malofeeva, Day, Saco, Young, & Ciancio, 2004). Therefore, include "race" games and other activities in your counting learning trajectory (see also Chapter 4).

Computer activities are another effective approach. After introducing numerals with games similar to "Tins," the *Building Blocks* computer activities often ask children to respond to questions by clicking on a numeral (numerals are written on "cards" that initially have fives-and-tens frame dot representations as well), or read a numeral to know what size collection to produce. Children using these and other activities outperformed comparison groups that also were taught numerals (Clements & Sarama, 2007c). For kindergartners and older children, use of Logo activities has similar facilitative effect on use of numerals, including connecting them to quantitative concepts (Clements, Battista, & Sarama, 2001; Clements & Meredith, 1993).

There are four pedagogically significant characteristics of these activities. First, the symbols have a quantitative meaning that children understand, and they build upon verbal representations. Second, children create their own representations initially. Third, the symbols are useful in the context of the activity. Fourth, children can translate from the situation to the symbols and back again.

Written numerals can play a valuable role in focusing children on representing and reflecting on numbers. The use of symbols with understanding may have an impact on number concepts through its role in providing a common cognitive model that facilitates communication about number, especially between young children and older people, and possibly in becoming part of the child's cognitive model of number (Munn, 1998; however, note that Munn privileges written symbols, de-emphasizing verbal words as symbols). However, children probably should have considerable experience with concrete situations and verbal problem-solving with numerical operations, such as adding and subtracting, before relying on symbols as the sole communicative tool. Slow, informal, meaningful uses in pre-K are more effective than traditional school methods, which lead to procedural approaches with less quantitative meaning (Munn, 1998).

Therefore, help children explicitly connect verbal and written symbols to each other and to sensory-concrete (see pp. 274–276 in Chap. 16) quantitative situations. Encourage them to use numerals as symbols *of* situations and symbols *for* reasoning. The emphasis should always be on thinking mathematically, using symbols to do so when appropriate.

Learning Trajectory for Counting

The learning trajectory for counting is more complex than that for subitizing in Chapter 2. First, there are many conceptual and skill advancements that makes levels more complicated. Second, there are *subtrajectories* within counting. For example, three subtrajectories for counting include verbal counting, object counting, and counting strategies. These are related, but can develop somewhat independently. Most of them deal with counting objects (and thus are not labeled further), but those that are mainly verbal counting skills are labeled "*Verbal*," and those that tend to begin as mainly verbal skills but also can be applied to object counting situations are labeled "*Verbal and Object*." Those labeled "*Strategy*" are particularly important in supporting arithmetic skills, and become increasingly integrated with (even identical to) the arithmetic strategies described in Chapter 5.

The importance of the *goal* of increasing children's ability to count verbally, count objects meaningfully, and learn increasingly sophisticated counting strategies is clear (see Figure 3.6). With that goal, Table 3.1 provides the two additional components of the learning trajectory, the

Pre-K

Number and Operations: Developing an understanding of whole numbers, including concepts of correspondence, counting, cardinality, and comparison

Children develop an understanding of the meanings of whole numbers and recognize the number of objects in small groups . . . by counting—the first and most basic mathematical algorithm. They understand that number words refer to quantity. They use one-to-one correspondence . . . in counting objects to 10 and beyond. They understand that the last word that they state in counting tells, "how many," they count to determine number amounts and compare quantities (using language such as "more than" and "less than") . . .

Kindergarten

Number and Operations: Representing, comparing, and ordering whole numbers and joining and separating sets

Children use numbers, including written numerals, to represent quantities and to solve quantitative problems, such as counting objects in a set, creating a set with a given number of objects . . . They choose, combine, and apply effective strategies for answering quantitative questions, including . . . counting and producing sets of given sizes, counting the number in combined sets, and counting backward.

Grade 1

Number and Operations and Algebra: Developing understandings of addition and subtraction and strategies for basic addition facts and related subtraction facts

Children develop strategies for adding and subtracting whole numbers on the basis of their earlier work with small numbers . . . Children understand the connections between counting and the operations of addition and subtraction (e.g., adding 2 is the same as "counting on" 2).

Number and Operations: Developing an understanding of whole number relationships, including grouping in tens and ones

Children . . . understand the sequential order of the counting numbers and their relative magnitudes and represent numbers on a number line.

Grade 2

Number and Operations and Algebra: Developing an understanding of the base-ten numeration system and place-value concepts

[Children's] understanding of base-ten numeration includes ideas of counting in units and multiples of hundreds, tens, and ones . . .

Children develop strategies for adding and subtracting whole numbers on the basis of their earlier work with small numbers . . . Children understand the connections between counting and the operations of addition and subtraction (e.g., adding 2 is the same as "counting on" 2).

Number and Operations: Developing an understanding of whole number relationships, including grouping in tens and ones

Children . . . understand the sequential order of the counting numbers and their relative magnitudes and represent numbers on a number line.

Figure 3.6 Curriculum focal points (NCTM, 2006) emphasizing counting in the early years.[1]

developmental progression and the instructional tasks. (Note that the ages in all the learning trajectory tables are only approximate, especially because the age of acquisition usually depends heavily on experience.)

Table 3.1 Learning Trajectory for Counting.

Age (years)	Developmental Progression	Instructional Tasks
1	**Pre-Counter** *Verbal* No verbal counting. Names some number words with no sequence. **Chanter** *Verbal* Chants "sing-song" or sometimes indistinguishable number words.	Associate number words with quantities (see the initial levels of the "Recognition of Number and Subitizing," learning trajectory in Chapter 2) and as components of the counting sequence. Repeated experience with the counting sequence in varied contexts.
2	**Reciter** *Verbal* Verbally counts with separate words, not necessarily in the correct order above "five". "one, two, three, four, five, seven." Puts objects, actions, and words in many-to-one (age 1;8) or overly rigid one-to-one (age 1; correspondence (age 2:6). Counts two objects "two, two, two." If knows more number words than number of objects, rattles them off quickly at the end. If more objects, "recycles" number words (inflexible list-exhaustion).	Provide repeated, frequent experience with the counting sequence in varied contexts. *Count and Race* Students verbally count along with the computer (up to 50) by adding cars to a racetrack one at a time.
3	**Reciter (10)** *Verbal* Verbally counts to ten, with *some* correspondence with objects, but may either continue an overly rigid correspondence, or exhibit performance errors (e.g., skipping, double-counting). Producing, may give desired number. "one [points to first], two [points to second], three [starts to point], four [finishes pointing, but is now still pointing to third object], five, . . . nine, ten, eleven, twelve, 'firteen,' fifteen . . ." Asked for 5, counts out 3, saying, "one, two, *five*." **Corresponder** Keeps one-to-one correspondence between counting words and objects (one word for each object), at least for small groups of objects laid in a line. ▢ ▢ ▢ ▢ "1, 2, 3, 4" May answer a "how many?" question by re-counting the objects, or violate 1–1 or word order to make the last number word be the desired or predicted word.	*Count and Move* Have all children count from 1–10 or an appropriate number, making motions with each count. For example, say, "one" [touch head], "two" [touch shoulders], "three" [touch head], etc. *Count and Move* also develops this competency. *Kitchen Counter* Students click on objects one at a time while the numbers from 1 to 10 are counted aloud. For example, they click on pieces of food and a bite is taken out of each as it is counted. 

Age (years)	Developmental Progression	Instructional Tasks

4 — **Counter (Small Numbers)**
Accurately counts objects in a line to 5 and answers the "how many" question with the last number counted. When objects are visible, and especially with small numbers, begins to understand cardinality.

□ □ □ □
"1, 2, 3, 4 . . . *four!*"

Cubes in the Box Have the child count a small set of cubes. Put them in the box and close the lid. Then ask the child how many cubes you are hiding. If the child is ready, have him/her write the numeral. Dump them out and count together to check.

Pizza Pizzazz 2 Students count items up to 5, putting toppings on a pizza to match a target amount.

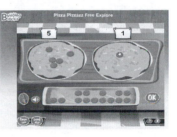

Pizza Pizzazz Free Explore Students explore counting and related number topics by adding toppings to pizzas. Give children challenges and projects! Have one child give a "model" for another to copy and so forth.

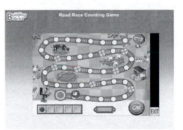

Which Color Is Missing? Assign each child in a small group a different color. Have each choose 5 crayons of that color. Once they have checked each other, have them put their crayons into the same large container. Then choose one child to be the "sneaky mouse." With everyone's eyes closed, the sneaky mouse secretly takes out one crayon and hides it. The other children have to count their crayons to see which color the mouse hid.

Road Race Counting Game Students identify number amounts (from 1 through 5) on a die (physical game board) or dot frame (computer version) and move forward a corresponding number of spaces on a game board.

Road Race Students identify numbers of sides (3, 4, or 5) on polygons and move forward a corresponding number of spaces on a game board.

Continued Overleaf

Age (years)	Developmental Progression	Instructional Tasks

Counter (10) Counts arrangements of objects to 10. May be able to write numerals to represent 1–10.

> Accurately counts a line of 9 blocks and says there are nine.

May be able to tell the number just after or just before another number, but only by counting up from 1.

> What comes after 4? "1, 2, 3, 4, 5. 5!"

Verbal counting to 20 is developing.

Counting Towers (Up to 10) A day before read *Shape Space*. Ask what shapes work well in which part of a tower (e.g., would the "tip on the triangle block" make it a good base?). Set up stations with different objects to stack. Encourage children to stack as many as they can, and count them to see how many they stacked.

Or, read Anno's counting book. Ask children if they ever count how many blocks they can stack in a tower. Have children work at a station and build a tower as high as they can. Ask them to estimate how many blocks are in their tower. Count the blocks with them before they knock it down. Try to get a larger number in the tower. Children then switch stations.

Counting Jar A counting jar holds a specified number of items for children to count without touching the items. Use the same jar all year, changing its small amount of items weekly. Have children spill out the items to count them.

Build Stairs 1 Students add stairs to a stair frame outline to reach a target height.

Dino Shop 1 Students identify the numeral that represents a target number of dinosaurs in a number frame.

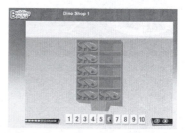

Dino Shop Free Explore Students explore counting and related number topics by putting party items on a table. Give children challenges and projects! Have one child give a "model" for another to copy and so forth.

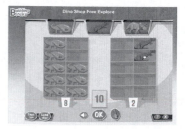

Age (years)	Developmental Progression	Instructional Tasks

Memory Number 1: Counting Cards Students match number cards (each with a numeral and corresponding dot cluster) within the framework of a "Concentration" card game.

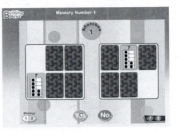

Number Line Race Give children number lines of different colors. Player 1 rolls a die and asks the banker for that many counters. The banker gives that number and Player 1 places the counters in order along her number line while counting. She then moves her playing piece along the counters, counting out loud again, until the piece is on the last counter. Eventually, ask children who are closest to the goal, and how they know it.

Before and After Math Students identify and select numbers that come either just before or right after a target number.

Producer (Small Numbers) Counts out objects to 5. Recognizes that counting is relevant to situations in which a certain number must be placed.

Produces a group of 4 objects.

Count Motions While waiting during transitions, have children count how many times you jump or clap, or some other motion. Then have them do those motions the same number of times. Initially, count the actions with children. Later, do the motions but model and explain how to count silently. Children who understand how many motions will stop, but others will continue doing the motions.

Pizza Pizzazz 3 Students add toppings to a pizza (up to 5) to match target numerals.

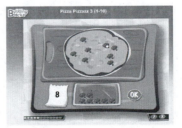

Continued Overleaf

Age (years)	Developmental Progression	Instructional Tasks

Pizza/Cookie Game 1 Children play in pairs. Player One rolls a number cube, and puts that many toppings (counters) on his/her plate. Player One asks Player Two, "Am I right?" Player Two must agree that Player One is correct. At that point, Player One moves the counters to the circular spaces for toppings on his/her pizza. Players take turns until all the spaces on their pizzas have toppings.

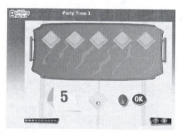

Numeral Train Game Students identify numerals (1–5) on a numeral cube (physical board game) or computer display and move forward a corresponding number of spaces on a game board.

Party Time 3 Students place items on a tray (up to 10) to match target numerals.

Counter and Producer (10+) Counts and counts out objects accurately to 10, then beyond (to about 30). Has explicit understanding of cardinality (how numbers tell how many). Keeps track of objects that have and have not been counted, even in different arrangements. Writes or draws to represent 1 to 10 (then, 20, then 30).

Counting Towers (Beyond 10) (See basic directions above.) To allow children to count to 20 and beyond, have them make towers with other objects such as coins. Children build a tower as high as they can, placing more coins, but not straightening coins already in the tower. The goal is to estimate and then count to find out how many coins are in your tallest tower. To count higher, have children make pattern "walls." They build a pattern block wall as long as they can. This allows them to count to higher numbers.

Age (years)	Developmental Progression	Instructional Tasks

Counts a scattered group of 19 chips, keeping track by moving each one as they are counted.

Gives next number (usually to 20s or 30s). Separates the decade and the ones part of a number word, and begins to relate each part of a number word/numeral to the quantity to which it refers.

Recognizes errors in others' counting *and* can eliminate most errors in own counting (point-object) if asked to try hard.

Alternatives:

1. Pairs can play a game in which they take turns placing coins.
2. Roll a number cube to determine how many coins to put on the tower.
3. Adopt this activity to any number of settings. For example, how many cans of food, such as soup (or other heavy objects) can two children hold when each holds two corners of a towel? Repeat this with very large or small cans. With your guidance, they could also try to make a tower of the cans (ordering them by size, with the largest on the bottom).

Number Jump with Numerals Hold up a numeral card and have children first say the numeral. Together, children do a motion you pick (such as jump, nod head, or clap) that number of times. Repeat with different numerals. Be sure and use 0 (zero).

Dino Shop 2 Students add dinosaurs to a box to match target numerals.

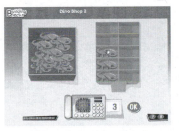

Mr. MixUp Counting Use an adult-like, somewhat goofy puppet, called "Mr. MixUp." Tell children Mr. MixUp frequently makes mistakes. Ask children to help Mr. MixUp count. They listen to Mr. MixUp, catch his mistake, correct him, and then count with him to help him "get it right." Have Mr. MixUp make mistakes such as the following, in approximately this developmental order.

Verbal counting mistakes
  Wrong order (1, 2, 3, 5, 4, 6)
  Skipping numbers (. . . 12, 14, 16, 17)
  Repeat numbers (. . . 4, 5, 6, 7, 7, 8)

Object counting mistakes
  One-to-one mistakes
    Skipping objects
    Count-point: Saying one number word but pointing twice or vice versa (but points are 1–1 with objects)
    Point-object: Pointing once but indicating more than one object or pointing more than once to one object (but counting words are 1–1 with pointing)

Cardinality/Last number mistakes
    Saying the wrong number as the "final count" (e.g., counting three objects, counting "1, 2, 3 [correctly, but then saying], there's 4 there!")

Keeping-track-of-what's-been-counted mistakes
    Double counting: "coming back" and counting an item again
    Skipping objects when counting objects not in a line

Continued Overleaf

Age (years)	Developmental Progression	Instructional Tasks

Memory Number 2: Count Cards to Numerals Students match cards with dot arrays to cards with the corresponding numerals within the framework of a "Concentration" card game, on and off computer.

Memory Number 3: Dots to Dots Students match cards with dots in frames to cards with the same number of dots, unframed, within the framework of a "Concentration" card game.

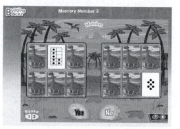

Counter Backward from 10 *Verbal and Object*

Counts backward from 10 to 1, verbally, or when removing objects from a group.

"10, 9, 8, 7, 6, 5, 4, 3, 2, 1!"

Count and Move—Forward and Backward Have all children count from 1–10 or an appropriate number, making motions with each count, and then count backward to zero. For example, they start in a crouch, then stand up bit by bit as they count up to 10. Then they count backwards to zero (sitting all the way down).

Blast Off! Children stand and count backward from 10 or an appropriate number, crouching down a bit with each count. After reaching zero, they jump up yelling, "Blast off!"

Countdown Crazy Students click digits in sequence to count down from 10 to 0.

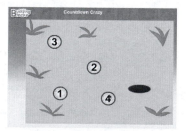

6   **Counter from N (N + 1, N − 1)** *Verbal and Object* Counts verbally and with objects from numbers other than 1 (but does not yet keep track of the *number* of counts).

Asked to "count from 5 to 8," counts "5, 6, 7, 8!"

Determines numbers just after or just before immediately.

One more! Counting on Have the children count two objects. Add one and ask, "How many now?" Have children count on to answer. (Count from 1 to check the first time or 2.) Add another and so on, until they have counted to 10. Start again with a different starting amount. When children are able, warn the children, "Watch out! I'm going to add more than 1 sometimes!" and sometimes add 2, and eventually 3, to the group. If children seem to need assistance, have a puppet model the strategy; for example, "Hmmm, there's fooour, one more makes it five, and one more makes it six. Six, that's it!"

Age (years)	Developmental Progression	Instructional Tasks
	Asked, "What comes just before 7?" says, "Six!"	*How Many in the Box Now?* Have the children count objects as you place them in a box. Ask, "How many are in the box now?" Add one, repeating the question, then check the children's responses by counting all the objects. Repeat, checking occasionally. When children are ready, sometimes add 2 objects.

How Many in the Box Now? Have the children count objects as you place them in a box. Ask, "How many are in the box now?" Add one, repeating the question, then check the children's responses by counting all the objects. Repeat, checking occasionally. When children are ready, sometimes add 2 objects.

> Variations: Place coins in a coffee can. Declare that a given number of objects is in the can. Then have the children close their eyes and count on by listening as additional objects are dropped in.
>
> Repeat this type of counting activity in a variety of settings, adding more objects at a time (starting with 0 to 3). Use story settings for the problems; for example, sharks eating small fish (children can be "sharks" eating actual fish crackers at the snack table), toy cars and trucks parking on a parking ramp, a superhero throwing bandits in jail, etc.

I'm Thinking of a Number Using counting cards, chose and hide a secret number. Tell children you hid a card with a number, and ask them to guess which it is. When a child guesses correctly, excitedly reveal the card. Until then, tell children whether a guess is more or less than the secret number. As children become more comfortable, ask why they made their guess, such as "I knew 4 was more than the secret number and 2 was less, so I guessed 3!" Repeat, adding clues, such as your guess is 2 more than my number. Do this activity during transitions.

X-Ray Vision 2 (see Chapter 4).

Build Stairs 2 Students identify the appropriate stacks of unit cubes to fill in a series of staircase steps. (Foundational for "Counting from N (N + 1, N – 1)") Build stairs with connecting cubes first.

Build Stairs 3 Students identify the numeral that represents a missing number in a sequence. Play with connecting cubes first.

Sea to Shore Students identify number amounts by (simple) counting on. They move forward a number of spaces on a game board that is *one more* than the number of dots in the fives and tens number frame. Play on and *off* computer.

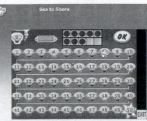

Continued Overleaf

Age (years)	Developmental Progression	Instructional Tasks

Skip Counter by 10s to 100 *Verbal and Object* Skip counts by tens up to 100 or beyond with understanding; e.g., "sees" groups of 10 within a quantity and count those groups by 10 (this relates to multiplication and algebraic thinking; see Chapters 7 and 13).

"10, 20, 30 . . . 100."

School Supply Shop Students count objects by tens to reach a target number up to 100.

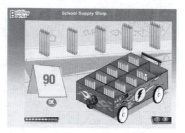

Counter to 100 *Verbal* Counts to 100. Makes decade transitions (e.g., from 29 to 30) starting at any number.

". . .78, 79. . .80, 81 . . ."

Counter On Using Patterns *Strategy* Keeps track of a few counting acts, but only by using numerical pattern (spatial, auditory, or rhythmic).

"How much is 3 more than 5?" Child feels 3 "beats" as counts, "5 . . . *6, 7, 8!*"

Count the Days of School. Each day of school, add a numeral to adding machine tape, taped to the wall, which will eventually surround the classroom. Count from 1 each day and then add that day's numeral. Write the multiples of 10 in red. Some days (e.g., on day 33), count just these red numerals—10, 20, 30 . . . and then continue with the final "ones"—31, 32, 33. Count the red numbers two ways: "ten, twenty, thirty, forty . . ." *and,* sometimes, as "one ten, two tens, three tens, four tens."

How Many in the Box Now? (Main directions above.)

Teacher Suggestion. Act incredulous, saying, "How do you *know* that? You can't even *see* them?" Have children explain.

Teaching Note. If they need help, suggest that children count and keep track using their fingers.

Bright Idea Students are given a numeral and a frame with dots. They count on from this numeral to identify the total amount, and then move forward a corresponding number of spaces on a game board.

Skip Counter *Verbal and Object* Counts by fives and twos with understanding.

Child counts objects, "2, 4, 6, 8 . . . 30."

Skip Counting Besides counting by tens, count groups of objects with skip counting, such as pairs of shoes by twos, or number of fingers in the class by fives.

Book Stacks Students "count on" (through one decade) from a given number as they load books onto a cart.

Age (years)	Developmental Progression	Instructional Tasks

Tire Recycling Students count objects by fives up to 100, or by twos up to 40.

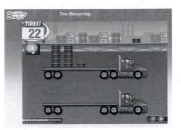

Counter of Imagined Items: *Strategy* Counts mental images of hidden objects.

> Asked, "There are 5 chips here and 5 under the napkin, how many in all?" says fiiiiive . . . then points to the napkin in 4 distinct points, [corners of an imagined square] saying, "6, 7, 8, 9."

How Many Hidden? Hide some objects, tell the child how many are hidden, and show other objects. Ask the child how many in all.

Counter On Keeping Track *Strategy* Keeps track of counting acts numerically, first with objects, then by "counting counts." Counts up 1 to 4 *more* from a given number.

> How many is 3 more than 6? "Six . . . 7 [puts up a finger], 8 [puts up another finger], 9 [puts up third finger]. *9.*"
>
> What is 8 take away 2? "Eight . . . 7 is one, and 6 is two. *6.*"

Easy as Pie On a (any) game board, using numeral cubes, students add two numerals to find a total number (sums of 1 through 10), and then move forward a corresponding number of spaces on a game board. The game encourages children to "count on" from the larger number (e.g., to add 3 + 4, they would count "four . . . 5, 6, 7!").

Lots of Socks Students add 2 numerals to find total number amounts (1 through 20), and then move forward a corresponding number of spaces on a game board. The game encourages children to count on from the larger number (e.g., to add 2 + 9, they would count "nine . . . 10, 11!").

Continued Overleaf

Age (years)	Developmental Progression	Instructional Tasks
		Eggcellent Students use strategy to identify which 2 of 3 numbers, when added together, will enable them to reach the final space on a game board in the fewest number of moves. Often that means the sum of the largest 2 numbers, but sometimes other combinations allow you to hit a positive or avoid a backward action space. 
	Counter of Quantitative Units/Place Value Understands the base-ten numeration system and place-value concepts, including ideas of counting in units and multiples of hundreds, tens, and ones. When counting groups of 10, can decompose into 10 ones if that is useful. Understands value of a digit according to the place of the digit within a number. Counts by tens and ones to determine. Counts unusual units, such as "wholes" when shown combinations of wholes and parts. Shown 3 whole plastic eggs and 4 halves, counts and says there are 5 whole eggs.	*How Many Eggs?* Using plastic eggs that break into halves, show some whole eggs and some halves and ask how many. Repeat in "play store" settings, with different materials (e.g., crayons and broken crayons), and so forth.
	Counter to 200 *Verbal and Object* Counts accurately to 200 and beyond, recognizing the patterns of ones, tens, and hundreds. "After 159 comes 160 because after 5 tens comes 6 tens."	*Count the Days of School* Extend the previous activity (p. 38).
7	**Number Conserver** Consistently conserves number (i.e., believes number has been unchanged) even in face of perceptual distractions such as spreading out objects of a collection. Counts 2 rows that are laid out across from each other and says they are the same. Adult spreads out 1 row. Says, "Both still have the same number, one's just longer."	*The Tricky Fox* Tell a story using stuffed animals. The fox is tricky, and tells the other animals that they should take the row of food with the most, but he spreads one row out and not the other, actually more numerous, row. Ask children how to avoid being tricked.

Age (years)	Developmental Progression	Instructional Tasks
	Counter Forward and Back *Strategy* Counts "counting words" (single sequence or skip counts) in either direction. Recognizes that decades sequence mirrors single-digit sequence.	*(See Chapter 5 for most activities for this competence.)*
	What's 4 less than 63? "62 is 1, 61 is 2, 60 is 3, 59 is 4, so 59."	*Math-O-Scope* Students identify numbers (representing values that are 10 more, 10 less, 1 more, or 1 less than a target number) within the hundreds chart to reveal a partially hidden photograph.
	What is 15 more than 28? "2 tens and 1 ten is 3 tens. 38, 39, 40, and there's 3 more, 43."	
	Switches between sequence and composition views of multidigit numbers easily.	*Figure the Fact* Students add numeric values from 1 through 10 to values from 0 through 99, to reach a maximum total of 100. That is, if they are "on" 33 and get an 8, they have to enter 41 to proceed to that space because the spaces are not marked with numerals, at least until they move through them.
	Counts backward from 20 and higher with meaning.	

Final Words

Chapter 2 described subitizing and this chapter described counting. These are the main ways children determine the number of a collection of objects. In many situations, they need to do more. For example, they may wish to compare 2 numbers or sequence several numbers. This is the topic we turn to in Chapter 4.

4
Comparing, Ordering, and Estimating

Jeremy and his sister Jacie were arguing about who had more dessert. "She has more!" declared Jeremy. "I do not!" said Jacie, "we have the same."

"No. See, I have one, two, three, four, and you have one, two, three, four, five."

"Listen, Jeremy. One of my cookies broke in half. You can't count each half. If you're counting pieces, I could break all yours in half, then you would have *way* more than me. Put the two halves back together and count. One, two, three, four. Four! We have the same."

Jacie went on to argue that she would prefer one whole cookie to the two broken halves anyway, but that's another story. Which "count"—Jeremy's or Jacie's—do you think was better, and why? In what situations should you count separate things, and in what situations might that lead you astray?

Chapter 2 introduced the notion that children possess or develop some ability to compare amounts in the first year of life. However, comparing accurately in many situations can be challenging, especially those in which people might think of either discrete quantities (countable items) or continuous quantities (magnitudes that are divisible, such as amount of matter), as in Jeremy's and Jacie's cookie debate. In this chapter, we discuss comparing, ordering, and estimating discrete quantity (Chapters 11 and 12 discuss continuous quantity).

Comparing and Equivalence

As we saw in Chapter 2, infants begin to construct equivalence relations between sets, possibly by intuitively establishing correspondences, as early as the first year of life. This ability develops considerably, especially as children learn number words, subitizing, and counting. For example, they can explicitly compare collections as early as 2 or 3 years of age in certain everyday situations, but show only the beginnings of such competence on teacher-given tasks at 2.5 to 3.5 years of age. They achieve success across a wide range of tasks, such as the number conservation task on pp. 19–20 of Chapter 3, only in primary school.

On number conservation tasks, even asking a child to count the 2 sets may not help her determine the correct answer. Or, if children deal out items to 2 puppets, and the teacher counts out 1 set, they still may not know how many the other puppet has. Such tasks may overwhelm their "working memory" and children may not know *how* to use counting for comparisons.

Ordering and Ordinal Numbers

The Mathematics of Ordering Numbers and Ordinal Numbers

Ordering numbers is the process of determining which of two numbers is "larger than" the other. Formally, given two whole numbers a and b, b is defined as larger than a if, in counting (see Chapter 3) a precedes b. One relationship must pertain to any such two numbers: $a = b$, $a < b$, or $b < a$. *Equals* in this case means *equivalent*, that is, not necessary "exactly the same" (some comparisons are equal in that sense, such as $6 = 6$), but equal in value ($4 + 2$ is equivalent in value to 6). This relationship of equivalence is *reflexive* (something equals itself, $x = x$), *symmetric* ($x = y$ means that $y = x$), and *transitive* (if $x = y$ and $y = z$ then $x = z$).

We can also define (and think about) ordering numbers on a *number line*—a line on which points are uniquely identified with numbers. This gives a geometric/spatial model for number. Usually the number line is constructed with a horizontal straight line, with a point designated as zero. To the right of 0, equally spaced points are labeled 1, 2, 3, 4 . . ., such as on a ruler. The whole numbers are identified with these points (see Figure 4.1). The line segment from 0 to 1 is called the *unit segment* and the number 1 is called the *unit*. Once we have determined this, all the whole numbers are fixed on the line (Wu, 2007).

Thus, $a < b$ also means that the point a on the number line is to the left of b as we define the number line. Statements such as $a < b$ and $b > a$ are called *inequalities*.

When whole numbers are used to put items in order, or in a sequence, they are *ordinal numbers*. Often we use the ordinal terms "first, second, third . . .," but not always: A person who is "number 5" in a line is labeled by a word that is no less ordinal in its meaning because it is not expressed as "fifth."

Ordering Numbers

> A female chimpanzee called Ai has learned to use Arabic numerals to represent numbers. She can count from zero to nine items, which she demonstrates by touching the appropriate number on a touch-sensitive monitor, and she can order the numbers from zero to nine in sequence (Kawai & Matsuzawa, 2000).

Well, the ability to sequence numbers is certainly not too developmentally advanced for preschoolers!

Relating ordering numbers to counting (see Chapter 3), we can see that if a and b are whole numbers and b has more digits than a, then $a < b$. If a and b have the same number of digits, then moving from the left, if for the first digit in which they do not agree, a's digit $<$ b's digit, then $a < b$ (Wu, 2007).

The ability to use this type of reason develops over years. Children develop the ability to order numbers by learning subitizing matching, and counting. For example, children can answer questions such as "which is more, 6 or 4?" only by age 4 or 5 years. Unlike middle-income children, low-income 5- and 6-year-olds may be unable to tell which of two numbers, such as 6 or 8, is bigger, or which number, 6 or 2, is closer to 5 (Griffin, Case, & Siegler, 1994). They may not have developed

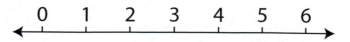

Figure 4.1 A section of a number line.

the "mental number line" representation of numbers as well as their more advantaged peers. All children must learn to reason that if the counts of two collections are 9 and 7, the collection with 9 has more because 9 comes later in the counting sequence than 7.

Finding out *how many* more (or fewer) there are in one collection than another is more demanding than simply comparing two collections to find which has more. Children have to understand that the number of elements in the collection with fewer items is contained in the number of items in the collection with more items. That is, they have to mentally construct a "part" of the larger collection (equivalent to the smaller collection) that is not visually present. They then have to determine the "other part" or the larger collection and find out how many elements are in this "left-over amount."

Ordinal Numbers

Ordinal numbers, usually (but not necessarily) involving the words "first, second. . ." indicate position in a series or ordering. As such, they have different features (e.g., their meaning is connected to the series they describe). Most children in traditional curricula learn terms such as "first," "second," and "last" early, but learn others only much later.

Estimation

An estimation is not merely a "guess"—it is at least a mathematically *educated* guess. Estimation is a process of solving a problem that calls for a rough or tentative evaluation of a quantity. There are many types of estimation, which—along with the common confusion between an estimates and (often wild) "guesses"—has resulted in poor teaching of this skill. The most common types of estimation discussed are measurement, numerosity, and computational estimation (Sowder, 1992a). Measurement estimation will be addressed in Chapters 11 and 12. Computational estimation has been most widely researched (see Chapter 6). Numerosity estimation often involves procedures similar in ways to measurement and computational estimation procedures. To estimate the number of people in a theater, for example, a person might take a sample area, count the people in it, and multiply by an estimate of the number of such areas in the theater. Early numerosity estimation may involve similar procedure (e.g., try to "picture 10" in a jar then count by tens), or even a straight-forward single estimate based on benchmarks (10 "looks like this"; 50 "looks like that") or merely intuition. One more type of estimation is "number line estimation"; for example, the ability to place numbers on a number line of arbitrary length, given that the ends are labeled (say, 0 to 100). Ability to build such a mental structure appears particularly important for young children, so we begin with this estimation type.

Number Line Estimation

The ability to build a "mental number line" is an important mathematical skill. Such skill supports development and performance of arithmetic, estimation, and other mathematical processes. The first skill after learning a mental number *list* may be to form a linear representation of numbers. But most people tend to exaggerate the distances between numbers at the lower end of a given number line—numbers that are more familiar—and underestimate the distances between numbers at the high end. So, rather than represent numbers as on a number line such as Figure 4.1, they tend to represent them as shown in Figure 4.2.

Improving children's number line estimation may have a broad beneficial effect on their representation, and therefore knowledge, of numbers. Further, the estimates of preschoolers from

Figure 4.2 Children initially *internally* represent smaller numbers as "farther apart" than larger numbers.

low-income families reveals poorer understanding of numerical magnitudes than do the estimates of preschoolers from higher-income families. So, facilitating the former children's learning of number line estimation is particularly important.

Estimation of Numerosities

Children's can subitize (Chapter 2) and count (Chapter 3), so can they estimate the number of objects in a collection? Surprisingly, not well. Children may need to learn such foundation skills well, and build mental images of both numbers and "benchmark" collections (e.g., what "10 objects" looks like) to perform numerosity estimation accurately.

Experience and Education

Comparing Numbers

Young children need to learn about the significance of the results of counting. To help them generalize, provide a variety of meaningful tasks and situations in which counting is a relevant strategy and inferences must be made. Prompt children to count in these comparing situations and then *verify* that counting led to correct judgments.

Of course, children also have to realize how to use counting to compare the number in two collections. They must be able to think, "I counted 6 circles and 5 squares, so there are more circles, because 6 comes after 5 when we count." To do this, children also must understand that each counting number is quantitatively one more than the one before (recall the "Counter from N (N + 1, N − 1)" level in Chapter 3, p. 36).

Language, even in supposedly "simple" situations, can be surprisingly complex but—used well—supportive of learning. A 5-year-old was told she had 7¢ and asked what she could buy (Lansdell, 1999). Later, she used the phrase "one more"; that is, an item costing 8 cents was "one more" than she had. Then, for an item costing one less cent, she said she had "one more less." She thought she could buy that item (for 6¢) with her 7¢. The teacher gave her the 7¢ to hold, and the girl talked herself into thinking that it was OK, she could buy the item. Then the teacher introduced the term *change*: "You'd have one penny left, wouldn't you. One penny change. So that would be nice. . . ." The teacher then asked about a 5¢ purchase, and the girl said, "I'd have two pennies change."

The next day she confused this terminology, but not concept. The teacher corrected her use of language, confirming her computational accuracy, but mirroring the correct language. Soon thereafter *change* was used to mean changing pennies to other coins. Impressively, the girl was still able to use *change* correctly and with increased confidence.

The researcher claimed that the informal talk and language were the most important aspects of these interactions, but the clarification or introduction of mathematical terminology is also important (Lansdell, 1999). Many mathematical terms may be ambiguous, usually due to their having non-mathematical meanings, and the teachers' closed questions and direct statements helped the child agree on specific new mathematical meanings. In addition, open questions helped the teacher understand the child's meanings and concepts.

Thus, we teachers need to be aware of such potentially ambiguous words, introduce new words and meanings after concepts are understood, and be careful and consistent in our use of the words. To do this, we should observe children's use of the words, build on the child's own language, and negotiate new meanings through practical experiences (Lansdell, 1999).

Order and Ordinal Numbers

Ordinal number words are potentially more confusing than the verbal counting words, and the two series are often difficult to relate. Repeated experiences with everyday activities are easy to implement, such as who is first, second, third . . . in lining up. Also, explicitly discuss the correspondences and plan activities that invite such connections. For example, in the *Building Blocks* curriculum (Clements & Sarama, 2007c), children build and label stairs with connecting cubes and, on the computer, with squares and numerals. They also insert missing steps. These activities encourage children to note that the second step is number 2, and so forth. Summative evaluations revealed strong effects on children's understanding and skill with ordinal relations and sequencing.

Children may also learn about ordinal relations from observing the consequences of adding and taking away objects (Cooper, 1984; Sophian & Adams, 1987). This suggests multiple experiences adding and subtracting small numbers (especially repeated additions/subtractions of 1). For children who have difficulty, including those with learning disabilities, analogies are helpful. For example, if children cannot identify which of two collections is more, relate the numbers to children's ages, as in, "Who is older, Jack who is 7 years old or Sue who is 5?"

Finally, experiences such as these help children understand and practice conservation of number. Surprisingly, strategy diversity also typifies children's approach to this task (Siegler, 1995). This study included 3 training conditions, correctness feedback, feedback with requests to justify one's reasoning, and feedback with requests to justify the *researcher's* reasoning. The last was the most effective (although order of feedback/explanation were confounded, as were, in the last condition, seeing another's perspective and explaining a correct response). Children use multiple types of explanations, and those explaining the researcher's reasons gave a greater variety than those who explained their own reasons. Again, then, the benefits of verbalizations and strategy diversity are evident.

Number Line Estimation

Having children place numerals on a number line may be helpful for first and second graders, but it can be confusing for younger children. Playing board ("race") games can develop all children's ability to do number line estimation, as well as to order magnitudes, count, and recognize numerals. Encourage parents to play such games at home as well.

Board games may be beneficial because they provide multiple cues to both the order of numbers and the numbers' magnitudes (Siegler & Booth, 2004). In such games, the greater the number in a square, the greater the distance that the child has moved the token, the number of discrete moves the child has made, the number of counting words the child has spoken, and the amount of time since the game began.

It is important to note that building number sense through number line estimation is *not the same as having children work with "number lines"* or to solve problems using number lines. That model is actually quite difficult for children to use, perhaps because children are confused by the dual representation of number as points and distances (or vectors) (Gagatsis & Elia, 2004).

Estimation of Numerosities

Although some have claimed success in promoting numerosity estimation through activities, the limited effects of others suggest caution in devoting much time to these activities in the earliest years of school. Any time that is given, probably in the primary grades, might best follow several guidelines. First, ensure that subitizing, counting, and especially number line estimation skills are well developed. Subitizing skills should be developed at least for small numbers, and counting and number line estimation skills should be developed at least up to the numbers to be estimated. Second, help children develop and understand benchmarks well. Again, benchmarks might beneficially be developed in number line estimation tasks initially, and then expanded to include images of collections of objects of those sizes. Third, within a short instructional unit, expect development to occur more within a level of the learning trajectory.

Learning Trajectories for Comparing, Ordering, and Estimating Numbers

The learning trajectory for comparing, ordering, and estimating numbers, like that for counting, is complex because there are many conceptual and skill advancements and, more obviously, there are *subtrajectories* for each subdomain.

The importance of *goals* for this domain is clear for comparing, ordering, and at least some aspects of estimation. Where these goals appear in NCTM's *Curriculum Focal Points* is shown in Figure 4.3. With those goals, Table 4.1 shows the two additional components of the learning trajectory, the developmental progression and the instructional tasks. (Note that the ages in all the learning trajectory tables are only approximate, especially because the age of acquisition usually depends heavily on experience.)

Pre-K

Number and Operations: Developing an understanding of whole numbers, including concepts of correspondence, counting, cardinality, and comparison

Children . . . use one-to-one correspondence to solve problems by matching sets and comparing number amounts . . . they count to determine number amounts and compare quantities (using language such as "more than" and "less than"), and they order sets by the number of objects in them.

Kindergarten

Number and Operations: Representing, comparing, and ordering whole numbers and joining and separating sets

Children use numbers, including written numerals, to represent quantities and to solve quantitative problems, such as comparing and ordering sets or numerals.

Grade 1

Number and Operations: Developing an understanding of whole number relationships, including grouping in tens and ones

Children compare and order whole numbers (at least to 100) to develop an understanding of and solve problems involving the relative sizes of these numbers. . . . They understand the sequential order of the counting numbers and their relative magnitudes and represent numbers on a number line.

Grade 2

Number and Operations and Algebra: Developing an understanding of the base-ten numeration system and place-value concepts

Children develop an understanding of the base-ten numeration system and place-value concepts (at least to 1000). Their understanding of base-ten numeration includes ideas of counting in units and multiples of hundreds, tens, and ones, as well as a grasp of number relationships, which they demonstrate in a variety of ways, including comparing and ordering numbers.

Figure 4.3 Curriculum Focal Points (NCTM, 2006). Emphasizing comparing, ordering, and estimating numbers in the early years.

Table 4.1 Learning Trajectory for Comparing, Ordering, and Estimating Numbers.

Age (years)	Developmental Progression	Instructional Tasks
0–1	**Many-to-One Corresponder** *Comparing* Puts objects, words, or actions in one-to-one or many-to-one correspondence or a mixture. Puts several blocks in each muffin tin.	Provide rich sensory, manipulative environments that include objects that provoke matching.
2	**One-to-One Corresponder** *Comparing* Puts objects in rigid one-to-one correspondence (age 2;0). Uses words to include "more," "less," or "same" Puts one block in each muffin tin, but is disturbed that some blocks left so finds more tins to put every last block in something. Implicitly sensitive to the relation of "more than/less than" involving very small numbers (from 1 to 2 years of age).	Provide *objects that provoke precise one-to-one correspondences* (e.g., egg carton and plastic eggs that fit exactly). Discuss the correspondences the child makes, or could make. "Does every doll have a block to sit on?"
	Object Corresponder *Comparing* Puts objects into one-to-one correspondence, although may not fully understand that this creates equal groups (age 2;8). Put a straw in each carton (doesn't worry if extra straws are left), but doesn't necessarily know there are the same numbers of straws and cartons.	Provide knob or simple shape puzzles in which each shape is to be placed inside a corresponding hole in the puzzle. *Get Just Enough—Match* Children get just enough of one group of objects to match another group; e.g., a paintbrush for each paint container. At this level, have the two groups next to each other to help children physically match one-to-one. *Setting the Table* Children set a table for dolls/toy animals, possibly in the dramatic play area, using a real or pretend table. Children should set out just enough paper (or toy) plates, cloth napkins, and plastic (or toy) silverware for the dolls/toy animals. Talk with children to establish the idea that one-to-one matching creates equal groups: if you know the number in one of the groups, then you know the number in the other.
	Perceptual Comparer *Comparing* Compares collections that are quite different in size (e.g., one is at least twice the other). Shown 10 blocks and 25 blocks, points to the 25 as having more. If the collections are similar, compares very small numbers. Compares collections using number words "one" and "two" (age 2;8). Shown groups of 2 and 4, points to the group of 4 as having more.	Informal discussions of which is more. *Pizza Pizzazz 1* Children choose the matching pizza.
3	**First-Second Ordinal Counter** *Ordinal Number* Identifies the "first" and often "second" objects in a sequence.	Discuss who wishes to be first and second in line. Gradually extend this to higher ordinal numbers.
	Nonverbal Comparer of Similar Items (1–4 items) *Comparing* Compares collections of 1–4 items verbally or nonverbally ("just by	*Is it Fair?* Show children a small number of objects given to two people (dolls, stuffed animals . . .) and ask if it's fair—if they both have the same number.

Continued Overleaf

Age (years)	Developmental Progression	Instructional Tasks
	looking"). The items must be the same. May compare the smallest collections using number words "two" and "three" (age 3;2), and "three" and others (age 3;6). Can transfer an ordering relation from one pair of collections to another. Identifies ••• and •ׂ• as equal and different from •• or •ׂ	*Compare Snapshots* asking children only to tell if it is the same number or not (see p. 51).
4	**Nonverbal Comparer of Dissimilar Items** *Comparing* Matches small, equal collections, showing that they are the same number. Matches collections of 3 shells and 3 dots, then declares that they "have the same number."	Same as above, with dissimilar objects.
	Matching Comparer *Comparing* Compares groups of 1–6 by matching. Gives one toy bone to every dog and says there are the same number of dogs and bones.	Ask children to determine whether there are the same number of spoons as plates (and many other similar situations). Provide feedback as necessary. Talk to them about how they knew "for sure" and how they figured it out. *Party Time 1* Students practice one-to-one correspondence by matching party utensils to placemats. *Goldilocks and the Three Bears* Read or tell *Goldilocks and the Three Bears* as a flannel board story. Discuss the one-to-one correspondence of bears to other things in the story. Ask: How many bowls are in the story? How many chairs? How do you know? Then ask: Were there just enough beds for the bears? How do you know? Summarize that one-to-one match can create equal groups. That is, if you know the number of bears in one group, then you know the number of beds in the other group. Tell children they can retell the story and match props later in center time.
	Counting Comparer (Same Size) *Comparing* Accurate comparison via counting, but only when objects are about the same size and groups are small (about 1–5). Counts two piles of 5 blocks each, and says they are the same. Not always accurate when larger collection's objects are smaller in size than the objects in the smaller collection.	

Age (years)	Developmental Progression	Instructional Tasks
	Accurately counts two equal collections, but when asked, says the collection of larger blocks has more.	*Compare Game* For each pair of children playing, 2 or more sets of counting cards (1–5) are needed. Teach children to mix the cards (e.g., by mixing them all up as they are face down), and then deal them evenly (one to the first player, then one to the second player . . .), face down to both players. Players simultaneously flip their top cards and compare to find out which is greater. Player with the greater amount says, "I have more," and takes the opponent's cards. If card amounts are equal, players each flip another card to determine a result. The game is over when all cards have been played, and the "winner" is the player with more cards.  Use cards with dot arrays and numerals at first, then just dot arrays. Start with small numbers and slowly add larger numbers. Play the game on computers as well, as below. *Number Compare 1: Dots and Numerals* In this Compare ("war") game, children compare two cars and choose the one with the greater value. 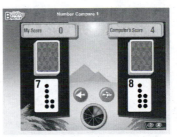 *Compare Snapshots* Secretly place three counters on a plate and five counters on another plate. Using a dark cloth, cover the plate with five counters. Show children both plates, one covered. Tell children to watch carefully and quietly, keeping their hands in their laps, as you quickly reveal the covered plate so they can compare it to the other plate. Uncover the plate for 2 seconds, and cover it again. Ask children: Do the plates have the same number of counters? Because the answer is "no," ask: Which plate has more? Have children point or say the number on the plate. Which plate has fewer counters? If needed, repeat the reveal. Uncover the plate indefinitely. Ask children how many counters are on each plate. Confirm that five is more than three because five comes after three when counting.
	Mental Number Line to 5 *Number Line Estimation* Uses knowledge of counting number relationships to determine relative size and position when given perceptual support.	Ask children who is older, a 2-year-old or a 3-year-old. Provide feedback as necessary. Ask them to explain how they know. *Race Game*: Board game with numbers 1 to 10 in consecutively numbered, linearly arranged, equal-size squares. Spin a "1" or a "2". Move that many, then say each number while you are moving your token.

Continued Overleaf

Age (years)	Developmental Progression	Instructional Tasks

Shown a 0 at one end of a line segment and 5 at the other, places a "3" approximately in the middle.

Road Race Counting Game Students identify number amounts (from one through five) on a dot frame and move forward a corresponding number of spaces on a game board.

Road Race Students identify numbers of sides (three, four, or five) on polygons and move forward a corresponding number of spaces on a game board.

What's the Missing Step?

Show children a growing and shrinking cube staircase tower 1,2,3,4,3,2,1. Have children close their eyes and remove the first tower of 3 cubes. Ask them what step they think is missing. Ask why they selected that step. Did they count? Did they just know? Show the missing step and count the cubes.

Repeat, but this time remove the second tower of 3 cubes. Ask for their answers, ask why they think that.

Build Stairs 3: What's the Missing Step? Children play this game on and off computer. A step is missing; they have to determine the number of the missing step.

Numeral Train Game Students identify numerals (1–5) and move forward a corresponding number of spaces on a game board. On physical or computer game boards, this builds knowledge of the relative size of numbers.

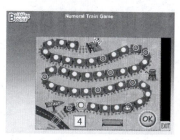

5 | **Counting Comparer (5)**
Comparing Compares with counting, even when larger collection's objects are smaller. Later, figures out *how many* more or less.

Memory Game—Number

For each pair of children, one set of Dot cards and one set of Numeral cards are needed.

Place card sets face down in two separate arrays. Players take turns choosing, flipping, and showing a card from each array.

Age (years)	Developmental Progression	Instructional Tasks

Accurately counts two equal collections, and says they have the same number, even if one collection has larger blocks.

If the cards do not match, they are returned face down to the arrays. If they match, that player keeps them.

Find the Number—Compare Before children get to the center, conceal several pizzas (paper plates), each under its own opaque container, each with a different number of pepperoni slices (round counters) under its own opaque container. Display one pizza with three to five pepperoni slices. The goal is for children to find the hidden match to the pizza on display.

Get Just Enough—Count Children get just enough of one group of objects to match another group; e.g., a scissors for each child at their table. At this level, make sure they have to go across the room to get the scissors, so they have to count. The same can be done with *Setting the Table* (see above)—make sure counting is necessary.

Ordinal Counter *Ordinal Number* Identifies and uses ordinal numbers from "first" to "tenth."

Can identify who is "third in line."

Ordinal Construction Company Students learn ordinal positions (first through tenth) by moving objects between the floors of a building.

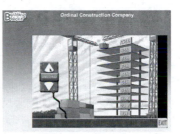

Spatial Extent Estimator—Small/ Big *Numerosity Estimation* Names a "small number" (e.g., 1–4) for sets that cover little space and a "big number" (10–20 or more; children classify numbers "little/big" idiosyncratically, and this may change with the size of the to-be-estimated collection, or TBE).

Shown 9 objects spread out for 1 second and asked, "How many?," responds, "Fifty!"

The Estimating Jar Put objects in a clear plastic jar as you did for the *Counting Jar* activity and secure the lid. Tell children it will now be an Estimating jar, and they will estimate how many items are in it, recording their estimates and their names on self-sticking notes to post by the jar. At the end of the week, spill the items out, count them, and compare the counts to the estimates.

Counting Comparer (10) *Comparing* Compares with counting, even when larger collection's objects are smaller, up to 10.

Accurately counts two collections of 9 each, and says they have the same number, even if one collection has larger blocks.

Compare Game For each pair of children playing, 2 or more sets of counting (with dots and numerals, and, soon thereafter, just dots) cards (1–10) are needed. Mix and deal cards evenly face down.

Players simultaneously flip their top cards and compare to find out which is greater.

Player with the greater amount says, "I have more," and takes the opponent's cards.

If card amounts are equal, players each flip another card to determine a result.

The game is over when all cards have been played.

Continued Overleaf

Age (years)	Developmental Progression	Instructional Tasks

Mr. MixUp—Comparing Tell children that Mr. MixUp needs help comparing.

Compare collections of objects of different sizes. For example, show four blocks and six much smaller items, and have Mr. MixUp say, "The blocks are bigger so the number is greater." Ask children to count to find out which group really has more items, and explain to Mr. MixUp why he is wrong.

Cube towers—which have more, which have fewer. Show two towers: one made of eight identical blocks on the floor and another made of seven similar identical blocks on a chair. Ask children which tower is taller. Discuss any strategies they invent. Summarize that, although the tower on the chair is higher, from the bottom of the tower to the top of the tower is shorter because it consists of fewer blocks than the tower on the floor.

Age (years)	Developmental Progression	Instructional Tasks
6	**Mental Number Line to 10** *Number Line Estimation* Uses internal images and knowledge of number relationships to determine relative size and position. Which number is closer to 6, 4 or 9?	*Compare Game* (see above) *What's the Missing Step?* (as above, 1–10) *I'm Thinking of A Number*

Using counting cards from 1 to 10, choose and hide a secret number.

Tell children you hid a card with a number, and ask them to guess which it is.

When a child guesses correctly, excitedly reveal the card.

Until then, tell children whether a guess is more or less than the secret number.

As children become more comfortable, ask why they made their guess, such as "I knew 4 was more than the secret number and 2 was less, so I guessed 3!

Repeat, adding clues, such as your guess is 2 more than my number.

Do this activity during transitions.

Rocket Blast 1 Students estimate the placement of a tick mark on a 1–20 number line to the nearest whole number.

Age (years)	Developmental Progression	Instructional Tasks

Space Race Students choose numbers that enable them to reach the final space on a game board in a designated number of moves. The better number is usually (but not always) the larger of the two presented.

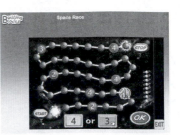

Serial Orderer to 6+
Comparing/Ordering Orders numerals, and collection (small numbers first).

Given cards with 1 to 5 dots on them, puts in order.

Orders lengths marked into units.

Given towers of cubes, puts in order, 1 to 10.

Build Stairs Have children make "stairs" with connecting cubes. Encourage them to count each step. Ask them to describe the numbers. Extensions:

Have someone hide one of the stairs and you figure out which one is hidden, then you insert it.

Have them mix up the steps and put them back in order.

Building Stairs 2 Order steps to fill in a series of staircase steps.

Building Stairs 3 Identify the numeral that represents a missing number in a sequence.

Order Cards Place Dot Cards 1–5 so they are left to right from the children's perspective. Ask children to describe the pattern. Tell children to keep counting out loud, predicting the next number as you continue to lay out the next Dot Card in the pattern. Explain that they will eventually put these cards in order on their own at the Hands On Math Center.

Continued Overleaf

Age (years)	Developmental Progression	Instructional Tasks
		X-Ray Vision 1 Place Counting Cards 1–10 in numerical order so that children see them in left-to-right order, and count them with children. Then place the cards face down, still in order.
		Ask a volunteer to point to any of the cards. Using your "x-ray vision" (really, counting from one to the chosen card), tell children which card it is. The volunteer flips the card to show you are correct, and then replaces it face down.
		Repeat with another card.
		Ask children to use their x-ray vision in a similar manner after you point to one of the cards. Remind them where "1" is, then point to "2." Have children spontaneously say what they think the card is. Turn it over to check.
		X-Ray Vision 2 This variation encourages counting forward and backward from numbers.
		Place Counting Cards 1–10 in numerical order, and count them with children. Then place the cards face down, still in order. Tell children this is a new way to play X-Ray Vision, keeping the cards showing after they are guessed.
		Point to any card. Ask children to use their x-ray vision to figure out which card it is. Flip the card to show they are correct and keep the card face up, telling children you are doing that on purpose.
		Point to the card right after the face-up card. Ask children to use their x-ray vision to determine what the card is. Ask children how they figured it out. Discuss that you could count forward from the face-up card.
		Keeping both cards face up, repeat with a face-down card that comes right before another card.
	Spatial Extent Estimator *Numerosity Estimation* Extends sets and number categories to include "small numbers" which are usually subitized, not estimated, "middle-size numbers" (e.g., 10–20) and "large numbers." The arrangement of the TBE affects the difficulty.	*The Estimating Jar* (see above)
		Estimate How Many In specifically designed instructional situations (e.g., a whole group lesson in which a large chart is covered with a number of dots) or other setting (e.g., noting a large flock of birds on the playground), ask children to estimate the number. Discuss strategies, having someone demonstrate each, then challenge children to apply them to new situations.
	Shown 9 objects spread out for 1 second and asked, "How many?," responds, "Fifteen."	
7	**Place Value Comparer** *Comparing* Compares numbers with place value understandings.	*Snapshots Compare* with place value models.
		See also activities in Chapter 6 dedicated to place value (pp. 89–90).
	"63 is more than 59 because 6 tens is more than 5 tens even if there are more than 3 ones."	
	Mental Number Line to 100 *Number Line Estimation* Uses internal images and knowledge of number relationships, including ones embedded in tens, to determine relative size and position.	*I'm Thinking of A Number* (as above, but done verbally or with an "empty number line"—a line segment initially labeled only with 0 to 100, filled in with each of the children's estimates).
		Rocket Blast 2 Students estimate the placement of a tick mark on a 1–100 number line to the nearest whole number.
	Asked, "Which is closer to 45, 30 or 50?," says, "45 is right next to 50, but fives, but 30 isn't."	*Lots of Socks* Students add two numerals to find total number amounts (1 through 20), and then move forward a corresponding number of spaces on a game. Although this and the next activity mainly teach addition, the movements on the (1 to 50, then 50 to 100) game board also helps build a mental number line.

Age (years)	Developmental Progression	Instructional Tasks

Figure the Fact Students add numeric values from 1 through 10 to values from 0 through 99, to reach a maximum total of 100. That is, if they are "on" 33 and get an 8, they have to enter 41 to proceed to that space, because the spaces are not marked with numerals, at least until they move through them. This is especially important in developing a mental number line.

Again, the activities in Chapter 6 dedicated to place value (pp. 89–90) and those at the higher levels of the learning trajectories in that chapter develop these abilities as well.

Scanning with Intuitive Quantification Estimator
Numerosity Estimation

Shown 40 objects spread out for 1 second and asked, "How many?," responds, "About thirty."

Estimate How Many In specifically designed instructional situations (e.g., a whole group lesson in which a large chart is covered with a number of dots) or other setting (e.g., noting a large flock of birds on the playground), ask children to estimate the number. Discuss strategies, having someone demonstrate each, then challenge children to apply them to new situations.

8   Mental Number Line to 1000s
Number Line Estimation Uses internal images and knowledge of number relationships, including place value, to determine relative size and position.

Asked, "Which is closer to 3500, 2000 or 7000?," says, "70 is double 35, but 20 is only 15 from 35, so 20 hundreds, 2000, is closer."

I'm Thinking of A Number (as above, 0 to 1000)

Rocket Blast 3 Students estimate the placement of a tick mark on a 1–1000 number line to the nearest whole number.

Benchmarks Estimator
Numerosity Estimation
Initially, a portion of the TBE is counted; this is used as a benchmark from which an estimate is made. Later, scanning can be linked to recalled benchmarks.

Estimate How Many (see above) Emphasize strategies at this level or the next.

Continued Overleaf

Age (years)	Developmental Progression	Instructional Tasks
	Shown 11, says, "It looked closer to 10 than 20, so I guess 12." Shown 45 objects spread out for 1 second and asked, "How many?," responds, "About 5 tens—fifty."	
	Composition Estimator *Numerosity Estimation* Initially for regular arrangements, subitizing is used to quantify a subset and repeated addition or multiplication used to produce an estimate. Later, the process is extended to include irregular arrangements. Finally, it includes the ability to *decompose* or *partition* the TBE into convenient subset sizes, then recompose the numerosity based on multiplication.	*Estimate How Many* (see above) Emphasize strategies at this level.
	Shown 87 objects spread out and asked for an estimate responds, "That's about 20—so, 20, 40, 60, 80. Eighty!"	

Final Words

In many situations, people wish to compare, order, or estimate the number of objects. Another common type of situation involves putting collections—and the numbers of these collections—together and taking them apart. These operations of arithmetic are the focus of Chapter 5.

5
Arithmetic
Early Addition and Subtraction and Counting Strategies

Alex is 5 years old. Her brother, Paul, is 3. Alex bounds into the kitchen and announces:

Alex: When Paul is 6, I'll be 8; when Paul is 9, I'll be 11; when Paul is 12, I'll be 14 [she continues until Paul is 18 and she is 20].
Father: My word! How on earth did you figure all that out?
Alex: It's easy. You just go "three-FOUR-five" [saying the "four" very loudly, and clapping hands at the same time, so that the result was very strongly rhythmical, and had a soft-LOUD-soft pattern], you go "six-SEVEN [clap]-eight," you go "nine-TEN [clap!]-eleven" (Davis, 1984, p. 154).

Is this small, but remarkable, scene a glimpse at an exceptional child? Or is it an indication of the potential *all* young children have to learn arithmetic? If so, how early could instruction start? How early *should* it start?

The Earliest Arithmetic

We saw that children have a sense of quantity from early in life. Similarly, they appear to have some sense of simple arithmetic. For example, they appear to expect that if you add one, you have one more. Figure 5.1 illustrates one such experiment. After seeing a screen hide one doll, then a hand place another doll behind the screen, 5-month-olds look longer when the removal of the screen reveals an incorrect, rather than a correct, outcome (a violation-of-expectations procedure, Wynn, 1992).

Research on subitizing (Chapter 2) and early arithmetic suggests that infants intuitively represent small collections (e.g., 2) as individual objects (that they "track") but not as groups. In contrast, they represent large numbers (e.g., 10) as groups but not as individual objects, but they can combine such groups and intuitively expect a certain outcome. For example, shown two groups of five dots combined, they discriminate between the outcome of 5 (incorrect) and 10 (correct). Also, by 2 years of age, children show signs of knowing that adding increases, and taking away decreases, quantity. The intuitive quantity estimators they use may be innate, and facilitate later-developing, explicit arithmetic. However, they do not directly lead to and determine this explicit, accurate arithmetic.

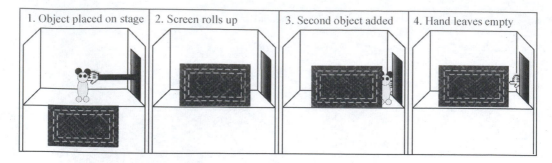

Then either...

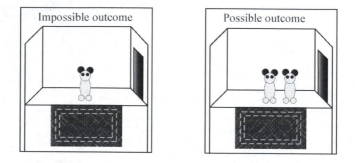

Figure 5.1 An experiment revealing 5-month-olds' sensitivity to adding one object.

Across many studies, research suggests that children develop an initial *explicit* understanding of addition and subtraction with small numbers by about 3 years of age. However, it is not until 4 years of age that most children can solve addition problems involving even slightly larger numbers with accuracy (Huttenlocher, Jordan, & Levine, 1994).

Most children do not solve larger-number problems without the support of concrete objects until 5½ years of age. However, *this is not so much a developmental, as an experiential, limitation.* With experience, preschoolers and kindergartners can learn "counting-all" and even beginning "counting-on" strategies.

Arithmetic: Mathematical Definitions and Properties

Mathematically, we can define addition in terms of counting (Wu, 2007). This connects arithmetic to counting (especially incrementation, also known as the successor operation, the addition of 1 to a number). The *sum* $3 + 8$ is the whole number that results from counting 8 numbers starting at 3—*3*... 4, 5, 6, 7, 8, 9, 10, 11 (Wu, 2007). One would not welcome the task, but the sum $37 + 739$ is the number that results from counting 739 numbers starting at 37—*37*... 38, 39 ... 774, 775, 776. In general, for any two whole numbers *a* and *b*, the sum $a + b$ is the number that results by counting *b* more numbers starting at the number *a* (Wu, 2007).

We can also skip-count. If we do skip-counting by 10s *ten times*, we have 100. Similarly, skip-counting by 100s *ten times* results in 1000, and so forth. All this is consistent with what we learned about counting in Chapters 3 and 4. Thus, $47 + 30$ can be solved by skip-counting by 10s—*47*... 57, 67, 77. Place value is fundamental to arithmetic, which we discuss in more detail in Chapter 6.

From the earliest levels, arithmetic depends on two properties.

The associative law of addition: $(a + b) + c = a + (b + c)$

For example, this allows a mental addition strategy that simplifies some computations, such as: $4 + 4 + 6 = 4 + (4 + 6) = 4 + 10 = 14$.

The commutative law of addition: $a + b = b + a$

Young children usually do not know these laws explicitly, but may use them intuitively (however, some studies indicate that children do understand the concept of commutativity when using it in counting strategies, Canobi, Reeve, & Pattison, 1998). Illustrating commutativity, think how odd it would be if the number of toy vehicles you put in an empty toy box depended on whether you put the trucks or the cars in first.

Subtraction does not follow these laws. Subtraction is defined mathematically as the inverse of addition; that is, subtraction is the *additive inverse* $-a$ for any a, such that $a + -a = 0$. Or, for $8 - 3$, the difference is the number that, when added to 3, results in 8. So, $c - a = b$ means that b is the number that satisfies $a + b = c$. Thus, although it seems cumbersome, one can think of $(8 - 3)$ as $((5 + 3) - 3) = 5 + (3 - 3) = 5 + 0 = 5$. Or, since we know that subtraction and addition are inverses of each other, saying

$8 - 3 = \_$

means the same as

$8 = 3 + \_.$

Subtraction can also be intuitively understood through counting: The *difference* $8 - 3$ is the whole number that results from counting *backward* 3 numbers starting at 8—8 . . . 7, 6, 5. That is, asking "what is $8 - 3$?" means the same as "what number added to 3 gives 8? And, we know that the *difference* $(8 - 3)$ is the whole number that results from counting *backward* 3 numbers starting at 8—8 . . . 7, 6, 5. This process is consistent with the "take away" notion of subtraction. All of these notions are equivalent, and to us they seem natural. For students coming to grips with subtraction, seeing them all as the "same thing" takes lots of time and practice.

Addition and subtraction can therefore be understood through counting, and that is one way children come to learn more about these arithmetic operations (building on the foundations discussed previously). This way of understanding arithmetic is the focus of this chapter.

Addition and Subtraction Problem Structures (and other factors that affect difficulty)

In most cases the larger the numbers, the more difficult the problem. This is so even for single-digit problems, due to the frequency one has experienced the arithmetic computations and the strategies one must use. For example, children use a more sophisticated strategy to solve subtraction combinations whose minuend (the "whole" from which a part is subtracted) are larger than 10 than for those that are smaller than 10.

Beyond the size of the number, it is the *type*, or *structure* of the word problem that mainly determines its difficulty. Type depends on the *situation* and the *unknown*. There are four different situations, shown in the four rows of Table 5.1 The names in quotation marks are those considered most useful in classroom discussions. For each of these categories, there are three quantities that play different roles in the problem, any one of which could be the unknown. In some cases, such as

Table 5.1 Addition and Subtraction Problem Types.

Category	Start/Part Unknown	Change/Difference Unknown	Result/Whole Unknown
Join ("Change Plus") An action of joining increases the number in a set.	*start unknown* $\Box + 6 = 11$ Al had some balls. Then he got 6 more. Now he has 11 balls. How many did he start with?	*change unknown* $5 + \Box = 11$ Al had 5 balls. He bought some more. Now he has 11. How many did he buy?	*result unknown* $5 + 6 = \Box$ Al had 5 balls and gets 6 more. How many does he have in all?
Separate ("Change Minus") An action of separating decreases the number in a set.	*start unknown* $\Box - 5 = 4$ Al had some balls. He gave 5 to Barb. Now he has 4. How many did he have to start with?	*change unknown* $9 - \Box = 4$ Al had 9 balls. He gave some to Barb. Now he has 4. How many did he give to Barb?	*result unknown* $9 - 5 = \Box$ Al had 9 balls and gave 5 to Barb. How many does he have left?
Part–Part–Whole ("Collection") Two parts make a whole, but there is no action—the situation is static.	*part ("partner") unknown* [bar model: 10 / □ 6] [tree: 10 branching to □ and 6] Al has 10 balls. Some are blue, 6 are red. How many are blue?	*part ("partner") unknown* [bar model: 10 / 4 □] [tree: 10 branching to 4 and □] Al has 10 balls; 4 are blue, the rest are red. How many are red?	*whole ("total") unknown* [bar model: □ / 4 6] [tree: □ branching to 4 and 6] Al has 4 red balls and 6 blue balls. How many balls does he have in all?
Compare The numbers of objects in two sets are compared.	*smaller unknown* [bar: 7] [bar: _ 2] Al had 7 balls. Barb has 2 fewer balls than Al. How many balls does Barb have? (More difficult language: "Al has 2 more than Barb.")	*difference unknown* [bar: 7] [bar: 5 _] "Won't get" Al has 7 dogs and 5 bones. How many dogs won't get a bone? Al has 6 balls. Barb has 4. How many more does Al have than Barb? (Also: How many fewer balls does Barb have?)	*larger unknown* [bar: empty] [bar: 5 2] Al has 5 marbles. Barb has 2 more than Al. How many balls does Barb have? (More difficult language: "Al has 2 balls less than Barb.")

the unknown parts of Part–Part–Whole problems, there is no real difference between the roles, so this does not affect the difficulty of the problem. In others, such as the result unknown, change unknown, or start unknown of Join problems, the differences in difficulty are large. Result unknown problems are easy, change unknown problems are moderately difficult, and start unknown are the most difficult. This is due in large part to the increasing difficulty children have in modeling, or "act outing," each type.

Arithmetic Counting Strategies

Most people can invent strategies for solving such problems. The strategies of children as young as preschool are notably creative and diverse. For example, preschool to first grade children can invent and use a variety of covert and overt strategies, including counting fingers, finger patterns (i.e., conceptual subitizing), verbal counting, retrieval ("just knowing" a combination), derived combinations ("derived facts"; e.g., "doubles plus 1": $7 + 8 = 7 + 7 + 1 = 14 + 1 = 15$). Children are flexible strategists; using different strategies on problems they perceive to be easier or harder.

Modeling and Counting Strategies

Strategies usually emerge from children's modeling the problem situation. That is, children as young as preschool and kindergarten can solve problems using concrete objects or drawings (see the section *Manipulatives and "Concrete" Representations* in Chapter 16). Children from lower-resource communities have more difficulty solving verbally presented problems.

Counting Strategies

Preschoolers, 3 and 4 years of age, were told stories in which they were asked, for example, to help a baker. They were shown an array of goods, which they counted. Then the array was hidden, and 1, 2, or 3 more goods were added or subtracted. Children were asked to predict, and then count to check. Even the 3-year-olds understood the difference between predicting and counting to check a prediction. All were able to offer a number that resulted from an addition or subtraction that was consistent with the principles that addition increases numerosity and subtraction decreases numerosity. They made other *reasonable* predictions. Their counts were usually correct and the answer was preferred to the prediction (Zur & Gelman, 2004).

Most initially use a *counting-all* procedure. As illustrated in Figure 5.2, given a situation of $5 + 2$, such children count out objects to form as set of 5 items, then count out 2 more items, and finally count all those and—if they made no counting errors—report "7." These children naturally use such counting methods to solve story situations as long as they understand the language and situation in the story.

After children develop such methods, they eventually *curtail* them. On their own, 4-year-olds may start "*counting-on*", solving the previous problem by counting, "Fiiiive . . . six seven. Seven!" The elongated pronunciation may be substituting for counting the initial set one by one. It is *as if* they counted a set of 5 items. Some children first use transitional strategies, such as the *shortcut-sum* strategy, which is like counting-all strategy, but involves only one count; for example, to solve $4 + 3$, 1, 2, 3, 4, 5, 6, 7 and answer 7.

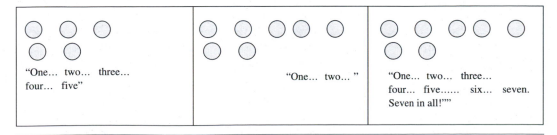

"One... two... three... four... five"

"One... two... "

"One... two... three... four... five...... six... seven. Seven in all!""

Figure 5.2 Using the *counting-all* procedure to solve an addition problem ($5 + 2$).

Children then move to the *counting-on-from-larger* strategy, which is preferred by most children once they invent it. Presenting problems such as 2 + 23, where counting on saves the most work, often prompts children to invent this strategy.

Thus, counting skills—especially sophisticated counting skills—play an important role in developing competence with arithmetic. Counting easily and quickly predicts arithmetic competence in kindergarten and later. Knowing the next number (see the level, "Counter from N (N + 1, N − 1)," in Chapter 3) predicts arithmetic achievement and addition speed in grades 1 and 2.

Counting-on when increasing collections and the corresponding *counting-back-from* when decreasing collections are powerful numerical strategies for children. However, they are only beginning strategies. In the case where the amount of increase is unknown, children use *counting-up-to* to find the unknown amount. If six items are increased so that there are now nine items, children may find the amount of increase by counting, "Siiiix; 7, 8, 9. Three." And if nine items are decreased so that six remain, children may count from nine down to six to find the unknown decrease (separate change unknown), as follows: "Nine; 8, 7, 6. Three." However, counting backward, especially more than three counts, is difficult for most children unless they have high-quality instruction in this competence.

Instead, children in many parts of the world learn *counting-up-to* the total to solve a subtraction situation because they realize that it is easier. For example, the story problem "8 apples on the table. The children ate 5. How many now?" could be solved by thinking, "I took away 5 from those 8, so 6, 7, 8 (raising a finger with each count), that's 3 more left in the 8." When children fully realize that they can find the amount of decrease (e.g., $9 − \_ = 6$) by putting the items back with the 6 and counting from 6 up to 9, they establish that subtraction is the inversion of addition and can use addition instead of subtraction. This understanding develops over several years, but may emerge in the preschool years and can be used by kindergartners with good instruction.

Metacognitive Strategies and Other Knowledge

There is much more to competence in solving even simple word problems than just knowing counting strategies. As stated, children must understand the language, including the semantics and the syntax, and be familiar with the situations the language represents.

Also, solutions of word problems occur in social-cultural contexts and those too, affect children's solutions. For example, schooling can lead to "coping strategies" that children use, or even direct teaching of unfortunate strategies, that limits children's problem-solving abilities. As an example, in low-quality environments, children come to use, or are taught to use, "key word" approaches, such as finding the word "left" or "less" in a problem and then subtracting a small from a larger number they find in the text.

When children consider problems for which they have no immediate strategy, they often do *not* apply "heuristics," or general strategies or representations that may serve as guides. Teaching of heuristics such as "make a drawing" or "break the problem down into parts" have not been remarkably successful. However, *metacognitive* or self-regulatory teaching, often including heuristics, shows more promise (Verschaffel, Greer, & De Corte, 2007). Chapter 13 focuses on such problem-solving processes.

Summary

Babies are sensitive to some situations that adults see as arithmetical. They may be using an innate subitizing ability that is limited to very small numbers, such as 2 + 1. Or they may be individuating and tracking individual objects. In any case, they possess a far richer foundation for arithmetic than traditional Piagetian accounts suggested.

Only years later can children solve problems with larger numbers (but not yet large; e.g., 3 + 2), using concrete objects and subitizing and/or counting. Later again, children develop more sophisticated counting and composition strategies as curtailments of these early solution strategies. That is, children learn to count from a given number (rather than starting only from one), generate the number before or after another number, and eventually embed one number sequence inside another. They think about the number sequence, rather than just saying it (Fuson, 1992a). Such reflection empowers counting to be an effective and efficient representational tool for problem-solving. Thus, educators must study the processes children use as well as the problems they can solve to understand both their strengths and limitations at various ages. Learning involves a complex development of knowledge, understanding, and skill, usually involving the use of a mix of strategies. More sophisticated strategies are learned, strategies are selected more effectively, and speed and accuracy of executing these strategies increases (NMP, 2008).

Experience and Education

At *every* age, children need opportunities to learn arithmetic. In the U.S., virtually all children need *better* opportunities than those presently provided—to solve addition and subtraction problems, building on their competencies with subitizing, modeling, and counting. Because this unfortunate state of affairs is so common, we begin this section by discussing roadblocks to high-quality instruction.

Roadblocks to High-quality Experience and Education

Limiting beliefs. Children can learn arithmetic from 3 years of age, and, in limited contexts, even earlier. Yet most preschool teachers and other professionals do not believe arithmetic is appropriate, and do not believe very young children can think arithmetically. Thus, it is unsurprising that young children do not receive high-quality educational experiences with arithmetic.

Typical instruction. Instruction often helps students perform arithmetic procedures, but *at the expense of conceptual understanding.* Children are initially competent at modeling different problem types. Schooling makes them ask, "What do I do, add or subtract?" and makes them perform more wrong-operation errors. Instead, informal modeling and understanding the situations need to be encouraged and instruction needs to build on informal knowledge (Frontera, 1994).

Textbooks. In too many traditional U.S. textbooks, only the simplest meanings are given for addition and subtraction problems join or separate, result unknown (Stigler, Fuson, Ham, & Kim, 1986). That is unfortunate, because (a) most kindergartners can already solve these problem types and (b) other countries' first grade curricula include *all* the types in Table 5.1 (p. 62).

Textbooks also do little with subitizing or counting, automatization of which aids arithmetical reasoning, and de-emphasize counting strategies. The younger the children, the more problematic these instructional approaches become. No wonder that American schooling has a positive effect on children's accuracy on arithmetic, but an inconsistent effect on their use of strategies.

In addition, textbooks offer an inadequate presentation of problems with anything but small numbers. In one kindergarten text, only 17 of the 100 addition combinations were presented, and each of these only a small numbers of times.

Teaching Arithmetic Counting Strategies

There are other reasons to believe that present practice is inadequate with regard to teaching arithmetic counting strategies. For example, longitudinal studies suggest that in spite of the gains many younger children make through adopting efficient mental strategies for computation in the first years of school, a significant proportion of them still rely on inefficient counting strategies to solve arithmetical problems mentally in the upper years of primary school (Carr & Alexeev, 2008; Clarke, Clarke, & Horne, 2006; Gervasoni, 2005; Perry, Young-Loveridge, Dockett, & Doig, 2008). Early use of more sophisticated strategies, including fluency and accuracy in second grade, appears to influence later arithmetical competence. Children using manipulatives continued to need to use manipulatives (Carr & Alexeev, 2008).

How might we do better? Teachers want children to advance in their sophistication, but effective advances usually do not involve replacing initial strategies with school-based algorithms, such as "column addition" (see Chapter 6). Instead, *effective teaching helps children curtail and adapt their early creations.*

General approaches. As we shall see repeatedly, one of the main lessons from research for arithmetic is to *connect children's learning of skills, facts, concepts, and problem-solving.* So, work with children to pose problems, make connections, and then work out these problems in ways that make the connections visible. Encourage children to use increasingly sophisticated counting strategies, seek patterns, and understand the relationship between addition and subtraction.

Other studies confirm the advantages in children inventing, using, sharing, and explaining *different strategies* for more demanding arithmetic problems. *The number of different strategies children understand and use predicts their later learning.*

Counting-on. Encourage children to invent new strategies. To begin, help children learn the "Counter from N (N + 1, N − 1)" level of counting well. This helps because children often use the knowledge that $n + 1$ tasks can be solved by the "number-after" strategy (the counting word after n is the sum) to invent the counting-on strategy. If children, especially those with a learning disability, need help with the number-after skill, provide and then fade a "running start." Also, to spur children to start using the counting-on-from-larger strategy, pose problems in which its use would save considerable effort, such as $1 + 18$ or $3 + 21$.

If some children do not then invent *counting-on* for themselves and always use *counting-all*, encourage understanding and use of the subskills. For example, lay out numerals "6" and "4" and ask a child to lay out that number of counters. Ask him to count to find how many in all. As he is counting, right as he reaches "six," point to last counter of the first group (the sixth object). When he counts that last counter, point to numeral card and say, "See this is 6 also. It tells how many counters there are here." Have him count again, and interrupt him sooner, until he understands that when he reaches that object, he will have counted 6. Next, point to the first counter of the second group (addend), and say, "See, there were *six* counters here, so *this* one (exaggerated jump from last counter in the first addend to first counter in the second addend) gets the number *seven.* If need be, interrupt the child's counting of the first addend with questions: "How many here (first addend)? So this dot (last of first) gets what number? And this one (first of second)?" Continue until the child understands these ideas and can answer easily. *Counting-on* and other strategies, such as *counting-up-to* and *counting-down-to* are not just good strategies for finding answers. They also develop part–part–whole relationships more effectively than teaching paper-and-pencil algorithms (B. Wright, 1991).

Adding zero (additive identity). This is simply the understanding that adding zero to any number results in that number, or $n + 0 = n$ (zero is called the additive identity). Children can learn this as a general rule, and thus do not need to practice combinations involving zero.

Commutativity often develops without explicit teaching. Presenting tasks such as 3 + 5 near the commuted problem 5 + 3, and doing so systematically and repeatedly, is useful.

Inversion. In a similar vein, children's use of arithmetical principles, such as the inverse principle, before formal schooling should be considered when planning curriculum and teaching. Once kindergartners can verbally subitize small numbers and understand the additive and subtractive identity principle, they can solve inversion problems using 1 ($n + 1 - 1 = \_?$) and slowly work up to 4. A useful teaching strategy is to first add or take away the *same* objects, discuss the inversion principle, and then pose problems in which you add several objects, and take away the same number, but not the same objects.

Invention or direct instruction? Some argue that children must invent their own arithmetic strategies. Others claim that *children making sense of mathematical relations is key*, but the exact teaching approach matters less. Our review of the research suggests the following:

- Challenge preschoolers to build subitizing, counting, and other competencies and then work on arithmetic problems in concrete settings.
- Later, ask children to solve semi-concrete problems, in which children reason about hidden but previously manipulated or viewed collections.
- Encourage children to invent their own strategies—with peers and with your *active* guidance—discussing and explaining their strategies.
- Encourage children to adopt more sophisticated, beneficial strategies as soon as possible.

Representations

Forms of representation are important factors in young children's arithmetic problem-solving.

Representations in curricula. Primary grade students tend to ignore *decorative* pictures and attend to, but are not always helped by, pictures containing information required for solution of the problem. Decorative pictures should be avoided. Students should be taught to use informational pictures.

Students often ignore, or are confused by, number line representations as well. If number lines are to be used to teach arithmetic, students should learn to move between number line and symbolic representations. One study suggested that carefully guided peer tutoring on using the number line to solve missing addend problems was successful and appreciated by both teachers and the students, who were low-performing first graders. The tutors were taught to use a teaching procedure, a shortened version of which follows.

1. What is the sign?
2. Which way do you go? [on the number line]
3. Is the blank before or after the equal sign? [the former is "tricky"]
4. What's the first number; put your pencil on it; it tells you where to start.
5. Identify the second number as the goal.
6. How many jumps?
7. Put that number in the blank and read the entire number sentence to check.

There are other important specifics. First, the intervention only helped when peer tutors demonstrated and guided use of the number line—the number line was not useful by itself. Also, the accuracy of children who just solved missing addend problems decreased, indicating that practicing errors is not helpful. Finally, there was some anecdotal evidence that it was important for peers to give feedback to the students they were tutoring. Thus, present, typical instruction on use of representations, especially geometry/spatial/pictorial representations, may be inadequate for most students and should receive more attention.

Manipulatives.[1] What about manipulatives, whether counters or fingers? Many teachers view these strategies as crutches and discourage their use too soon (Fuson, 1992a). Paradoxically, those who are best at solving problems *with* objects, fingers, or counting are *least* likely to use those less sophisticated strategies *in the future*, because they are confident in their answers and so move toward accurate, fast retrieval or composition (Siegler, 1993). Thus, help and encourage all children, and especially those from lower-income communities, to use these strategies until they are confident. Trying to move children too fast to retrieval ironically makes this development slow and painful. Instead, move when possible to counting strategies, and discuss how and why strategies work and why it is desirable to help build meaning and confidence.

For what period are manipulatives necessary? For children at any age they can be necessary at certain levels of thinking. Preschoolers initially need them to give meaning to arithmetical tasks and the number words involved. In certain contexts, older children require concrete representations as well. For example, Les Steffe asked first grader Brenda to count six marbles into his hand. Then he covered them up, showed one more, and asked how many he had in all. She said one. When he pointed out he had six marbles hidden, Brenda said adamantly, "I don't see no six!" For Brenda, there could be no number without things to count (Steffe & Cobb, 1988). Successful teachers interpret what the child is doing and thinking and attempt to see the situation from the child's point of view. Based on their interpretations, they conjecture what the child might be able to learn or abstract from his or her experiences. Similarly, when they interact with the child, they also consider their own actions from the child's point of view. Brenda's teacher, for example, might hide four marbles and then encourage Brenda to put up four fingers and use them to represent the hidden marbles.

Fingers—the best manipulative? Teaching useful *finger* addition methods accelerates children's single-digit addition and subtraction as much as a year over traditional methods in which children count objects or pictures (Fuson, Perry, & Kwon, 1994). The particular strategy in this study was to use the non-writing hand to performing counting-on-keeping-track (even for subtraction). The index finger represents 1, the middle finger 2, and so forth up to 4. The thumb represents 5 (all other fingers are raised), the thumb and index finger 6, and so forth. Children would then count on using fingers to keep track of the second addend. Most children moved to mental methods by second grade; more low-income children used the finger method throughout the second grade, but they were proud to be able to add and subtract large numbers. Educators should note that different cultures, such as traditional U.S., Korean, Latino, and Mozambican have different informal methods for representing numbers with fingers (Draisma, 2000; Fuson et al., 1994).

As we saw previously, if teachers try to eliminate use of fingers too soon, children just put them "under the desk" where they are not visually helpful, or they adopt less useful and more error-prone methods. Further, the most sophisticated methods are *not* crutches that held children back.

Moving beyond manipulatives. Once children have established successful strategies using objects as manipulatives, they can often solve simple arithmetic tasks without them. To encourage this, ask children to count out five toys and place them into an opaque container, count out four more toys and place them into the container, and then figure out how many toys in all without looking at them.

Drawings and diagrams that children produce are important representational tools. For example, to solve 6 + 5, children might draw 6 circles, then 5 circles, and then circle 5 of the 6 along with the second 5 to make 10, and then announce that the total is 11. As another example, consider the diagrams in Table 5.1 on p. 62. Karen Fuson found that the second diagrams for the "Collections" problem types were more useful for children (Fuson & Abrahamson, in press). They called them "math mountains" and introduced them with stories of "Tiny Tumblers," some of whom tumbled down one side and some the other side of the mountain. They would draw dots in circles on each side and then make different combinations. Their number sentences for this problem type started with the total (e.g., $10 = 4 + 6$) and would record all the combinations they could make ($10 = 0 + 10$; $10 = 1 + 9 \ldots$). Chapter 13 presents other research on children's use of diagrams in problem-solving.

Teaching Arithmetic Problem-Solving

A main issue for teaching is knowing the sequence in which to present the problem types. The broad developmental progression is as follows.

1. *(a) join, result unknown (change plus); (b) part–part–whole, whole unknown; and (c) separate, result unknown (change minus).* Children can *directly model* these problems' actions, step by step. For example, they might solve a join problem as follows: "Morgan had 3 candies [child counts out 3 counters] and then got 2 more [child counts out 2 more]. How many does he have in all?" (the child counts the counters and announces "five"). Attention should be paid to the mathematical vocabulary, for example, that "altogether" means "in all" or "in total."

2. *join, change unknown and part–part–whole, part unknown.* A three phase developmental progression occurs leading to the ability to solve these types. First, children learn to solve the first two problems types (a and b in #1 above) with *counting-on*. Second, they learn to solve the last problem type (c in #1), separate, result unknown problems, using *counting-on* (thinking of $11 - 6$ as $6 + — = 11$, and *counting-up-to* 11, keeping track of the 5 counts) or *counting-back* (which students can do *if* they have well-developed skill in counting backward). In either case, intentional instruction is needed. The counting backward solution might work best if all early childhood teachers, preschool and up, developed that skill conscientiously. The *counting-up* method might work best if you explicitly help children see how to transform the subtraction to a missing-addend addition problem. This represents another advantage of this approach: the relationship between addition and subtraction is highlighted.

Third and finally, they learn to apply that strategy to solve these new types; for example, counting on from the "start" number to the total, keeping track of the number of counts on the fingers, and reporting that number.

3. *"start unknown."* Children can use commutativity to change the join, start unknown problems to those that yield to *counting-on* (e.g., $\_ + 6 = 11$ becomes $6 + \_ = 11$, and then count on and keep track of the counts). Or, reversal is used to change $\_ - 6 = 5$ to $6 + 5 = \_$. At this point, all of these types of problems can be solved by new methods that use derived combinations, which are discussed in more detail in Chapter 6.

One type of problem, comparison, presents children with several unique difficulties, including vocabulary challenges. Many children interpret "less" or "fewer," as synonyms for "more" (Fuson & Abrahamson, in press). They hear the larger term in many situations (taller, longer) more frequently than the smaller term (shorter), so they need to learn several vocabulary terms. Comparisons can be expressed in several ways, and one way is easier. The order "Jonah has 6 candies," then "Juanita has 3 more than Jonah" is easier than "He has 3 fewer than Juanita" in figuring out how many candies Juanita has. Research shows that for "There are 5 birds and 3 worms," the question, "How many birds won't get a worm?" is easier than "How many more birds than worms are there?" (Hudson, 1983). Thus, such wording might be used to introduce these problems. Children also can be encouraged to draw matching diagrams, such as Figure 5.3

Later, children could use the type of bar diagrams shown in Table 5.1 on p. 62.

Similar wording changes in initial presentations of comparison problems help children, such as changing the question, "How many more does A have than B?" to "How many would B have to get

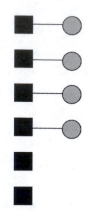

Figure 5.3. A matching diagram for comparison problems.

to have the same number as A?" Eventually, ask students to rephrase questions, including changing a "fewer" to a "more" statement. Further, although textbooks often model the use of subtraction to solve comparison problems, more students think of comparisons using an unknown addend *count-on* or *add-on*. Counting or adding on models the comparison situation because the two addends (the small quantity and the difference quantity) are added on one side of the equation and they then balance the large quantity which is written alone on the other side of the equation.

In summary, children benefit from instruction in two aspects of problems. First is understanding *situations*, including understanding "what's going on" in the contexts as well as the language used to describe them. Second is understanding the *mathematical structure*, such as learning part–whole relationships via fact families or solving missing addend problems such as _ + 3 − 8 − 2. Children who are novices, poor performers, or who have cognitive impairments or learning difficulties, may benefit particularly from situational training. More experienced and higher-performing children may profit from mathematical training. Such mathematical training should be combined with help transferring their part–whole knowledge to problem settings by including both in the same instructional settings and discussing the similarities.

As a similar combination, specifically-designed story contexts can help students develop an abstract understanding of part–whole problems. For example, one teacher told stories about a grandfather who sent presents to his two grandchildren or, later, about the two children sending presents to him. Another story was about children who live on two islands and travel by boat to school. Children represented these with a part–part–whole board (similar to the part–part–whole diagrams in Table 5.1).

Implications—A Brief Summary

Provide a full range of activities appropriate to the age (from 3 years on), covering subitizing, counting, counting strategies, and an increasing range of addition and subtraction situations (problem types), which should cover all problem types by the end of first grade. Emphasis should be on meaning and understanding, enhanced through discussions. Slow and inefficient learning occurs when principles are not understood. The tedious and superficial learning of school-age children is too often the product of not understanding the goals and relationships in problems. *Meaning for the child must be the consistent focus.* A few additional implications are highlighted below and, of course, they are woven into the chapter's learning trajectory.

- For the youngest children, use physical objects related to the problem (rather than structured "math manipulatives"), which supports their use of informal knowledge to solve the arithmetic problems.
- Begin instruction with children's solution methods, ensuring initial semantic analysis of problems, and build more sophisticated numerical and arithmetic strategies in tandem with the development of conceptual understanding.
- Build multiple supporting concepts and skills. Subitizing is an important support to counting strategies such as *counting-on*, and, as discussed in the following section, for small-number composition/decomposition approaches to addition and subtraction. Simple counting practice transfers to addition and subtraction, but counting skills should also include effortlessly counting forward and backward, counting in either direction starting with any number, naming the number before or after another number, *counting-on-using-patterns*, *counting-on-keeping-track* of the number of counts, and eventually embedded quantities within counting sequences.
- Provide a variety of experiences, including children creating, using, sharing, and explaining different strategies to help children develop their adaptive expertise with arithmetic.
- Avoid decorative pictures and illustrations, as they are ignored by (or confuse) children and do not support problem-solving, but only add to the length of textbooks (NMP, 2008).
- Provide instruction on the use of representations, especially geometry/spatial/pictorial representations.
- Ask children to explain and justify solutions rather than to "check" their work. Checking is not helpful to most young children, but justification both builds concepts and procedures and serves as a meaningful introduction to checking one's work.
- Choose curricula that avoid the difficulties of too many U.S. textbooks; instruction should mitigate any limitations of any curriculum used.

In summary, present children with a range of addition and subtraction types and encourage them to invent, adapt, use, discuss, and explain a variety of solution strategies that are meaningful to them. For example, most children can begin to do this even in pre-K, and most all can develop such understandings and skills through the kindergarten and first grade years. Children at the level of counting perceptual units may need to be encouraged to put two collections into one box and count all the items to establish the act of uniting and quantifying the sum. Most children can quickly learn to reprocess two collections and conceive of it as one quantifiable collection. They can then solve problems with an increasingly diverse range of strategies. Having them add one or two more to a collection encourages their awareness of increasing the number in a collection and encourages them to connect their counting and adding schemes (similar for subtraction). Some children need to re-count, but most, even in the pre-K year, can learn to count up with experience. In all cases, the emphasis should be on children's use of strategies that are meaningful to them. Approaches that emphasize understanding, meaningfulness, patterns, relations, and invention of strategies, if used consistently and patiently, also work with special needs children (Baroody, 1996). Informal strategies such as knowing how to add 0 or 1 should be encouraged; research shows that, if paced appropriately, children classified as learning-disabled can be taught to use such patterns and strategies (see Chapters 15 and 16 for more on children with special needs). Additional specific implications are woven into the following learning trajectories.

Learning Trajectories for Adding and Subtracting (Emphasizing Counting Strategies)

As others we have seen, the learning trajectory for adding and subtracting is complex because there are many conceptual and skill advancements. The importance of *goals* for this domain is clear: Arithmetic is a main focus of elementary education. Where these goals appear in NCTM's *Curriculum Focal Points* is shown in Figure 5.4. Accepting those goals, Table 5.2 provides the two additional components of the learning trajectory, the developmental progression and the instructional tasks. Remember that the ages in all the learning trajectory tables are only approximate, especially because the age of acquisition usually depends heavily on experience. A final important note: *Most strategies will be used successfully for smaller numbers (totals 10 or less) a year or more before they are used successfully for larger numbers* (Frontera, 1994). *This should be considered when constructing tasks for children.*

Pre-K

Connection to the Focal Points Number and Operations: Children use meanings of numbers to create strategies for solving problems and responding to practical situations.

Kindergarten

Focal Point Number and Operations: **Representing, comparing, and ordering whole numbers and joining and separating sets**

Children use numbers, including written numerals, to represent quantities and to solve quantitative problems, such as . . . modeling simple joining and separating situations with objects. They choose, combine, and apply effective strategies for answering quantitative questions, including . . . counting the number in combined sets and counting backward.

Grade 1

Focal Point Number and Operations and Algebra: **Developing understandings of addition and subtraction and strategies for basic addition facts and related subtraction facts**

Children develop strategies for adding and subtracting whole numbers on the basis of their earlier work with small numbers. They use a variety of models, including discrete objects, length-based models (e.g., lengths of connecting cubes), and number lines, to model "part–whole," "adding to," "taking away from," and "comparing" situations to develop an understanding of the meanings of addition and subtraction and strategies to solve such arithmetic problems. Children understand the connections between counting and the operations of addition and subtraction (e.g., adding 2 is the same as "counting-on" 2). They use properties of addition (commutativity and associativity) to add whole numbers, and they create and use increasingly sophisticated strategies based on these properties (e.g., "making tens") to solve addition and subtraction problems involving basic facts. By comparing a variety of solution strategies, children relate addition and subtraction as inverse operations.

Grade 2

Focal Point Number and Operations and Algebra: **Developing quick recall of addition facts and related subtraction facts and fluency with multidigit addition and subtraction**

Children use their understanding of addition to develop quick recall of basic addition facts and related subtraction facts. They solve arithmetic problems by applying their understanding of models of addition and subtraction (such as combining or separating sets or using number lines), relationships and properties of number (such as place value), and properties of addition (commutativity and associativity). Children develop, discuss, and use efficient, accurate, and generalizable methods to add and subtract multidigit whole numbers. They select and apply appropriate methods to estimate sums and differences or calculate them mentally, depending on the context and numbers involved. They develop fluency with efficient procedures, including standard algorithms, for adding and subtracting whole numbers, understand why the procedures work (on the basis of place value and properties of operations), and use them to solve problems.

Connection to the Focal Points Number and Operations: Children use place value and properties of operations to create equivalent representations of given numbers (such as 35 represented by 35 ones, 3 tens and 5 ones, or 2 tens and 15 ones) and to write, compare, and order multidigit numbers. They use these ideas to compose and decompose multidigit numbers. Children add and subtract to solve a variety of problems, including applications involving measurement, geometry, and data, as well as nonroutine problems. In preparation for grade 3, they solve problems involving multiplicative situations, developing initial understandings of multiplication as repeated addition.

Figure 5.4 Curriculum Focal Points for addition and subtraction.

Table 5.2 Learning Trajectory for Addition and Subtraction (emphasizing counting strategies).

Age (years)	Developmental Progression	Instructional Tasks
1	**Pre-Explicit** +/− Sensitivity to adding and subtracting perceptually combined groups. No formal adding. Shows no signs of understanding adding or subtracting.	Besides providing rich sensory, manipulative environments, use of words such as "more" and actions of adding objects directs attention to comparisons and combinations.
2–3	**Nonverbal** +/− Adds and subtracts very small collections nonverbally. Shown 2 objects then 1 object going under a napkin, identifies or makes a set of 3 objects to "match."	*Nonverbal join result unknown or separate, result unknown (take-away), using the smallest numbers.* For example, children are shown 2 objects then 1 object going under a napkin, and then asked to show how many. *Pizza Pazzazz 4.* Students add and subtract numbers up to totals of 3 (with objects shown, but then hidden), matching target amounts. 

4	**Small Number** +/− Finds sums for joining problems up to 3 + 2 by counting-all with objects.
	
	Asked, "You have 2 balls and get 1 more. How many in all?" counts out 2, then counts out 1 more, then counts all 3: "1, 2, 3, 3!."
		Join result unknown or separate, result unknown (take-away) problems, numbers < 5.
		  "You have 2 balls and get 1 more. How many in all?"
		
		Word Problems. Tell children to solve simple addition problems with toys that represent the objects in the problems. Use totals up to 5.
		  Tell children you want to buy 3 toy triceratops and 2 toy tyrannosauruses. Ask how many dinosaurs that is altogether.
		  Ask children how they got their answer and repeat with other problems.
		
		Finger Word Problems. Tell children to solve simple addition problems with their fingers. Use very small numbers. Children should place their hands in their laps between each problem.
		  To solve the problems above, guide children in showing 3 fingers on one hand and 2 fingers on the other and reiterate: How many is that altogether?
		  Ask children how they got their answer and repeat with other problems.
		
		Dinosaur Shop 3. At a customer's request, students add the contents of 2 boxes of toy dinosaurs (number frames) and click a target numeral that represents the sum.
		
		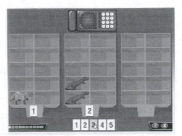

4–5	**Find Result** +/− Finds sums for joining (you had 3 apples and get 3 more, how many do you have in all?) and part–part–whole (there are 6 girls and 5 boys on the playground,	*Word Problems.* Children solving all the above problem types using manipulatives or their fingers to represent objects. For *Separate, result unknown (take-away),* "You have 5 balls and give 2 to Tom. How many do you have left?" Children might count out 5 balls, then take away 2, and then count remaining 3.

Continued Overleaf

Age (years)	Developmental Progression	Instructional Tasks

how many children were there in all?) problems *by direct modeling, counting-all, with objects.*

Asked, "You have 2 red balls and 3 blue balls. How many in all?" counts out 2 red, then counts out 3 blue, then counts all 5.

Solves take-away problems by separating with objects.

Asked, "You have 5 balls and give 2 to Tom. How many do you have left?" counts out 5 balls, then takes away 2, and then counts remaining 3.

For *Part–part–whole, whole unknown* problems, they might solve "You have 2 red balls and 3 blue balls. How many in all?"

Note: In all teacher-directed activities, present commuted pairs one after the other: 5 + 3 then 3 + 5. With such experiences, most children learn to incorporate commutativity into their strategies. Also, encourage children who can to use the shortcut-sum strategy (to solve 5 + 3, "1, 2, 3, 4, 5, 6, 7, 8 . . . 8!") which serves as a transition to counting-on.

Places Scenes (Addition)—Part–Part–Whole, Whole Unknown Problems. Children play with toy on a background scene and combine groups. For example, they might place 4 tyrannosaurus rexes and 5 apatosauruses on the paper and then count all 9 to see how many dinosaurs they have in all.

Dinosaur Shop 3. Customers at the shop ask students to combine their 2 orders and add the contents of 2 boxes of toy dinosaurs (number frames) and click a target numeral that represents the sum.

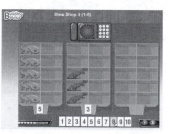

Off the Tree. Students add 2 amounts of dots to identify their total number value, and then move forward a corresponding number of spaces on a game board, which is now marked with numerals.

Compare Game (Adding). For each pair of children, use two or more sets of counting cards 1–10. Mix and deal cards evenly, face down.

Players simultaneously flip 2 cards to add and then compare which is greater. The player with more says, "I have more!" and takes the opponent's cards. If cards are equal, each player flips another card to break the tie.

The game ends when all cards have been played, and the winner is the player with more cards. Or, play this game without a winner by not allowing players to collect cards.

Age (years)	Developmental Progression	Instructional Tasks

Find a Five. Children make groups of 1 to 5 beans then hide them under cups. Then, they mix up the cups. In pairs, children try to find 2 cups that equal 5. When ready, increase to a higher sum.

Make It N Adds on objects to "make one number into another," without needing to count from "1." Does not (necessarily) represent how many were added (this is not a requirement of this intermediate-difficulty problem type) (Aubrey, 1997).

Make it Right. Children solve problems such as, "This puppet has 4 balls but she should have 6. Make it 6."

Dinosaur Shop 4. Students start with x dinosaurs in a box and add y more to reach a total of z dinosaurs (up to 10).

Asked, "This puppet has 4 balls but she should have 6. Make it 6," puts up 4 fingers on one hand, immediately counts up from 4 while putting up 2 more fingers, saying, "5, 6."

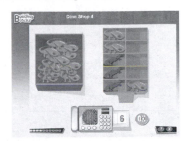

Pizza Pazzazz 5. Students add toppings to a pizza (up to 10) to make the required amount.

Sea to Shore. Students identify number amounts by (simple) counting-on. They move forward a number of spaces on a game board that is **one more** than the number of dots in the fives and tens number frame.

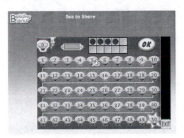

Note that *I'm Thinking of a Number* in Chapter 3 helps develop the relevant counting skills.

Find Change +/− Finds the missing addend (5 + _ = 7) by adding on objects.

Join Change Unknown problems such as, "You have 5 balls and then get some more. Now you have 7 in all. How many did you get?" Children solve using balls of 2 colors.

Join-To—Count-All-Groups. Asked, "You have 5 balls and then get some more. Now you have 7 in all. How many did you get?" counts out 5, then counts those 5 again starting at 1,

Part–Part–Whole, Part Unknown. "There are 6 children on the playground. 2 are boys and the rest are girls. How many are girls?"

This problem type may be more difficult for most students, and not solvable independently until the next level because it requires keeping the added-on objects

Continued Overleaf

Age (years)	Developmental Progression	Instructional Tasks

then adds more, counting "6, 7," then counts the balls added to find the answer, 2. (Some children may use their fingers, and attenuate the counting by using finger patterns.)

Separate-To—Count-All-Groups. Asked, "Nita had 8 stickers. She gave some to Carmen. Now she has 5 stickers. How many did she give to Carmen?" counts 8 objects, separates until 5 remain, counts those taken away.

Compares by matching in simple situations.

Match—Count Rest. Asked, "Here are 6 dogs and 4 balls. If we give a ball to each dog, how many dogs won't get a ball?" counts out 6 dogs, matches 4 balls to 4 of them, then counts the 2 dogs that have no ball.

separate from the initial objects. Children might use fingers and finger patterns. They might use "adding-on" if they make one part first, or "separating-from" if they count out 6, then remove 2, then count the remaining objects. With supportive phrasing and guidance, however, many children can learn to solve them. For example, using "boys and girls" in the above problem helps. So does saying "and the rest are." Finally, saying the known sum first helps.

5–6 **Counting Strategies** +/− Finds sums for joining (you had 8 apples and get 3 more . . .) and part–part–whole (6 girls and 5 boys . . .) problems with finger patterns and/or by counting on.

Counting-on. "How much is 4 and 3 more?" "Fourrrrr . . . five, six, seven [uses rhythmic or finger pattern to keep track]. Seven!"

Counting-up-to May solve missing addend (3 + _ = 7) or compare problems by counting up; e.g., counts "4, 5, 6, 7" while putting up fingers; and then counts or recognizes the 4 fingers raised.

Asked, "You have 6 balls. How many more would you need to have 8?" says, "Six, seven [puts up first finger], eight [puts up second finger]. Two!"

How Many Now? Have the children count objects as you place them in a box. Ask, "How many are in the box now?" Add 1, repeating the question, then check the children's responses by counting all the objects. Repeat, checking occasionally. When children are ready, sometimes add 2, and eventually more objects.

Variations: Place coins in a coffee can. Declare that a given number of objects are in the can. Then have the children close their eyes and count on by listening as additional objects are dropped in.

More Toppings. Children use cutout "pizzas" and brown disks for toppings. The teacher asks them to put 5 toppings on their pizzas, and then asks how many they would have in all if they put on 3 more. They count on to answer, then actually put the toppings on to check.

Double Compare. Students compare sums of cards to determine which sum is greater. Encourage children to use more sophisticated strategies, such as counting-on.

Join Result Unknown and *Part–Part–Whole, Whole Unknown.* "How much is 4 and 3 more?"

Encouraging the use of counting-on. Children often use counting-on instead of direct modeling (counting-all strategies) when easy to apply, such as when first addend is very large (23) and second one very small (2).

Teaching counting-on skills. If children need assistance to use counting-on, or do not spontaneously create it, explicitly teach the subskills.

Lay out the problem with numeral cards (e.g., 5 + 2). Count out objects into a line below each card.

Point to the last object of the first addend. When child counts that last object, point to numeral card and say, "See this is 5 also. It tells how many dots there are here."

Age (years)	Developmental Progression	Instructional Tasks

Solve another problem. If the child counts the first set starting with one again, interrupt them sooner and ask what number they will say when they get to the last object in the first set. Emphasize it will be the same as the numeral card.

Point to first dot of set and say (e.g., for 5 + 2) "See, there are 5 here, so this one (exaggerated jump from last object in the first set to first object in the second set) gets the number *six*.

Repeat with new problems. If children need more assistance, interrupt their counting of the first set with questions: "How many are here (first set)? So *this* (last of first) gets what number? And what number for *this* one (first of second set)"?

Word Problems. Students solve word problems (totals to 10) off and on the computer.

Turn Over Ten and *Make Tens.* See Chapter 6. Many children will, especially at first, use counting strategies to solve the tasks in these games.

Bright Idea. Students are given a numeral and a frame with dots. They count on from this numeral to identify the total amount, and then move forward a corresponding number of spaces on a game board.

Easy as Pie: Students add 2 numerals to find a total number (sums of 1 through 10), and then move forward a corresponding number of spaces on a game board. The game encourages children to count on from the larger number (e.g., to add 3 + 4, they would count "four . . . 5, 6, 7!").

Lots of Socks: Students add 2 numerals to find total number amounts (1 through 20), and then move forward a corresponding number of spaces on a game board. The game encourages children to count on from the larger number (e.g., to add 2 + 9, they would count "nine . . . 10, 11!").

Continued Overleaf

Age (years)	Developmental Progression	Instructional Tasks
6	**Part-Whole** +/−: Has initial part–whole understanding. Solves all previous problem types using flexible strategies (may use some known combinations, such as 5 + 5 is 10). Sometimes can do start unknown (_ + 6 = 11), but only by trial and error. Asked, "You had some balls. Then you get 6 more. Now you have 11 balls. How many did you start with?" lays out 6, then 3 more, counts and gets 9. Puts 1 more with the 3, . . . says 10, then puts 1 more. Counts up from 6 to 11, then re-counts the group added, and says, "Five!"	*Separate Result Unknown.* "You have 11 pencils balls and give 7 away. How many do you still have?" Encourage children to use counting-down or, especially with the numbers in this example, counting-up, to determine the difference. Discuss when each of these and other strategies would be most efficient. Also *Join Change Unknown, Part–Part–Whole Part Unknown, and Compare Difference Unknown* ("Nita has 8 stickers. Carmen has 5 stickers. How many more does Nita have than Carmen?"). *Barkley's Bones.* Students determine the missing addend in problems such as 4 + _ = 7.  *Word Problems 2.* Students solve word problems (single-digit addition and subtraction) off and on the computer.  *Hidden Objects.* Hide 4 counters under the dark cloth and show students 7 counters. Tell them that 4 counters are hidden and challenge them to tell you how many there are in all. *Or*, tell them that there are 11 in all and ask how many are hidden. Have them discuss their solution strategies. Repeat with different sums. *Eggcellent.* Students use strategy to identify which 2 of 3 numbers, when added together, will enable them to reach the final space on a game board in the fewest number of moves. Often that means the sum of the largest 2 numbers, but sometimes other combinations allow you to hit a positive or avoid a backward action space. 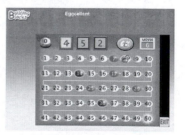

Age (years)	Developmental Progression	Instructional Tasks

6–7

Numbers-in-Numbers +/− Recognizes when a number is part of a whole and can keep the part and whole in mind simultaneously; solves start unknown (_ + 4 = 9) problems with counting strategies.

Asked, "You have some balls, then you get 4 more balls, now you have 9. How many did you have to start with?" Counts, putting up fingers, "Five, six, seven, eight, nine." Looks at fingers, and says, "Five!"

Start Unknown Problems. "You have some balls, then you get 4 more balls, now you have 9. How many did you have to start with?"

Flip the Cards. Take turns. Students roll 2 numeral cubes (1–6), add them, and flip over numeral cards 1 to 12. Students can flip over any combination of cards whose sum equals the cube sum. Students continue until they cannot flip over any cards. Then, the sum of the cards still face up is recorded. The lowest final sum wins. Available commercially as *Wake Up Giants* or *Shut the Box.*

Guess My Rule. Tell the class that they have to guess your rule. Students give a number (say 4), the teacher records:

$$4 \longrightarrow 8$$

Students might guess the rule is "doubling." However, as the game continues:

$$4 \longrightarrow 8$$
$$10 \longrightarrow 14$$
$$1 \longrightarrow 5 \ldots$$

The students then guess the rule is "add 4." *But they cannot say this.* If they think they know, *they* try to give the number to the right of the arrow. The teacher records it if they are right. Only when (most) all of the students can do this do they discuss the rule.

Function Machine. Students identify a math function (rule) by observing a series of operations that apply a consistent addition or subtraction value $(+2, -5,$ etc.$)$.

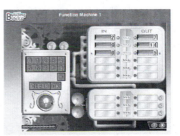

Deriver + −: Uses flexible strategies and derived combinations (e.g., "7 + 7 is 14, so 7 + 8 is 15) to solve all types of problems. Includes Break-Apart-to-Make-Ten (BAMT—explained in Chapter 6). Can simultaneously think of 3 numbers within a sum, and can move part of a number to another, aware of the increase in one and the decrease in another.

Asked, "What's 7 plus 8?" thinks: 7 + 8 → 7 + [7 + 1] → [7 + 7] + 1 = 14 + 1 = 15.

Or, using BAMT, thinks, 8 + 2 = 10, so separate 7 into 2 and 5, add 2 and 8 to make 10, then add 5 more, 15.

Solves simple cases of multidigit addition (sometimes subtraction) by incrementing tens and/or ones.

"What's 20 + 34?" Student uses connecting cube to count up 20, 30, 40, 50 plus 4 is 54.

All types of single-digit problems.

Tic-Tac-Total. Draw a tic-tac-toe board and write the numbers 0 2 4 6 8 0 and 1 3 5 7 9 nearby. Players take turns crossing out one of the numbers and writing it on the board. One player uses only even numbers, the other only odd numbers. Whoever makes 15 first as a sum of three numbers in a row (column, diagonal) wins (Kamii, 1985). Change the total to 13 for a new game.

21. Play cards, where Ace is worth either 1 or 11 and 2 to 10 are worth their values.

Dealer gives everyone 2 cards, including herself.

On each round, each player, if sum is less than 21, can request another card, or "hold."

If any new card makes the sum more than 21, the player is out.

Continue until everyone "holds."

The player whose sum is closest to 21 wins.

Variations: Play to 15 at first.

Multidigit addition and subtraction. "What's 28 + 35?" (See Chapter 6.)

Continued Overleaf

Age (years)	Developmental Progression	Instructional Tasks
7	**Problem Solver** +/− Solves all types of problems, with flexible strategies and known combinations. Asked, "If I have 13 and you have 9, how could we have the same number?" says, "9 and 1 is 10, then 3 more to make 13. 1 and 3 is 4. I need 4 more!" Multidigit may be solved by incrementing or combining tens and ones (latter not used for join, change unknown). "What's 28 + 35?" Incrementer thinks: 20 + 30 = 50; +8 = 58; 2 more is 60, 3 more is 63. Combining tens and ones: 20 + 30 = 50. 8 + 5 is like 8 plus 2 and 3 more, so, it's 13. 50 and 13 is 63.	*All types* of problem structures for single-digit problems. (See Chapter 6 for multidigit problems.)

Final Words

In Chapters 2 and 3, we saw that children quantify groups with different processes, such as subitizing and counting. They can also solve arithmetic tasks with different processes. This chapter emphasized a counting-based approach to arithmetic. Chapter 6 describes a composition-based approach. Children often use both, and even combine them, as has been suggested by the more sophisticated strategies already described (e.g., Deriver +/−).

6
Arithmetic
*Composition of Number, Place Value, and
Multidigit Addition and Subtraction*

> I find it easier not to do it [simple addition] with my fingers because
> sometimes I get into a big muddle with them [and] I find it much
> harder to add up because I am not concentrating on the sum. I am
> concentrating on getting my fingers right . . . which takes a while. It can
> take longer to work out the sum than it does to work out the sum in
> my head. ["In her head" Emily imagined dot arrays. Why didn't she
> just use those?] If we don't use our fingers, the teacher is going to
> think, "Why aren't they using their fingers . . . they are just sitting there
> thinking" . . . we are meant to be using our fingers because it is easier
> . . . which it is not.
>
> (Gray & Pitta, 1997, p. 35)

Do you think the teacher should have Emily use concrete objects? Or should she encourage children
such as Emily to use increasingly sophisticated arithmetic reasoning? For example, should she
help Emily decompose and recompose numbers, such as using "doubles-plus-one" (7 + 8 is solved
as 7 + 7 = 14, and 14 + 1 = 15). This chapter discusses three topics involving increasingly
sophisticated composition of number: arithmetic combinations ("facts"), place value, and multidigit addition and subtraction.

Composing Number

Composing and decomposing numbers is another approach to addition and subtraction, one that
is often used alongside with counting strategies, as the "doubles-plus-one" strategy illustrates.
Conceptual subitizing *is* an important case of composition of number (see Chapter 2).

Initial Competencies with Part–whole Relationships

Toddlers learn to recognize part–whole relations in nonverbal, intuitive, perceptual situations and can nonverbally represent parts that make a specific whole (e.g., •• and •• make ••••). Between 4 and 5 years of age, children learn from everyday situations that a whole is made up of smaller parts and thus is bigger than its parts; however, they may not always accurately quantify that relationship.

Toddlers learn to recognize that sets can be combined in different orders (even if they do not explicitly recognize that groups are composed of smaller groups). Preschoolers show intuitive knowledge of commutativity (adding a group of 3 to a group of 1 yields a group with the same number as adding the group of 1 to a group of 3) and, later, associativity (adding a group of 3 to a group of 2, and then adding that group to a group of 1, yields a group with the same number as adding the group of 3 *after* combining the groups of 2 and the 1).

Then children learn these same ideas apply in more abstract contexts, including specific arithmetic problems, for example, that "two" and "two" make "four." At that point, children can develop the ability to recognize that the numbers 2 and 3 are "hiding inside" 5, as are the numbers 4 and 1 (Fuson & Abrahamson, in press). That is, they can develop explicit knowledge of part–whole relations at 4 or 5 years of age.

In brief, children develop an early, primitive understanding of commutativity, then additive composition (large groups are made up of smaller groups), commutativity of combined groups, and then associativity. So, at least by 5 years of age, children are ready to solve problems that require part–whole reasoning, such as join or separate, change unknown problems. However, teachers may need to help children see the relevance in and apply their understandings of part–whole relationships to these types of problems.

Building on their part–whole understandings, children can learn to separate a group into parts in various ways, producing (eventually, all of) the number combinations composing a given number; for example, 8 as 7 + 1, 6 + 2, 5 + 3, and so on. This approach to arithmetic combinations builds on and complements the counting-based strategies of the previous chapter.

Learning Basic Combinations ("Facts") and Fluency

Recommendations for high-quality mathematics education have never ignored the need for children to eventually become fluent in knowledge of basic number combinations, such as 4 + 7 = 11. Those reading many reports in the media may be surprised by this, given articles that declared that NCTM "reversed direction" to emphasize "basic facts" both in their 2000 *Principles and Standards for School Mathematics* and their 2006 *Curriculum Focal Points*. Regardless, both the *Curriculum Focal Points* and the National Math Panel report (NMP, 2008) make it clear that everyone agrees the goal is important. That does not mean that the exact nature of the goal and when and how it might best be achieved garner similar agreement. Let us examine what the research tells us.

Getting your facts straight: Misconceptions that harm children. World-wide research shows that the way most people in the U.S. think about arithmetic combinations and children's learning of them, and the language they use *may harm more than help* (Fuson, personal communication, 2007). For example, we hear about "memorizing facts" and "recalling your facts." This is misleading regarding what goes on in the learning process (this section) and the teaching process (the following section). As we saw in Chapter 5, children move through a long developmental progression to reach the point where they can compose numbers. Further, they also should learn about arithmetic properties, patterns, and relationships as they do so, *and that knowledge, along with intuitive magnitude and other knowledge and skills, ideally is learned simultaneously and in an integrated fashion with knowledge of arithmetic combinations.* That is one reason we do not even use the term "fact"—knowing an arithmetic combination well means far more than knowing a simple, isolated "fact." For example, children notice that the sum of n and 1 is simply the number after n in the counting sequence, resulting in an integration of knowledge of combinations with the well-practiced counting knowledge.

Research suggests that producing basic combinations is not just a simple "look-up" process. Retrieval is an important part of the process, but many brain systems help. For example, systems that involve working memory, executive (metacognitive) control, and even spatial "mental number lines" support knowledge of arithmetic combinations. Further, for subtraction calculations, both the region specializing in subtraction *and* that specializing in addition are activated. So, when children *really know* $8 - 3 = 5$, they also know that $3 + 5 = 8$, $8 - 5 = 3$, and so forth, and all these "facts" are *related*.

Implications are that children need considerable practice, distributed across time. Also, because counting strategies did not activate the same systems, we need to guide children to move to more sophisticated composition strategies. Finally, practice should not be "meaningless drill" but should occur in a context of making sense of the situation and the number relationships. Multiple strategies help build that number sense, and children who are strong in calculations know and use multiple strategies. If ever educators needed an argument against teaching "one correct procedure," this is it.

Experience and Education

So, children should be able to reason strategically, adapting strategies for different situations and easily and quickly retrieve the answer to any arithmetic combination when that is appropriate. What do we know about facilitating such adaptive expertise?

*What does **not** work?* Some recent large-scale efforts have tried to teach memorization of facts directly, with disastrous results. Textbooks in California in 2008 had to teach children to memorize all the facts in first grade, with little guidance for second grade. Only 7% demonstrated adequate progress.

What happened? Two instructional practices were *negatively* related to basic-combinations retrieval:

- Use of California State-approved textbooks demanding retrieval in first grade.
- Timed tests.

Flash card use didn't hurt, but didn't help either. Neither did extensive work on small sums. We can see that memorization without understanding or strategies is a bad idea. Another bad idea is presenting easier arithmetic problems far more frequently than harder problems. That's what most U.S. textbooks do. The opposite is the case in countries with higher mathematics achievement, such as East Asian countries (NMP, 2008).

*What **does** work?* The California study found that some approaches were successful, such as using thinking strategies. Such strategies include the following.

Conceptual subitizing: The earliest school addition. Teachers of children as young as 4 years can use *conceptual subitizing* to develop composition-based ideas about addition and subtraction (see Chapter 2). Such experience provides an early basis for addition, as students "see the addends and the sum as in 'two olives and two olives make four olives' " (Fuson, 1992b, p. 248). A benefit of subitizing activities is that different arrangements suggest different views of that number. Children can come to see all of the different number combinations for a given number by working with

Figure 6.1 Building Blocks software activity "Number Pictures."

objects (e.g., 5 objects). Within a story context (e.g., animals in two different pens), children can separate the 5 objects into different partners (4 and 1; 3 and 2). Similarly, on and off the computer, children can make "number pictures"—as many different arrangements of a given number as possible, with the subsets labeled, as in Figure 6.1 (Baratta-Lorton, 1976).

Commutativity and associativity. Teachers can do a lot to develop those understandings and skills earlier and more dependably. Preschool and kindergarten teachers can pose problems that children model with manipulatives, ensuring that a problem such as "3 and 2 more" is followed by "2 and 3 more." Many games in which children separate sets of a given number in many different ways and name the subsets may be particularly helpful. For example, children lay 4 cubes along their line of sight and use a clear plastic sheet to "hide" 1 and then read "one *and* three." They then hide 3 and read "three *and* one" (Baratta-Lorton, 1976).

Ensure that children understand that the sum of 6 and 3 is 9 no matter what the order of the addends. Many children will build these understandings and strategies for themselves. Others will if the curriculum and teacher present problems in commuted pairs (6 + 7 and then, immediately after 7 + 6, as mentioned previously for small numbers). Still others may need explicit instruction on the principle. Help children relate their physical understandings, based on equivalence of groups of objects in various combinations and orders, to the *manipulations* of them that resulted in this different arrangement, and then to explicit numerical generalizations. In any of these forms, such instruction may help children develop more sophisticated strategies and thus relate their knowledge of arithmetic principles and their problem-solving, which they often do not do. Especially fruitful might be ensuring children understand that larger groups are additively composed of smaller groups and using commutativity to learn to count on from a larger addend.

Whether they are subitizing or subitizing and counting, children as young as kindergarten age benefit from finding all the decompositions for a number—all pairs of numbers "hiding inside" other numbers. Listing them can help children see patterns *and* can illustrate a way of representing equations that expands the traditional, limited, view of an equal sign as meaning "the answer comes next" (Fuson, in press; Fuson & Abrahamson, in press):

$$6 = 0 + 6$$
$$6 = 1 + 5$$

$6 = 2 + 4$
$6 = 3 + 3$
$6 = 4 + 2$
$6 = 5 + 1$
$6 = 6 + 0$

"Doubles" and the n + 1 *rule.* Special patterns can be useful and easy for children to see. One of these involves "doubles" (3 + 3, 7 + 7), which can also allow access to combinations such as 7 + 8 ("doubles-plus-one"). Children can learn the doubles (e.g., 6 + 6 = 12) surprisingly easily. They appear to develop doubles plus (or minus) one (7 + 8 = 7 + 7 + 1 = 14 + 1 = 15) on their own or from brief discussions or practice on computer software. However, ensure that rules such as $n + 1$ (adding one to any number is simply the next counting word) are well established *first.*

Fives and tens frames. Another special pattern is the spatial one of fives and tens frames. These encourage decomposition into fives and tens (e.g., 6 made as 5 + 1, 7 as 5 + 2), as illustrated in Figure 6.2.

Break-Apart-to-Make-Ten (BAMT) strategy. Japanese students often proceed through the same general developmental progression as U.S., and other researchers have identified moving from *counting-all,* to *counting-on,* and to derived combinations and decomposing-composing strategies. However, their learning trajectory at that point differs. They come together around a single powerful strategy—*Break-Apart-to-Make-Ten (BAMT).*

Before these lessons, children work on several related learning trajectories. They develop solid knowledge of numerals and counting (i.e., move along the counting learning trajectory). This includes the number structure for teen numbers as 10 + another number, which, as we learned, is more straightforward in Asian languages ("thirteen" is "ten and three"). They learn to solve addition and subtraction of numbers with totals less than 10 (i.e., Find Result +/− in the learning trajectory in Chapter 5), often chunking numbers into 5 (e.g., 7 as 5-plus-2, as Fig. 6.2 illustrated).

With these levels of thinking established, children develop several levels of thinking within the composition/decomposition developmental progression (what we call "composer to 4, then 5 . . . up to Composer to 10 in the learning trajectory at the end of this chapter). For example, they work on "break-apart partners" of numbers less than or equal to 10. They solve addition and subtraction

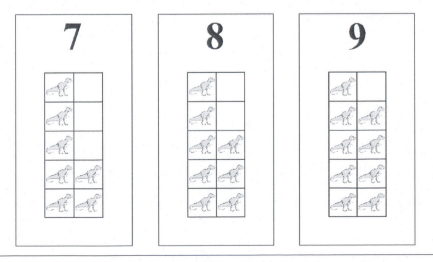

Figure 6.2 Fives and tens frames can help children decompose numbers and learn combinations.

problems involving teen numbers using the 10s structure ($10 + 2 = 12$; $18 - 8 = 10$), and addition and subtraction with three addends using 10s (e.g., $4 + 6 + 3 = 10 + 3 = 13$ and $15 - 5 - 9 = 10 - 9 = 1$).

At this point the "*break-apart-to-make-ten*" (*BAMT*) strategy is developed. The entire process (to fluency) follows four instructional phases. In Phase 1, teachers elicit, value, and discuss child-invented strategies and encourage children to use these strategies to solve a variety of problems. Supports to connect visual and symbolic representations of quantities are used extensively, and curtailed and phased out as children learn. For example, in step 1, 9 counters (or fingers) and 4 counters are shown, then 1 moved from the 4 to make a group of 10. Next, the 3 left are highlighted. Then children are reminded that the 9 and 1 made 10. Last, they see 10 counters and 3 counters and think ten-three, or count on "ten-one, ten-two, ten-three." Later, representational drawings serve this role, in a sequence such as shown in Figure 6.3.

In Phase 2, teachers focus on mathematical properties and mathematically advantageous methods, especially *BAMT*. In Phase 3, children gain fluency with the *BAMT* (or other) methods. In Phase 4, distributed practice is used to increase retention and efficiency and to generalize the use of the method in additional contexts and as a component of more complex methods.

Of the means of assistance in Tharp and Gallimore's model (1988), the teacher used questioning and cognitive restructuring extensively, and used feeding back, modeling, instructing, and managing to a lesser extent. He also used an additional strategy, engaging and involving. Lessons were based first on children's ideas and contributions. All strategies were accepted and appreciated. Students were expected to try to express their ideas and strategies as well as understand those of others. Strategies were often named for the students who created them. Children then voted for the "most useful" strategy; the majority liked the *BAMT* strategy.

In the following phase, the teacher reviewed different methods, compared the methods mathematically, and voted on the easiest method. New problem types (e.g., adding to 8) are connected to previously solved problems (adding to 9). The teacher also moved his conceptual emphasis from the initial to later steps in the *BAMT* process (as illustrated in Fig. 6.3 below). For homework, children reviewed that day's work and previewed the work to come the following day, supported by families.

In the third phase, children practiced the *BAMT* method to achieve fluency. "Practice" in Japanese means "kneading" different ideas and experiences together to "learn." Children do not just drill but engage in whole group (choral responding), individual-within-whole-group, and independent practice. In individual-within-whole-group practice, individual students answered, but then asked the class, "Is it OK?" They shouted their response back. All practice emphasized

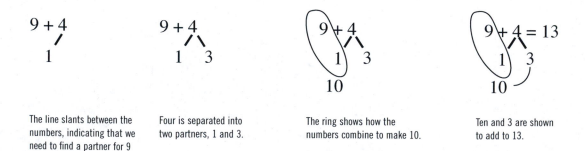

The line slants between the numbers, indicating that we need to find a partner for 9 to make 10.

Four is separated into two partners, 1 and 3.

The ring shows how the numbers combine to make 10.

Ten and 3 are shown to add to 13.

Figure 6.3 Phases of instruction to teach the "Break-Apart-to-Make Tens" or *BAMT* strategy.

conceptual links. "Kneading knowledge" to "learn" was always about fluency *and* understanding. The fourth and final phase is delayed practice. This is not rote learning or rote practice but a clear, high-quality use of the concepts of learning trajectories.

Combined strategies. Further, learning a variety of such strategies are good for children of all ability levels. Further, although *BAMT* is a powerful strategy and more helpful than others for later multidigit computation, it should not be the only strategy children learn. Therefore, *doubles ± 1* and other strategies are also worthwhile learning objectives.

Thus, good strategies should all work together, of course, to form adaptive expertise. For example, see the activity in Chapter 2's "Learning Trajectory for Recognition of Number and Subitizing" for the level, Conceptual Subitizer to 20 (p. 17). Notice how the fives and tens frames are used to give imagistic support for what is, basically, the *BAMT* strategy—all while encouraging conceptual subitizing.

Children at risk. At several points in this book we argue that some children fail to make progress in the learning trajectories in Chapter 5 and in this chapter. Here we emphasize that if children are not making progress in grade 1, and especially grade 2, they need intensive interventions (see Chapters 14, 15, and 16).

Achieving fluency. Research establishes several guidelines for helping children achieve fluency with arithmetic combinations, that is, correct and accurate knowledge *and* concepts and strategies that promote *adaptive expertise.*

1. Follow learning trajectories so that *children develop the concepts and strategies of the domain first. Understanding should precede practice.*

2. Ensure practice is *distributed,* rather than massed. For example, rather than studying $4 + 7$ for 30 seconds, it is better to study it once, then study another combination, then return to $4 + 7$. Further, practice on all combinations is best done in short but frequent sessions. For long-term memory, a day or more should eventually separate these sessions.

3. Use drill and practice software that includes research-based strategies (see the companion book).

4. Ensure practice continually develops relationships and strategic thinking. For example, at least some practice should occur on all forms of all possible combinations. This may help children understand properties, including commutativity, additive inverse, and equality, as well as supporting students' retrieval of basic combinations:

$$5 + 3 = 8 \qquad 3 + 5 = 8 \qquad 8 - 5 = 3 \qquad 8 - 3 = 5$$
$$8 = 5 + 3 \qquad 8 = 3 + 5 \qquad 3 = 8 - 5 \qquad 5 = 8 - 3$$

As an illustration, teachers make "math mountain" cards such as those in Figure 6.4 (Fuson & Abrahamson, in press). Students cover any of the three numbers and show them to their partner, who tells what number is covered.

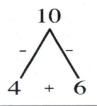

Figure 6.4 "Math Mountain" cards for practicing arithmetic combinations.

This suggests that it is not just the arithmetic combinations that should be automatic. *Students should also be fluent with the related reasoning strategies.* For example, the *Building Blocks* software not only provides the drill problems following these guidelines but also presents each group of combinations based on the strategy that is most helpful in a particular type of solution. As a specific illustration, the software initially groups together all those combinations that yield nicely to the *BAMT* strategy.

Summary. An important goal of early mathematics is students' growth of flexible, fluent, accurate knowledge of addition and subtraction combinations. Learning these combinations is not only about rote memorization. Seeing and using patterns, and building relationships, can free children's cognitive resources to be used in other tasks. Children generalize the patterns they learn and apply it to combinations that were not studied (Baroody & Tiilikainen, 2003). Number combination instruction that focuses on encouraging children to look for patterns and relations can generalize to problem-solving situations and can free attention and effort for other tasks.

Science is facts; just as houses are made of stones, so is science made of facts; but a pile of stones is not a house and a collection of facts is not necessarily science.

(Jules Henri Poincairé)

Grouping and Place Value

What determines children's development of base-ten understandings? Not age but classroom experience. Use of the BAMT strategy, for example, helps children group into tens to solve addition and subtraction problems and to develop place value concepts. Place value has been a part of the learning trajectories of Chapters 2, 3, 4, and 5, but here we focus on the concepts of grouping and place value.

Development of Grouping and Place Value Concepts

Extending the mathematics. Grouping underlies multiplication and measuring with different units. A special grouping organizes collections into groups of ten. That is, a numerical collection can be measured using units of one, ten, one hundred, or one thousand, and, in a written multidigit numeral, the value of a digit depends on its position in the numeral because different digit positions indicate different units. To build understanding of numbers greater than ten, children must build on their early numerical knowledge and decomposing/composing to understand even the teen numbers as 1 ten and some extras and later to understand numbers above 19 as some number of groups of ten and some extras. Beginning with the teen numbers, the written numerals and the number words both refer to groups of ten (e.g., 11 is 1 group of ten and 1 one).

From what we saw about counting, comparing, and addition in Chapters 3, 4, and 5, we know that 35 is the number that results from counting 5 more than 30. Similarly, 435 is the number that results from counting 35 more than 400. So, 435 = 400 + 30 + 5 (Wu, 2007). The symbol "435" illustrates a deep idea in the Hindu-Arabic number system: Each digit represents different magnitudes, depending on its *place* in the symbol. The *place value* of the digit means its value, or magnitude, as in "4" meaning "400" in "435" (but "4" means "40" in "246"). The sum of 400 + 30 + 5, used to represent the separate place value of each digit, is called the number's *expanded notation.*

Children's knowledge of grouping and place value. Preschool children begin to understand the process of making groups with equal numbers of objects. Such grouping, and knowledge of the special grouping into tens, appears not to be related to counting skill. However, experience with additive composition does appear to contribute to knowledge of grouping and place value.

Teachers often believe that their students understand place value because they can, for example, put digits into "tens and ones charts." However, ask these students what the "1" in "16" means and they are as likely to say "one" (and mean 1 singleton) as they are to say "one ten." This is one of many tasks that illustrate the difference between children with little, and children with developing or strong, knowledge of place value. Several classifications systems have been used to describe the levels of thinking children develop from moving from little or no, to strong knowledge of place value.

- Students who say only "one" have little or no knowledge of place value. They will usually make a group of 16 objects to represent "16," but they do not understand the place value of the numeral.
- Students understand that "26" means a group of 20 cubes along with a group of 6 cubes, but for "twenty-six" might write "206."
- Students create a group of 26 cubes by counting two groups of 10 (10, 20), and then counting up by ones (21, 22, 23, 24, 25, 26).
- Students count "1 ten, 2 tens . . ." (or even "1, 2 tens") and then count the ones as before.
- Students connect the number words (twenty-six), numerals (26), and quantities (26 cubes); they understand that 546 is equal to 500 plus 40 plus 6, and can use a variety of strategies for solving multidigit number problems.

Students may be at a higher level for small numbers (e.g., up to 100) than they are for numbers with which they are less familiar (e.g., numbers to 1000). Students eventually need to understand that 500 is equal to 5 times 100, 40 is equal to 4 times 10, and so forth. They need to know that all adjacent places have the same exchange values: exchange 1 unit to the left for 10 units to the right and vice versa.

Language and place value. As we saw previously, English has thirteen rather than "threeteen" or, better, "ten-three"; twenty rather than "twoty" or, better, "two tens." Other languages, such as Chinese, in which 13 is read as "ten-and-three," are more helpful to children. Also, neither "teen" nor "ty" say ten, although they mean ten in different ways. The written numbers are clearer in their pattern, but the written numerals are so succinct that they mislead children: a 52 looks like a 5 and a 2 side by side, without suggesting fifty or five tens to the beginner. It is especially unfortunate that the first two words following ten do not even feature the "teen" root at all. Instead, "eleven" and "twelve" stem from Old English words meaning "one left" (after ten) and "two left."

Experience and Education

Children learn to understand the ten-structured groupings named by our number words and written numbers as they see and work with quantities grouped into tens linked to number words and to written numbers. They may count 52 blocks into their own units of tens and ones, but counting and stacking blocks cannot take the place of working with the ideas and the symbols. That is, children have to discuss these ideas. They might also pretend to make stacks of blocks, while counting, "11 is one ten and one, 12 is one ten and two . . . 20 is two tens" and so forth. They have to engage in many experiences to establish ten as a benchmark and, more important, as a new unit (1 ten that contains 10 ones). Regular tens and ones words (52 is "five tens two ones") used along with the ordinary words can help establish a language that symbolizes decomposing and composing. Further, solving simple addition problems in the pre-K and kindergarten years helps form a foundation for understanding place value. Following the counting, comparing, and addition learning trajectories in Chapters 3, 4, and 5 is consistent with these findings.

So, there are two complementary approaches to learning grouping and place value. The first focuses directly on learning place value for numbers of a certain range (the teens, or numbers to 100). The second is using arithmetic problem-solving as a good context for the learning of place value, which we discuss in the following section.

In the first approach, students work with place value ideas before arithmetic. For example, they might play "banking" games in which they roll two number cubes and take that many pennies (or play money single-dollar bills), *but* if they have 10 or more pennies, they have to trade 10 pennies for a dime before their turn is over. The first one to get to 100 wins. There are many such activities. Students could take an inventory of classroom supplies, count chairs for an assembly, get reading for a party, or conduct a science experiment—in each, grouping items to be counted into tens and ones. Similar games can involve throwing a ring or other object onto a target and accumulating scores or any other similar activity.

In one project, students also represented tens and ones with cardboard or paper "penny stripes" with ten pennies separated into two groups of five on the front and one dime on the back (base-ten blocks were deemed too expensive). Eventually, students used drawings to solve problems. They drew columns of ten circles or dots, counted them by tens and by ones, and then connected the columns of ten by a 10-stick (or quick-ten). When they understood the 10-sticks as meaning ten ones, they just drew the 10-sticks and ones. Tens and ones were drawn using 5-groups to minimize errors and help students see the numbers at a glance. A space was left after the first five 10-sticks, and five ones circles (or dots) were drawn horizontally and then the rest of the ones circles drawn below these in a row.

During this work, the teacher called 78 "seventy-eight" but *also "seven-tens, eight ones."* Some children still viewed and operated on digits in a multidigit number as if they were singletons; therefore, "secret code cards" were introduced such as have been used by many educators. They were placed in front of each other to illustrate the place value system, as shown in Figure 6.5.

High-quality instruction often uses manipulatives or other objects to demonstrate and record quantities. Further, such manipulatives are used consistently enough that they become tools for thinking (see Chapter 16). They are *discussed* to explicate the place-value ideas. They are used to solve problems, including arithmetic problems. Finally, they are replaced by symbols.

Multidigit Addition and Subtraction

Almost all, who have ever fully understood arithmetic, have been obliged to learn it over again in their own way.

(Warren Colburn, 1849)

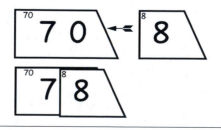

Figure 6.5 Place value "secret code cards."

Conceptual knowledge, especially of the base-ten system, influences how students understand, learn, and use algorithms. Recall that an algorithm is a step-by-step procedure that is guaranteed to solve a specific category of problems. A computation algorithm is a cyclic algorithm that solves computational problems, such as arithmetic problems, in a limited number of steps. Efficient, accurate, multidigit computation methods use the decomposition of the numbers into their place value quantities (they are "cyclic" because they then operate on one place, then the next . . .), the commutative and associative properties in adding or subtracting like values, and, again, composition and decomposition whenever there are too many (when adding) or not enough (when subtracting) of a given value. (Recall the discussion in "Arithmetic: Mathematical Definitions and Properties," Chapter 5, pp. 60–61.)

Strategies involving counting by tens and ones (see Chapter 3) can be altered along with children's developing understanding of numeration and place value to lead up to explicit multidigit addition and subtraction knowledge. Altering students' increasingly sophisticated counting strategies is a natural site for developing their understanding of place value in arithmetic. Rather than count by tens and ones to find the sum of 38 and 47, children might decompose 38 into its tens and ones and 47 into its tens and ones. This encourages the children to reason with ten as a unit like the unit of one and compose the tens together into 7 tens, or 70. After composing the ones together into 15 ones, they have transformed the sum into the sum of 70 and 15. To find this sum, the children take a 10 from the 15 and give it to the 70, so the sum is 80 and 5 more, or 85. Strategies such as this are modifications of counting strategies involving tens and ones just as certain strategies for finding the sum of 8 and 7 (e.g., take 2 from 7 and give it to 8, then add 10 and 5) are modifications of counting strategies involving only counting by ones.

To use such strategies, students need to conceptualize numbers both as wholes (as units in themselves) and composites (of individual units). For example, students can repeatedly answer what number is "10 more" than another number. "What is ten more than 23?" "33!" "Ten more?" "43!"

This, then, is the second approach (mentioned previously) to moving along the developmental progression for learning explicit place values, along with multidigit arithmetic. Like other developmental progressions, the levels of understanding of place value are not absolute or lockstep. Students might use a strategy based on a flexible combination of decomposition–composition strategies and counting-based, or sequence, strategies when solving a horizontally-formatted arithmetic problem, such as 148 + 473. For example, they might say, "100 and 400 is 500. And 70 and 30 is another hundred, so 600. Then 8, 9, 10, 11 . . . and the other 10 is 21. So, 621."

However, these same students regress to an earlier level when solving problems in a vertical format.

```
  148
+473
  511
```
(the student ignored the numbers that needed to be regrouped)

The vertical format can lead students to just think of each number as singles, even if they understand place value in different contexts. The extensive historical work on "bugs" in algorithms provides many additional examples, such as the following.

```
  73
−47
  34
```
(the student subtracted the smaller from the larger *digit* in each case)

802

−47

665 (the student first ignored the zero "borrowing" from the 8 two times).

All these have several lessons for us. Teaching arithmetic is much more than teaching procedures. It involves relationships, concepts, and strategies. Indeed, *if taught conceptually, most students will not make these types of errors.* Also, teaching arithmetic does more than teach "computation"—it lays the groundwork for much of future mathematics, including algebra.

Experience and Education

The previous section showed that possessing strong knowledge of the properties and processes of counting, place value, and arithmetic helps students use algorithms adaptively and transfer their knowledge to new situations. Without this knowledge, children often make errors such as subtracting the smaller from the larger digit regardless of which is actually to be subtracted from which. Many of these errors stem from children's treatment of multidigit numbers as a series of single-digit numbers, without consideration of their place value and role in the mathematical situation (Fuson, 1992b). Thus, U.S. children learn to carry out the steps of algorithm, but do not develop conceptual understanding of place value. This is a national problem.

Some have argued that standard algorithms are actually *harmful* to children. For example, in classrooms where standard algorithms were *not* taught, second and third grades performed better on problems such as mental addition of 7 + 52 + 186 than students in classrooms in which standard algorithms were taught, *even when the latter were in fourth grade* (Kamii & Dominick, 1997, 1998). Further, when they did make errors, the non-algorithm students' answers were more reasonable. The fourth grade algorithm classes gave answers that were nonsensical, with sums above 700 or even 800. They also gave answers such as "four, four, four" indicating they thought about the numbers not as having place value but rather just as a series of separate digits. The researchers argue that algorithms are harmful because they encourage children to cease their own thinking and because they "unteach" place value.

This may be due to poor curricula and teaching. As traditionally taught, divorced from children's own strategies and from conceptual understanding, algorithms appear to replace quantitative reasoning. Algorithms purposefully work on one "column" after another without a concern for the place value of the numbers. Too often, teachers directly teach standard algorithms regardless of their students' developmental progressions in counting strategies, allowing the students to perform meaningless but prescribed procedures unconnected to their understandings of counting and other number concepts.

In contrast, *curricula and teaching that emphasize both conceptual understanding simultaneously with procedural skill, and flexible application of multiple strategies, lead to equivalent skill, but more fluent, flexible use of such skills, as well as superior conceptual understanding.*

In general, then, high-quality teaching addresses concepts, procedures, and connections, but *also* emphasizes *students' sense making.* For example, the use of visual representations of quantities, and explication of the relationships between concepts and skills can be important. Teachers say, "Here, 8 tens and 7 tens are 15 tens. This equals 1 *hundred* and 5 *tens,*" modeling with base-ten manipulatives as necessary. Such teaching is often necessary, but alone is not sufficient. *Students need to make sense of the procedures for themselves.* They need to describe and explain what they are doing in natural and then mathematical language. At certain levels of understanding, especially, they need to be able to adapt procedures.

This is one of the main reasons that some argue that students should create their own strategies to solve multidigit arithmetic problems before formal instruction on algorithms. That is, children's informal strategies may be the best starting points for developing both place value and multidigit arithmetic concepts and skills. These strategies differ significantly from formal, paper-and-pencil algorithms. For example, children prefer working right to left, whereas the formal algorithms work left to right (Kamii & Dominick, 1997, 1998). The reason for this is not just that it encourages children's creative thinking—that *is* a remarkable finding of this area of research. As stated, one group of researchers believes that algorithms harm students' thinking. As another example, one teacher gave her class *only* problems in which one addend ended with "99" or "98" (e.g., 366 + 199). For most of the session, all the students used the standard algorithm. One student, who had not been taught these algorithms in previous grades, said that he changed 366 + 199 to 365 + 200 and then added to find 565. However, only three students adopted such methods—all the rest kept "lining up the digits" and computing each of these problems digit by digit.

Kamii blamed standard algorithms for students' reticence to *think* about problems. When the teachers stopped teaching them the differences were called "astounding" (Kamii & Dominick, 1998). For example, they convinced teachers to stop teaching standard algorithms and rely only on students' thinking. In one year, correct answers on 6 + 53 + 185 went from 3 of 16 students, all of whom used the standard algorithm, to only two using the standard algorithm (both incorrectly) and 18 using their own strategies, with 15 of the 18 getting the correct answer.

Thus, Kamii is convinced that, at least for whole number addition and subtraction, algorithms introduced early do more harm than good. But what, many ask, if children make mistakes? The argument is that the logic of the mathematics in this case, with the reasoning of the students, is adequate to *self*-correct any such errors. One second grade class was asked a challenging problem, to add 107 and 117. A first group of students added from the right and got 2114. A second said 14 was two-digit and could not be written in the ones place; you should only write the 4 there, so the answer is 214. A third group said the 1 in 14 should be written because it was more important so answer was 211. The fourth group added the tens and said the answer was 224. Individual students argued. The inventor of each approach defended it vigorously. At the end of the 45-minute period, the only thing the class could agree on was that is was impossible to have four different correct answers. (This is the point at which many teachers hearing the story worry the most—Isn't it unethical to send them home without the right answer?)

Over the next session, all students in this class constructed the "correct" algorithm. They made mistakes, but were encouraged to defend their opinion until they were convinced that the procedures they had used were wrong. They learned by modifying their ideas, not just "accepting" a new procedure.

These and similar studies support the notion that inventing one's own procedures is usually a good first phase. They also illustrate the approach, mentioned previously, of teaching place value in the context of solving multidigit addition and subtraction problems (Fuson & Briars, 1990).

Is student invention necessary? Some contend that invention at this level is not the critical feature. Rather, they argue for the importance of the *sense*-making in which students engage whether or not they invent, adapt, or copy a method.

Sense-making is probably the essence; however, we believe *the bulk of research indicates that initial student invention develops multiple interconnecting concepts, skills, and problem-solving.* This does not mean that children must invent every procedure but that conceptual development, adaptive reasoning, and skills are developed simultaneously and that initial student invention may be a particularly effective way of achieving these goals. Finally, we believe that student invention is a creative act of mathematical thinking that is valuable in its own right.

Mental procedures before algorithms. Many researchers believe that use of written algorithms is introduced too soon and that a more beneficial approach is the initial use of mental computation.

Kamii's extensive writings and research, already discussed, exemplify this approach. Standard written algorithms intentionally relieve the user of thinking about where to start, what place value to assign to digits, and so forth. *This is efficient for those who already understand, but often has negative effects on initial learning.* In comparison, mental strategies are derived from and support underlying concepts. Conventionally taught students usually take a long time to master algorithms and often never master them. Students learn better if mental computation is taught and performed before written algorithms (and practiced throughout education), along with appropriate work with concrete materials and drawings.

Such mental computation creates *flexible* thinkers. Inflexible students mostly use mental images of standard paper-and-pencil algorithms. For 246 + 199, they compute as follows: 9 + 6 = 15, 15 = 1 ten and 5 ones; 9 + 4 + 1 = 14, 14 tens = 1 hundred and 4 tens; 1 + 2 + 1 = 4. Four hundreds; so, 445—and, frequently, they make errors.

Flexible students instead might compute as follows: 199 is close to 200; 246 + 200 = 446, take away 1; 445. The flexible students also used strategies such as the following to compute 28 + 35:

- *compensation*: 30 + 35 = 65, 65 − 2 = 63 (or 30 + 33 = 63)
- *decomposition*: 8 + 5 = 13, 20 + 30 = 50, 63
- *jump*, or "begin-with-one-number": 28 + 5 = 33, 33 + 30 = 63 (28 + 30 = 58, 58 + 5 = 63).

Compensation and decomposition strategies aligned with base-ten blocks and other such manipulatives, whereas the jump strategy is aligned with 100s charts or number lines (especially the empty number line, discussed later in this chapter). For many students, the jump strategies are more effective and accurate. For example, in subtraction, students using standard algorithms often show the "smaller-from-larger" bug, as, for 42 − 25, giving the answer 23.

Games can give targeted practice with the jump strategy. For example, in *The 11 Game*, students spin two spinners (partially unbent paper clips can be spun around a pencil point). If they get what is illustrated in Figure 6.6, for example, they must subtract 11 from 19. They then can put one of

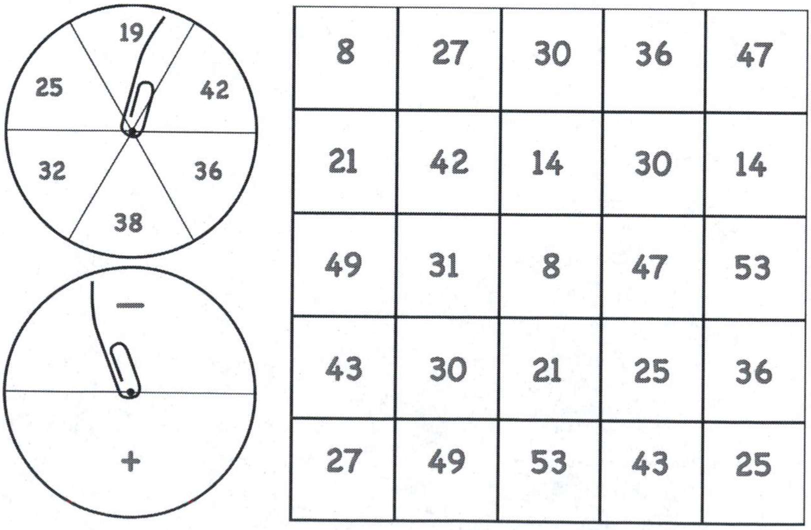

8	27	30	36	47
21	42	14	30	14
49	31	8	47	53
43	30	21	25	36
27	49	53	43	25

Figure 6.6 The 11 Game.

their counters on the result, 8 (which appears in two locations)—as long as one is open. Their goal is to be the first to get four in a row (horizontal, vertical, or oblique). The emphasis on adding or subtracting only 1 ten and 1 one helps children understand and establish a strong use of the jump strategy. Many variations are, of course, possible, such as changing 11 to 37 or adding or subtracting only multiples of 10.

In a similar vein, a buying-and-selling situation embodied in a modified game of lotto was used successfully as a context to motivate and guide first graders in two-digit subtraction (Kutscher, Linchevski, & Eisenman, 2002). Students transferred their knowledge to the classroom context.

The Dutch more recently have promoted the use of the "empty number line" as a support for the jump strategies. Use of this model has been reported as supporting more intelligent arithmetical strategies. The number line is "empty" in that it is not a ruler with all numbers marked but simply keeps the order of numbers and the size of "jumps" recorded, such as shown in Figure 6.7.

Other researchers/developers believe that both the decomposition and jump strategies are worthwhile, and neither has to be learned first (R. J. Wright, Stanger, Stafford, & Martland, 2006). The jump strategy is preferred as a *mental arithmetic* strategy, with the empty number line as a recording, not a computational, device. That is, in their view, students should use the empty number line to record what they have already done mentally, so it becomes a written representation and a way to communicate their thinking to their peers and the teacher.

Students also create combinations of these strategies. For example, students might first decompose a bit and then jump: 48 + 36—40 + 30 = 70; 70 + 8 = 78; 78 + 2 = 80; 80 + 4 = 84. They might also use compensation or other transformational strategies, such as: 34 + 59 —> 34 + 60 − 1, so 94 − 1 = 93 (R. J. Wright et al., 2006).

Do not just "do both strategies," but also help students *connect* them. For example, the jump strategy may de-emphasize decade structures but maintain number sense. Decomposition strategies emphasize place value but often lead to errors. Using and connecting both, intentionally addressing the mathematics they each develop, may be the most effective pedagogical approach.

Other spinner games can provide substantial and enjoyable practice with these strategies. For example, "Spin Four" is similar to the "The 11 Game" except that the second spinner shows the amount added or subtracted from the number spun on the first spinner. This can be done in many ways. Figure 6.8 features subtraction with no regrouping. Other games can easily be constructed to feature subtraction with regrouping, addition with and without regrouping, or a combination of addition and subtraction.

"Four in a Row" is a similar game, but here each player has 12 chips of one color ("see through" if possible). Each chooses two numerals in the square on the left, summing them and covering them (just for this turn) with chips (see Figure 6.9). The player also covers the sum on the square on the right (this chip stays). The first to make four in a row with his/her chips is the winner (from Kamii, 1989, who credits Wheatley and Cobb for this version; Kamii's work includes many other games).

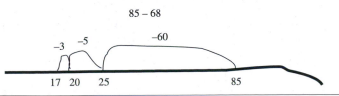

Figure 6.7 The empty number line supporting arithmetic.

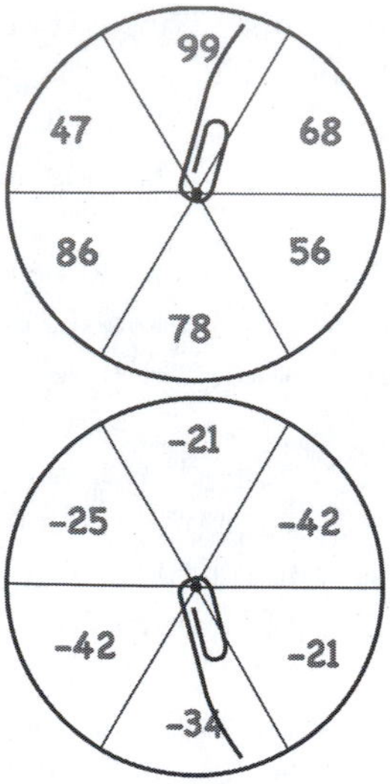

78	47	52	65	57
57	72	14	22	44
36	31	53	57	43
34	22	61	65	26
5	26	13	53	35

Figure 6.8 Spin Four.

5	6	7
8	9	10
11	12	13

16	21	18	13	18
19	20	12	20	23
22	24	19	21	16
17	11	23	22	14
14	15	15	17	25

Figure 6.9 Four in a Row.

Before we leave this topic, we note that it may be inaccurate to say a child "uses" a "jump" strategy when strategies are just barely forming (i.e., the youngest child). That is, they may not be deliberately choosing and applying strategies but basing computations on their familiarity with certain numbers relations. A second grader may add 39 + 6 by deciding to add one to 39, then the "rest" of the 6 (i.e., 5) to the 40 to get 45, without conscientiously thinking—or even knowing about, "jump strategies." Such explicit knowledge and decision-making might emerge *from* repeated experiences using number relationships. At first these are "theorems-in-action" (Vergnaud, 1978) and are explicit strategies until the are redescribed. Instructionally, this would imply that the initial goal is not so much to teach the strategies as to develop schemes of number relationships and then use them to construct strategies, discussing these strategies to highlight the mathematical principles involved.

Which algorithms? There are many arguments about whether to teach *the* standard algorithms. Too often, such arguments have generated more heat than light, for several reasons:

- There is no single standard algorithm. Many different ones have been used in the U.S. and around the world (e.g., see algorithms *a* and *b* in Table 6.1). All of these are valid (Kilpatrick et al., 2001).
- What are taken as different "standard" algorithms by teachers and lay people are often *not* viewed as different by mathematicians, who believe they are all just simple *modifications* (often in the way numbers are recorded) of general place-value based algorithms. That is, the algorithms in Table 6.1 all subtract in same-place-value columns and compose/ decompose as necessary; they just do these processes and notate them in slightly different ways.

Several modifications of the standard U.S. algorithm (Table 6.2) are useful (Fuson, in press). For beginners, or those having difficulty, recording each addition showing its full place value, as in Table 6.2, can develop their understanding and skill. Once this is attained, the accessible and mathematically desirable algorithm shown in Table 6.2 is superior to the standard shown in Table 6.1*a* for several reasons. First, the numeral (e.g., "13") is written with the digits close to each other, maintaining for the children the origin of the "13." Second, with students "adding from the top," the (usually larger) numerals are added first, freeing students' memory from holding an altered

Table 6.1 "Different" Standard Algorithms.

a. Decomposition—Traditional U.S.

4 5 6
 −1 6 7
	4
	 4 5^1 6
	 −1 6 7
		4
		 4 5^1 6
		 −1 6 7
		     9
			3^1 4
			 4 5^1 6
			 −1 6 7
			     9
				3^1 4
				 4 5^1 6
				 −1 6 7
				 2 8 9

	Add 10 to 6 ones, "borrowing" from 5 tens.	Subtract 16 − 7.	Add 10 tens to 4 tens, borrowing from 4 hundreds.	Subtract 14 − 6 (tens) and 3 − 1 (hundreds).

b. Equal Addends—From Europe and Latin America

4 5 6
 −1 6 7
	4 5^1 6
	 −1^1 6 7
		4 5^1 6
		 −1^1 6 7
		     9
			4^1 5^1 6
			 −1^1 6 7
			     9
				4^1 5^1 6
				 −1^1 6 7
				 2 8 9

	Add 10 to 6 ones to make 16 ones, and 1 ten to 6 tens (here it is 1 *plus* 6 tens, *not* 16 tens).	Subtract 16 − 7.	Add 10 tens to 5 tens, 1 hundred to 1 hundred.	Subtract 15 − 7 (tens) and 4 − 2 (hundreds).

c. Accessible and mathematically desirable—a modification of the U.S. algorithm (Fuson, in press)

4 5 6 −1 6 7	3^1 4 4 5^1 6 −1 6 7	3^1 4 4 5^1 6 −1 6 7 2 8 9
	Regroup everywhere needed.	Subtract everywhere.

numeral (which was added to the "carried" 1). Instead, the larger numerals are first added first, and the easy-to-add "1" is added last.

Similarly, notice the subtraction algorithm back in Table 6.1*c* (compared to Table 6.1*a*, see p. 97). Regrouping everywhere *first* helps students concentrate *just* on the need to regroup and the regrouping itself. Once that has been completed, then the subtraction operations are performed one after the other. *Not* having to "switch" between the two processes allows better focus on each one.

These "accessible and mathematically desirable algorithms," are simple variations of the standard U.S. algorithms. However, they can significantly help students build both skill and understanding (Fuson, in press).

Table 6.2 Variations on the Standard Addition Algorithm.

a. Traditional U.S.

	1	11	11
456	456	456	456
+167	+167	+167	+167
	3	23	623

| | Add 6 + 7, enter 3 in ones place, "carry" the 10 ones to create 1 ten. | Add 6 + 5 + 1 (tens), enter 2 in tens place, "carry" the 10 tens to create 1 hundred. | Add 1 + 4 + 1 (hundreds), enter 6 in hundreds place. |

b. Transitional algorithm—write all totals (Fuson, in press)

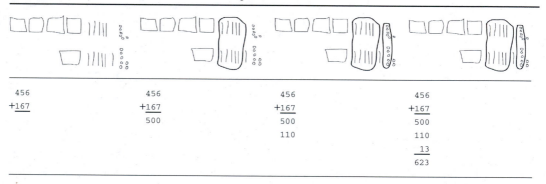

456	456	456	456
+167	+167	+167	+167
	500	500	500
		110	110
			13
			623

c. Accessible and mathematically desirable algorithm—a modification of the U.S. algorithm (Fuson, in press)

456	456	456	456
+167	+167	+167	+167
	3	23	623

| | Add 6 + 7, enter "13" but with the 3 in the ones place and the 1 ten *under* the tens column. | Add 5 + 6 + 1 ten, enter "2" in the tens place and the 1 hundred under the hundreds column. | Add 4 + 1 + 1 hundreds. |

For any variation, base-ten manipulatives and drawing can support the learning of composition and decomposition methods—especially in maintaining a connection between concepts and procedures. Use of drawings is illustrated in Tables 6.2*b* and *c*. (Notice there are two basic differences between the two, the order in which values are grouped and the way they are grouped.) Manipulatives or drawings help illustrate that different place value quantities need to be added separately and that certain quantities need to be composed to make a unit of a higher place value.

Research shows that the key is *teaching for meaning and understanding.* Instruction that focuses on flexible application of a variety of strategies helps students build robust concepts and procedures. They learn to adaptively fit their strategies to the characteristics of the problems. In contrast, instruction that focuses only on routines results in students blindly following those routines. Understanding the mathematics, and students' thinking about mathematics, including the varied strategies and algorithms they might use, helps students create and use adaptive calculations. If students invent their own strategies first, they have fewer errors than students who were taught algorithms from the start.

In summary, *conceptually-based instruction supports mathematical proficiency.* Teach conceptual knowledge first, and alongside, procedural knowledge. Have students develop their own methods first, the earlier in their educational lives the better. When standard algorithms are developed, the modified algorithms we present here can help children build concepts and procedures simultaneously. On that note, let us turn to this chapter's learning trajectories.

Learning Trajectory for Composing Number and Multidigit Addition and Subtraction

The importance of the *goal* of increasing children's ability in these arithmetic abilities is clear. With that goal, Table 6.3 provides the two additional components of the learning trajectory, the developmental progression and the instructional tasks. There are three important notes on this learning trajectory:

- Unlike other learning trajectories, Table 6.3 is split into two parts, first composing, and then multidigit addition and subtraction. This was done to emphasize that the second part is a *copy* of the developmental progression already included in the learning trajectory in Chapter 5, enhanced with the instructional tasks from this chapter.
- Note that place value is fundamental to all number domains, so it is embedded in the learning trajectories in Chapters 2, 3, 4, and 5, as well as this one. This chapter simply has the most specific focus on place value.
- Recall again that the ages in all the learning trajectory tables are only approximate, especially because the age of acquisition usually depends heavily on experience.

Table 6.3 Learning Trajectory for Composing Number and Multidigit Addition and Subtraction.

Age (years)	Developmental Progression	Instructional Tasks
	Composing Number	
0–2	**Pre-Part–Whole Recognizer** Only nonverbally recognizes parts and wholes. Recognizes that sets can be combined in different orders, but may not explicitly recognize that groups are additively composed of smaller groups.	Basic early childhood experiences are helpful, as described in previous chapters.

Continued Overleaf

Age (years)	Developmental Progression	Instructional Tasks
	When shown 4 red blocks and 2 blue blocks, intuitively appreciates that "all the blocks" include the red and blue blocks, but when asked how many there are in all, may name a small number, such as 1.	
3–4	**Inexact Part–Whole Recognizer** Knows that a whole is bigger than parts, but may not accurately quantify. (Intuitive knowledge of commutativity, and, later, associativity, with physical groups, later in more abstract contexts, including numbers.)	Experiences in learning trajectories from other chapters are appropriate to developing these abilities. Especially relevant are subitizing (Chapter 2), counting (Chapters 3 and 5), comparing (Chapter 4), and sorting (Chapter 12).
	When shown 4 red blocks and 2 blue blocks and asked how many there are in all, names a "large number," such as 5 or 10.	
4–5	**Composer to 4, then 5** Knows number combinations. Quickly names parts of any whole, or the whole given the parts.	*Finger Games* Ask children to make numbers with their fingers (hands should be placed in their laps between tasks). These sessions should be short and fun, spread out as needed.
	Shown 4, then 1 is secretly hidden, and then is shown the 3 remaining, quickly says "1" is hidden.	Ask children to show 4 with their fingers. Tell your partner how you did it. Now in a different way. Tell your partner.
		Now make 4 with the same number on each hand.
		Ask children to show 5 with their fingers and discuss responses. (Did they use one hand only or two? Can they do it a different way? and so on).
		Ask them to show another way to make 5, using both hands if they did not yet.
		Repeat the above tasks, but "you can't use thumbs."
		Challenge children by asking them to show 3 or 5 using the same number of fingers on each hand. Discuss why it cannot be done.
		Bunny Ears. In this modification, have children make the numbers as "bunny ears"—holding their hands above their heads to make numbers 1–5 in different ways.
		Up and Down. In another session, ask children to show 4 on one hand. Ask how many fingers are up and how many are down (all on one hand only). Repeat with 0, 1, 2, 3, and 5 across several days.
		Snap! (to 5) Agree on a number from 3 to 5. Make a train of that number of connecting cubes, all of one color. Put them behind your back and snap off some. Show the rest. Have students determine how many are behind your back. Discuss their solution strategies.
		Students work in pairs playing *Snap!*, taking turns making the connecting cube train and snapping. Students should ask their partner to guess how many you have, then show them to check.
	Composer to 7 Knows number combinations to totals of 7. Quickly names parts of any whole, or the whole given parts. Doubles to 10.	*Snap!* (to 7) (see above)
		Make a Number. Children decide on a number to make, say 7. They then get 3 decks of cards and take out all the cards numbered 7 or more, shuffling the remaining cards. The children take turns drawing a card and try to make a 7 by combining it with any other face-up card—if they can, they can keep both cards. If they can't, they must place it face up beside the deck. When the deck is gone, the player with the most pairs wins.
	Shown 6, then 4 are secretly hidden, and shown the 2 remaining, quickly says "4" are hidden.	Play again by changing the number to make.

Age (years)	Developmental Progression	Instructional Tasks

Number Snapshots 6. Students identify an image that correctly matches a target image from four multiple-choice selections.

Composer to 10 Knows number combinations to totals of 10. Quickly names parts of any whole, or the whole given parts. Doubles to 20.

"9 and 9 is 18."

Finger Games Ask children to make numbers with their fingers (hands should be placed in their laps between tasks).

Ask children to show 6 with their fingers. Tell your partner how you did it. Now in a different way. Tell your partner.

Now make 6 with the *same number* on each hand. Repeat with other even numbers (8, 10).

Ask children to show 7 with their fingers and discuss responses. Can they do it a different way?

Repeat the above tasks, but "you can't use thumbs." (Can you make 10?)

Challenge children by asking them to show 3, 5, or 7 using the same number of fingers on each hand. Discuss why it cannot be done.

Bunny ears. In this modification, have children make the numbers as "bunny ears"—holding their hands above their heads to make numbers 6–10 in different ways.

Up and down. Ask children to show 6. Ask how many fingers are up and how many are down (all on one hand only). Repeat with all numbers 0 to 10 across many days.

Turn Over Ten. The goal is to accumulate the most pairs of cards that sum to 10. Provide each group of children with 3 collections of 0–10 cards.

10 cards are dealt to each player, who assembles them in one pile, face down.

The remaining cards are placed face down in a "pick-up pile" between the two players. The top card of this pile is flipped over, face up.

Player 1 turns over his/her top card. If this card forms a sum of ten together with the card in the pick-up pile, that player takes and keeps the pair. (Whenever the card on top of the pick-up pile is used, a new one is turned over.)

If the sum of ten is not reached, the player places this top card next to the pick-up pile, so that these cards can be seen and used by players in subsequent turns (therefore, there may be a row of "discards" face up between the two players).

In either case (pair formed or card discarded) the turn passes to the next player, who turns over his/her top card.

If any of the cards showing can be used to form a pair of ten, the player keeps that pair.

If a player sees a pair of cards showing that form ten, he can choose that pair during his/her turn instead of turning over the top card in his/her pile.

Turns alternate until each player has turned over all of his or her cards. The player with the most pairs accumulated is the winner.

Make Tens. The goal is to make tens with all your cards and avoid being left with the extra card. Provide each group of children a deck of cards made of 2 collections plus one other card of any number between 0 and 10 (this will eventually be the "Old Maid" card that cannot make a 10). For example, use one of the following:

Continued Overleaf

Age (years)	Developmental Progression	Instructional Tasks

1. Two collections of number cards 0–10 with dots and numerals, with one extra 5 card.
2. Collections of numeral (only) cards 0–10 with one extra 5 card.

Introduce this two-player game. All the cards are dealt out to both players.

Both players first form all possible pairs of 10 in their own hands and set these pairs aside in their score pile. They keep the extras in their hand.

They take turns choosing (without looking) one card from the other player's hand. If they can use it to make 10, they place that pair in their score pile. If they cannot use it, the card remains in their hand.

At the end of the game, one player will be left with the odd card.

Slap a Ten. The goal is to make tens with all your cards and be the first one "out." Provide each group of children a deck of cards made of 4 decks of 1–10 cards.

Introduce this 2- to 4-player game.

Six cards are dealt out to each player. The remaining cards are placed in the middle, face down.

One player turns the top card over. The other players quickly determine if they can make a 10 with that and one card in their hand. If they can, they slap the card. The player who slaps it first must use it to make a ten. If they cannot, they keep the card and must take another card off the pile.

Players take turns turning over the top card.

The game ends when player goes "out" or the pile is gone. The player who went "out" or the one with the fewest cards in their hand wins.

Modification: If children are having a problem trying to slap the card at the same time . . .

If they can make a ten with the card shown, they slap their own card down. The player who slapped it down first will ask "Is it 10?"

All players must agree that the two cards make 10.

Tens Memory Game

For each pair of children, two sets of Numeral cards 1–9 are needed.

Place card sets face down in two separate 3-by-3 arrays. Players take turns choosing, flipping, and showing a card from each array.

If the cards do not sum to 10, they are returned face down to the arrays. If they do, that player keeps them.

Use more cards to make a longer game.

Snap! (to 10) (see above)

Make a Number (to 10) (see above)

Number Snapshots 8. Students identify an image that correctly matches a target image from four multiple-choice selections.

Age (years)	Developmental Progression	Instructional Tasks
7	**Composer with Tens and Ones** Understands 2-digit numbers as tens and ones; count with dimes and pennies; 2-digit addition with regrouping. "17 and 36 is like 17 and 3, which is 20, and 33, which is 53."	*Note: All games above involving tens can be played with larger sums to extend children's knowledge of arithmetic combinations.* *Make the Sum.* Six 1–10 decks of numeral cards are mixed and dealt out to players. Three number cubes are thrown by one player, who announces to sum. All plays try to make this sum in as many ways as possible. The first player to use up all her or his cards wins. *Salute!* With a deck of cards with the face cards removed, and Ace as 1, cards are dealt to 2 of the 3 players (Kamii, 1989). The two players sit facing each other with their cards face down. The third player says, "Salute!" and the two players take the top card from their piles and hold them on their foreheads so that the other two players can see them, but they cannot. The third player announces the sum of the two cards. Each of the other players tries to be the first to announce the value of their *own* cards. The person who is first takes both cards. The winner is the person who collects the most cards. *Composing 10s and 1s.* Show students connecting cubes—4 tens and 3 ones—for 2 seconds only (e.g., hidden under a cloth). Ask how many they saw. Discuss how they knew. Repeat with new amounts. Tell students you have a real challenge for them. Tell them there are 2 tens and 17 ones hidden. How many are there in all? Once they tell you, uncover them to check. Place 4 blue tens, 1 red tens, and 4 red singles. Tell students you have 54 cubes in all, and 14 are red. Ask them how many are blue. *Number Snapshots 10: Dots to Numerals up to 50.* Students identify an image that correctly matches a target image from four multiple-choice selections. 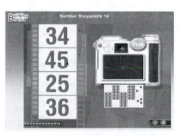 *From this point, the most important activities are included in the subitizing learning trajectory. See Chapter 2, pp. 16–17, especially the levels* **Conceptual Subitizer with Place Value and Skip Counting** *and* **Conceptual Subitizer with Place Value and Multiplication.**

Multidigit Addition and Subtraction

6–7	**Deriver** +/−: Uses flexible strategies and derived combinations (e.g., "7 + 7 is 14, so 7 + 8 is 15) to solve all types of problems. Includes Break-Apart-to-Make-Ten (BAMT). Can simultaneously think of 3 numbers within a sum, and can move part of a number to another, aware of the increase in one and the decrease in another. Asked, "What's 7 plus 8?" thinks: 7 + 8 → 7 + [7 + 1] → [7 + 7] + 1 = 14 + 1 = 15. Or, using BAMT, thinks, 8 + 2 = 10, so separate 7 into 2 and 5, add 2 and 8 to make 10, then add 5 more, 15.	*All types* of single-digit problems, using derived and, increasingly, known combinations. *(Note: Students should have achieved the level of* **Skip Counter by 10s to 100** *and* **Counter to 100** *before the following tasks; see Chapter 3's learning trajectory, p. 38.)* *Adding and subtracting 10s.* Present problems such as 40 + 10, initially by using separate fives and tens frames or connecting cubes in trains of 10. Ask how many dots (cubes) are there? How many tens? Add a ten and ask again. Progress to adding more than 1 ten at a time. *Repeat and fade:* Repeat as above until the students are fluent. Model the solution process yourself if necessary. As soon as possible, *hide* those placed out so children build visual, *mental* models. Eventually, present the problems only orally. Then take away tens (e.g., 80 − 10).

Continued Overleaf

Age (years)	Developmental Progression	Instructional Tasks
	Solves simple cases of multidigit addition (and often subtraction) by incrementing tens and/or ones. "What's 20 + 34?" Student uses connecting cube to count up 20, 30, 40, 50 plus 4 is 54.	*Adding to a decade.* Present problems such as 70 + 3 and 20 + 7. Use the same strategy as above as placing 2 tens and then 7 ones out. If students need additional assistance, lay the ones out one at a time while counting by ones. Note the result ("27 . . . that means 2 tens and 7 ones") and encourage students to solve another one a faster way. *Repeat and fade* as above. *Adding and subtracting multiples of 10s off the decade.* Present problems such as 73 + 10 and 27 + 20. Use the same strategy as above, placing 7 tens and 3 ones out, then adding tens one (or more) at a time. *Adding and subtracting within decades.* Present problems such as 2 + 3, then 22 + 3, then 72 + 3 and so forth (include 12 + 3 once the pattern is well established). Repeat. *Math-O-Scope.* Students identify numbers (representing values that are ten more, ten less, one more, or one less than a target number) within the hundreds chart to reveal a partially hidden photograph. 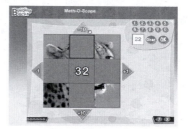
7	**Problem Solver** +/− Solves all types of problems, with flexible strategies and known combinations. Asked, "If I have 13 and you have 9, how could we have the same number?" says, "Nine and one is ten, then three more to make 13. One and three is four. I need four more!" Multidigit may be solved by incrementing or combining tens and ones (latter not used for join, change unknown). "What's 28 + 35?" Incrementer thinks: 20 + 30 = 50; +8 = 58; 2 more is 60, 3 more is 63. Combining tens and ones: 20 + 30 = 50. 8 + 5 is like 8 plus 2 and 3 more, so, it's 13. 50 and 13 is 63.	*All types* of problem structures for single-digit problems. *Adding across decades.* Present problems that bridge decades, such as 77 + 3 and 25 + 7. As above, use manipulatives and modeling as necessary, until children can solve this mentally, or with drawings such as the empty number line. *Repeat and fade* as above. *Figure the Fact.* Students add numeric values from 1 through 10 to values from 0 through 99, to reach a maximum total of 100. That is, if they are "on" 33 and get an 8, they have to enter 41 to proceed to that space, because the spaces are not marked with numerals, at least until they move through them. (See also Chapter 6.)  *Subtracting across decades.* Present problems that bridge decades, such as 73 + 7 and 32 − 6. As above, use manipulatives and modeling as necessary, until children can solve this mentally, or with drawings such as the empty number line. *Adding and subtracting 10s and 1s with manipulatives.* Present addition problems using fives and tens frames or connecting cubes. Show 1 ten and 4 ones. Ask how many dots (cubes) are there? Add a ten *and* 3 ones and ask

Age (years)	Developmental Progression	Instructional Tasks

again. Continue to add 1 to 3 tens and 1 to 9 ones each time until you are close to 100. Then ask, "How many do we have in all? How many would we need to reach 100?"

Use different manipulatives, such as imitation currency or coins.

Repeat and fade as above.

Adding and subtracting tens with the empty number line. Present addition (and then subtraction) problems under an empty number line (see top figure below) and have students "talk aloud" to solve the problem, representing their thinking on the empty number line (see bottom figure).

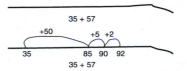

Move from problems such as 45 + 10 to 73 − 10, then 27 + 30 and 53 − 40, then move to . . .

Adding tens and ones. Present addition problems under an empty number line, as above.

Start with problems without regrouping such as 45 + 12, 27 + 31, and 51 + 35, then move to . . .

Problems with regrouping, such as 49 + 23, 58 + 22, 38 + 26.

Problems that suggest transformations such as compensation (e.g., 57 + 19 —> 56 + 20 or 57 + 20 − 1), such as 43 + 45 (44 + 44), 22 + 48, and so forth.

Allow students to use strategies that "work" for them, but encourage them to move from counting singles to more sophisticated strategies.

Present similar problems with place value manipulatives or drawings, such as base-ten blocks, or drawings of them (see the text).

Use different manipulatives, such as imitation currency or coins.

Repeat and fade as above.

Subtracting tens and ones. Present subtraction problems under an empty number line, as above.

Start with problems without regrouping such as 99 − 55, 73 − 52, and 59 − 35, then move to . . .

Present problems with regrouping, such as 81 − 29, 58 − 29, 32 − 27, and so on.

Problems that suggest transformations such as compensation, such as 83 − 59 (84 − 60, or 83 − 60 + 1), 81 − 25, 77 − 28, and so forth.

Watch for "subtract smaller digit from larger digit" errors (e.g., in 58 − 29, subtracting 9 − 8 rather than the correct 8 − 9).

Present similar problems with place value manipulatives or drawings, such as base-ten blocks, or drawings of them (see the text).

Use different manipulatives, such as imitation currency or coins.

Repeat and fade as above.

The 11 Game. See p. 94 and Figure 6.5.

Continued Overleaf

Age (years)	Developmental Progression	Instructional Tasks
7–8	**Multidigit** +/– Uses composition of tens and all previous strategies to solve multidigit +/– problems. Asked, "What's 37 − 18?" says, "I take 1 ten off the 3 tens; that's 2 tens. I take 7 off the 7. That's 2 tens and zero . . . 20. I have one more to take off. That's 19." Asked, "What's 28 + 35?" thinks, 30 + 35 would be 65. But it's 28, so it's 2 less—63.	*Hidden 10s and 1s.* Tell students you have hidden 56 red connecting cubes and 21 blue cubes under a cloth. Ask them how many there are altogether. Progress to problems with regrouping, such as 47 + 34. Move to problems with subtraction without (85 − 23), then with (51 − 28) regrouping. *Spin Four.* See p. 95 and Figure 6.7. *Four in a Row.* See p. 95 and Figure 6.8. Variations are to make the game Five in a Row and to use larger addends. Variation: Have 2 small squares, one with larger numerals, the other with smaller. Students subtract. *Word Problems:* Students solve multidigit word problems off and on the computer. (See Chapter 6.) *Jumping to 100.* Using numeral cubes, one with the numerals 1 to 6 and other with 10, 20, 30, 10, 20, 30, two teams take turns throwing the cubes and—starting at 0—adding that number to their position on an empty number line. Whoever reaches or passes 100 first wins. Variation: Jump down from 100 to 0. *Calculator "Make Me 100."* One student (or team) enters a two-digit number. The other has to enter a single addition which will make the display "100." Points can be kept. As a variation, students (or teams) can only add a number from 1 to 10. They take turns, and the winner is the first team to display 100. Higher-digit addition and subtraction. Pose problems such as, "What's 374 − 189?," "What's 281 + 35?"

Final Words

To this point, our discussions have emphasized number. Especially in early number, however, there appeared to be a strong spatial component. For example, some studies suggest that children's earliest quantification is *spatial* at its core. Further, knowledge of space and shape is important for its own sake. Spatial thinking is addressed in Chapter 7, and more specific geometric thinking in Chapters 8 and 9.

7
Spatial Thinking

Before reading on, when you read the title of this chapter, what did you think "spatial thinking" would involve? What ways do you "think spatially" in a typical week? Which of those might you consider "mathematical"?

Spatial thinking is important because it is an essential human ability that contributes to mathematical ability. However, the relationship between spatial thinking and mathematics is not straightforward. Sometimes, "visual thinking" is "good" but sometimes it is not. For example, many studies have shown that children with specific spatial abilities are more mathematically competent. However, other research indicates that students who process mathematical information by verbal-logical means outperform students who process information visually.

Also, *limited* imagery in mathematical thinking can cause difficulties. As we shall discuss in more detail in Chapter 8, an idea can be *too* closely tied to a single image. For example, connecting the idea of "triangles" to a single image such as an equilateral triangle with a horizontal base restricts young children's thinking.

Therefore, spatial ability is important in learning many topics of mathematics. The role it plays, however, is elusive and, even in geometry, complex. Two major abilities are spatial orientation and spatial visualization (A. J. Bishop, 1980; Harris, 1981; McGee, 1979). We first discuss spatial orientation, which involves an extensive body of research, then spatial visualization and imagery.

Spatial Orientation

Dennis the Menace is shown on a map where his family has driven. He looks aghast, and says, "*Two days?* Just to go *three inches?*" (from Liben, 2008, p. 21)

Spatial orientation is knowing where you are and how to get around in the world; that is, understanding relationships between different positions in space, at first with respect to your own position and your movement through it, and eventually from a more abstract perspective that includes maps and coordinates. This essential competence is not only linked to mathematics knowledge but also how we *remember* things.

Like number, spatial orientation has been postulated as a core domain with some abilities present from birth. For example, infants focus their eyes on objects and then begin to follow moving objects. Toddlers use geometric information about the overall shape of their environment to solve location tasks. Again, as with number, such early competencies develop with experience, and socio-cultural influences. What can young children understand and represent about spatial relationships and navigation? When can they represent and ultimately mathematize this knowledge?

Spatial Location and Intuitive Navigation

What kind of "mental maps" do young children possess? Neither children nor adults actually have "maps in their heads"—that is, their "mental maps" are not like a mental picture of a paper map. But, people do build up private and idiosyncratic knowledge as they learn about space. They do this by developing two categories of spatial knowledge. The first based on their own bodies—self-based systems. The second is based on other objects—external-based reference systems. The younger the child, the more loosely linked these systems are. Within each category, there is an early-developing type and a later-developing type. Let's look at each in turn.

Early Self- and External-based Systems

Self-based spatial systems are related to the child's own position and movements. The early-developing type is *response learning*, in which the child notes a pattern of movements that have been associated with a goal. For example, the child might get used to looking to the left from a high chair to see a parent cooking.

External-based reference systems are based on landmarks in the environment. The landmarks are usually familiar and important objects. In *cue learning*, children associate an object with a nearby landmark, such as a toy on a couch. Children possess both these types in the first months of life.

Later-developing Self- and External-based Systems

The later-developing type of self-based systems is *path integration*, in which children record the approximate distance and direction of their own movements. That is, they remember the "path they walked." As early as 6 months, and certainly by 1 year of age, children can use this strategy with some accuracy when they move themselves.

The more powerful type of external-based systems, *place learning*, comes closest to people's intuition of "mental maps." Children store locations by remembering distances and directions to landmarks. For example, children might use the walls of a room as a frame of reference to find a toy. This illustrates an early, implicit foundation for later learning of coordinate systems. This ability first develops during the second year of life and continues to be refined through life. As children develop, they get better at using—including knowing when to use—each of these types of spatial knowledge. They also *integrate* knowledge from each of these four types.

Spatial Thought

In their second year, children develop the critical capacity for *symbolic thought*. This supports many types of mathematical knowledge, including explicit spatial knowledge. As one example, children learn to take others' perspectives in viewing objects. They learn to coordinate different viewpoints on objects, but also use an external frame of reference (as in place learning) to work out different viewpoints.

Navigation Through Large-scale Environments

Children also learn to navigate in large environments. This also requires integrated representations, because one can see only some landmarks at any given point. Only older preschoolers learn scaled routes for familiar paths; that is, they know about the relative distances between landmarks. Even young children, however, can put different locations along a route into some relationship, at least in certain situations. For example, they can point to one location from another even though they never walked a path that connected the two.

Children as young as 3.5 years can learn to accurately walk along a path that replicates the route between their seat and the teacher's desk in their classroom. *Self-produced* movement is important. Kindergartners could not *imagine* similar movements or point accurately without moving, but they could imagine and recreate the movements and point accurately when they actually walked and turned. Thus, children can build mental imagery of locations and use this imagery, but they must physically move to show their competence. Preschoolers to first grades need landmarks or boundaries to succeed at such tasks. By third grade, children can use larger, encompassing frameworks that include the observer in the situation.

Thus, children develop these complex ideas and skills over years. However, even adults do not have perfectly accurate ideas about space. For example, all people intuitively view space as centered at one's home or other familiar place. They also view space as increasingly dense as they approach this center, so that distances seem larger the closer they get.

The Language of Space

Children learning English show a strong tendency to *ignore* fine-grained shape when learning novel *spatial* terms such as "on" or "in front of" or when interpreting known spatial terms. They show an equally strong tendency to *attend* to fine-grained shape when learning novel *object* names. For example, 3-year-olds shown an unusual object placed near a box and told, "This is acorp my box" tend to ignore the shape of the object and instead attend to its *location* relative to the box. They believe that "acorp" refers to a spatial *relation*. If they had instead been told "This *is* a prock" they would attend to the unusual object's *shape*.

The first spatial words English-speaking children learn are "in," "on," and "under," along with such vertical directionality terms as "up" and "down." These initially refer to transformations of one spatial relationship into other. For example, "on" initially does not refer to one object on top of another, but only to the act of making an object become physically attached to another.

Second, children learn words of proximity, such as "beside" and "between." Third, children learn words referring to frames of reference such as "in front of," "behind." The words "left" and "right" are learned much later, and are the source of confusion for many years, usually not well understood until 6 to 8 years of age (although specific attention to those words helps preschoolers orient themselves).

By 2 years of age, children have considerable spatial competence on which language might be based. Further, in contrast to many who emphasize children's naming of objects, children use spatial relational words more frequently, and often earlier, than names. Moreover, the use of even a single-word utterance by a 19-month-old, such as "in," may reflect more spatial competence than it first appears when the contexts differ widely, such as saying, "in" when about to climb into the child seat of a shopping cart and saying "in" when looking under couch cushions for coins she just put in the crack between cushions.

Models and Maps

At what age can children use and make representations of space? Even 2-year-olds can find their mother behind a barrier after observing the situation from above. But only by 2½ can they locate a toy shown a picture of the space. By 3 years, children may be able to build simple, but meaningful, models with landscape toys such as houses, cars, and trees, although this ability is limited through the age of 6 years. For example, in making models of their classroom, kindergartners cluster furniture correctly (e.g., they put the furniture for a dramatic play center together), but may not relate the clusters to each other.

In a similar vein, beginning about 3, and more so at 4, years of age, children can interpret arbitrary symbols on maps, such as a blue rectangle standing for blue couch, or "x marks the spot." On another map they may recognize lines as roads . . . but suggest that the tennis courts were doors. They can benefit from maps and can use them to guide navigation (i.e., follow a route) in simple situations.

Coordinates and Spatial Structuring

Even young children can use coordinates if adults provide the coordinates and guide children in their use. However, when facing traditional tasks, they and their older peers may not yet be able or predisposed to spontaneously make and use coordinates for themselves.

To understand space as organized into grids or coordinate systems, children must learn *spatial structuring*. Spatial structuring is the mental operation of constructing an organization or form for an object or set of objects in space. Children may first view a grid as a collection of squares, rather than as sets of perpendicular lines. They only gradually come to see them as organized into rows and columns, learning the order and distance relationships within the grid. For coordinates, labels must be related to grid lines and, in the form of ordered pairs of coordinates, to points on the grid. Eventually these, too, must be integrated with the grid's order and distance relationships to be understood as a mathematical system.

Imagery and Spatial Visualization

Visual representations are central to our lives, including most domains of mathematics. Spatial images are internal representations of objects that appear to be similar to real-world objects. People use four processes: generating an image, inspecting an image to answer questions about it, maintaining an image in the service of some other mental operation, and transforming an image.

Thus, spatial visualization abilities are processes involved in generating and manipulating mental images of two- and three-dimensional objects, including moving, matching, and combining them. Such visualization might guide the drawing of figures or diagrams on paper or computer screens. For example, children might create a mental image of a shape, maintain that image, and then search for that same shape, perhaps hidden within a more complex figure. To do this, they may need to mentally rotate the shapes, one of the most important transformations for children to learn. These spatial skills directly support children's learning of specific topics, such as geometry and measurement, but they can also be applied to mathematical problem-solving across topics.

Children do have to develop the ability to move mental images. That is, their initial images are static, not dynamic. They can be mentally re-created, and even examined, but not necessarily transformed. Only dynamic images allow children to mentally "move" the image of one shape (such as a book) to another place (such as a bookcase, to see if it will fit) or mentally move (slide) and turn an image of one shape to compare that shape to another one. Slides appear to be the easiest motions for children, then flips and turns. However, the direction of transformation may affect the relative difficulty of turn and flip. Results depend on specific tasks, of course; even 4- to 5-year-olds can do turns if they have simple tasks and cues, such as having a clear mark on the edge of a shape and no "flipped" shape as a distractor.

Probably due to reading instruction, first graders discriminate between mirror-image reversals (b vs. d) better than kindergartners. But they also treat orientation as a meaningful difference between *geometric shapes*, which it is not. So, explicitly discuss when orientation is and is not relevant to calling a shape "the same" in different contexts.

From research with people who are congenitally blind, we know that their imagery is in some ways similar and some ways different from normally sighted people. For example, only sighted people image objects of different size at different distances, so the image will not overflow a fixed image space. They image objects at distances so that the objects subtend the same visual angle. Thus, some aspects of visual imagery are visual, and not present in blind people's images, but some aspects of imagery may be evoked by multiple modalities (Arditi, Holtzman, & Kosslyn, 1988).

Types of images and mathematical problem-solving. There are different types of images, and they range from *helpful* to *harmful*, depending on their nature and the way children use them. High-achieving children build images with a conceptual and relational core. They are able to link different experiences and abstract similarities. Low-achieving children's images tended to be dominated by surface features. Instruction might help them develop more sophisticated images.

- The *schematic images* of high-achieving children are thus more general and abstract. They contain the spatial relationships relevant to a problem and thus support problem-solving (Hegarty & Kozhevnikov, 1999).
- The *pictorial images* of low-achieving children do not aid problem-solving and actually can impede success. They represent mainly the visual appearance of the objects or persons described in a problem. Thus, just using pictures or diagrams, encouraging children to "visualize" may not be at all useful. Instead, educators should help students develop and use specific types of schematic images. The diagrams for arithmetic in Chapters 5 (e.g., Table 5.1) and 6 (e.g., Figures 6.3 and 6.7) illustrate that such images are useful in many mathematics contexts.

Experience and Education

Teaching isolated spatial skills, especially to children with special needs, has a long history, most of which has been *unsuccessful*. Here we examine integrated approaches that may have more promise.

Spatial Orientation, Navigation, and Maps

For children of all ages, but especially the youngest, moving oneself around leads to later success in spatial thinking tasks. This suggests the benefit of maximizing such experience for all young children and may seem obvious, but there may be opportunities that are not presently pursued. In some communities, for example, young girls are allowed to play only in their yard, but same-age boys are allowed to explore the neighborhood.

To develop children's spatial orientation, plan school environments that include interesting layouts inside and outside classrooms. Also include incidental and planned experiences with land-marks and routes, and frequent discussion about spatial relations on all scales, including dis-tinguishing parts of children's bodies and spatial movements (forward, back), finding a missing object ("under the table that's next to the door"), putting objects away, and finding the way back home from an excursion. Rich language is important.

Children need specific instruction to learn about models and maps. School experiences are limited and fail to connect map skills with other curriculum areas, including mathematics. Most students do not become competent users of maps even beyond their early childhood years.

Research provides suggestions. Provide instruction on using maps that explicitly connects real-world space and maps, including one-to-one connection between objects and icons on the map, helps children understand maps—and symbols. Using oblique maps, on which tables are shown with legs, helps preschoolers' subsequent performance on plan ("bird's-eye view") maps. Telling very young children that a model was the result of putting a room in a "shrinking machine" helped them see the model as a symbolic representation of that space.

Informally, too, encourage children working with model toys to build maps of the room with these toys. Children might use cutout shapes of a tree, swing set, and sandbox in the playground and lay them out on a felt board as a simple map. These are good beginnings, but models and maps should eventually move beyond overly simple iconic picture maps, and challenge children to use geometric correspondences. Help children connect the abstract and sensory-concrete meanings of map symbols (Clements, 1999a; see also Chapter 16 for a discussion of these terms).

Similarly, many of young children's difficulties do not reflect misunderstanding about space but the conflict between such sensory-concrete and abstract frames of reference. Guide children to (a) develop abilities to build relationships among objects in space, (b) extend the size of that space, (c) link primary and secondary meanings and uses of spatial information, (d) develop mental rotation abilities, (e) go beyond "map skills" to engage in actual use of maps in local environments (A. J. Bishop, 1983), and (f) develop an understanding of the mathematics of maps.

Work with children to raise four mathematical questions: Direction—which way?, distance—how far?, location—where?, and identification—what objects? To answer these questions, children need to develop a variety of skills. Children must learn to deal with mapping processes of abstraction, generalization, and symbolization. Some map symbols are icons, such as an airplane for an airport, but others are more abstract, such as circles for cities. Children might first build with objects such as model buildings, then draw pictures of the objects' arrangements, then use maps that are "miniaturizations" and those that use abstract symbols. Some symbols may be beneficial even to young children. Over-reliance on literal pictures and icons may hinder understanding of maps, leading children to believe, for example, that certain actual roads are red (Downs, Liben, & Daggs, 1988). Similarly, children need to develop more sophisticated ideas about *direction* and *location*. Young children should master environmental directions, such as above, over, and behind. They should develop navigation ideas, such as front, back, "going forward," and turning. Older children might represent these ideas in simple route maps within the classroom.

Children can develop navigation ideas, such as left, right, and front, and global directions such as north, east, west, and south, from these beginnings. Perspective and direction are particularly important regarding the alignment of the map with the world. Some children of any age will find it difficult to use a map that is not so aligned. Also, they may need specific experiences with perspective. For example, challenge them to identify block structures from various viewpoints, matching views of the same structure that are portrayed from different perspectives, or to find the viewpoint from which a photograph was taken. Such experiences address such confusions of perspective as preschoolers "seeing" windows and doors of buildings in vertical aerial photographs (Downs & Liben, 1988). Introduce such situations gradually. Realistic Mathematics Education in geometry makes extensive use of interesting spatial and map tasks (Gravemeijer, 1990), but, unfortunately, research on the effects of this specific strand is lacking.

Primary grade students can approach map creation mathematically, learning to represent position and direction. One third grade class moved from initial, intuitively-based drawings to the use of polar coordinates (determining a position by an angle and a distance) in creating a map of the playground (Lehrer & Pritchard, 2002). Walking encouraged characterization of length in a direction and drawing the maps led students to render space. Students learned about the usefulness of concepts such as origin, scale, and the relationship of multiple locations.

Combining physical movement, paper-and-pencil, and computer work can facilitate learning of mathematics and map skills. Such spatial learning can be particularly meaningful because it can be consistent with young children's way of moving their bodies (Papert, 1980). For example, young children can abstract and generalize directions and other map concepts working with the Logo turtle. Giving the turtle directions such as forward 10 steps, right turn, forward 5 steps, they learn orientation, direction, and perspective concepts, among others. For example, Figure 7.1 shows a "scavenger hunt" activity in which children are given a list of items the turtle has to get. From the center of the grid, they commanded the turtle to go forward 20 steps, then turn right 90 degrees, then go forward 20 more steps—that's where the car was. They have the car now, and will give the turtle other commands to get other objects.

Walking paths and then recreating those paths on the computer help them abstract, generalize, and symbolize their experiences navigating. For example, one kindergartner abstracted the geometric notion of "path" saying, "A path is like the trail a bug leaves after it walks through purple paint" (Clements et al., 2001). Logo can also control a floor turtle robot, which may have special benefits for certain populations. For example, blind and partially sighted children using a computer-guided floor turtle developed spatial concepts such as right and left and accurate facing movements.

Many people believe that maps are "transparent"—that anyone can "see through" the map immediately to the world that it represents. This is not true. Clear evidence for this is found in children's misinterpretations of maps. For example, some believe that a river is a road or that a pictured road is *not* a road because "it's too narrow for two cars to go on."

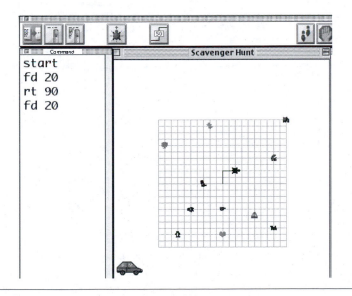

Figure 7.1 The "Scavenger Hunt" activity from Turtle Math (Clements & Meredith, 1994).

Coordinates. Students should learn to understand and eventually quantify what grid labels represent. To do so, they need to connect their counting acts to those quantities and to the labels. They need to learn to mentally structure grids as two-dimensional spaces, demarcated and measured with "conceptual rulers" ("mental number lines"—see Chapter 10). That is, they need to understand coordinates as a way to organize 2D space by coordinating two perpendicular number lines—every location is the place where measures along each of these two number lines meet.

Real-world contexts can be helpful in teaching coordinates initially, but mathematical goals and perspectives should be clearly articulated throughout instruction and the contexts should be faded from use as soon as students no longer need them (Sarama, Clements, Swaminathan, McMillen, & González Gómez, 2003). Computer environments can additionally aid in developing children's ability and appreciation for the need for clear conceptions and precise work. Turning the coordinate grid on and off can help children create a *mental* image of coordinates. Coordinate-based games on computers, such as versions of "Battleship," can help older children learning location ideas (Sarama et al., 2003). When children enter a coordinate to move an object but it goes to a different location, the feedback is natural, meaningful, non-evaluative, and so particularly helpful.

Indeed, Logo can help children learn both "path" (self-based systems based on ones own movement and the routes one follows) and "coordinate" (external-based) concepts, as well as how to differentiate between them. One way to move the Logo turtle is to give it commands such as "forward 100" and "right 90." This path perspective is distinct from coordinate commands, such as "setpos [50 100]" (set the position to the coordinates (50, 100)). Figure 7.2 shows Monica's layer cake project. She is not only competent at using both path-based commands, including her "rect"

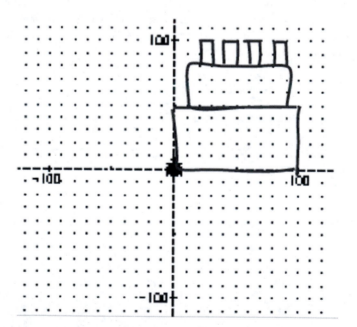

Monica chose the layer cake task as her project. She drew a plan on dot paper, as shown.

She wrote a rectangle procedure for the layers and the candles without any problems, counting the spaces on the dot paper to determine the lengths and widths.

After drawing the bottom layer on the computer, she tried the commands `jumpto [0 10]` and `jumpto [0 50]`, saying, "I've always had a little problem with that." She carefully counted by tens and figured out that she needed a `jumpto [10 50]`.

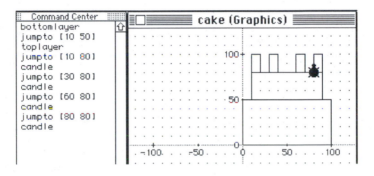

At this point she switched the grid tool on, saying, "Now it's gonna be hard." She had planned `jumpto [10 70]`, but seeing where the turtle ended up, she changed the input to `[10 80]` and then to `[20 80]`.

She entered her `candle` procedure. She looked back at her figure and decided that she did not like the way her candles were spread apart on the paper and decided not to do it like in her drawing. She counted on from (20, 80), entered `jumpto [40 80]` then her candle procedure. The teacher asked her if she could figure out the next jumpto from her commands without counting. She said that it would be `jumpto [80 80]`, probably adding 40 to her previous `jumpto`. But when she saw it, she changed the input to `[70 80]` and then to `[60 80]`. A final `jumpto [80 80]` and `candle` completed the first cake.

She wasn't satisfied with the location of her candles and wanted to move two over. She moved directly to the correct `jumpto` commands, changing the inputs to `[10 80]` and `[30 80]`. Her confidence indicated that she understood the connection between each command and its effect.

Figure 7.2 Monica's use of path and coordinate logo commands.

procedure but she shows understanding of the connection between each command and its graphic effect, the effects of changing each coordinate, and the distinction between path and coordinate commands. Monica initially struggled to differentiate between regions and lines, made erroneous, perceptually-based judgments of path length, and interpreted two coordinate pairs as four separate numbers. So, her work on the layer cake project represented a substantial mathematical advance.

This study also suggests cautions regarding some popular teaching strategies. For example, phrases such as "over and up" and "the x-axis is the bottom," which we recorded on numerous occasions, do not generalize well to a four-quadrant grid. The "over and up" strategy also hinders the integration of coordinates into a coordinate *pair* representing *one* point (Sarama et al., 2003).

Building Imagery and Spatial Visualization

As early as the preschool years, U.S. children perform lower than children in countries such as Japan and China on spatial visualization and imagery tasks. There is more support for spatial thinking in

Figure 7.3 Snapshots—geometry.

these countries. For example, they use more visual representations and expect children to become more competent in drawing.

So, we can and should do more. Use manipulatives such as unit blocks, puzzles, and tangrams—intelligently (see Chapter 16). Encourage children to play with blocks and puzzles at school and home. Encourage girls to play with "boys' toys," helping them to develop higher visual-spatial skills.

Use geometric "Snapshot" activities to build spatial visualization and imagery. Children see a simple configuration on the overhead or chalk board for 2 seconds, then try to draw what they saw. They then compare their drawings and *discuss* what they saw. In Figure 7.3, different children see three triangles, "a sailboat sinking," a square with two lines through it, and a "y in a box." The discussions are especially valuable in developing vocabulary and the ability to see things from other points of view. Younger children can view combinations pattern blocks for 2 seconds and then construct a copy with their own pattern blocks.

These also generate good discussions, emphasizing the *properties* of shapes. Such imagistic/memory tasks also engender interesting discussions revolving around "what I saw." (Clements & Sarama, 2003a; Razel & Eylon, 1986, 1990; Wheatley, 1996; Yackel & Wheatley, 1990). Having children use many different media to represent their memories and ideas with the "hundred languages of children" (Edwards, Gandini, & Forman, 1993) will help them build spatial visualization and imagery.

Tactile kinesthetic tasks ask children to identify, name, and describe objects and shapes placed in a "feely box" (Clements & Sarama, 2003a). In a similar vein, executing geometric motions on the computer helped children as young as kindergartners learn these concepts (Clements et al., 2001). Activities that involve motion geometry—slides, flips, and turns—whether doing puzzles (see Chapter 9) or Logo, improve spatial perception. Constructing shapes from parts with multiple media builds imagery as well as geometric concepts (see Chapter 8). Composing and decomposing 2D shapes and 3D shapes (e.g., block building) is so important that Chapter 9 is dedicated to these processes.

Building spatial abilities early is effective and efficient. For example, grade 2 children benefitted more than grade 4 children from lessons taught to develop spatial thinking (Owens, 1992). In 11 lessons, children described the similarities and differences of shapes, made shapes from other shapes, made outlines using sticks, compared angles, made pentomino shapes and found their symmetries. Those children outperformed a control group in a randomized field trial on a spatial thinking test, with differences attributable to the grade 2 children. No difference was found between groups that worked cooperatively or individually, with whole-class discussions. Nearly all interactions that lead to heuristics about what to do or to conceptualizations were between the teacher and the student, not between students (Owens, 1992). So, teach actively.

Learning Trajectories for Spatial Thinking

The *goal* of increasing children's knowledge of geometry and space is second in importance only to numerical goals and all these are (or should be) strongly interrelated. The Curriculum Focal Points includes the goals in Figure 7.4. Goals for the primary grades feature specific geometric ideas included in later chapters.

With those goals, Table 7.1 provides the two additional learning trajectory components, the developmental progression and the instructional tasks for *two* learning trajectories for spatial thinking: spatial orientation (maps and coordinates) and spatial visualization and imagery. The learning trajectory for maps becomes increasingly connected to children's development of *spatial structuring*, the ability to organize space into two dimension, which is discussed in detail in Chapter 12 (because it is just as critical for understanding area). The reader may notice that the instructional tasks in this learning trajectory tend not to be specific activities, but global suggestions. This difference reflects our belief that (a) there is as yet too little evidence on the specific role of this learning trajectory in maths, (b) such activities may be conducted in other subject matter

Pre-K

Geometry: Geometry: Identifying shapes and describing spatial relationships

Children develop spatial reasoning by working from two perspectives on space as they examine the shapes of objects and inspect their relative positions. They find shapes in their environments and describe them in their own words. They build pictures and designs by combining two- and three-dimensional shapes, and they solve such problems as deciding which piece will fit into a space in a puzzle. They discuss the relative positions of objects with vocabulary such as "above," "below," and "next to."

Kindergarten

Geometry: Geometry: Describing shapes and space

Children interpret the physical world with geometric ideas (e.g., shape, orientation, spatial relations) and describe it with corresponding vocabulary. They identify, name, and describe a variety of shapes, such as squares, triangles, circles, rectangles, (regular) hexagons, and (isosceles) trapezoids presented in a variety of ways (e.g., with different sizes or orientations), as well as such three-dimensional shapes as spheres, cubes, and cylinders. They use basic shapes and spatial reasoning to model objects in their environment and to construct more complex shapes.

Grade 1

Geometry: Composing and decomposing geometric shapes

Children compose and decompose plane and solid figures (e.g., by putting two congruent isosceles triangles together to make a rhombus), thus building an understanding of part–whole relationships as well as the properties of the original and composite shapes. As they combine figures, they recognize them from different perspectives and orientations, describe their geometric attributes and properties, and determine how they are alike and different, in the process developing a background for measurement and initial understandings of such properties as congruence and symmetry.

Grade 2

Geometry Connection

Children estimate, measure, and compute lengths as they solve problems involving data, space, and movement through space. By composing and decomposing two-dimensional shapes, intentionally substituting arrangements of smaller shapes for larger shapes or substituting larger shapes for many smaller shapes, they use geometric knowledge and spatial reasoning to develop foundations for understanding area, fractions, and proportions.

Grade 3

Geometry: Describing and analyzing properties of two-dimensional shapes

Students describe, analyze, compare, and classify two-dimensional shapes by their sides and angles and connect these attributes to definitions of shapes. Students investigate, describe, and reason about decomposing, combining, and transforming polygons to make other polygons. Through building, drawing, and analyzing two-dimensional shapes, students understand attributes and properties of two-dimensional space and the use of those attributes and properties in solving problems, including applications involving congruence and symmetry.

Figure 7.4 Curriculum focal points for geometry and spatial thinking (for Chapters 7, 8, and 9).

Table 7.1 Learning Trajectories for Spatial Thinking.

a. Spatial Orientation (including maps and coordinates)

Age (years)	Developmental Progression	Instructional Tasks
0–2	**Landmark and Path User** Uses a distance landmark to find an object or location near it, if they have not personally moved relative to the landmark. Understands initial vocabulary of spatial relations and location.	Provide a rich sensory, manipulative environment, and the freedom and encouragement to manipulate it and move through it. Infants who crawl more learn more about spatial relationships. Use spatial vocabulary to direct attention to spatial relations. Initially emphasize "in," "on," and "under," along with such vertical directionality terms as "up" and "down."
2–3	**Local-Self Framework User** Uses distant landmarks to find objects or location near them, even after they have moved themselves relative to the landmarks, *if* the target object is specified ahead of time. Orient a horizontal or vertical line in space (Rosser, Horan, Mattson, & Mazzeo, 1984).	Walk different routes and discuss the landmarks you see. Ask children to point to where different landmarks are at various points along the path. Use spatial vocabulary to direct attention to spatial relations. Emphasize words of proximity, such as "beside" and "between." Ask 3-year-olds to find an object shown a picture of its location. Have children build with blocks to represent simple scenes and locations (see Chapter 9 for much more on block building). If children are interested, make a model of the classroom and point to a location in it that represents a place where a "prize" is hidden in the actual classroom. Use the notion of a "shrinking machine" to help them understand the model as a representation of the classroom space.
4	**Small Local Framework User** Locates objects after movement, even if target is not specified ahead of time. Searches a small area comprehensively, often using a circular search pattern. Extrapolates lines from positions on both axes and determines where they intersect if meaningful contexts.	Use spatial vocabulary to direct attention to spatial relations. Emphasize words referring to frames of reference such as "in front of " and "behind." Initiate the learning of "left" and "right." Also encourage parents to avoid pointing or showing when possible, but instead to give verbal directions ("it's in the bag *on the table*"). Have students pose verbal problems for each other, such as finding a missing object ("under the table that's next to the door"), putting objects away, and finding the way back from an excursion. During free time, challenge children to follow simple maps of the classroom or playground to find secret "treasures" you have hidden. Interested children can draw their own maps. Start with oblique maps (e.g., in which chairs and tables are shown with legs). Explore and discuss outdoor spaces, permitting children (both sexes) as much freedom in self-directed movement as safely possible. Encourage parents to do the same. Walk different routes and discuss different paths, and which would be shorter, which would be longer. Ask *why* one path is shorter. Encourage children to build models of the room or playground with toys.
5	**Local Framework User** Locates objects after movement (relates several locations separately from own position), maintaining the overall shape of the arrangement of objects. Represents objects' positions relative to landmarks (e.g., about halfway in between two landmarks) and keeps track of own location in open areas or mazes. Some use coordinate labels in simple situations.	Plan and discuss different routes, and which would be the best route to take and why. Draw maps of routes, illustrating what will be "passed" or seen from different routes. Use spatial vocabulary to direct attention to spatial relations. Emphasize all words listed previously, including the learning of "left" and "right." Encourage children to make models of their classroom, using blocks or play furniture to represent objects in the classroom. Discuss which ones go "near each other" and other spatial relationships. Maps of the playground: Children might use cutout shapes of a tree, swing set, and sandbox in the playground and lay them out on a felt board as a simple map. They can discuss how moving an item in the schoolyard, such

Age (years)	Developmental Progression	Instructional Tasks
		as a table, would change the map of the yard. On the map, locate children shown sitting in or near the tree, swing set, and sandbox. In scavenger hunts on the playground, children can give and follow directions or clues.
		Explore and discuss outdoor spaces, permitting children (both sexes) as much freedom in self-directed movement as safely possible. Encourage parents to do the same. (This recommendation extends through the grades.)
		Encourage children to mark a path from a table to the wastebasket with masking tape. With the teacher's help, children could draw a map of this path (some teachers take photographs of the wastebasket and door and glue these to a large sheet of paper). Items appearing alongside the path, such as a table or easel, can be added to the map.
		Logo Engage children in age-appropriate "turtle math" environments (Clements & Meredith, 1994; Clements & Sarama, 1996). Have them tutor each other in those environments.
		Ask children to solve two-dimensional matrices (e.g., placing all objects where colors are sorted into rows and shapes are sorted into columns) or use of coordinates on maps.
6	**Map User** Locates objects using maps with pictorial cues. Can extrapolate two coordinates, understanding the integration of them to one position, as well as use coordinate labels in simple situations.	Use spatial vocabulary to direct attention to spatial relations. Emphasize all words listed previously and the various interpretations of "left" and "right." **Maps** Continue the previous activities, but emphasize the four questions (see p. 112): Direction—which way?, distance—how far?, location—where?, and identification—what objects? Notice the use of coordinates on maps.
		Challenge students to find their house or school in Internet-based aerial photographs, once you have accessed that location on the computer.
		Ask students to plan routes around the school using maps, then follow those routes.
		Logo Engage children in age-appropriate "turtle math" environments (Clements & Meredith, 1994; Clements & Sarama, 1996). Have them tutor each other in those environments.
		Use coordinates in all applicable situations; for example, to label locations ("pegs") on geoboards as students build shapes.
7	**Coordinate Plotter** Reads and plots coordinates on maps.	Ask students to draw simple sketch-maps of the area around their houses, classroom, playground, or area around the school. Discuss differences among representations of the same spaces. Present tasks in which maps must be aligned with the space. Showing children several maps and models, and explicitly comparing them using language and visual highlights, helps them build representational understandings.
		"Battleship"-type games are useful. Guide children in the following competencies in all coordinate work. • interpreting the grid structure's components as line segments or lines rather than regions • appreciating the precision of location of the lines required, rather than treating them as fuzzy boundaries or indicators of intervals • learning to trace closely-packed vertical or horizontal lines that were not axes • integrating two numbers into single coordinate • conceptualizing labels as signs of location and distance ((a) to quantify what the grid labels represent, (b) to connect their counting acts to those quantities and

Continued Overleaf

Age (years)	Developmental Progression	Instructional Tasks
		to the labels, (c) to subsume these ideas to a part–whole scheme connected to both the grid and to counting/arithmetic, and finally (d) to construct proportional relationships in this scheme) (Sarama et al., 2003)
		Logo and coordinate games and activities on computer benefit children's understanding and skills with coordinates (Clements & Meredith, 1994; Clements & Sarama, 1996).
8+	**Route Map Follower** Follows a simple route map, with more accurate direction and distances.	Engage students in practical map-using and map-making tasks similar to "find the treasure" in an environment with which children are familiar, then less familiar. Include coordinate maps. (See pp. 114–115: Lehrer, 2002.)
	Framework User Uses general frameworks that include the observer and landmarks. May not use precise measurement even when that would be helpful, unless guided to do so. Can follow and create maps, even if spatial relations are transformed.	**Logo** Engage children in "turtle math" environments in which maps are translated to computer programs (Clements & Meredith, 1994; Clements & Sarama, 1996).

b. Spatial Visualization and Imagery

Age (years)	Developmental Progression	Instructional Tasks
0–3	**Simple Slider** Can move shapes to a location.	**Make My Picture** Ask children to use building blocks or pattern blocks to duplicate a simple "picture."
4	**Simple Turner** Mentally turns object in easy tasks. Given a shape with the top marked with color, correctly identifies which of three shapes it would look like if it were turned "like this" (90° turn demonstrated) before physically moving the shape.	**Make My Picture—Hidden Version** Ask children to use building blocks or pattern blocks to duplicate a simple "picture" that they see for 5 to 10 seconds and then is covered. (See also Geometry Snapshots in Chapter 8.) Ask children to show how a circular object should be rotated to make it appear circular or elliptical. Work with shadows to make a rectangle appear as a non-rectangular parallelogram ("rhomboid") or vice versa. **Puzzles** Have children solve jigsaw, pattern block, and simple tangram puzzles and discuss how they are moving the shapes to make them fit (see more in Chapter 8). Encourage parents to engage children in all types of puzzles and talk to them as they solve the puzzles (especially girls). **Feely Boxes** Use "feely boxes" to identify shapes by touch (see more in Chapter 8). Challenge children to turn a well-marked shape to align it with another, congruent, shape. **Snapshots—Geometry** Students copy a simple configuration of pattern blocks shown for 2 seconds. (See Chapter 9 for more details.)
5	**Beginning Slider, Flipper, Turner** Uses the correct motions, but not always accurate in direction and amount. Knows a shape has to be flipped to match another shape, but flips it in the wrong direction.	**Feely Boxes** Use "feely boxes" to identify a wide variety of shapes by touch (see more in Chapter 8). **Tangram Puzzles** Have children solve tangram puzzles and discuss how they are moving the shapes to make them fit (see more in Chapter 8). **Geometry Snapshots 2** Shown a simple configuration of shapes for just 2 seconds, students match that configuration to four choices from memory (imagery).

Age (years)	Developmental Progression	Instructional Tasks
		Geometry Snapshots 3 Students identify an image that matches the "symmetric whole" of a target image from four multiple-choice selections. 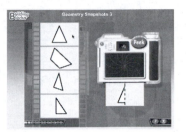
6	**Slider, Flipper, Turner** Performs slides and flips, often only horizontal and vertical, using manipulatives. Performs turns of 45, 90, and 180 degrees. Knows a shape must be turned 90° to the right to fit into a puzzle.	**Snapshots—Geometry** Students draw one or more shapes shown for 2 seconds. **Geometry Snapshots 4** Students identify an image that matches one of four moderately complex configurations from memory (imagery). 
7	**Diagonal Mover** Performs diagonal slides and flips. Knows a shape must be turned flipped over an oblique line (45° orientation) to fit into a puzzle.	**Geometry Snapshots 6** Students match geometric figures that differ on angle measure from memory (imagery). 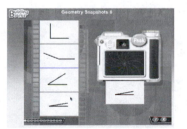
8+	**Mental Mover** Predicts results of moving shapes using mental images. "If you turned this 120°, it would be just like this one."	**Pattern Block Puzzles** and **Tangram Puzzles** Ask students how many of a certain shape it would take to cover another shape (or configuration of shapes). Students predict, record their prediction, then try to to check. (See Chapter 9 for more.)

areas (e.g., social studies), and (c) similarly, these activities are often best done informally, as part of everyday activity.

However, these two learning trajectories represent only a small bit of the role of spatial thinking in mathematics. We saw that spatial and structural thinking is critical in (visual) subitizing, counting strategies, and arithmetic. Such spatial knowledge is central to geometry, measurement, patterning, data presentation, and the other topics discussed in forthcoming chapters. Thus, attention to spatial thinking should be woven throughout the curriculum and is explicitly included in the learning trajectories in those chapters.

Final Words

Visual thinking is thinking that is tied down to limited, surface-level, visual ideas. Children can learn to move beyond that kind of visual thinking as they learn to manipulate dynamic images, as they enrich their store of images for shapes, and as they connect their spatial knowledge to verbal, analytic knowledge. In this way, instruction discussed in the next two chapters, on shapes and composing shapes, also makes a strong contribution to children's spatial thinking.

8
Shape

One kindergartner impressed his teacher saying he knew that a shape (Figure 8.1a) was a triangle because it had "three straight lines and three angles." Later, however, she said Figure 8.1b was not a triangle.

Teacher: Doesn't it have three straight sides?
Child: Yes.
Teacher: And what else did you say triangles have to have?
Child: Three angles. It has three angles.
Teacher: Good! So . . .
Child: It's *not* a triangle. It's upside down!

Did this kindergartner know triangles or not? What was *driving* her thinking about triangles, do you think? In general, how should we as educators help children develop the mathematics of geometric shape? Why should we?

Shape is a fundamental concept in cognitive development. For example, infants use mainly shape to learn the names of objects. Shape is also a fundamental idea in geometry, but in other areas of mathematics, too. Unfortunately, geometry is one of U.S. students' weakest topics in mathematics. Even in the preschool years, children in the U.S. know less about shape than children in other countries. The good news is: They know enough to build upon, they can learn a lot quickly, and they enjoy engaging with shapes.

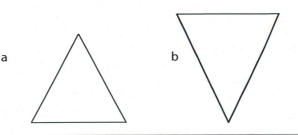

Figure 8.1 Two triangles.

Young Children's Learning about Shape

Although it may seem obvious that we learn about shapes by seeing them and naming them, some—such as Jean Piaget—say that isn't the whole story. He claims that it isn't even the main story. For Piaget, children do not "read off" of their spatial environment but rather *construct* their ideas about shape by actively manipulating shapes in their environment. Further, even if children can name a square, their knowledge might be limited. For example, if they cannot feel a hidden square and name it after exploring it with their hands, Piaget would claim they do not really understand the *concept* "square."

A husband-and-wife team of researchers, Pierre and Dina van Hiele, agree that children construct their geometric ideas. They also describe levels of thinking through which children do so. For example, at first children can't distinguish between one shape and another. Later, they can, but only visually—they recognize shapes as wholes. They might call a shape a "rectangle" because "it looks like a door." They do not think about the defining attributes or properties of shapes.

The Mathematics of 2D Shapes

Before we move on, let's take a side trip to define some of these terms. We use *attributes* to mean any characteristic of a shape. Some are *defining attributes*. To be a square, a shape must have *straight* sides. Others are *non-defining attributes*. A child might consider a shape "right side up" or describe it as "red" but neither of these attributes is relevant to whether the shape is a square or not. Some defining attributes describe the parts of a shape—as a square has *four sides*. Others are special attributes we call *properties*, which describe a *relationship between parts*. A square must have four *equal-length* sides.

At the next level of geometric thinking, then, students recognize and characterize shapes *by their defining attributes*. For instance, a child might think of a square as a plane (flat) figure that has four equal sides and four right angles. Properties are established by observing, measuring, drawing, and model-making. Not until later, often middle school or later, do students see relationships between *classes of figures* (see Figure 8.2). For example, most children incorrectly believe that a figure is not a rectangle because it is a square (whereas actually a square is a special type of rectangle).

Definitions related to shapes. The following definitions are intended to help teachers both understand preschooler's development of specific mathematical concepts, and talk to them about these concepts. They are not formal math definitions but rather simple descriptions using a mixture of mathematics and everyday vocabulary. The shapes below are taken to be two-dimensional (plane) shapes.

angle   Two lines that meet to make a corner, or vertex.

circle   A two-dimensional figure that consists of all points a fixed distance from a point called its center. Circles are "perfectly round;" that is, they have a constant curvature.

closed   A two-dimensional figure is closed when it is made up of several line segments that are joined together; exactly two sides meet at every vertex, and no sides cross each other. (Similarly for curved figures.)

congruent   Exactly alike in shape and size, so they can be superposed.

hexagon   A shape (polygon) with six straight sides.

kite   A four-sided figure with two pairs of *adjacent* sides that are the same length.

line symmetry   Plane figures have line, or mirror, symmetry when their shape is reversed on opposite sides of a line, like R | Я. If the plane is folded at the line, the figures will fit together.

octagon   A shape (polygon) with eight straight sides.

orientation   How a figure is turned compared to a reference line.

parallel lines   Lines that remain the same distance apart like railroad tracks.

parallelograms   Quadrilaterals with two pairs of opposite parallel sides.

pentagons   Polygons with four straight sides.

plane   A flat surface.

polygon   A plane figure bounded by three or more straight sides.

quadrilateral   A shape (polygon) with four straight sides.

rectangle   A polygon with four straight sides (i.e., a quadrilateral) and four right angles. As with all parallelograms, a rectangle's opposite sides are parallel and the same length.

rhombus   A plane figure with four straight sides (i.e., a quadrilateral) that are all the same length.

right angle   Two lines that meet like a corner of a typical doorway. Often informally called "square corner," right angles measure 90 degrees. Lines intersecting at a right angle are perpendicular.

rotational symmetry   A figure has rotational symmetry when it can be turned less than a full turn to fit on itself exactly.

shape   Informal name for a geometric figure two- or three-dimensional made up of points, lines, or planes.

square   A polygon that has four equal straight sides and all right angles. Note that a square is both a special kind of rectangle and a special kind of rhombus.

trapezoid   A quadrilateral with one pair of parallel sides. (Some insist trapezoids have *only* one pair of parallel sides; that is how they are categories in Figure 8.2a. Others say they have to have *at least* one pair, which would then make all parallelograms a subset of the trapezoids.)

triangle   A polygon with three sides.

Relationships between shapes. The diagrams on p. 126 show the relationships between classes of shapes. For example, all the shapes in Figure 8.2a are quadrilaterals. A *proper subset* of them are parallelograms, all of which have two pairs of opposite parallel sides. Parallelograms in turn include other subclasses. If all of a parallelogram's sides are the same length, they are also called *rhombuses*. If all of a parallelogram's angles are the same, then they must all be right angles, and they are also called *rectangles*. If both are true—if they are rhombuses and rectangles—they are also called *squares*.

Thinking and Learning about Specific Shapes

Children are sensitive to shape from the first year of life. And they prefer closed, symmetric shapes, such as those in Figure 8.3, as do most people from many cultures, even those with little or no exposure to other civilizations.

Culture influences these preferences. We conducted an extensive examination of materials that teach children about shapes from books, toy stores, teacher supply stores, and catalogs. With few exceptions (and with signs that this is changing in recent years), these materials introduce children to triangles, rectangles, and squares in rigid ways. Triangles are usually equilateral or isosceles and have horizontal bases. Most rectangles are horizontal, elongated shapes about twice as long as they

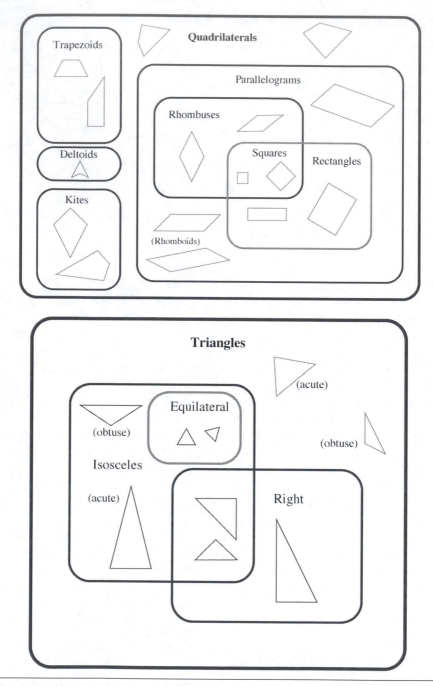

Figure 8.2 Venn diagrams of relationships between quadrilaterals (a) and triangles (b).

are wide. No wonder so many children, even throughout elementary school, say that a square turned is "not a square anymore, it's a diamond" (Clements, Swaminathan, Hannibal, & Sarama, 1999; Lehrer, Jenkins, & Osana, 1998).

So, children tend only to see only typical forms of each shape—what we will call "exemplars" (the shapes in Figure 8.3 are exemplars for each of four classes of shapes). They do not frequently

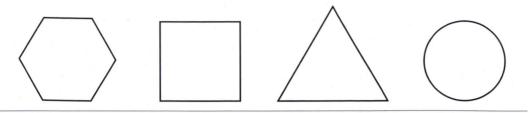

Figure 8.3 Examples of two-dimensional figures that are closed and are symmetric, preferred by most people.

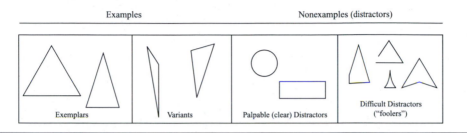

Figure 8.4 Exemplars, variants, palpable distractors, and difficult distractors for triangles.

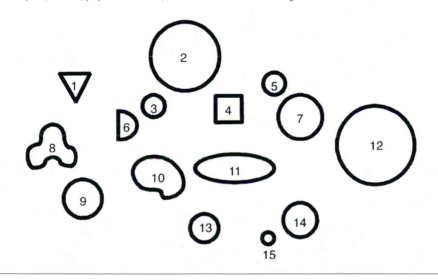

Figure 8.5 Student marks circles.

see and discuss other examples of the shapes, what we will call "variants." Nonexamples—usually called "distractors" in assessments or instruction—are not members of that shape class. They are called "palpable distractors" if they have little or no *overall resemblance* to the exemplars and "difficult distractors" (for the children, we call them "foolers") if they are highly visually similar to exemplars but lack at least one defining attribute. Figure 8.4 illustrates these for triangles.

What visual prototypes and ideas do young children form about common shapes? Circles—which only have one basic prototype, because they can only vary in size—are the easiest shape for children to identify. From 92% of 4-year-olds to 99% of 6-year-olds accurately identify circles as those shown in Figure 8.5 (Clements et al., 1999). Only a few of the youngest children chose the ellipse and another curved shape (shapes 11 and 10). Most children described circles as "round," if they described them at all. Thus, the circle was easily recognized but relatively difficult to describe for these children.

Children also identified squares fairly well: 82%, 86%, and 91% for 4-, 5-, and 6-year-olds, respectively. Younger children tended to mistakenly choose non-square rhombi ("diamonds" such as shape 3 in Figure 8.6); however, they were no less accurate in classifying squares without horizontal sides (shapes 5 and 11). This confusion—that turning a shape changes its name—can last until age 8 if not well addressed educationally. Children are less likely misled by orientation (the way a shape is "turned") when manipulatives are used, or when they walk around large shapes placed on the floor. Children are more likely to be accurate when their justifications for selection were based on the shape's defining attributes, such as the number and length of the sides.

Children were less accurate at recognizing triangles and rectangles. However, their scores were not low; about 60% correct for triangles (Figure 8.7). Across the years from 4 to 6, children go through a phase in which they accept many shapes as triangles, then another in which they "tighten" their criteria to reject some distractors but also some examples. The children's visual prototype seems to be of an isosceles triangle. Especially when not exposed to high-quality geometry education, they are misled by lack of symmetry or an aspect ratio—the ratio of height to base—not near one (e.g., a "long, skinny" triangle, such as shape 11).

Young children tended to accept "long" parallelograms or right trapezoids (shapes 3, 6, 10, and 14 in Figure 8.8) as rectangles. Thus, children's visual prototype of a rectangle is a four-sided figure with two long parallel sides and "close to" square corners.

Only a few children correctly identified the squares (shapes 2 and 7) as rectangles. Because they have all the properties of rectangles, these squares should be chosen. This is upsetting to many adults who have never been provided good geometry instruction themselves. But it is a good opportunity to encourage children to think *mathematically* and *logically*—even when the wider culture does not.

Although young children in this study were less accurate at recognizing triangles and rectangles, their performance shows considerable knowledge, especially given the abstract nature of the test and the variety of shapes employed. Depressingly, they learn very little from these early years to sixth grade (see graphs in the companion book).

In their play, children showed interest and involvement with "pattern and shape" more

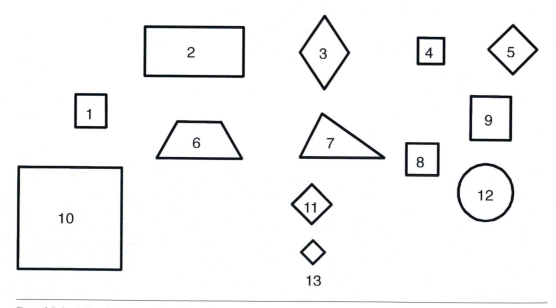

Figure 8.6 Student marks squares. Adapted from (Razel & Eylon, 1991).

Figure 8.7 Student marks triangles. (Adapted from Burger & Shaughnessy, 1986 and Clements & Battista, 1991).

frequently than any of the six other categories. About 47% of these behaviors involved recognizing, sorting, or naming shapes. They also develop in their ability to draw shapes (see the companion book for details). Finally, children do far more than just name shapes; they are an important part of much of children's play. Of course, that play involves three-dimensional shapes.

3D Figures

As with 2D figures, children do not perform well in school-based tasks involving three-dimensional shapes. The reason is much like that about plane figures. They refer to a variety of attributes, such as "pointyness" and comparative size or slenderness that are often non-geometric or non-defining. They use names for 2D shapes, probably indicating that they do not distinguish between two and three dimensions. Learning only plane figures in textbooks during the early primary grades may cause some initial difficulty in learning about solids.

Two related studies asked children to match solids with their nets (arrangements of 2D shapes that "fold up into" the 3D shape). Kindergartners had reasonable success when the solids and nets both were made from the same interlocking materials (Leeson, 1995). An advanced kindergartner

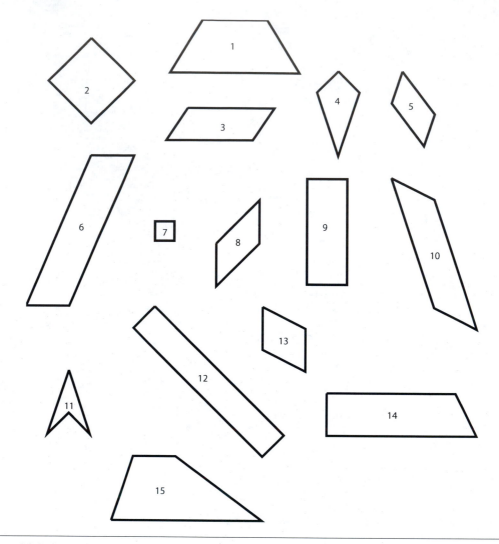

Figure 8.8 Student marks rectangles. (Adapted from Burger & Shaughnessy, 1986 and Clements & Battista, 1991).

had more difficulty with drawings of the nets (Leeson, Stewart, & Wright, 1997), possibly because he was unable to visualize the relationship with the more abstract materials.

The Mathematics of 3D Shapes

Definitions related to shapes. As with 2D shapes, the following definitions of 3D shapes are intended to help teachers both understand preschooler's development of specific mathematical concepts, and talk to them about these concepts. They are not formal math definitions but rather simple descriptions of a mixture of mathematics and everyday vocabulary.

cone   A 3D shape that has one base that is a circle (actually a *circular cone* because other curved shapes are possible bases) that is connected to a single point, the *vertex* that lies over the base, creating a curved surface.

cube   A special type of right prism whose faces are all squares.

cylinder A 3D shape that has two identical (congruent) parallel bases that are circles (or other shapes, usually curved) connected by a curved surface. (Most cylinders we deal with are right cylinders, but, as with prisms, they can be oblique.)

prism A 3D shape that has two identical (congruent) parallel bases that are polygons (2D shapes with straight sides), with corresponding sides of the bases connected with rectangles (in a *right prism*, those we usually deal with—if the sides are connected with parallelograms, it is an *oblique prism*).

pyramid A 3D shape that has one base that is a polygon that is connected to a single point, the *vertex* that lies over the base, with triangles.

sphere A 3D shape is a "perfectly round ball;" that is, all the points a fixed distance from a point called its center.

Congruence, Symmetry, and Transformations

Young children develop beginning ideas not just about shapes but also about symmetry, congruence, and transformations. As we saw, even infants are sensitive to at least some symmetric figures. Preschoolers often use and refer to rotational (⬡) symmetry as much as they do line, or mirror (⬻), symmetry in working with pattern blocks, such as remarking that an equilateral triangle was "special, because when you turn it a little it fits back on itself" (Sarama, Clements, & Vukelic, 1996). They also produce symmetry in their play (Seo & Ginsburg, 2004). For example, preschooler Jose puts a double unit block on the rug, two unit blocks on the double unit block, and a triangle unit on the middle, building a symmetrical structure.

Many young children judge congruence (Are these two shapes "the same"?) based on whether they are, overall, more similar than different. However, children younger than kindergarten may not do an exhaustive comparison and may consider rotated shapes as "different." Until about 7 years of age, students may not attend to the spatial relationships of all the parts of complex figures. Not until later, at age 11, did most children perform as adults.

With guidance, however, even 4-year-olds and some younger children can generate strategies for verifying congruence for some tasks. They gradually develop a greater awareness of the type of differences between figures that are geometrically relevant and move from considering only some of the shapes' parts to considering the spatial relationships of these parts. In about first grade, they begin to use superposition—moving one shape on top of another to see if it fits exactly.

In summary, teaching both shape recognition and transformations may be important to children's mathematical development. Traditional teaching of separate categories of "squares" and "rectangles" may underlie children's difficulties in relating these shape classes and their attributes. The use of the strategy of increasing one dimension of a rectangle may allow children to develop dynamic intuition that a square may thus be produced.

Experience and Education

A toddler, after some experimentation, puts a square peg into a square hole. What does she know of shapes? What more will she learn in preschool and elementary school? What might she learn?

Shapes: 2D. Experiences and instruction play a large role in shaping children's knowledge of geometry. If the examples and nonexamples children experience are rigid, not including a variety of variants of that shape class, their mental images and ideas about that shape will also be rigid and limited. For example, many children learn to accept as triangles only isosceles triangles with a horizontal base, such as the "exemplars" in Figure 8.4. Others learn richer concepts, even at a young age; for example, one of the youngest 3-year-olds scored higher than every 6-year-old on the shape recognition tasks discussed previously.

This is important. *Children's ideas stabilize as early as 6 years of age.* It is therefore *critical to provide better opportunities to learn about geometric figures* to all children between 3 and 6 years of age.

Of course, it is always important to get the language straight. Many 4-year-olds say that they know triangles have "three points and three sides." Half of these children, however, were not sure what a "point" or "side" is (Clements et al., 1999)! As with the number word sequence, the English language presents more challenges than others, such as East Asian languages. For example, in those languages, every "quadrilateral" is called simply "four-side-shape." An acute angle is simply a "sharp angle." Those teaching in English or Spanish need rich discussions.

Further, although appearances usually dominate children's decisions, they are also learning and sometimes using verbal knowledge. Using such verbal knowledge accurately takes time and can initially appear as a regression. Children may initially say a square has "four sides the same and four points." Because they have yet to learn about perpendicularity, some accept any rhombus as a square. Their own description convinces them even though they feel conflicted about the "look" of this "new square." With guidance, however, this conflict can be beneficial, as they come to understand the properties of squares.

So, *provide varied examples and nonexamples to help children understand attributes of shapes that are mathematically relevant as well as those (orientation, size) that are not.* Include "difficult distractors" of triangles (e.g., Figure 8.4) and rectangles.

Doing this, you will be a welcome exception. U.S. educational practice usually does not reflect these recommendations. Children often know as much about shapes entering school as their geometry curriculum "teaches" them in the early grades. This is due to teachers and curriculum writers' assumptions that children in early childhood classrooms have little or no knowledge of geometric figures. Further, teachers have had few experiences with geometry in their own education or in their professional development. Thus, it is unsurprising that most classrooms exhibit limited geometry instruction. One early study found that kindergarten children had a great deal of knowledge about shapes and matching shapes before instruction began. Their teacher tended to elicit and verify this prior knowledge but did not add content or develop new knowledge. That is, about two-thirds of the interactions had children repeat what they already knew in a repetitious format as in the following exchange:

Teacher: Could you tell us what type of shape that is?
Children: A square.
Teacher: Okay. It's a square (B. Thomas, 1982).

Even worse, when they did say something, teachers often make incorrect statements saying, for example, that every time you put two triangles together you get a square. Instruction does not improve in the primary grades. Children actually *stop* counting the sides and angles of shapes to differentiate one from another. *Avoid these common poor practices.* Learn more about geometry and challenge children to learn more every year.

Families and the wider culture do not promote geometry learning either. On a geometry assessment, 4-year-olds from America scored 55% compared to those from China at 84%.

Recall that story about the two triangles (Figure 8.1) at the beginning of this chapter. This example illustrates the research finding on "concept images" that shows that certain visual prototypes can rule children's thinking. That is, even when they know a definition, children's ideas of shapes are dominated by mental images of a "typical" shape.

To help children develop accurate, rich concept images, provide experiences of many different examples of a type of shape. For example, Figure 8.9a shows a rich variety of triangles that would be sure to generate discussion. Show nonexamples that, when compared to similar examples, help focus attention on the critical attributes. For example, the nonexamples in Figure 8.9b are close to the examples to their left, differing in just one attribute. Use such comparisons to focus on each defining attribute of a triangle.

Mary Elaine Spitler's study of *Building Blocks* reveals that children felt quite *powerful* knowing and using definitions of triangles (Spitler, Sarama, & Clements, 2003). One preschooler said of the second figure from the top in Figure 8.9a, "That's not a triangle! It's too skinny!" But his *Building Blocks* friend responded, "I'm telling you, it is a triangle. It's got three straight sides, see? One, two, three! It doesn't matter that I made it skinny." Similar studies around the world confirm that children can learn much more—at earlier ages.

Summary—Four guiding features. Children can learn richer concepts about shape if their educational environment includes four features: varied examples and nonexamples, discussions about shapes and their attributes, a wider variety of shape classes, and a broad array of geometric tasks. First, ensure that children experience many different examples of a type of shape, so that they do not form narrow ideas about any class of shapes. Use of prototypes may bootstrap initial learning, but examples should become more diverse as soon as possible. Showing nonexamples and comparing them to similar examples helps focus children's attention on the critical attributes of shapes and prompts discussion. This is especially important for classes that have more diverse examples, such as triangles.

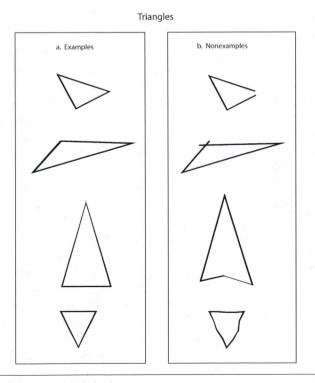

Triangles

a. Examples

b. Nonexamples

Figure 8.9 Examples and matched nonexamples of triangles.

Second, encourage children's descriptions while encouraging the development of language. Visual (prototype-based) descriptions should, of course, be expected and accepted, but attribute and property responses should also be encouraged. They may initially appear spontaneously for shapes with stronger and fewer prototypes (e.g., circle, square). Again, they should be especially encouraged for shape categories such as triangles. Children can learn to explain why a shape belongs to a certain category—"It has three straight sides" or does not belong ("The sides aren't straight!"). Eventually, they can internalize such arguments; for example, saying, "It is a weird, long, triangle, but it has three straight sides!"

Third, include a wide variety of shape *classes*. Early childhood curricula traditionally introduce shapes in four basic-level categories: circle, square, triangle, and rectangle. The idea that a square is not a rectangle is rooted by age 5. We suggest presenting many examples of squares and rectangles, varying orientation, size, and so forth, *including squares as examples of rectangles*. If children say, "That's a square," teachers might respond that it is a square, which is a special type of rectangle, and they might try double-naming ("It's a square-rectangle"). Older children can discuss "general" categories, such as quadrilaterals and triangles, counting the sides of various figures to choose their category. Also, teachers might encourage them to describe why a figure belongs or does not belong to a shape category. Then, teachers can say that because a triangle has all equal sides, it is a special type of triangle, called an equilateral triangle. Children might also "test" right angles on rectangles with a "right-angle checker," (thumb and index finger held apart at 90°, or a corner of a piece of paper).

Use computer environments to engage and develop children's thinking about relationships between classes of shapes, including squares and rectangles. In one large study (Clements et al., 2001), some kindergartners formed their own concept (e.g., "It's a square rectangle") in response to their work with Logo microworlds.

Also, teachers might encourage them to describe why a figure belongs or does not belong to a shape category. Then, teachers can say that because a triangle has all equal sides, it is a special type of triangle, called an equilateral triangle. Further, children should experiment with and describe a wider variety of shapes, including but not limited to semicircles, quadrilaterals, trapezoids, rhombi, and hexagons.

Fourth, challenge children with a broad array of interesting tasks. Experience with manipulatives and computer environments are often supported by research, if the experiences are consistent with the implications just drawn. Activities that promote reflection and discussion might include building models of shapes from components. Matching, identifying, exploring, and even making shapes with computers is particularly motivating (Clements & Sarama, 2003b, 2003c). Work with Logo's "turtle graphics" is accessible even to kindergartners (Clements et al., 2001), with results indicating significant benefits for that age group (e.g., more than older children, they benefitted in learning about squares and rectangles). See Figure 8.10.

Shapes: 3D. Play and other activities with blocks is beneficial for many reasons. For geometric learning, *mathematize* such activity. Engage children in fruitful discussions of blocks and other solids, and using specific terminology for solids, faces, and edges. Much more is known about building with blocks and other 3D shapes (see Chapter 9).

Geometric motions, congruence, and symmetry. Encouraging children to perform and discuss geometric motions improves their spatial skills. Computers are especially helpful, as the screen tools make motions more explicit. Use computer environments to help children learn congruence and symmetry (Clements et al., 2001). There is undeveloped potential in generating curricula that seriously consider children's intuitions, preference, and interest in symmetry. Children's painting and constructions can be used as models in introducing symmetry, including two-dimensional creations of painting, drawing, and collage, and three-dimensional creations of clay and blocks.

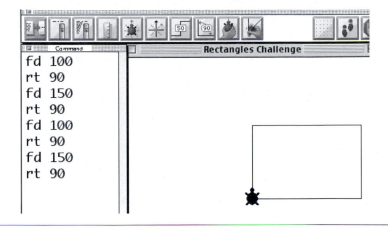

Figure 8.10 Using the Logo turtle to draw a rectangle in Turtle Math (Clements & Meredith, 1994).

Angle, parallelism, and perpendicularity. Angles are critical but often are not learned or taught well. Children have many varied and often incorrect ideas about what angles are. To understand angles, children must discriminate angles as critical parts of geometric figures, compare and match angles, and construct and mentally represent the idea of turns, integrating this with angle measure. These processes can begin in early childhood; for example, 5-year-olds can match angles. The long developmental process of learning about turns and angles can begin informally in the early and elementary classrooms, as children deal with corners of figures, comparing angle size, and turns. Computer-based shape manipulation and navigation environments can help mathematize these experiences. Especially important is understanding how turning one's body relates to turning shapes and turning along paths in navigation and learning to use numbers to quantify these turn and angle situations. For example, even 4-year-olds learn to click on a shape to turn it and say, "I need to turn it three times!" (Sarama, 2004, and Chapter 12).

Mitchelmore and his colleagues have proposed the following sequence of tasks. Begin by providing practical experiences with angles in various contexts, including corners, bends, turns, openings, and slopes. The first examples for each should have two "arms of the angle" physically present, such as in scissors, road junctions, a corner of a table. Corners are the most salient for children and should be emphasized first. The other physical models can follow. Experience with bending (e.g., a pipe cleaner) and turning (e.g., doorknobs, dials, doors) would be introduced last in this early phase.

Then help children understand the angular relationships in each context by discussing the common features of similar contexts, such as bends in lines or in paths on maps. Next, help students bridge the different contexts by representing the common features of angles in each context. For example, that they can be represented by two line segments (or rays) with a common endpoint. Once turns are understood, use the dynamic notion of turning to begin measuring the size of the angles.

The Spirit of Math—A Final Logo Example

High-quality implementations of Logo experiences places as much emphasis on the spirit of mathematics—exploration, investigation, critical thinking, and problem-solving—as it does on geometric ideas. Consider first grader Andrew (Clements et al., 2001). At the final interview, he was quite sure of himself. When asked to explain something he thought clearly evident, Andrew would always preface his remarks with an emphatic, "Look!" On one item, he was asked, "Pretend you are talking on the telephone to someone who has never seen a triangle. What would you tell this person to help them make a triangle?"

Andrew: I'd ask, "Have you seen a diamond?"

Interviewer: Let's say that they said, "Yes."

Andrew: Well, cut out a triangle. [Pause.] No, I made a mistake.

Interviewer: How?

Andrew: They have never seen a triangle. Well, cut it off in the middle. Fold it in the middle, on top of the other half, then tape it down, and you'll have a triangle. Then hang it on the wall so you'll know what a triangle is!

Interviewer: What if they said they hadn't seen a diamond?

Andrew: Make a slanted line over, then another slant the other way down, then another slanted line up, then another slanted line to the beginning.

Interviewer: [Thinks he is trying to describe a triangle] What?

Andrew: [Repeats the directions. Then] That's a diamond. Now, do what I told you before!

Andrew had done what mathematicians are so fond of doing. He had reduced the problem to one that was already solved! At the end, he asked, "Will this test be on my report card? 'Cause I'm doing really good!" Throughout the interview, it was apparent that Andrew was sure of his own reasoning and knowledge from his experience. Although Andrew is not typical of students in our project, it is important to note that students such as Andrew may later become mathematicians, scientists, and engineers. Andrew had been reflecting greatly on the ideas in the curriculum and relished the opportunity to discuss them so that he could demonstrate the results of his thought.

Learning Trajectory for Shapes

As others we have seen, the learning trajectory for shapes is complex. First, there are several conceptual and skill advancements that make levels more complicated. Second, there are four *subtrajectories* that are related, but can develop somewhat independently: (a) The *Comparing* subtrajectory involves matching by different criteria in the early levels and determining congruence. (b) The *Classifying* subtrajectory includes recognizing, identifying ("naming"), analyzing, and classifying shapes. (c) The *Parts* subtrajectory involves distinguishing, naming, describing, and quantifying the components of shapes, such as sides and angles. (d) The closely related *Representing* subtrajectory involves building or drawing shapes.

The *goal* of increasing children's ability to name, describe, analyze, and classify is second in importance only to numerical goals. The Curriculum Focal Points includes the goals already described in Table 8.1 (see pp. 137–147). (The specific goals in grade 1 are discussed in Chapter 9.)

With those goals, Table 8.1 provides the two additional components of the learning trajectory, the developmental progression and the instructional tasks. As we have stated in previous chapters, the ages in all the learning trajectory tables are only approximate, especially because the age of acquisition usually depends heavily on experience. This is especially true in the domain of geometry, where most children receive low-quality experiences.

Table 8.1 Learning Trajectory for Shapes.

Age (years)	Developmental Progression	Instructional Tasks
0–2	**"Same Thing" Comparer** *Comparing* Compares real-world objects (Vurpillot, 1976). Says two pictures of houses are the same or different. **Shape Matcher—Identical** *Comparing* Matches familiar shapes (circle, square, typical triangle) with *same size and orientation.* Matches  . **—Sizes** Matches familiar shapes with *different sizes.* Matches . **—Orientations** Matches familiar shapes with *different orientations.* Matches .	**Match and Name Shapes** Sit in a circle with children. Using familiar (prototypical) shapes from the Shape Sets in two colors, give each child a shape from one Shape Set. Choose a shape from the other Shape Set, which is a different color, that exactly matches a child's shape. Ask children to name who has an exact match for your shape. After a correct response is given, follow up by asking how the child knows his or her shape is a match. The child might offer to fit his or her shape on top of your shape to "prove" the match. Have children show their shapes to others seated near them, naming the shape whenever they can. Observe and assist as needed. Repeat once or twice. Afterward, tell children they will be able to explore and match shapes later during Work Time. **Mystery Pictures 1** Children build pictures by selecting shapes that match a series of target shapes. The skill children practice is matching, but the program *names* each shape so shape names are introduced. Shapes are familiar at this level. 
3	**Shape Recognizer—Typical** *Classifying* Recognizes and names typical circle, square, and, less often, a typical triangle. May physically rotate shapes in atypical orientations to mentally match them to a prototype. Names this a square [ ] . Some children correctly name different sizes, shapes, and orientations of rectangles, but also call some shapes rectangles that look rectangular but are not rectangles. Names these shapes "rectangles" (including the non-rectangular parallelogram). **"Similar" Comparer** *Comparing* Judges two shapes the same if they are more visually similar than different. "These are the same. They are pointy at the top."	**Circle Time!** Have children sit in the best circle they can make. Show and name a large, flat circle, such as a hula hoop. As you trace the circle with your finger, discuss how it is perfectly round; it is a curved line that always curves the same. Ask children to talk about circles they know, such as those found in toys, buildings, books, tri- or bicycles, and clothing. Distribute a variety of circles for children's exploration—rolling, stacking, tracing, and so on. Have children make circles with their fingers, hands, arms, and mouths. Review a circle's attributes: round and curves the same without breaks. **Match and Name Shapes**, above, includes the naming of these shapes. Do this activity in small groups, as well as in whole groups. **Mystery Pictures 2** Children build pictures by identifying shapes that are *named* by the *Building Blocks* software program. (**Mystery Pictures 1** is appropriate before this activity, as it teaches the shape names.) 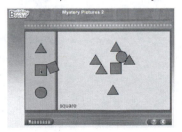
3–4	**Shape Matcher—More Shapes** *Comparing* Matches a wider variety of shapes with *same size and orientation.*	**Match and Name Shapes** As above, but using a wider variety of shapes from the Shape Sets in different orientations. **Match Blocks** Children match various block shapes to objects in the classroom. Have different block shapes in front of you with all the children

Continued Overleaf

Age (years)	Developmental Progression	Instructional Tasks

—Sizes and Orientations Matches a wider variety of shapes with *different sizes and orientations*.

Matches these shapes.

—Combinations Matches *combinations* of shapes to each other.

Matches these shapes.

in a circle around you. Show one block, and ask children what things in the classroom are the same shape. Talk children through any incorrect responses, such as choosing something triangular but saying it has the shape of a quarter circle.

Mystery Pictures 3 Children build pictures by selecting shapes that match a series of target shapes. The skill children practice is matching, but the program *names* each shape, so shape names are introduced. Shapes are more varied and include new (less familiar) shapes at this level.

Memory Geometry

Place two sets of memory geometry cards face down, each in an array.

Players take turns exposing one card from each array.

Cards that do not match are replaced face down; cards that match are kept by that player.

Players should name and describe the shapes together.

Use new shape cards that feature additional shapes from the Shape Set.

Feely Box (Match) Secretly hide a shape in the Feely Box (a decorated box with a hole large enough to fit a child's hand but not so large that you can see into the box). Display five shapes, including the one that exactly matches the one you hid. Have a child put his or her hand in the box to feel the shape; that child should then point to the matching shape on display.

Match and Name Shapes, above, includes the naming of these shapes.

Circles and Cans Display several food cans, and discuss their shape (round) with children. Shift focus to the bottom and top, collectively the bases, of each can. Point out to children that these areas are circular; the edges are circles. Show the large sheets of paper on which you have traced the bases of a few cans that vary substantially in size. Trace one or two other cans to show children what you did, and then shuffle the papers and cans. Ask children to match the cans to the traced circles. For children who are unsure of their choice, have them place the can directly on the traced circle to check. Tell children they can all have a turn matching circles and cans during free time and store the activity's materials in a center for that purpose.

Is It or Not? (Circles) Draw a true circle on a surface where the entire class can view it. Ask children to name it, and then tell why it is a circle. Draw an ellipse (an oval) on the same surface. Ask children what it looks like, and then ask them to tell why it is not a circle. Draw several other circles and shapes that are not circles but could be mistaken for them, and discuss their differences. Summarize by reviewing that a circle is perfectly round and consists of a curved line that always curves the same.

Shape Show: Triangles Show and name a large, flat triangle. Walk your fingers around its perimeter, describing and exaggerating your actions: straaiiight side . . . turn, straaiiight side . . . turn, straaiiight side . . . stop. Ask children how many sides the triangle has, and count the sides with them.

4 | **Shape Recognizer—Circles, Squares, and Triangles** + *Classifying* Recognizes some less typical squares and triangles and may recognize some rectangles, but usually not rhombuses (diamonds). Often doesn't differentiate sides/corners.

Names these as

triangles

Age (years)	Developmental Progression	Instructional Tasks

Emphasize that a triangle's sides and angles can be different sizes; what matters is that its sides are straight and connected to make a closed shape (no openings or gaps). Ask children what things they have at home that are triangles. Show different examples of triangles. Have children draw triangles in the air. If available, have children walk around a large triangle, such as one marked with colored tape on the floor.

Shape Hunt: Triangles

- Tell children to find one or two items in the room with at least one triangle face. For variety, hide Shape Set triangles throughout the room beforehand.
- Encourage children to count the shape's sides and, if possible, show the triangle to an adult, discussing its shape. For example, triangles have three sides, but the sides are not always the same length. After discussion, have the child replace the triangle so other children can find it.
- You may choose to photograph the triangles for a class shape book.

Is It or Not? (Triangles) As above p 138. Include variants (e.g., "skinny triangles") and, as distractors that are visually similar to triangles ("difficult distractors" or "foolers") such as those in Figure 8.9b.

Feely Box (Name) Similar to Feely Box (Match) (p. 138), but now encourage the child to name the shape and explain how he or she figured it out.

Part Comparer *Comparing* Says two shapes are the same after matching one side on each (Beilin, 1984; Beilin, Klein, & Whitehurst, 1982).

"These are the same" (matching the two sides).

Geometry Snapshots 1 Shown a shape for just 2 seconds, students match that to one of four multiple-choice selections.

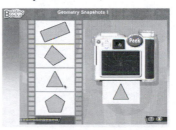

Constructor of Shapes from Parts—Looks Like *Parts*. Uses manipulatives representing parts of shapes, such as sides, to make a shape that "looks like" a goal shape. May think of angles as a corner (which is "pointy").

Asked to make a triangle with sticks, creates the following.

Build Shapes/Straw Shapes includes the naming of these shapes. In a small group lesson with the teacher, children use plastic stirrers of various lengths to make shapes they know. Ensure that they build shapes with correct attributes, such as all sides the same length and all right angles for squares. All stirrers should be "connected" (touching) at their endpoints. Discuss attributes as children build. If children need help, provide a model for them to copy or a drawing on which to place stirrers. Can they choose the correct amount and sizes of stirrers to make a given shape? If children excel, challenge them to get a shape "just right." Can they place pieces with little trial and error?

Straw Shapes: Triangles In a free-choice center, children use plastic stirrers to make triangles and/or to create pictures and designs that include triangles.

Some Attributes Comparer *Comparing* Looks for differences in attributes, but may examine only part of shape.

"These are the same" (indicating the top halves of the shapes are similar by laying them on top of each other).

Match Shapes Children match the Shape Set shapes (i.e., find the yellow shape that is exactly the same size and shape as each of the blue shapes).

Continued Overleaf

Age (years)	Developmental Progression	Instructional Tasks

4–5 | **Shape Recognizer—All Rectangles**

Classifying Recognizes more rectangle sizes, shapes, and orientations of rectangles.

Correctly names these shapes "rectangles".

Guess My Rule Tell children to watch carefully as you sort Shape Set shapes into piles based on something that makes them alike.

Ask children to silently guess your sorting rule, such as circles versus squares or four-sided shapes versus round.

Sort shapes one at a time, continuing until there are at least two shapes in each pile.

Signal "shhh," and pick up a new shape. With a look of confusion, gesture to children to encourage all of them to point quietly to which pile the shape belongs. Place the shape in its pile.

After all shapes are sorted, ask children what they think the sorting rule is.

Repeat with other shapes and new rules.

Circles versus squares (same orientation).

Circles versus triangles.

Circles versus rectangles.

Triangles versus squares.

Triangles versus rectangles.

Etc.

Mystery Pictures 4 Children build pictures by identifying a wide variety of shapes that are *named* by the *Building Blocks* software program. (**Mystery Pictures 3** is appropriate anytime before this activity, as it teaches the shape names.)

Shape Show: Rectangles Show and name a large, flat rectangle. Walk your fingers around its perimeter, describing and exaggerating your actions: short straaiiight side . . . turn, long straaiiight side . . . turn, short straaiiight side . . . turn, long straaiiight side . . . stop. Ask children how many sides the rectangle has, and count the sides with them. Emphasize that opposite sides of a rectangle are the same lengths, and all "turns" are right angles. To model this, you may place a stirrer that is the same length as one pair of sides on top of each of those sides, and repeat for the other pair of opposite sides. To illustrate right angles, talk about the angle—like an uppercase L—in a doorway. Make uppercase Ls with children using thumbs and index fingers. Fit your L on the angles of the rectangle. Ask children what things they have at home that are rectangles. Show different examples of rectangles. Have children walk around a large, flat rectangle, such as a rug. Once seated, have children draw rectangles in the air.

Shape Hunt: Rectangles As above p. 139, but involving rectangles.

Build Shapes / Straw Shapes As above p. 139, but involving rectangles.

Straw Shapes: Rectangles As above p. 139, but involving rectangles.

Shape Show: Squares Show and name a large, flat square. Walk your fingers around its perimeter, describing and exaggerating your actions: straaiiight side . . . turn, straaiiight side . . . turn, straaiiight side . . . turn, straaiiight side . . . stop. Ask children how many sides the square has, and count the sides with them. Review that all sides of a square are the same length, and all

Age (years)	Developmental Progression	Instructional Tasks
		"turns" are right angles. To model this, you may place stirrers that are the same length as each side on each side. Remind children about right angles (uppercase Ls or the corner of a doorway). Make uppercase Ls with children using thumbs and index fingers. Fit your L on the angles of the square. Ask children what things they have at home that are squares. Show different examples of squares. Have children walk around a large, flat square, such as a floor tile. Once seated, have children draw squares in the air.

Is It or Not? As above p. 138, with rectangles or squares.

I Spy Beforehand, place various Shape Set shapes throughout the classroom in plain view. Name the shape of something in the room. You may wish to start with something easily recognizable, such as "three sides." Have children guess the item or shape you are thinking about. If able, have the child who guessed correctly think of the next item or shape for you and the class to guess. As a variation, try the properties version: describe a shape's attributes and see whether children can guess which item or shape you mean. This can also be done with Shape Sets, actual objects in the room, and/or other shape manipulative. |
| | **Side Recognizer** *Parts.* Identifies sides as distinct geometric objects.

Asked what this shape is ⟨image⟩, says it is a quadrilateral (or has four sides) after counting each, running finger along the length of each side.

Most Attributes Comparer *Comparing* Looks for differences in attributes, examining full shapes, but may ignore some spatial relationships.

"These are the same." | **Rectangles and Boxes** Draw a large rectangle for the entire class to see, and trace it, counting each side as you go. Challenge children to draw a rectangle in the air as you count, reminding them that each side should be straight. Show a variety of boxes to children, such as toothpaste, pasta, and cereal boxes, and discuss their shape. Eventually focus on the faces of the boxes, which should mostly be rectangles. Talk about the sides and right angles. On large paper, place two boxes horizontally and trace their faces. Have children match the boxes to the traced rectangles. Trace more boxes and repeat. Help children consider other box face shapes, such as triangles (candy and food storage), octagons (hat and gift boxes), and circles/cylinders (toy and oats containers).

Name Faces of Blocks During circle or free playtime, children name the faces (sides) of different building blocks. Tell children which classroom items are the same shape.

Feely Box (Describe) As above, but now children must describe the shape *without* naming it, well enough that their peers can figure out the shape they are describing. Have children explain how he or she figured out which shape. They should describe the shape, emphasizing straightness of the sides and the number of sides and angles. |
| | **Corner (Angle) Recognizer**—*Parts* Recognizes angles as separate geometric objects, at least in the limited context of "corners."

Asked why is this a triangle, says, "It has three angles" and counts them, pointing clearly to each vertex (point at the corner). | **Shape Parts 1** Students use shape parts to construct a shape that matches a target shape. They must place every component exactly, so it is a skill that is actually at the **Constructor of Shapes from Parts—Exact** level, but some children can begin to benefit from such *scaffolded* computer work at this level.

 |

Continued Overleaf

Age (years)	Developmental Progression	Instructional Tasks
5	**Shape Recognizer—More Shapes** *Classifying* Recognizes most familiar shapes and typical examples of other shapes, such as hexagon, rhombus (diamond), and trapezoid. Correctly identifies and names all the following shapes  .	**Shape Step** Make shapes on the floor with masking or colored tape or chalk shapes outdoors. Tell children to step on a certain class of shapes (e.g., rhombuses) only. Have a group of five children step on the rhombuses. Ask the rest of the class to watch carefully to make sure the group steps on them all. Whenever possible, ask children to explain why the shape they stepped on was the correct shape ("How do you know that was a rhombus?"). Repeat the activity until all groups have stepped on shapes. **Mystery Pictures 4** Children build pictures by identifying a wide variety of shapes that are *named* by the *Building Blocks* software program. This activity includes the hexagon, rhombus (diamond), and trapezoid. 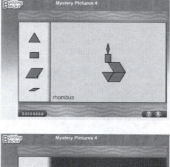  **Geometry Snapshots 2** Shown a simple configuration of shapes for just 2 seconds, students match that configuration to four choices from memory (imagery). 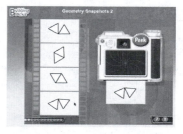 **Guess My Rule** As above, with "rules" appropriate for this level. Circles versus triangles versus squares (all different orientations). Triangles versus rhombuses. Trapezoids versus rhombuses. Trapezoids versus not trapezoids. Hexagons versus trapezoids. Triangles versus not triangles. Squares versus not squares (for example, all other shapes). Rectangles versus not rectangles. Rhombuses versus not rhombuses.

Age (years)	Developmental Progression	Instructional Tasks
6	**Shape Identifier** *Classifying* Names most common shapes, including rhombuses, without making mistakes such as calling ovals circles. Recognizes (at least) right angles, so distinguishes between a rectangle and a parallelogram without right angles. Correctly names all the following shapes 	**Trapezoids and Rhombuses** Show pattern block shapes, one after another, having children name each one. Focus especially on the rhombus and trapezoid. Ask children what they could make with such shapes. Have children describe the properties of the shapes. A trapezoid has one pair of parallel sides; a rhombus has two pairs of parallel sides all the same length. **Mr. MixUp (Shapes)** Explain that children are going to help Mr. MixUp name shapes. Remind children to stop Mr. MixUp right when he makes a mistake to correct him. Using Shape Set shapes, have Mr. MixUp start by confusing the names of a square and a rhombus. After children have identified the correct names, ask them to explain how their angles are different (squares must have all right angles; rhombuses may have different angles). Review that all rhombuses and squares, which are actually a special kind of rhombus with all right angles, have four straight sides of equal length. Repeat with a trapezoid, a hexagon, and any other shapes you would like children to practice. **Geometry Snapshots 4** Students identify an image that matches one of four moderately complex configurations from memory (imagery). 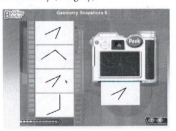
7	**Angle Recognizer—More Contexts** *Parts* Can recognize and describe contexts in which angle knowledge is relevant, including corners (can discuss "sharper" angles), crossings (e.g., a scissors), and, later, bent objects and bends (sometimes bends in paths and slopes). Only later can explicitly understand how angle concepts relate to these contexts (e.g., initially may not think of bends in roads as angles; may not be able to add horizontal or vertical to complete the angle in slope contexts; may even see corners as more or less "sharp" without representing the lines that constitute them). Often does not relate these contexts and may represent only some features of angles in each (e.g., oblique line for a ramp in a slope context).	**Geometry Snapshots 6** Students match geometric figures that differ on angle measure from memory (imagery). **Mr. MixUp (Shapes)** As above, confuse sides and corners; make sure children explain which is which.

Continued Overleaf

Age (years)	Developmental Progression	Instructional Tasks

Parts of Shapes Identifier *Classifying* Identifies shapes in terms of their components.

> "No matter how skinny it looks, that's a triangle *because* it has three sides and three angles."

Congruence Determiner *Comparing* Determines congruence by comparing all attributes and all spatial relationships.

> Says that two shapes are the same shape and the same size after comparing every one of their sides and angles.

Congruence Superposer *Comparing* Moves and places objects on top of each other to determine congruence.

> Says that two shapes are the same shape and the same size because they can be laid on top of each other.

Constructor of Shapes from Parts— Exact *Representing*. Uses manipulatives representing parts of shapes, such as sides and angle "connectors," to make a shape that is completely correct, based on knowledge of components and relationships.

> Asked to make a triangle with sticks, creates the following △.

Shape Shop 1 Students identify shapes by their attributes or number of parts (e.g., number of sides and angles).

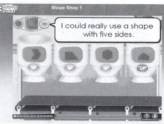

Build Shapes/Straw Shapes As above, but involving any of the shapes in the Shape Set, *or* a verbally-named set of properties (e.g., make a shape that has (a) two pairs of adjacent sides the same length or (b) all four sides the same length but no right angles).

> Give other challenges, such as: Can you make a triangle with any three of these straw (lengths)? (No, not if one straw is longer than the sum of the lengths of the other two.)

> How many different shapes (classes) can you make with two pairs of straws the same length?

Shape Parts 2 Students use shape parts to construct a shape that matches a target shape. They must place every component exactly.

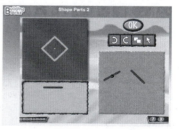

Warm-Up: Snapshots (Shape Parts) Give children a set of Straws of Various Lengths. Secretly make a shape using the "straws," such as a rectangle, and cover it with a dark cloth. Tell children to look carefully and take a snapshot in their minds as you show your shape for two seconds, and then cover it again—immediately after—with a dark cloth. Have children build what they saw with their straws. Show your shape for two more seconds so children can check and change their shapes if necessary. Then have children describe what they saw and how they built their own. Repeat with other secret shapes, making them more complex as children's ability allows.

Age (years)	Developmental Progression	Instructional Tasks
8+	**Angle Representer** *Parts.* Represents various angle contexts as two lines, explicitly including the reference line (horizontal or vertical for slope; a "line of sight" for turn contexts) and, at least implicitly, the size of the angle as the rotation between these lines (may still maintain misconceptions about angle measure, such as relating angle size to the length of side's distance between endpoints and may not apply these understandings to multiple contexts).	**Logo** See Logo examples and suggestions in this and the previous chapter. **As the World Turns** Have students estimate, then measure, and draw and label different real-world angle measures, such as a door opening, a radio control turning, a doorknob, head turning, turning a faucet on, and so forth.
	Congruence Representer *Comparing* Refers to geometric properties and explains with transformations. "These must be congruent, because they have equal sides, all square corners, and I can move them on top of each other exactly."	
	Shape Class Identifier *Classifying* Uses class membership (e.g., to sort), not explicitly based on properties. "I put the triangles over here, and the quadrilaterals, including squares, rectangles, rhombuses, and trapezoids over there."	**Guess My Rule** As above, with "rules" appropriate for this level, including all classes of shapes. **Shape Step (Properties)** As above, with students told a property rather than a shape name and asked to justify that the shape they selected has that property.
	Shape Property Identifier *Classifying* Uses properties explicitly. Can see the invariants in the changes of state or shape, but maintaining the shapes' properties. "I put the shapes with opposite sides parallel over here, and those with four sides but not both pairs of sides parallel over there."	**Guess My Rule** As above, with "rules" appropriate for this level, including sorts such as "has a right angles vs. has no right angle" or "regular polygons (closed shapes with all straight sides) vs. any other shapes, symmetrical vs. non-symmetrical shapes, etc." **I Spy** As above, but giving properties such as "I spy a shape with four sides and with opposite sides the same length, but no right angles." **Legends of the Lost Shape** Students identify target shapes using textual clues provided, such as having certain angle sizes. 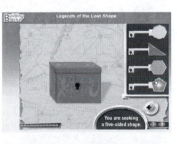 **Shape Shop 2** Students identify shapes by their *properties* (number of, and relationships between, sides and angles). 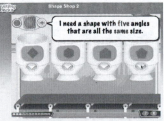

Continued Overleaf

Age (years)	Developmental Progression	Instructional Tasks

Property Class Identifier *Classifying* Uses class membership for shapes (e.g., to sort or consider shapes "similar") explicitly based on properties, including angle measure. Is aware of restrictions of transformations and also of the definitions and can integrate the two. Sorts hierarchically, based on properties.

> "I put the equilateral triangles over here, and scalene triangles over here. The isosceles triangles are all these . . . they included the equilaterals."

Mr. MixUp (Shapes) As above, but focus on class memberships and defining properties (e.g., Mr. MixUp says that a rectangle has two pairs of equal and parallel sides but [erroneously] "could not be a parallelogram because it's a rectangle").

Which Shape Could It Be? Slowly reveal a shape from behind a screen. At each "step," ask children what class of shapes it could be and how certain they are.

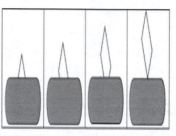

Shape Parts 3 Students use shape parts to construct a shape that matches a target shape, which is rotated, so the construction is at a different orientation. They must place every component exactly. Depending on the problem and the way it is approached, these activities can be useful at several levels.

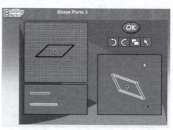

Shape Parts 4 As above, but with multiple embedded shapes.

Shape Parts 5 As above, but no model is provided.

Age (years)	Developmental Progression	Instructional Tasks

Shape Shop 3 Students identify shapes by their *properties* (number of, and relationships between, sides and angles) with more properties named at this level.

Angle Synthesizer *Parts* Combines various meanings of angle (turn, corner, slant), including angle measure.

"This ramp is at a 45° angle to the ground."

Shape Parts 6 As above, but the student must use sides *and* angles (manipulable "corners").

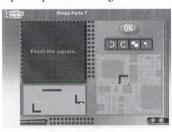

Shape Parts 7 As above, and more properties/problem-solving involved.

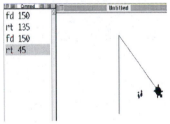

Using the Logo turtle to draw challenging shapes, such as creating an isosceles triangle in *Turtle Math* (Clements & Meredith, 1994).

```
fd 150
rt 135
fd 150
rt 45
```

Final Words

As this chapter showed, children can learn a considerable amount about several aspects of geometric shapes. There is one more important competency, so important that we dedicate Chapter 9 to it: shape composition.

9
Composition and Decomposition of Shapes

Zachary's grandmother was walking him out of pre-school. He looked at the tiled walkway and yelled, "Look, grandma! Hexagons! Hexagons all over the walk. You can put them together with no spaces!"

What does Zachary show he knows about shapes and geometry? Zachary and his friends have been working on the *Building Blocks* curriculum which emphasizes putting shapes together. Children enjoy playing with puzzles and shapes, with challenges such as tangram puzzles provide. If such experiences are organized into learning trajectories, they can benefit and enjoy these experiences even more. Teachers report such experiences can change the way children see their world.

The ability to describe, use, and visualize the effects of composing and decomposing geometric regions is important in and of itself. It also provides a foundation for understanding other areas of mathematics, especially number and arithmetic, such as part–whole relationships, fractions, and so forth.

In this chapter we examine three related topics. First, we discuss composition of three-dimensional shapes in the restricted but important early childhood setting of building with blocks. Second, we discuss composition and decomposition of two-dimensional shapes. Third, we discuss disembedding of two-dimensional shapes, such as in embedded (hidden) figures problems.

Composition of 3D Shapes

Children initially build block structures one block at a time and only later explicitly put together these 3D shapes to create new 3D shapes. In their first year, they pound, clap together, or slide the blocks, or they use single blocks to represent an object, such as a house or vehicle. Children's first combinations are simple pairs. At about 1 year of age, they stack blocks then make a "road." At about 2 years, they place each successive block congruently on or next to the one previously placed (see the companion book for more details and for illustrations). Around 2 to 3 years of age, children begin to extend their building to two dimensions, covering to extend a plane in creating a floor or wall. At 3 to 4 years of age, children regularly build vertical and horizontal components within a building, even making a simple arch. At 4 years, they can use multiple spatial relations, extending in multiple directions and with multiple points of contact among components, showing flexibility in how they generate and integrate parts of the structure. A small number of children will build a tower with all blocks; for example, by composing the triangular blocks to make rectangular blocks. Although the available research on 3D is limited, it is consistent with the research on composing 2D shapes, to which we turn.

Composition and Decomposition of 2D Shapes

Research on 3D shapes, especially dealing with their *composition*, is limited. In contrast, we have created and tested a developmental progression for the composition of 2D shapes (again, more detail can be found in the companion book).

Pre-Composer. Children manipulate shapes as individuals, but are unable to combine them to compose a larger shape. For example, children might use a single shape for a sun, a separate shape for a tree, and another separate shape for a person.

Piece Assembler. Children at this level are similar to Pre-Composers, but they place shapes contiguously to form pictures, often touching only at vertices. In free-form "make a picture" tasks, for example, each shape used represents a unique role, or function in the picture (e.g., one shape for one leg). Children can fill simple outline puzzles using trial and error, but do not easily use turns or flips to do so; they cannot use motions to see shapes from different perspectives.

Picture Maker. Children can concatenate shapes contiguously to form pictures in which several shapes play a single role, but use trial and error and do not anticipate creation of new geometric shapes.

Shape Composer. Children combine shapes to make new shapes or fill puzzles, with growing intentionality and anticipation ("I know what will fit"). Children use angles as well as side lengths. Rotation and flipping are used intentionally to select and place shapes.

Substitution Composer. Children deliberately form composite units of shapes and recognize and use substitution relationships among these shapes (e.g., two trapezoid pattern blocks can make a hexagon).

Shape Composite Iterater. Children construct and operate on composite units (units of units) intentionally. They can continue a pattern of shapes that leads to a "good covering."

Shape Composer with Superordinate Units. Children build and apply (iterate and otherwise operate on) units of units of units.

This developmental progression is the core of the learning trajectory for the composition of 2D shapes, of course, but also helped inform the learning trajectory for the composition of 3D shapes.

Disembedding 2D Shapes

Children develop over years in learning how to separate structures within embedded figures (see illustrations and a description in the companion book)—that is, finding "hidden shapes" within more complex diagrams. Few 4-year-olds could find embedded circles or squares embedded in square structures, but many 5-year-olds were more likely to do so. Before 6 years of age, what children perceive is organized in a rigid manner into basic structures. Children grow in the flexibility of the perceptual organizations they can create. They eventually integrate parts and can create and use "imaginary components." Of course, we all know that embedded pictures can be very complex, and can stump people of any age, who have to build them up piece by piece. The learning trajectory puts this body of research into a developmental progression.

Experience and Education

Composition of 3D Shapes

Block building has long been a staple of high-quality early childhood education (at least in theory). It supports children's learning of shape and shape composition ability, to say nothing of the general reasoning that it may help develop. Amazingly, block building in preschool predicts mathematics achievement in high school (although, like most research of this nature, this is "correlation, not causation"). Block building also helps develop spatial skills. Research provides several other useful guidelines, as follows:

- Have younger children build with or alongside older preschoolers; in that context, they develop block-building skills more rapidly.
- Provide materials, facilitative peer relationships, and time to build, and also incorporate *planned, systematic* block building into their curriculum. Children should have open exploratory play *and* solve semi-structured and well-structured problems, with intentional teaching provided for each.
- Understand and apply children's developmental progressions in the levels of complexity of block-building. More effective teachers provide verbal scaffolding for the children based on those levels (e.g., "sometimes people use a block to join . . ."), but avoid directly assisting children, or engaging in block building themselves.
- Understand full learning trajectories—that is, the goal, developmental progression, *and* matched activities improve in block-building skill. Children of teachers who understand all three improve more than control groups who receive an equivalent amount of block-building experience during unstructured free-play sessions.
- Address equity. As with other types of spatial training, intentional instruction in block building may be more important for girls than boys.

Structured and sequenced block-blocking interventions will help provide boys and girls with equitable, beneficial opportunities to learn about the structural properties of blocks and thus spatial skills. For example, activities can be designed to encourage spatial and mathematical thinking and sequenced to match developmental progressions. In one study, the first problem was to build an enclosure with walls that were at least two blocks high and included an arch. This introduced the problem of bridging, which involves balanced measurement, and estimation. The second problem was to build more complex bridges, such as bridges with multiple arches and ramps or stairs at the end. This introduced planning and seriation. The third problem was to build a complex tower with at least two floors, or stories. Children were provided with cardboard ceilings, so they had to make the walls fit the constraints of the cardboard's dimensions.

Unit blocks also provide a window into the geometry of young children's play. These blocks allow children to explore a world where objects have predictable similarities and relationships. Children create forms and structures that are based on mathematical relationships. For example, children have to struggle with length relationships in finding a roof for a building. Length and equivalence are involved in substituting two shorter blocks for one long block.

Children also consider height, area, and volume. The inventor of today's unit blocks, Caroline Pratt, tells a story of children making enough room for a horse to fit inside a stable. The teacher told Diana that she could have the horse when she had made a stable for it. She and Elizabeth began to build a small construction, but the horse did not fit. Diana had made a large stable with a low roof. After several unsuccessful attempts to get the horse in, she removed the roof, added blocks to the walls to make the roof higher, and replaced the roof. She then tried to put into words what she had done. "Roof too small." The teacher gave her new words, "high" and "low" and she gave a new explanation to the other children.

Just building with blocks, children form important ideas. These intuitive ideas can be fostered by teachers, such as Diana's, who discuss these ideas with children, giving words to their actions. For example, children can be helped to distinguish between different quantities such as height, area, and volume. Three preschoolers made towers and argued about whose was the biggest. Their teacher asked them if they meant whose was tallest (gesturing) or widest, or used the most blocks? The children were surprised to find that the tallest tower did not have the most blocks.

In many situations, you help children see and discuss the similarities and differences among the blocks they use and the structures they make. You can also pose challenges that will focus children's actions on these ideas. At the right time, you might challenge the children to do the following:

- Put the blocks in order by length.
- Use other blocks to make a wall as long as the longest block.
- Use 12 half-units (square) blocks to make as many differently-shaped (rectangular) floors as they can.
- Make a box that is four blocks square.

Learning Trajectory for Composition of 3D Shapes

The goal for the area of composing and decomposing shapes, as expressed in the Curriculum Focal Points were described in Table 8.1 (see pp. 137–147). Although the emphasis for 2D composition is in Grade 1, all grades include work in this area.

The learning trajectories for the composition of three-dimensional geometric shapes are presented in Table 9.1. This is *only* for the set of unit blocks; composition of more complex and less familiar 3D shapes would follow the same developmental progression but at later ages and more dependence on specific educational experiences.

Table 9.1 A Learning Trajectory for the Composition of 3D Shapes.

Age (years)	Developmental Progression	Instructional Tasks
	Pre-Composer (3D). Manipulates shapes as individuals, but does not combine them to compose a larger shape. May pound, clap together, or use slide blocks or single blocks to represent an object, such as a house or truck.	This level is not an instructional goal level.
1	**Stacker.** Shows use of the spatial relationship of "on" to stack blocks, but choice of blocks is unsystematic.	
1.5	**Line Maker.** Shows use of relationship of "next to" to make a line of blocks.	

Age (years)	Developmental Progression	Instructional Tasks

| 2 | **Congruency Stacker.** Shows use of relationship of "on" to stack congruent blocks, or those that show a similarly helpful relationship to make stacks or lines. | 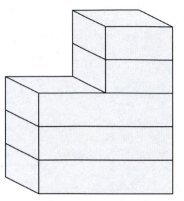 |

| 2 | **Piece Assembler (3D).** Builds vertical and horizontal components within a building, but within a limited range, such as building a "floor" or simple "wall." | 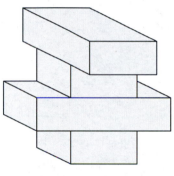 |

| 3–4 | **Picture Maker (3D).** Uses multiple spatial relations, extending in multiple directions and with multiple points of contact among components, showing flexibility in integrating parts of the structure. Produce arches, enclosures, corners, and crosses, but may use unsystematic trial and error and simple addition of pieces. | 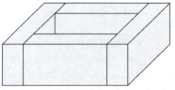
See also Figure 9.3 in the companion book. |

| 4–5 | **Shape Composer (3D).** Composes shapes with anticipation, understanding what 3D shape will be produced with a composition of 2 or more other (simple, familiar) 3D shapes. Can produce arches, enclosures, corners, and crosses systematically. Builds enclosures and arches several blocks high (Kersh, Casey, & Young, in press). | 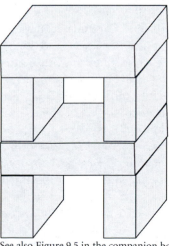
See also Figure 9.5 in the companion book. |

Continued Overleaf

Age (years)	Developmental Progression	Instructional Tasks
5–6	**Substitution Composer and Shape Composite Repeater (3D).** Substitutes a composite for a congruent whole. Builds complex bridges with multiple arches, with ramps and stairs at the ends.	 See also Figure 9.6 in the companion book.
6–8+	**Shape Composer—Units of Units (3D).** Makes complex towers or other structures, involving multiple levels with ceilings (fitting the ceilings), adult-like structures with blocks, including arches and other substructures.	 See also Figure 9.7.

Composition and Decomposition of 2D Shapes

Young children move through levels in the composition and decomposition of 2D figures. From lack of competence in composing geometric shapes, they gain abilities to combine shapes into pictures, then synthesize combinations of shapes into new shapes (composite shapes), eventually operating on and iterating those composite shapes. Early foundations for this learning appear to be formed in children's experiences. Few curricula challenge children to move through these levels. Our theoretical learning trajectory guides the selection of puzzles for children at different levels of the trajectory. The content and effects of one program illustrate the importance of shape and shape composition. An artist and collaborating educational researchers developed the Agam program to develop the "visual language" of children ages 3 to 7 years. The activities begin by building a visual alphabet. For example, the activities introduce horizontal lines in isolation. Then, they teach relations, such as parallel lines. In the same way, teachers introduce circles, then concentric circles, and then a horizontal line intersecting a circle. The curriculum also develops verbal language, but always following a visual introduction. Combination rules involving the visual alphabet and ideas such as large, medium, and small, generate complex figures. As words combine to make sentences, the elements of the visual alphabet combine to form complex patterns and symmetric forms. The Agam approach is structured, with instruction proceeding from passive identification to memory to active discovery, first in simple form (e.g., looking for plastic circles hidden by the teacher), then in tasks that require visual analysis (e.g., finding circles in picture books). Only then does the teacher present tasks requiring reproduction of combinations from memory. The curriculum repeats these ideas in a large number of activities featuring multiple modes of representation, such as bodily activity, group activity, and auditory perception.

The results of using the program, especially for several consecutive years, are positive. Children gain in geometric and spatial skills and show pronounced benefits in the areas of arithmetic and writing readiness. Supporting these results, emphasis on the learning trajectory for composition of shape in the *Building Blocks* program (we borrowed heavily from the Agam program in designing *Building Blocks*) led strong effects in this area—equivalent to benefits often found for individual tutoring. In a follow-up, large-scale randomized field trial with 36 classrooms, the *Building Blocks* curriculum made the most substantial gains compared to both a non-treatment and another pre-school math curriculum, in shape composition (and several other topics). Especially because the other curriculum also included shape composition activities, we believe that the greater gains provided by the *Building Blocks* curriculum can be attributed to its explicit use of the sequenced activities developed from, and the teachers' knowledge of, the learning trajectory, to which we turn.

Learning Trajectories for the Composition and Decomposition of Geometric Shapes (2D)

Because the learning trajectories for the composition and decomposition of two-dimensional geometric shapes are closely connected, we present them together, in Table 9.2.

Table 9.2 A Learning Trajectory for the Composition and Decomposition of 2D Shapes.

Age (years)	Developmental Progression	Instructional Tasks
0–3	**Pre-Composer** Manipulates shapes as individuals, but is unable to combine them to compose a larger shape. Make a picture.	These levels are not instructional goal levels. However, several preparatory activities may orient 2- to 4-year-old children to the task, and move them toward the next levels that do represent (some) competence. In "Shape Pictures," children play with physical pattern blocks and Shape Sets, often making simple pictures. Recall that the "Mystery Pictures" series (see pp. 137–142) sets the foundation for this learning trajectory and would be the first task for the following level. Children only match or identify shapes, but the *result* of their work is a picture made up of other shapes—a demonstration of composition.
	Pre-DeComposer Decomposes only by trial and error. Given *only* a hexagon formed by two trapezoids, can break it apart to make this simple picture, by random placement.	
4	**Piece Assembler** Makes pictures in which each shape represents a unique role (e.g., one shape for each body part) and shapes touch. Fills simple "Pattern Block Puzzles" using trial and error. Make a picture.	In the first "Pattern Block Puzzles" tasks, each shape is not only outlined, but touches other shapes only at a point, making the matching as easy as possible. Children merely match pattern blocks to the outlines. **Pattern Block Puzzles**

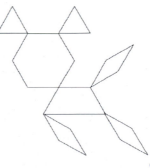

Continued Overleaf

Age (years)	Developmental Progression	Instructional Tasks
		Then, the puzzles move to those that combine shapes by matching their sides, but still mainly serve separate roles.

Pattern Block Puzzles

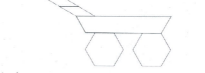

| 5 | **Picture Maker** Puts several shapes together to make one part of a picture (e.g., two shapes for one arm). Uses trial and error and does not anticipate creation of new geometric shape. Chooses shapes using "general shape" or side length. Fills "easy" "Pattern Block Puzzles" that suggest the placement of each shape (but note in the example on the right that the child is trying to put a square in the puzzle where its right angles will not fit). | The "Pattern Block Puzzles" at this level start with those where several shapes are combined to make one "part," but internal lines are still available. |

Make a picture.

Later puzzles in the sequence require combining shapes to fill one or more regions, without the guidance of internal line segments.

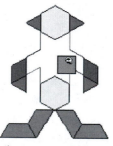

"Piece Puzzler 3" is a similar computer activity. In the first tasks, children must concatenate shapes, but are helped with internal line segments in most cases; these internal segments are faded in subsequent puzzles.

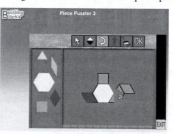

Snapshots (Shapes) Give children Pattern Blocks. Secretly make a simple house with a square (foundation) and triangle (roof). Tell children to look carefully and take a snapshot in their minds as you show your house for 2 seconds, and then cover it immediately after with a dark cloth. Have children build what they saw with Pattern Blocks. Show your house for 2 more seconds so children can check and change their pictures, if necessary. During the final reveal, have children describe what they saw and how they built their own. Repeat with other secret pictures, making them more complex as children's ability allows.

Age (years)	Developmental Progression	Instructional Tasks

Simple DeComposer Decomposes ("takes apart" into smaller shapes) simple shapes that have obvious clues as to their decomposition.

> Given hexagons, can break it apart to make this picture.

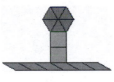

"Super Shape 1" is like "Piece Puzzler" with an essential difference. Children only have *one* shape in the shape palette and they must *decompose* that "super" (superordinate) shape and then recompose those pieces to complete the puzzle. The tool they use for decomposition is a simple "break apart" tool; when applied, a shape breaks into its canonical parts.

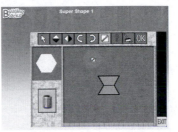

Shape Composer Composes shapes with anticipation ("I know what will fit!"). Chooses shapes using angles as well as side lengths. Rotation and flipping are used intentionally to select and place shapes. In the "Pattern Block Puzzles" below, all angles are correct, and patterning is evident.

> Make a picture.

The "Pattern Block Puzzles" and "Piece Puzzler" activities have no internal guidelines and larger areas; therefore, children must compose shapes accurately.

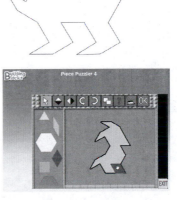

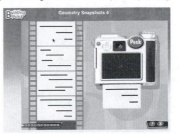

Geometry Snapshots 4 Students identify an image that matches one of four moderately complex configurations from memory (imagery).

Snapshots (Shapes) As above, but use several copies of the same shape, so children have to compose mentally. Also, try simple outlines and see if they can compose the same shape with pattern blocks. Tangrams can provide additional challenges.

Continued Overleaf

Age (years)	Developmental Progression	Instructional Tasks

6 | **Substitution Composer** Makes new shapes out of smaller shapes and uses trial and error to substitute groups of shapes for other shapes to create new shapes in different ways.

At this level, children solve "Pattern Block Puzzles" in which they must substitute shapes to fill an outline in different ways.

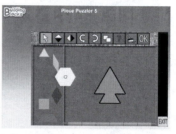

Make a picture with intentional substitutions.

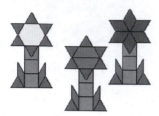

"Piece Puzzler" tasks are similar; the new task here is to solve the same puzzle in several different ways.

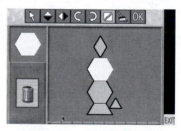

Pattern Block Puzzles and **Tangram Puzzles** Ask students how many of a certain shapes it would take to cover another shape (or configuration of shapes). Students predict, record their prediction, then try to check.

Shape DeComposer (with Help) Decomposes shapes using imagery that is suggested and supported by the task or environment.

SuperShape 2 (and several additional levels) requires multiple decompositions.

Given hexagons, can break one or more apart to make this shape.

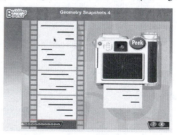

Geometry Snapshots 4 Students identify an image that matches one of four moderately complex configurations from memory (imagery).

Age (years)	Developmental Progression	Instructional Tasks

7   **Shape Composite Repeater**

Constructs and duplicates units of units (shapes made from other shapes) intentionally; understands each as being both multiple small shapes *and* one larger shape. May continue a pattern of shapes that leads to tiling.

Children use a shape composition repeatedly in constructing a design or picture.

Children are asked to repeat a structure they have composed.

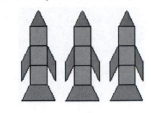

Shape DeComposer with Imagery

Decomposes shapes flexibly using independently generated imagery.

Given hexagons, can break one or more apart to make shapes such as these.

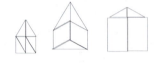

In "Super Shape 6" children again only have one shape in the shape palette and they must decompose that shape and then recompose those pieces to complete the puzzle. The tool they use for decomposition is a scissors tool in which they must specific two points for a "cut." Therefore, their decompositions must be more intentional and anticipatory.

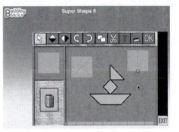

Geometry Snapshots 7 Students identify an image that matches one of four complex configurations from memory (imagery).

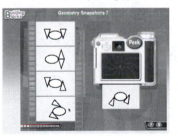

8   **Shape Composer—Units of Units**

Builds and *applies* units of units (shapes made from other shapes). For example, in constructing spatial patterns, extend patterning activity to create a tiling with a new unit shape—a unit of unit shapes that they recognize and consciously construct.

Builds a large structure by making a combination of pattern blocks over and over and then fitting them together.

In this "Tetrominoes" task, the child must repeatedly build and repeat superordinate units. That is, as in the illustration here, the child repeatedly built "Ts" out of four squares, used 4 Ts to build squares, and used squares to tile a rectangle.

Continued Overleaf

Age (years)	Developmental Progression	Instructional Tasks

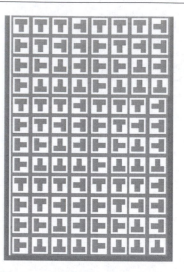

Shape Parts 4 Students use shape parts to construct a shape that matches a target shape, including multiple embedded shapes.

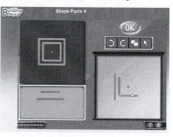

Shape DeComposer with Units of Units Decomposes shapes flexibly using independently generated imagery and planned decompositions of shapes that themselves are decompositions.

Given only squares, can break them apart—*and then break the resulting shapes apparent again*—to make shapes such as these.

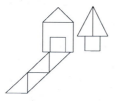

In "Super Shape 7" children only get exactly the number of "super shapes" they need to complete the puzzle. Again, multiple applications of the scissors tool is required.

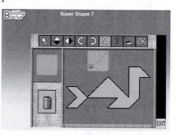

Geometry Snapshots 8 Students identify a configuration of cubes that matches one of four complex configurations from memory (imagery).

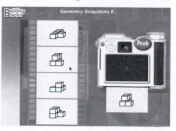

Disembedding 2D Shapes

More research is needed before suggesting a solid recommendation as to how much time to spend and how to approach the disembedding of 2D shapes. The motivating nature of disembedding activities (cf. "hidden pictures" activities in children's magazines) may indicate, however, that such activities may be interesting to children as extra work, such as might be added to learning centers or taken home.

The primary task we present in the learning trajectory is straightforward—to find figures in increasingly complex geometric figures, including embedded figures. It may be wise to have children embed figures themselves before finding already embedded figures.

Learning Trajectories for Embedded Geometric Figures (2D)

Table 9.3 presents a tentative learning trajectory for disembedding geometric shapes.

Table 9.3 A Learning Trajectory for the Disembedding of Geometric Shapes.

Age (years)	Developmental Progression	Instructional Tasks
3	**Pre-Disembedder** Can remember and reproduce only one or small collection of non-overlapping (isolated) shapes.	See Chapters 7 and 8.
4	**Simple Disembedder** Identifies frame of complex figure. Finds some shapes in arrangements in which figures overlap, but not in which figures are embedded in others.	
5–6	**Shapes-in-shapes Disembedder** Identifies shapes embedded within other shapes, such as concentric circles and/or a circle in a square. Identifies primary structures in complex figures.	

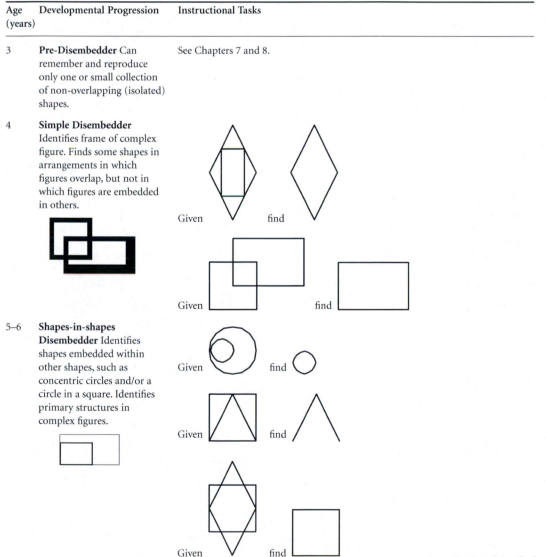

Continued Overleaf

Age (years)	Developmental Progression	Instructional Tasks
7	**Secondary Structure Disembedder** Identifies embedded figures even when they do not coincide with any primary structures of the complex figure.	
8	**Complete Disembedder** Successfully identifies all varieties of complex arrangements.	

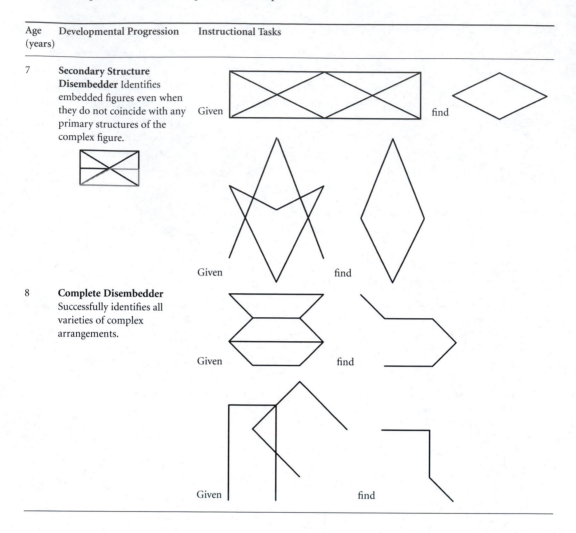

Final Words

The ability to describe, use, and visualize the effects of composing, decomposing, embedding, and disembedding shapes is an important mathematical competence. It is relevant to geometry but also related to children's ability to compose and decompose numbers. Further, it underlies knowledge and skill with art, architecture, and the sciences. Thus, it helps people solve a wide variety of problems, from geometric proofs to the design of a floor space. Of course, such designs also require geometric measurement, the topic of the next two chapters.

10
Geometric Measurement
Length

First graders were studying mathematics through measurement, rather than counting discrete objects. They described and represented relationships among and between quantities, such as comparing two sticks and symbolizing the lengths as "A < B." This enabled them to reason about relationships. For example, after seeing the following statements recorded on the board, if V > M, then M ≠ V, V ≠ M, and M < V, one first grader noted, "If it's an inequality, then you can write four statements. If it's equal, you can only write two." (Slovin, 2007)

Do you think this (true) episode is of a gifted class? If not, what does is suggest about young children's mathematical thinking? Do you think the context—thinking and talking about the length of sticks—contribute to these first graders' remarkable mathematical insights?

Measurement is an important real-world area of math. We use lengths consistently in our everyday lives. Further, as the introductory story shows, it can help develop other areas of mathematics, including reasoning and logic. Also, by its very nature it connects the two most critical domains of early mathematics, geometry and number.

Unfortunately, typical measurement instruction in the U.S. does not accomplish any of these goals. Many children measure in a rote fashion. In international comparisons, U.S. students' performance in measurement is very low. By understanding measurement learning trajectories, we can do better for children.

Learning Measurement

Measurement can be defined as the process of assigning a number to a magnitude of some attribute of an object, such as its length, relative to a unit. These attributes are *continuous quantities*. That is, up to this point we have talked about *discrete quantity*, a number of separate things that can be determined exactly by counting with whole numbers. Measurement involves *continuous quantities*—amounts that can always be divided in smaller amounts. So, we can count 4 apples exactly—that is a discrete quantity. We can add those to 5 different apples and know that the result is exactly 9 apples. However, the *weight* of those apples varies continuously, and scientific measurement with tools can give us only an approximate measure—to the nearest pound (or, better, kilogram) or the nearest 1/100th of a pound, but always with some error.

As in the domain of discrete number, research shows that even infants are sensitive to continuous quantities such as length. At 3 years of age, children know that if they have some clay and then are given more clay, they have more than they did before. However, they cannot reliably make judgments about which of two amounts of clay is more. For example, if one of two equal amounts is rolled into a long "snake," they will say that is "more clay."

Children also do not reliably differentiate between continuous and discrete quantity. For example, they may try to share equally by dividing the number of cookie pieces rather than the amount of the cookies. Or, to give someone with fewer pieces of cookie "more," they may simply break one of that person's pieces into two smaller pieces!

Despite such challenges, young children can be provided with appropriate measurement experiences. They discuss amounts in their everyday play. They are ready to learn to measure, connecting number to the quantity. In this chapter we discuss length. In the next chapter, we discuss other continuous quantities, such as area, volume, and angle size.

Length Measurement

Length is a characteristic of an object found by quantifying how far it is between the endpoints of the object. "Distance" is often used similarly to quantify how far it is between any two points in space. The discussion of the number line is critical here because this defines the number line used to measure length (see Chapter 4). Measuring length or distance consists of two aspects, identifying a unit of measure and *subdividing* (mentally and physically) the object by that unit, placing that unit end to end (*iterating*) alongside the object. Subdividing and unit iteration are complex mental accomplishments that are too often ignored in traditional measurement curriculum materials and instruction. Therefore, many researchers go beyond the physical act of measuring to investigate children's understandings of measuring as covering space and quantifying that covering.

We discuss length in the following three sections. First, we identify several key concepts that underlie measuring (Clements & Stephan, 2004; Stephan & Clements, 2003). Second, we discuss early development of some of these concepts. Third, we describe research-based instructional approaches that were designed to help children develop the concepts and skills of length measurement.

Concepts in Linear Measurement

Measuring is a difficult *skill*, but it also involves many *concepts*. Foundational concepts include understanding of the attribute, conservation, transitivity, equal partitioning, iteration of a standard unit, accumulation of distance, origin, and relation to number.

Understanding of the attribute of length includes understanding that lengths span fixed distances.

Conservation of length includes understanding that as a rigid object is moved, its length does not change.

Transitivity is the understanding that if the length of a red pencil is greater than the length of a blue pencil and the length of the blue pencil is greater than that of the black pencil, then the red pencil is longer than the black pencil. A child with this understanding can use a third object to compare the lengths of two other objects.

Equal partitioning is the mental activity of slicing up an object into the same-sized units. This idea is not obvious to children. It involves mentally seeing the object as something that can be partitioned (or "cut up") into smaller lengths before even physically measuring. Some children who do *not* yet have this competence, for instance, may understand "5" as a single mark on a ruler, rather than as a length that is cut into five equal-sized units.

Units and unit iteration. Unit iteration is the ability to think of the length of a small unit such as a block as *part* of the length of the object being measured and count how many times you can place the length of the smaller block repeatedly, without gaps or overlaps, along the length of the larger object. Young children do not always see the need for equal partitioning and thus the use of *identical* units.

Accumulation of distance and additivity. Accumulation of distance is the understanding that, as you iterate a unit, the counting word represents the length covered by all units. Additivity is the idea lengths can be put together (composed) and taken apart.

Origin is the notion that any point on a ratio scale can be used as the origin. Young children who lack this understanding often begin a measurement with "1" instead of zero.

Relation between number and measurement. Children must understand of the items they are counting to measure continuous units. They make measurement judgments based upon counting ideas, often based on experiences counting discrete objects. For example, Inhelder and Piaget showed children two rows of matches. The matches in each row were of different lengths, but there was a different number of matches in each so that the rows were the same length (see Figure 10.1). Although, from the adult perspective, the lengths of the rows were the same, many children argued that the row with six matches was longer because it had more matches. They counted *discrete* quantities, but in measurement of *continuous* quantities, the size of the unit must be considered. Children must learn that the larger the unit, the fewer number of units in a given measure, that is, the inverse relation between the size of the unit and the number of those units.

Early Development of Length Measurement Concepts

Even children as young as 1 year old can make simple judgments of length. However, even many primary grade children do not yet explicitly conserve length or use transitive reasoning. As was the case with number, however, such logical ideas appear to be important for understanding some ideas, but their lack does not prohibit learning of beginning ideas. For example, students who conserve are more likely to understand the idea we just discussed, the inverse relation between the size of the unit and the number of those units. However, with high-quality education experience, even some preschoolers understand the inverse relation, so conservation may not be a rigid prerequisite, just a "supportive" idea. In a similar vein, children who conserve are more likely to understand the need to use equal length units when measuring. All in all, though, children can learn many ideas about comparing continuous quantities and measuring before they conserve.

This learning, however, is challenging and occurs over many years. The learning trajectory at the end of this chapter describes the levels of thinking that develop. Here we only briefly describe some common misconceptions and difficulties children have:

- To determine which of two objects is "longer," children may compare the objects at one end only.
- Children may leave gaps between units or overlap units when measuring.
- As old as 5 or 6 years, children may write numerals haphazardly to make a "ruler," paying little attention to the size of the spaces.
- Children may begin measuring at "1" rather than "0" or measure from the wrong end of the ruler.

Figure 10.1 An experiment to see if children focus more on discrete or continuous units.

- Children may mistakenly think of marks on a ruler or heel-to-toe steps not as covering space but just a "point" that is counted.
- Some children find it necessary to iterate the unit until it "fills up" the length of the object and will not extend the unit past the endpoint of the object they are measuring.
- Many children do not understand that units must be of equal size (e.g., measuring one length with paper clips of different sizes).
- Similarly, children may combine units of different size (e.g., 3 feet and 2 inches is "5 long").

Experience and Education

Young children naturally encounter and discuss quantities in their play (Ginsburg, Inoue, & Seo, 1999). Simply using labels such as "Daddy/Mommy/ Baby" and "big/little/tiny" helps children as young as 3 years of age to become aware of size and to develop seriation abilities.

Traditionally, the goal of measurement instruction has been to help children learn the skills necessary to use a conventional ruler. In contrast, research and recent curriculum projects suggest that, in addition to such skills, developing the conceptual *foundation* for such skills is critical to develop both understanding and procedures.

Many suggest an instructional sequence in which children compare lengths, measure with non-standard units to see the need for standardization, incorporate the use of manipulative standard units, and measure with a ruler. For example, children might pace from one point to another. As they discuss their strategies, ideas concerning iterating units and using equal-length units emerge. Children progress from counting paces to constructing a unit of units, such as a "footstrip" consisting of traces of their feet glued to a roll of adding-machine tape. Children may then confront the idea of expressing their result in different-sized units (e.g., 15 paces or 3 footstrips each of which has 5 paces). They also discuss how to deal with leftover space, to count it as a whole unit or as part of a unit. Measuring with units of units helps children think about length as a composition of these units. Furthermore, it provided the basis for constructing rulers.

However, several studies suggest that early experience measuring with several different units may be the *wrong* thing to do. Until they understand measurement better, using different arbitrary units often confuses children. If they do not understand measurement well, or the role of *equal-length* units, switching units frequently—even if the *intent* is to show the need for *standard* units—may send the wrong message—that any combination of any lengths-as-"units" is as good as any other. In contrast, measuring with standard units—even on rulers—is less demanding and is often more interesting and meaningful for young children. Consistent use of these units may develop a model and a context for children's construction of the *idea* of and *need* for equal-length units, as well as the wider notion of what measurement is all about. Later, after they understand the idea of unit and the need for units to be equal in size (otherwise, they are not units!), different units can be used to emphasize the need for *standard* equal-length units (centimeters or inches).

We suggest a sequence of instruction based on recent research (see the companion volume). With the youngest children, listen carefully to see how they are interpreting and using language (e.g., "length" as distance between endpoints or as "one end sticking out"). Also *use* language to distinguish counting-based terms, such as "a toy" or "two trucks," and measurement-based terms, such as "some sand" or "longer."

Once they understand these concepts, give children a variety of experiences comparing the length of objects. Once they can line up endpoints, children might use cut pieces of string to find all the objects in the classroom the same length as, shorter than, or longer than the height of their seat. Ideas of transitivity should be explicitly discussed.

Next, engage children in experiences that allow them to connect number to length. Provide children with both conventional rulers and manipulative units using standard units of length, such as edges of centimeter cubes, specifically labeled "length units." As they explore with these tools, discuss the ideas of length-unit iteration (not leaving space between successive length units, for example), correct alignment (with a ruler) and the zero-point concept. Having children draw, cut out, and use their own rulers can be used to highlight these ideas.

In all activities, focus on the meaning that the numerals on the ruler have for children, such as enumerating lengths rather than discrete numbers. In other words, classroom discussions should focus on "What are you counting?" with the answer in "length units." Given that counting discrete items often correctly teaches children that the size of the objects does not matter (i.e., for counting discrete objects), plan experiences and reflections on the nature of properties of the length-unit in various discrete counting and measurement contexts. Comparing results of measuring the same object with manipulatives and with rulers and using manipulative length units to make their own rulers helps children connect their experiences and ideas. In second or third grade, teachers might introduce the need for standard length units and the relation between the size and number of length units. The relationship between the size and number of length units, the need for standardization of length units, and additional measuring devices can be explored at this time. The use of *multiple nonstandard* length units could be helpful *at this point*. Instruction focusing on children's interpretations of their measuring activity can enable children to use flexible starting points on a ruler to indicate measures successfully. Without such attention, children often just read off whatever ruler number aligns with the end of the object into the intermediate grades.

Children must eventually learn to subdivide length units. Making one's own ruler and marking halves and other partitions of the unit may be helpful in this regard. Children could fold a unit into halves, mark the fold as a half, and then continue to do so, to build fourths and eighths.

Computer experiences also can help children link number and geometry in measurement activities and build measurement sense. Turtle geometry provides both motivation and meaning for many length measurement activities. This illustrates an important general guideline: Children should use measurement as a means for achieving a goal not as an end in itself only. Note that even young children can abstract and generalize measurement ideas working with computers if the interface is appropriate and activities well planned. Giving the turtle directions such as forward 10 steps, right turn 90°, forward 5 steps, they learn both length and turn and angle concepts. In Figure 10.2, children have to "finish the picture" but figuring out the missing measures (more challenging examples are shown in the learning trajectory at the end of the chapter).

Whatever the specific instructional approach taken, research has four general implications, with the first the most extensive. First, teach measurement as more than a simple skill—measurement is a complex combination of concepts and skills that develops over years. Understand the foundational concepts of measurement so that you will be better able to interpret children's understanding and ask questions that will lead them to construct these ideas. For example, when children count as they measure, focus children's conversations on that to *what* they are counting—not "points" but equal-sized units of length. That is, if a child iterates a unit five times, the "five" represents five units of length. For some students "five" signifies the hash mark next to the numeral five instead of the amount of space covered by five units. In this way, the marks on a ruler "mask" the intended

Figure 10.2 "Missing measure" problem with the Logo Turtle.

conceptual understanding involved in measurement. Children need to understand what they are measuring and why a unit on a ruler is numbered at its end, as well as the full suite of principles. Many children see no problem mixing units (e.g., using both paper clips and pen tops) or using different-sized units (e.g., small and large paper clips) as long as they covered the entire length of the object in some way (Clements, Battista, & Sarama, 1998; Lehrer, 2003). Both research with children and interviews with teachers support the claims that (a) the principles of measurement are difficult for children, (b) they require more attention in school than they are usually given, (c) time needs first to be spent in informal measurement, where use of measurement principles is evident, and (d) transition from informal to formal measurement needs much more time and care, with instruction in formal measure always returning to basic principles (cf. Irwin, Vistro-Yu, & Ell, 2004).

Eventually, children need to create an abstract unit of length (Clements, Battista, Sarama, Swaminathan, & McMillen, 1997; Steffe, 1991). This is not a static image but rather an interiorization of the process of moving (visually or physically) along an object, segmenting it, and counting the segments. When consecutive units are considered a unitary object, the children have constructed a "conceptual ruler" that can be projected onto unsegmented objects (Steffe, 1991). In addition, the U.S. mathematics curriculum does not adequately address the notion of unit. And measurement is a fruitful domain in which to turn attention away from separate objects and toward the unit we are counting (cf. Sophian, 2002).

Second, use initial informal activities to establish the attribute of length and develop concepts such as "longer," "shorter," and "equal in length" and strategies such as direct comparison. Third, encourage children to solve real measurement problems, and, in so doing, to build and iterate units, as well as units of units.

Fourth, help children closely connect the use of manipulative units and rulers. When conducted in this way, measurement tools and procedures become tools for mathematics and tools for thinking about mathematics (Clements, 1999c; Miller, 1984, 1989). Well before first grade, children have begun the journey toward that end.

Learning Trajectory for Length Measurement

The importance of *goals* for length measurement is shown by their frequent appearance in NCTM's *Curriculum Focal Points* as shown in Figure 10.3. Accepting those goals, Table 10.1 provides the two additional components of the learning trajectory, the developmental progression and the instructional tasks.

Pre-K

Measurement: Identifying measurable attributes and comparing objects by using these attributes

Children identify objects as "the same" or "different," and then "more" or "less," on the basis of attributes that they can measure. They identify measurable attributes such as length and weight and solve problems by making direct comparisons of objects on the basis of those attributes.

Kindergarten

Measurement: Ordering objects by measurable attributes

Children use measurable attributes, such as length or weight, to solve problems by comparing and ordering objects. They compare the lengths of two objects both directly (by comparing them with each other) and indirectly (by comparing both with a third object), and they order several objects according to length.

Grade 1

Connections: Measurement and Data Analysis

Children strengthen their sense of number by solving problems involving measurements and data. Measuring by laying multiple copies of a unit end to end and then counting the units by using groups of tens and ones supports children's understanding of number lines and number relationships. Representing measurements and discrete data in picture and bar graphs involves counting and comparisons that provide another meaningful connection to number relationships.

Grade 2

Measurement: Developing an understanding of linear measurement and facility in measuring lengths

Children develop an understanding of the meaning and processes of measurement, including such underlying concepts as partitioning (the mental activity of slicing the length of an object into equal-sized units) and transitivity (e.g., if object A is longer than object B and object B is longer than object C, then object A is longer than object C). They understand linear measure as an iteration of units and use rulers and other measurement tools with that understanding. They understand the need for equal-length units, the use of standard units of measure (centimeter and inch), and the inverse relationship between the size of a unit and the number of units used in a particular measurement (i.e., children recognize that the smaller the unit, the more iterations they need to cover a given length).

Figure 10.3 Curriculum focal points for length measurement.

Table 10.1 A Learning Trajectory for Length Measurement.

Age (years)	Developmental Progression	Instructional Tasks
2	**Pre-Length Quantity Recognizer** Does not identify length as attribute. "This is long. Everything straight is long. If it's not straight, it can't be long."	Children intuitively compare, order, and build with many types of materials, and increasingly learn vocabulary for specific dimensions.
3	**Length Quantity Recognizer** Identifies length/distance as attribute. May understand length as an absolute descriptor (e.g., all adults are tall), but not as a comparative (e.g., one person is taller than another). "I'm tall, see?" May compare non-corresponding parts of shape in determining side length.	Teachers listen for and extend conversations about things that are "long," "tall," "high," and so forth.
4	**Length Direct Comparer** Physically aligns two objects to determine which is longer or if they are the same length.	In many everyday situations, children compare heights and other lengths directly (who has the tallest tower, the longest clay snake, etc.). *Continued Overleaf*

Age (years)	Developmental Progression	Instructional Tasks

Stands two sticks up next to each other on a table and says, "This one's bigger."

In "As Long As My Arm," children cut a ribbon the length of their arms and find things in the classroom that are the same length.

In "Comparisons," children simply click on the object that is longer (or wider, etc.).

In "Compare Lengths," teachers encourage children to compare lengths throughout the day, such as the lengths of block towers or roads, heights of furniture, and so forth.

In "Line Up By Height," children order themselves (with teacher's assistance) by height in groups of 5 during transitions.

Indirect Length Comparer
Compares the length of two objects by representing them with a third object.

Compares length of two objects with a piece of string.

When asked to measure, may assign a length by guessing or moving along a length while counting (without equal-length units).

Moves finger along a line segment, saying 10, 20, 30, 31, 32.

May be able to measure with a ruler, but often lacks understanding or skill (e.g., ignores starting point).

Measures two objects with a ruler to check if they are the same length, but does not accurately set the "zero point" for one of the items.

Children solve everyday tasks that require indirect comparison, such as whether a doorway is wide enough for a table to go through.

Children often *cover* the objects to be compared, so that indirect comparison is actually not possible. Give them a task with objects such as felt strips so that, if they cover them with the third object such as a (wider) strip of paper (and therefore have to visually guess) they can be encouraged to then directly compare them. If they are not correct, ask them how they could have used the paper to better compare. Model laying it next to the objects if necessary.

In "Deep Sea Compare," children move the coral to compare the lengths of two fish, then click on the longer fish.

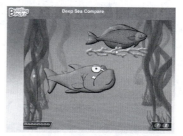

Children should connect their knowledge of number to length, as when they have to find the missing stair in "Build Stairs 3."

Age (years)	Developmental Progression	Instructional Tasks
5	**Serial Orderer to 6+** Orders lengths, marked in 1 to 6 units. (This develops in parallel with "End-to-End Length Measurer".) Given towers of cubes, puts in order, 1 to 6.	In "What's the Missing Step?" Children see stairs made from connecting cubes from 1 to 6. They cover their eyes and the teacher hides one step. They uncover their eyes and identify the missing step, telling how they knew. In a connection to number, "X-Ray Vision 1," children place Counting Cards, 1 to 6 or more, in order, face down. Then they take turns pointing to the cards, and using their "x-ray vision" to tell which card it is.
6	**End-to-End Length Measurer** Lays units end to end. May not recognize the need for equal-length units. The ability to apply resulting measures to comparison situations develops later in this level. (This develops in parallel with "Serial Orderer to 6+"). Lays 9 inch cubes in a line beside a book to measure how long it is.	"Length Riddles" ask questions such as, "You write with me and I am 7 cubes long. What am I?"  Measure with physical or drawn units. Focus on long, thin units such as toothpicks cut to 1 inch sections. Explicit emphasis should be given to the *linear nature* of the unit. That is, children should learn that, when measuring with, say, centimeter cubes, it is the *length of one edge* that is the *linear* unit—not the area of a face or volume of the cube. Measuring with rulers can begin. In this computer activity, "Reptile Ruler", children have to place a reptile on the ruler. The software snaps the reptile to a whole number, and gives helpful feedback if, for example, they do not align it to the zero point.  Making pictures of rulers and discussing key aspects of measurement that are or are not represented in these pictures can help children understand and apply these concepts. Children should also be asked to make a ruler using a particular unit, such as an inch or centimeter cube. They should learn to carefully mark each unit length and then add the correct numeral. Again, explicit emphasis should be given to the *linear nature* of the unit.
7	**Length Unit Relater and Repeater** Measures by repeated use of a unit (but initially may not be precise in such iterations). Relates size and number of units explicitly (but may not appreciate the need for identical units in every situation). Relates size and number of units explicitly.	Repeat "Length Riddles" (see above) but provide fewer cues (e.g., only the length) and only one unit per child so they have to iterate (repeatedly "lay down") a single unit to measure. "Mr. MixUp's Measuring Mess" can be used at several levels, adapted for the levels before and after this one. For example, have the puppet leave gaps between units used to measure an object (for the End-to-End Length Measurer level, gaps are between multiple units; for this level, gaps would be between iterations of one unit). Other errors include overlapping units and not aligning at the starting point (this is important with ruler use as well).

Continued Overleaf

Age (years)	Developmental Progression	Instructional Tasks
	"If you measure with centimeters instead of inches, you'll need more of them, because each one is smaller." Can add up two lengths to obtain the length of a whole. "This is 5 long and this one is 3 long, so they are 8 long together." Iterates a single unit to measure. Recognizes that different units will result in different measures and that identical units should be used, at least intuitively and/or in some situations. Uses rulers with minimal guidance. Measures a book's length accurately with a ruler.	Children may be able to *draw* a line to a given length before they measure objects accurately (Nührenbörger, 2001). Use line-drawing activities to emphasize how you start at the 0 (zero point) and discuss how, to measure objects, you have to align the object to that point. Similarly, explicitly discuss what the intervals and the number represent, connecting these to end-to-end length measuring with physical units. Children confront measurement with different units and discuss how many of each unit will fill a linear space. They make an explicit statement that the longer the unit the fewer are needed.
8	**Length Measurer** Considers the length of a bent path as the sum of its parts (not the distance between the endpoints). Measures, knowing need for identical units, relationship between different units, partitions of unit, zero point on rulers, and accumulation of distance. Begins to estimate. "I used a meter stick three times, then there was a little left over. So, I lined it up from 0 and found 14 centimeters. So, it's 3 meters, 14 centimeters in all."	Children should be able to use a physical unit and a ruler to measure line segments and objects that require both an iteration and subdivision of the unit. In learning to subdivide units, children may fold a unit into halves, mark the fold as a half, and then continue to do so, to build fourths and eighths. Children create units of units, such as a "footstrip" consisting of traces of their feet glued to a roll of adding-machine tape. They measure in different-sized units (e.g., 15 paces or 3 footstrips each of which has 5 paces) and accurately relate these units. They also discuss how to deal with leftover space, to count it as a whole unit or as part of a unit.
	Conceptual Ruler Measurer Possesses an "internal" measurement tool. Mentally moves along an object, segmenting it, and counting the segments. Operates arithmetically on measures ("connected lengths"). Estimates with accuracy. "I imagine 1 meter stick after another along the edge of the room. That's how I estimated the room's length is 9 meters."	In "Missing Measures," students have to figure out the measures of figures using given measures. This is an excellent activity to conduct on the computer using Logo's turtle graphics. 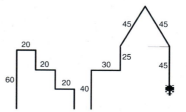 Children learn explicit strategies for estimating lengths, including developing benchmarks for units (e.g., an inch-long piece of gum) and composite units (e.g., a 6-inch dollar bill) and mentally iterating those units.

Final Words

This chapter addressed the learning and teaching of length measurement. Chapter 11 addresses other geometric attributes we need to measure, including area, volume, and angle.

11

Geometric Measurement
Area, Volume, and Angle

I had a student who basically understood the difference between area and perimeter. I drew this rectangle on a grid. To figure the area, she counted down like this (Figure 11.1a), then she counted across like this (11.1b). Then she multiplied three times four and got twelve. So, I asked her what the perimeter was. She said it was "the squares around the outside." She counted like this (11.1c). She understood the perimeter, she just counted wrong. She was always off by four.

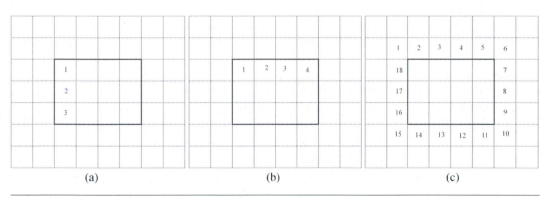

(a)	(b)	(c)

Figure 11.1 A student works with a perimeter problem.

Do you agree with this teacher? Does the student understand area and perimeter and distinguish between them? What would you have asked the student to find out for sure?

Area Measurement

Area is an amount of two-dimensional surface that is contained within a boundary. Area is complex, and children develop area concepts over time. Sensitivity to area is present in the first year of life, as is sensitivity to number. However, infants' approximate number sense is more accurate than their corresponding sense of area. So, even infants find area challenging!

Area understandings do not develop well in typical U.S. instruction and have not for a long time. Young children show little explicit understanding of measurement. Primary graders, asked how much space a square would cover, used a ruler (once) to measure. Even with manipulatives, many measured a length of a side of a square, then moved the ruler to a parallel position slightly toward the opposite side, and, repeating this process, adding the values of the lengths (Lehrer, Jenkins et al., 1998). Limitations in knowledge are also shown by preservice teachers, as the opening story illustrates.

To learn area measurement, children must develop a notion of what area is, as well as the understanding that decomposing and rearranging shapes does not affect their area. Later, children can develop the ability to build an understanding of two-dimensional arrays and then to interpret two lengths as measures of the dimensions of those arrays. Without such understandings and abilities, older students often learn a rule, such as multiplying two lengths, without understanding area concepts. Although area measurement is typically emphasized in the elementary grades, the literature suggests that there are some less formal aspects of area measurement that can be introduced in earlier years.

Concepts of Area Measurement

Understanding of area measurement involves learning and coordinating many ideas. Many of these ideas, such as transitivity and relation between number and measurement, are similar to those involved in length measurement. Other foundational concepts follow.

Understanding the attribute of area involves giving a quantitative meaning to the amount of 2D space, or surface. Children's first awareness of area can be seen in informal observations, such as when a child asks for more pieces of colored paper to cover their table. One way to intentionally assess children's understanding of area as an attribute is through comparison tasks. Preschoolers may compare the areas of two shapes by comparing only the length of their sides. With age or good experience, they move valid strategies, such as one shape on top of the other.

To measure, a unit must be established. This brings us to the following foundational concepts.

Equal partitioning is the mental act of "cutting" two-dimensional space into parts of equal area (usually congruent). Teachers often assume that "multiplying length times width" is the goal for understanding area. However, young children often cannot partition and conserve area, and use counting as a basis for comparing. For example, when it was determined that one share of pieces of paper cookie was too little, preschoolers cut one of that share's pieces into two and handed them both back, apparently believing that that share was now "more" (Miller, 1984). These children may not understand any foundational concept for area; the point here is that, eventually, children must learn the concept of partitioning surfaces into equal units of area.

Units and unit iteration. As with length measurement, children often cover space, but do not initially do so without gaps or overlapping and tend to keep all manipulatives inside the surface, refusing to extend units beyond a boundary, even when subdivisions of the unit are necessary (e.g. using square units to measure a circle's area). They prefer units that physically resemble the region they are covering; for example, choosing bricks to cover a rectangular region and beans to cover an outline of their hands. They also mix shapes of different shape (and areas), such as rectangular and triangular, to cover the same region and accept a measure of "7" even if the seven covering shapes were of different sizes. These concepts have to be developed before they can use iteration of equal units to measure area with understanding. Once these problems have been solved, students need to structure two-dimensional space into an organized array of units to achieve multiplicative thinking in determining area.

Accumulation and additivity. Accumulation and additivity of area operate similarly as they do in length. Primary grade students can learn that shapes can be decomposed and composed into regions of the same area.

Structuring space. Children need to *structure an array* to understand area as truly two-dimensional. That is, they need to understand how a surface can be tiled with squares that line up in rows and columns. Although this is taken as "obvious" by most adults, most primary grade students have not yet built up this understanding. For example, consider the levels of thinking portrayed by different children as they attempted to complete a drawing of an array of squares, given one column and row, as illustrated in Figure 11.2) (discussed in detail in the companion book). At the lowest level of thinking, children see shapes inside the rectangle, but the entire space is not covered. Only at the later levels do all the squares align vertically and horizontally, as the students learn to compose two-dimensional shapes in terms of rows and columns of squares.

Conservation. Similar to linear measurement, conservation of area is an important idea. Students have difficulty accepting that, when they cut a given region and rearrange its parts to form another shape, the area remains the same.

Experience and Education

Typical U.S. instruction does not build area concepts and skills well. One group of children were followed for several years (Lehrer, Jenkins et al., 1998). They improved in space-filling and additive composition by grade 4, but not in other competencies, such as distinguishing area and length, using identical area-units, and finding measures of irregular shapes.

In comparison, research-based activities taught second graders a wide range of area concepts and skills (Lehrer, Jacobson et al., 1998). The teacher presented rectangles (1×12, 2×6, 4×3) and asked which covers the most space. After disagreeing initially, the students transformed the shapes by folding and matching and came to agreement that these rectangles covered the same amount of space. Folding the 4 by 3 rectangle along each dimension led to the recognition that the rectangle—and ultimately all three—could be decomposed into 12 squares (intentionally, these were the same as the unit squares in previous quilting activities). Thus, children moved from decomposition to measurement using area-units.

Next, the teacher asked students to compare the areas of "hand prints," intending children to measure with squares in a counterintuitive context. Children tried superimposition first and then dismissed that strategy. Beans were used as the area-unit, but were rejected as having inadequate

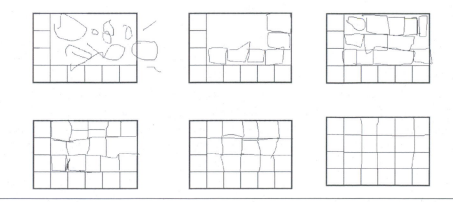

Figure 11.2 Levels of thinking for spatial structuring of two-dimensional space.

space-filling properties (they "left cracks"). The teacher introduced grid paper. The children initially resisted using this tool, probably because they wanted units whose shape was more consistent with the shape of the hands. Eventually, however, the grid paper was adopted by the children. They created a notional system in which fractions of a unit were color-coded for the same denomination (e.g., $\frac{1}{3}$ and $\frac{2}{3}$ were the same color, and then could be combined into a single unit easily). Thus, they learned about space filling, the irrelevance of the resemblance of the unit shape and the object to be measured, notation, and non-integer measures.

The final task was to compare the area of zoo cages, given shapes (some rectangular, other composites) and their dimensions, but no internal demarcations (e.g., no grid paper). Children learned to build a multiplicative understanding of area. These children displayed substantial learning of all aspects of area measurement. Starting with approximately the same knowledge of measurement in second grade as the longitudinal children (Lehrer, Jenkins et al., 1998), they surpassed, by the end of second grade, the performance of the longitudinal children, even when the latter were in their fourth grade year.

Thus, many more children could learn more about area, and learn formulas meaningfully, than presently do. Children should learn initial area concepts such as these, and also learn to structure arrays, laying the foundation for learning all area concepts and, eventually, learn to understand and perform accurate area measurement. As another approach, children could compare regions directly to see which covers more surface. Such enjoyable activities as paper folding, or origami, encourage the more sophisticated strategy of superposition—placing one shape on top of the other.

In meaningful contexts, have children explore and discuss the consequences of folding or rearranging pieces to establish that one region, cut and reassembled, covers the same space (conservation of area). Then challenge children to tile a region with a two-dimensional unit of choice and, in the process, discuss issues of leftover spaces, overlapping units, and precision. Guide discussion of these ideas to lead children to mentally partition a region into subregions that can be counted. Counting equal area-units will move the discussion to area measurement itself. Help children realize that there are to be no gaps or overlapping and that the entire region should be covered.

Ensure children learn how to structure arrays. Playing with structured materials such as unit blocks, pattern blocks, and tiles can lay the groundwork for this understanding. Building on these informal experiences, children can learn to understand arrays and area explicitly in the primary grades.

In summary, the too–frequent practice of simple counting of units to find area (achievable by preschoolers) leading directly to teaching formulas is a recipe for disaster for many children (Lehrer, 2003). A more successful approach is building upon young children's initial spatial intuitions and appreciating the need for children to construct the idea of measurement units (including development of a measurement sense for standard units; for example, finding common objects in the environment that have a unit measure); experience covering quantities with appropriate measurement units and counting those units; and spatially structure the object they are to measure (e.g., linking counting by groups to the structure of rectangular arrays; building two-dimensional concepts), thus to build a firm foundation for formulas.

The long developmental process usually only begins in the years before first grade. However, we should also appreciate the importance of these early conceptualizations. For example, 3- and 4-year-olds can intuitively compare areas in some contexts.

Learning Trajectory for Area Measurement

The goals for area and volume are not well established for the early years, but some experiences, especially basic concepts of covering and spatial structuring, are probably important. Table 11.1 provides the two additional components of the learning trajectory, the developmental progression and the instructional tasks.

Table 11.1 A Learning Trajectory for Area Measurement.

Age (years)	Developmental Progression	Instructional Tasks
0–3	*Area/Spatial Structuring:* **Pre-Area Quantity Recognizer**. Shows little specific concept of area. Uses side matching strategies in comparing areas (Silverman, York, & Zuidema, 1984). May draw approximation of circles or other figures in a rectangular tiling task (Mulligan, Prescott, Mitchelmore, & Outhred, 2005). Draws mostly closed shapes and lines with no indication of covering the specific region. 	Children intuitively compare, order, and build with many types of materials, and increasingly learn vocabulary for covering and amount of 2D space.
4	**Area Simple Comparer** May compare areas using only one side of figures, or estimating based on length plus (not times) width. Asked which rectangular "candy" is the "same amount" as a bar 4 cm by 5 cm, one child chooses the 4 by 8 by matching the sides of the same length. Another child chooses the 2 by 7, intuitively summing the side lengths. Measures area with ruler, measuring a length, then moving the ruler and measuring that length again, apparently treating length as a 2D space-filling attribute (Lehrer, Jenkins et al., 1998). *May* compare areas if task suggests superposition or unit iteration. Given square tiles and asked how many fit in a 4 by 5 area, child guesses 15. A child places one sheet of paper over the other and says, "This one."	Children are asked which piece of paper will let them paint the biggest picture.
	Area/Spatial Structuring: **Side-to-Side Area Measurer.** Covers a rectangular space with physical tiles. However, cannot organize, coordinate, and structure 2D space without such	Students' first experiences with area might include tiling a region with a two-dimensional unit of their choosing and, in the process, discuss issues of leftover spaces, overlapping units and precision. Discussions of these ideas lead students to mentally partition a region into subregions that can be counted.

Continued Overleaf

Age (years)	Developmental Progression	Instructional Tasks
	perceptual support. In drawing (or imagining and pointing to count), can represent only certain aspects of that structure, such as approximately rectangular shapes next to one another. Covers a region with physical tiles, and counts them by removing them one by one. Draws within the region in an attempt to cover the region. May fill only next to existing guides (e.g., sides of region). 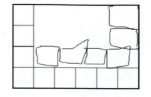 May attempt to fill region, but leave gaps and not align drawn shapes (or only align in one dimension). 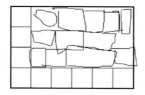	After experience quilting, children are given three rectangles (e.g., 1 × 12, 2 × 6, 4 × 3) and asked which covers the most space. They are guided to transform the shapes by folding and matching and ultimately transforming them into 12 1-unit squares.
5	*Area/Spatial Structuring:* **Primitive Coverer**. Draws a complete covering, but with some errors of alignment. Counts around the border, then unsystematically in the interiors, counting some twice and skipping others. 	Children cover a rectangle by tiling with physical square tiles and then learn the drawing convention to represent 2 contiguous edges with a single line. They discuss how to best represent a tiling that there must be no gaps.
	Area/Spatial Structuring: **Area Unit Relater and Repeater**. Draws as above. Also, counts correctly, aided by counting one row at a time and, often, by perceptual labeling.	Children discuss, learn, and practice systematic counting strategies for enumerating arrays.
6	*Area/Spatial Structuring:* **Partial Row Structurer**. Draws and counts some, but not all, rows as rows. May make several rows and then revert to making individual	Children use squared paper to measure areas to reinforce the use of the unit square, as well as non-integer values. Shown an array, children are asked how many in a row (5—use number that can easily be skip-counted). Sweep hand across the next row and repeat the question. Continue.

Age (years)	Developmental Progression	Instructional Tasks

squares, but aligns them in columns. Does not coordinate the width and height. In measurement contexts, does not necessarily use the dimensions of the rectangle to constrain the unit size.

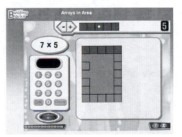

Fill in every greater numbers of missing sections. Use language such as "bringing down" or "up" a row.

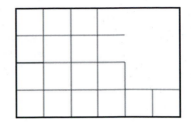

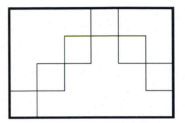

Children learn that the units must be aligned in an array with the same number of units in each row by representing their actions of fitting successive squares into the rectangle. Apart from the squares along the edges of the rectangle, each additional square must match two of its sides to sides of squares already drawn. A child who uses a ruler to draw lines across the rectangle has surely become aware of the alignment of the squares but may still be unaware of the congruence of the rows, so discussion and checking may be important.

In "Arrays in Area," children create a "row" the size they want, and repeatedly pull rows down to cover the area. They then put in their answer. This may help them solve the problems above.

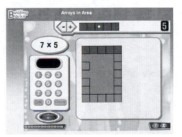

Continued Overeelaf

Age (years)	Developmental Progression	Instructional Tasks
7	*Area/Spatial Structuring:* **Row and Column Structurer.**	To progress, children need to move from local to global spatial structuring, coordinating their ideas and actions so see squares as part of rows and columns.

Area/Spatial Structuring: **Row and Column Structurer.**

Draws and counts rows as rows, drawing with parallel lines. Counts the number of squares by iterating the number in each row, either using physical objects or an estimate for the number of times to iterate. Those who count by ones usually do so with a systematic spatial strategy (e.g., by row).

If the task is to measure an unmarked rectangular region, measures one dimension to determine the size of the iterated squares and eventually measures both, to determine the number of rows needed in drawing. May not need to complete the drawing to determine the area by counting (most younger children) or computation (repeated addition or multiplication).

Area Conserver. Conserves area and reasons about additive composition of areas (e.g., how regions that look different can have the same area measure) and recognize need for space-filling in most contexts.

To progress, children need to move from local to global spatial structuring, coordinating their ideas and actions so see squares as part of rows and columns.

Children are encouraged to "fill in" open regions by mentally constructing a row, setting up a 1–1 correspondence with the indicated positions, and then repeating that row to fill the rectangular region.

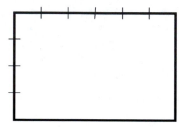

Children learn that the length of a line specifies the number of unit lengths that will fit along it. Given rectangles with no markings. Discuss that, provided you put the zero mark against one end of the line, the number you read off the other end gives the number of units that would fit along the line.

In "Arrays in Area," (see above) children are challenged to visualize their responses without covering the entire rectangle.

8 *Area/Spatial Structuring:* **Array Structurer.** With linear measures or other similar indications of the two dimensions, multiplicatively iterates squares in a row or column to determine the area.

Drawings are not necessary. In multiple contexts, children can compute the area from the length and width of rectangles *and* explain how that multiplication creates a measure of area.

Give children two rectangles (later, shapes made from several rectangles) and ask them how much more space is in one than the other.

Volume

Volume introduces even more complexity. First, the third dimension presents a significant challenge to students' spatial structuring, but the very nature of fluid materials that are measured with volume presents another complexity. This leads to two ways to physically measure volume, illustrated by "packing" a space such as a three-dimensional array with cubic units and "filling" a three-dimensional space with iterations of a fluid unit that takes the shape of the container. Filling is easier for children, about the same difficulty as measuring length. At first this might seem surprising, but we can see why, especially in the situation of filling a cylindrical jar in which the (linear) height corresponds with the volume.

On the other hand, "packing" volume is more difficult than length and area but also leads to more sophisticated understandings and to formulas for volume. Preschoolers may learn that fewer large objects will fit in a container than smaller objects. However, to understand packing volume, they have to understand spatial structuring in three dimensions. For example, understanding the spatial structure of one "layer" of a cube building is similar to understanding the spatial structure of the area of a rectangle. With many layers, the situation is complex, especially as some objects in a 3D array are "inside" and therefore hidden from view. Many younger students count only the faces of the cubes, often resulting in counting some cubes, such as those at the corners, multiple times and not counting cubes in the interior. Only a fifth of third graders in one study understood arrays of cubes as consisting of rows and columns in each of several layers.

Experience and Education

As with length and area, how students represent volume influences how they think of structuring volume. For example, compared to only a fifth of students without focused work on spatial structuring, *all* third graders with a wide range of experiences and representations of volume successfully structured space as a three-dimensional array (Lehrer, Strom, & Confrey, 2002). Most even developed the conception of volume as the product of the *area* (i.e., length times width) and the height. One third grader, for example, used squared grid paper to estimate the area of the base of a cylinder, then found the volume by multiplying this estimate by the height of the cylinder "to draw it [the area of the base] through how tall it is." This indicates that a developmental progression for spatial structuring, including packing volume, could reasonably be far more progressive than some cross-sectional studies of students in typical U.S. instructional sequences would indicate.

Learning Trajectory for Volume Measurement

Table 11.2 provides the two additional components of the learning trajectory, the developmental progression and the instructional tasks.

Table 11.2 A Learning Trajectory for Volume Measurement.

Age (years)	Developmental Progression	Instructional Tasks
0–3	*Volume/Capacity:* **Volume Quantity Recognizer.** Identifies capacity or volume as attribute. Says, "This box holds a lot of blocks!"	Teachers listen for and extend conversations about things that hold a lot (objects, sand, water).

Continued Overleaf

Age (years)	Developmental Progression	Instructional Tasks
4	**Capacity Direct Comparer.** Can compare two containers. Pours one container into another to see which holds more.	In "Compare Capacities," children compare how much sand or water about eight containers will hold. Ask children to show you which holds more and how they knew. Eventually, ask which holds the most.
5	**Capacity Indirect Comparer.** Can compare two containers using a third container and transitive reasoning. Pours one container into two others, concluding that one holds less because it overflows, and the other is not fully filled.	Ask children to show you which of two containers holds more when they use a third container to fill each of the others. Discuss how they knew.
6	*Volume/Spatial Structuring:* **Primitive 3D Array Counter.** Partial understanding of cubes as filling a space. Initially, may count the *faces* of a cube building, possibly double-counting cubes at the corners and usually not counting internal cubes. Eventually counts one cube at a time in carefully structured and guided contexts, such as packing a small box with cubes.	Students use cubes to fill boxes constructed so a small number of cubes fit well. They eventually predict how many cubes they will need, fill the box, and count to check.
7	**Capacity Relater and Repeater.** Uses simple units to fill containers, with accurate counting. Fills a container by repeatedly filling a unit and counting how many. With teaching, understands that fewer larger than smaller objects or units will be needed to fill a given container.	In "Measure Capacities," provide three half-gallon containers labeled "A," "B," and "C" in three different colors, cut to hold two, four, and eight cups, a one-cup measuring cup, and water or sand. Ask children to find the one that holds only four cups. Help them to fill to the "level top" of the measuring cup.
7	*Volume/Spatial Structuring:* **Partial 3D Structurer.** Understands cubes as filling a space, but does not use layers or multiplicative thinking. Moves to more accurate counting strategies. Counts unsystematically, but attempts to account for internal cubes. Counts systematically, trying to account for outside and inside cubes. Counts the numbers of cubes in one row or column of a 3D structure and using skip-counting to get the total.	Students use cubes to fill boxes constructed so a small number of cubes fit well. They eventually predict how many cubes they will need, fill the box, and count to check.
8	*Area/Spatial Structuring:* **3D Row and Column Structurer.** Counts or computes (row by column) the number of cubes in one row, and then uses addition or skip-counting to determine the total. Computes (row times column) the number of cubes in one row, and then multiplies by the number of layers to determine the total.	Predict how many cubes will be needed to fill the box, then count and check. Students first get a net, or pattern (below on the left) and a picture.

Age (years)	Developmental Progression	Instructional Tasks
9	*Area/Spatial Structuring:* **3D Array Structurer**. With linear measures or other similar indications of the two dimensions, multiplicatively iterates squares in a row or column to determine the area. Constructions and drawings are not necessary. In multiple contexts, children can compute the volume of rectangular prisms from its dimensions *and* explain how multiplication creates a measure of volume.	Ask students how many cubes are needed to fill *only a picture* of a box such as that above, and then just the dimensions. Later, non-integer measures should be used.

Relationships Among Length, Area, and Volume

Research indicates that there is no strict developmental sequence for length, area, and volume, but overlapping progress, except in one sense. Spatial structuring appears to develop in order in one, then two, and three dimensions. So, it is reasonable to develop length first, emphasizing the iteration of a unit. Experiences with "filling" volume could be used as another domain in which to discuss the importance of basic measurement concepts (e.g., iterations of equal-size units). Informal experiences constructing arrays with concrete objects could develop spatial structuring of 2D space, on which area concepts could be built. Packing volume would follow. Throughout, teachers should explicitly discuss the similarities and differences in the unit structures of length, area, and volume measurement.

Angle and Turn Measure

Methods of measuring the size of angles are based on the division of a circle. As with length and area, children need to understand concepts such as equal partitioning and unit iteration to understand angle and turn measure. In addition, there are several unique challenges in the learning of angle measure. Mathematically, angle has been defined in distinct but related ways. For example, an angle can be considered the figure formed by two rays extending from the same point or as the amount of turning necessary to bring one line or plane into coincidence with or parallel to another. The former involves the composition of two components, or parts, of a geometric figure and the latter—the measurement of angle size that concerns us here—involves a *relationship* between two components. Therefore, both are geometric *properties* (see Chapter 8, p. 124) and both are difficult for students to learn. They are also difficult to relate to each other. Students in the early and elementary grades often form separate concepts of angles, such as angle-as-a-shape and angle-as-movement. They also hold separate notions for different turn contexts (e.g., unlimited rotation as a fan vs. a hinge) and for various "bends" in roads, pipe cleaners, or figures.

Children hold many misconceptions about angles and angle measure. For example, "straight" may mean "no bend" but also "not up and down" (vertical). Many children correctly compare angles if all the line segments are the same length (see #1 in Figure 11.3), but, when the length of the line segments are different (#2), only less than half of primary grade students do so. Instead, they base their judgments on the length of the segments or the distance between their endpoints.

Other misconceptions include children's belief that a right angle is an angle that points to the right or that two right angles in different orientations are not equal.

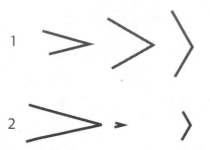

Figure 11.3 Angles with (1) the same and (2) different length line segments.

Experience and Education

The difficulties children encounter might imply that angle and turn measure need not be introduced to young children. However, there are valid reasons to include these as goals for early childhood mathematics education. First, children can and do compare angle and turn measures informally. Second, use of angle size, at least implicitly, is necessary to work with shapes; for example, children who distinguish a square from a non-square rhombus are recognizing angle size relationships, at least at an intuitive level. Third, angle measure plays a pivotal role in geometry throughout school, and laying the groundwork early is a sound curricular goal. Fourth, the research indicates that, although only a small percentage of students learn angles well through elementary school, young children *can* learn these concepts successfully.

Perhaps the most difficult step for students is to understand angle measure dynamically, as in turning. One useful instructional tool is the computer. Certain computer environments help children quantify angles and especially turns, attaching numbers to these quantities to achieve true measurement. Here we examine two types of computer environments. The first type is the computer manipulatives, perhaps the more appropriate of the two for younger children. For example, software can encourage children to use turn and flip tools meaningfully to make pictures and designs and to solve puzzles. Just using these tools helps children bring the concept of a turn to an explicit level of awareness (Sarama et al., 1996). For example, 4-year-old Leah first called the tool the "spin" tool, which made sense—she clicked it repeatedly, "spinning" the shape. Within one week, however, she called it the turn tool and used the left or right tool deliberately. Similarly, when a kindergarten boy worked off-computer, he quickly manipulated the pattern block pieces, resisting answering any questions as to his intent or his reasons. When he finally paused, a researcher asked him how he had made a particular piece fit. He struggled with the answer and then finally said that he "turned it." When working on-computer, he seemed aware of his actions, in that when asked how many times he turned a particular piece (in 30° increments), he correctly said, "Three," without hesitation (Sarama et al., 1996). A second computer environment is Logo's turtle geometry. Logo can also assist children in learning ideas of angle and turn measurement. A young children explained how he turned the turtle 45°: "I went 5, 10, 15, 20 . . . 45! [rotating her hand as she counted]. It's like a car speedometer. You go up by fives!" (Clements & Battista, 1991). This child mathematized turning: She applied a unit to an act of turning and used her counting abilities to determine a measurement.

Logo's "turtle" needs exact turn commands, such as "RT 90" for "turn right 90 degrees." *If* they work under the guidance of a teacher on worthwhile tasks, children can learn a lot about angle and turn measure by directing the Logo turtle. Discussions should focus on the difference between the angle of rotation and the angle formed as the turtle traced a path. For example, Figure 11.4 shows

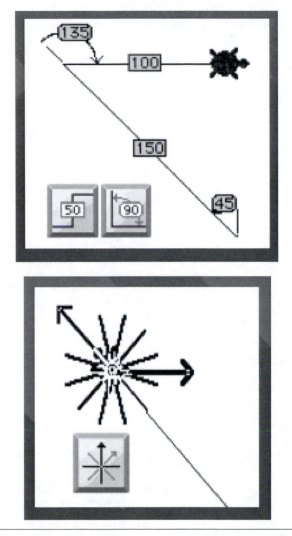

Figure 11.4 Turtle Math Tools: (a) "label lines" and "label turn" tools (inserts) and (b) "angle measure" tool.

several tools. The "Label Turns" tool shows the measure of each turn, reminding children that the command "RT 135" created an *external* angle of 135°, creating an *angle* of 45° (the *internal* angle formed by the two lines, 100 and 150 units long). Figure 11.4b shows a tool that allows children to measure a turn they desire. These tools were built into Turtle Math (Clements & Meredith, 1994), but teachers using any Logo, or turtle geometry environment, should ensure students understand the relationships among these ideas. Encourage children to turn their bodies and discuss their movements, then to visualize such movements mentally, using "benchmarks" such as 90° and 45°.

Learning Trajectory for Angle and Turn Measurement

To understand angles, children must understand the various aspects of the angle concept. They must overcome difficulties with orientation, discriminate angles as critical parts of geometric figures, and represent the idea of turns and their measure. They must learn to *connect* all these ideas. This is a difficult task that might best start early, as children deal with corners of figures, comparing angle size, and turns. A learning trajectory for angle measurement is shown in Table 11.3.

Table 11.3 Learning Trajectory for Angle (and Turn) Measurement.

Age (years)	Developmental Progression	Instructional Tasks
2–3	**Intuitive Angle Builder** Intuitively uses some angle measure notions in everyday settings, such as building with blocks. Places blocks parallel to one another and at right angles (with the perceptual support of the blocks themselves) to build a "road."	Block-building with structured materials (e.g., unit blocks). Everyday navigation.
4–5	**Implicit Angle User** Implicitly uses some angle notions, including parallelism and perpendicularity, in physical alignment tasks, construction with blocks, or other everyday contexts (Mitchelmore, 1989, 1992; Seo & Ginsburg, 2004). May identify corresponding angles of a pair of congruent triangles using physical models. Uses the word "angle" or other descriptive vocabulary to describe some of these situations. Moves a long unit block to be parallel with another blocks after adjusting the distance between them so as to accurately place perpendicular block across them, in anticipation of laying several other blocks perpendicularly across them.	Ask children who are building with blocks to describe why they placed blocks as they did, or challenge them to reroute a block "road," to help them reflect on parallelism, perpendicularly, and non-right angles. Use the term "angle" to describe a variety of contexts in which angle is used, from corners of shapes to bending wire, bends in a road, or ramps. Ask children to find and describe other things in the world that "have similar angles." Thus, children might relate a door opening to a scissors, a ramp made with blocks to a ladder against a wall, and so forth. The focus here should be on the size of the "opening" (for a scissors) or angle (to the horizontal, for a ramp).
6	**Angle Matcher** Matches angles concretely. Explicitly recognizes parallels from non-parallels in specific contexts (Mitchelmore, 1992). Sorts angles into "smaller" or "larger" (but may be misled by irrelevant features, such as length of line segments). Given several non-congruent triangles, finds pairs that have one angles that is the same measure, by laying the angle on top of one another.	Children use Shape Set to find shapes that have the same angles, even if the shapes are not congruent. Solve shape puzzles that require attention to angle size (i.e., Shape Composer level or above; see Chapter 9).
7	**Angle Size Comparer** Differentiates angle and angle size from shapes and contexts and compares angle sizes. Recognizes right angles, and then equal angles of other measures, in different orientations (Mitchelmore, 1989). Compares simple turns. (Note that without instruction, this and higher levels may not be achieved even by the end of the elementary grades.) "I put all the shapes that have right angles here, and all the ones that have bigger or smaller angles over there." Turns Logo turtle, using degree measurements.	Children use the Logo turtle to make or follow paths and construct shapes (Clements & Meredith, 1994). Similarly, talk about turns and their measures in a variety of movement contexts, such as taking walks and making maps. Relate a variety of angle size contexts to a common metaphor, such as a clock, noting the two sides of the angle (clock "hands"), the center of rotation, and the amount of turning from one side to the other. Talk about "foolers" in which an angle with a smaller measure is represented with longer line segments to address students' persistent *misconception* that the length of the segments, or the resulting length between the endpoints, is an appropriate indication of angle size.

Age (years)	Developmental Progression	Instructional Tasks
8+	**Angle Measurer** Understands angle and angle measure in both primary aspects and can represent multiple contexts in terms of the standard, generalizable concepts and procedures of angle and angle measure (e.g., two rays, the common endpoint, rotation of one ray to the other around that endpoint, and measure of that rotation).	Students calculate the measure (internal) of angles formed by the Logo turtle's turns (exterior angle). See *Angle Representer*, p. 145.

Final Words

Measurement is one of the principal real-world applications of mathematics. It also helps connect the two other critical realms of early mathematics, geometry and number. Chapter 12 also deals with content domains that are important in connecting mathematical ideas and in solving real-world problems. These include patterns, structures, and early algebraic processes, and data analysis.

12
Other Content Domains

What mathematics is shown in Figure 12.1?

Figure 12.1 What mathematics have these two preschoolers used?

NCTM's *Principles and Standards for School Mathematics* (2000) included five content domains for all grade bands: Number and Operations, Geometry, Measurement, Algebra, and Data Analysis and Probability. Previous chapters have treated the first three in depth. What of the last two? What role do they play?

Patterns and Structure (including algebraic thinking)

The breadth of ways the term "patterns" is used illustrates a main strength and weakness of the notion as a goal in mathematics. Consider some examples from other chapters:

- Perceptual patterns, such as subitized domino patterns, finger patterns, or auditory patterns (e.g., three beats) (see Chapter 2).
- Patterns in the number words of counting (Wu, 2007, see also Chapter 3).
- The "one-more" pattern of counting (Chapter 3), which also connects counting with arithmetic.
- Numerical patterns, such as a mental representation of 3 as a triangle; or a similar pattern of 5 that can be broken into 2 and 3 and then put them back together to make 5 again (see Chapters 2, 3, 5, and 6).
- Arithmetic patterns that are especially powerful and easy for children to see: doubles (3 + 3, 7 + 7), which allow access to combinations such as 7 + 8, and fives (6 made as 5 + 1, 7 as 5 + 2, etc.), which allow for decomposition into fives (see also Chapter 6, as well as other examples in Parker & Baldridge, 2004).
- Spatial patterns, such as the spatial pattern of squares (Chapter 8) or the composition of shapes (Chapter 9), including array structures (Chapter 11).

None of these examples of patterns in early mathematics illustrates the most typical practice of "doing patterns" in early childhood classrooms. Typical practice involves activities such as making paper chains that are "red, blue, red, blue . . ." and so forth. Such sequential repeated patterns may be useful, but educators should be aware of the *role* of patterns in mathematics and mathematics education and of how sequential repeated patterns such as the paper chains fit into (but certainly do not, alone, constitute) the large role of patterning and structure.

To begin, mathematician Lynne Steen referred to mathematics as the "science of patterns"—patterns in number and space (1988). The theory of mathematics, according to Steen, is built on relations among patterns and on applications derived from the fit between pattern and observations.

So, the concept of "pattern" goes far beyond sequential repeated patterns. *Patterning is the search for mathematical regularities and structures.* Identifying and applying patterns helps bring order, cohesion, and predictability to seemingly unorganized situations and allows you to make generalizations beyond the information in front of you. Although it can be viewed as a "content area," *patterning is more than a content area it is a process, a domain of study, and a habit of mind.* From this broad perspective, children begin this development from the first year of life, as previous chapters have shown. Here we limit ourselves mainly to sequential and other types of repeated patterns and their extension to algebraic thinking—the NCTM content domain most clearly linked to early work with patterns. But we should not forgot that this is just one small aspect of Steen's "science of patterns."

From the earliest years, children are sensitive to patterns—of actions, behaviors, visual displays, and so forth. An explicit understanding of patterns develops gradually during the early childhood years. For example, about ¾ of those entering school can copy a repeating pattern, but only ⅓ can extend or explain such patterns. Preschoolers can learn to copy simple patterns and, at least by kindergarten, children can learn to extend and create patterns. Further, children learn to recognize the relationship between different representations of the same pattern (e.g., between visual and motoric, or movement, patterns; red, blue, red, blue . . . and snap, clap, snap, clap . . .). This is a crucial step in using patterns to make generalizations and to reveal common underlying structures. In the early years of school, children benefit from learning to identify the core unit (e.g., AB) that either repeats (ABABAB) or "grows" (ABAABAAAB), and then use it to generate both these types of patterns. Little else is known, except that patterns are one of many elements of teaching visual literacy with positive long-term impact in the Agam program (Razel & Eylon, 1990).

Where is "algebra" in patterns? Having one thing stand for another is the beginnings of algebraic representation. Note that by the pre-K or kindergartner year, many children can name patterns with conventions such as "ABAB." This is potentially another step to algebraic thinking, as it involves using variable names (letters) to label or identify patterns that involve different physical embodiments. Such naming helps children recognize that mathematics focuses on underlying structure, not physical appearances. Further, making a one-to-one correspondence is a primitive version of the basic algebraic notion of mapping—like a function table. Perhaps most clear is that even preschoolers and kindergartners can make certain "early algebraic generalizations, such as "subtracting zero from any number gives that number," or that "subtracting a number from itself gives zero." Such algebraic generalizations can be further developed in the primary grades, although students usually become conscious of these only with explicit guidance from the teacher.

This body of research on young children's understanding of patterns may be used to establish developmentally appropriate learning trajectories for pattern instruction in early mathematics education, at least for simple sequential repeated patterns. The research is even thinner regarding patterning as a way of thinking. The next section includes some promising approaches.

Experience and Education

Approaches to teaching the most typical type of patterning in early childhood, sequential repeated patterns, have been documented in several curriculum projects in the U.S. (see Chapter 15). The *Building Blocks* learning trajectories for this type of pattern is presented in Table 12.1. These activities show that, in addition to placing shape or other objects in sequential patterns, young children can also engage in rhythmic and musical patterns. They can learn more complicated patterns than the simple ABABAB pattern. For example, they may begin with "clap, clap, slap; clap, clap slap. . . ." They can talk about this pattern, representing the pattern with words and other motions, so that "clap, clap slap . . ." is transformed to jump, jump, fall down; jump, jump, fall down . . . and soon symbolized as an AABAAB pattern. Several curricula have successfully taught such patterns to 4- to 5-year-olds.

Young children's play and informal activities can be effective vehicles for learning mathematical patterning in meaningful and motivating contexts. However, teachers need to understand how to take advantage of such opportunities. One teacher, for example, asked children to make clothing patterns for a paper doll. Unfortunately, her examples were colorful, but all had complex random designs that did not include patterns!

In another study, a teacher observed a child paint four iterations of a green, pink, and purple pattern core. The child said, "Look at my patterns." The teacher observed this and called out, "Looks like you are doing some lovely art work." She did not seem to be aware of the opportunity she had missed (Fox, 2005, p. 317). In another preschool, a child was working with a hammer and nails construction kit. Chelsea was tapping shapes on to the corkboard and described it to other children at the table. "It is a necklace with diamonds—diamond, funny shape, diamond, funny shape, diamond, funny shape." The teacher questioned Chelsea about her creation. After the teacher intervened, another child, Harriet, began to use the equipment to make a repeating pattern (yellow circle–green triangle). A second child, Emma, joined the table and created a necklace utilizing an ABBA pattern. Chelsea's explicit interest in mathematical patterning, and the teacher's involvement and intervention, encouraged other children to join her in creating patterns. This was useful mathematical patterning in a play-based context (p. 318).

Extending the conclusions of these research projects, we believe that teachers need to understand the learning trajectories of patterning in all its forms and the wider implications of patterning as a habit of mind. We agree that in patterning, as in all mathematical areas, there is a need to help teachers plan specific experiences and activities, capitalize on relevant child-initiated activities, and elicit and guide mathematically generative discussions in all settings.

Illustrating this approach, additional projects from Australia show the power of emphasizing a broad range of activities focusing on *mathematical pattern and structure*. The instructional activities developed students' visual memory as they observed, recalled and represented numerical and spatial structures in processes such as counting, partitioning, subitizing, grouping and unitizing (this implies that *many of the most important patterning activities in this book are in other chapters*, as the introduction to this chapter suggested). These activities were regularly repeated in varied form to encourage children to generalize. For example, children reproduced patterns, including sequential repeating patterns and simple grids and arrays of varying sizes (including triangular or square numbers). They explained why patterns are "the same" and described repeating patterns with ordinal numbers (e.g., "every third block is blue"). They reproduced grid patterns when part of the pattern was hidden, or from memory.

Thus, these "pattern and structure" activities included visual structures such as those used in subitizing (Chapter 2) and spatial structuring (Chapters 7 and 11); structuring linear space (Chapter 10) and the structure of numbers connected to these (Chapters 3 to 6). Thus, this view of pattern and structure includes, but goes far beyond, simple linear patterns, and connects seemingly separate areas of mathematics. *Children who do not develop this type of knowledge tend to make little progress in mathematics.*

Moving into the elementary school years, children benefit from describing patterns with numbers. Even sequential repeating patterns can be described as "two of something, then one of something else." The patterns of counting, arithmetic, spatial structuring, and so forth have been emphasized in other chapters. Here we re-emphasize that children should be helped to make and use arithmetic generalizations, such as the following:

- When you add zero to a number the sum is always that number.
- When you add one to a number the sum is always the next number in the counting sequence.
- When you add two numbers it does not matter which number "comes first."
- When you add three numbers it does not matter which two you add first.

For many, these are the first clear links among patterns, number, and algebra. One student's use of a strategy might prompt another student to ask why it would work, which would lead to discussions of general statements about a given operation. However, Carpenter and Levi found this did not occur regularly in first and second grade classrooms, so they used Bob Davis' activities from the Madison Project, in particular his activities involving true and false and open number sentences. For example, students were asked to verify the truth of "true/false number sentences" such as $22 - 12 = 10$ (true or false?), and others such as $7 + 8 = 16$, $67 + 54 = 571$. They also solved open number sentences of a variety of forms. The open number sentences involved single variables, such as $x + 58 = 84$, multiple variables such as $x + y = 12$, and repeated variables, such as $x + x = 48$. Certain cases were selected to prompt discussion of basic properties of numerical operations and relations; for example verifying the truth of $324 + 0 = 324$ led students to generalizations about zero (Note: when you say adding a zero to a number does not change that number, you must mean adding "just plain zero," not concatenating a zero, such as $10 \longrightarrow 100$ or adding numbers that include zero, such as $100 + 100$; Carpenter & Levi, 1999). Students also enjoyed and benefitted from creating and trading their own true/false number sentences. Another case is sentences in the form of

$15 + 16 = 15 + x$. This may prompt students to recognize they do not have to compute, and then to use more sophisticated strategies for problems such as $67 + 83 = x + 82$ (Carpenter, Franke, & Levi, 2003, pp. 47–57).

These researchers also indicated several practices to *avoid* (Carpenter et al., 2003). For example, avoid using the equal sign to list objects and numbers (e.g., John = 8, Marcie = 9 . . .). Do not use it to give a number in a collection (III = 3) or to indicate that the same number is in two collections. Finally, do not use it to represent strings of calculations, such as $20 + 30 = 50 + 7 = 57 + 8 = 65$. This last one is a common, but perhaps the most egregious case. It could be replaced with series of equations, if they are really needed, such as $20 + 30 = 50$; $50 + 7 = 57$; $57 + 8 = 65$.

There are a few more research-based instructional suggestions on the equal sign, which is often badly taught. One project introduces it *only* in the context of finding all the decompositions for a number, and they place that number (e.g., 5) first: $5 = 5 + 0$, $5 = 4 + 1$, $5 = 3 + 2$ (Fuson & Abrahamson, in press). Children then write equations chains in which they write a number in many varied ways (e.g., $9 = 8 + 1 = 23 - 14 = 109 - 100 = 1 + 1 + 1 + 1 + 5 = . . .$). Such work helps avoid limited conceptualizations.

Another study found that kindergartners and first graders knowledge could recognize legitimate number sentences, such as $3 + 2 = 5$, but only first graders could *produce* such sentences. However, they found it more difficult to recognize number sentences such as $8 = 12 - 4$. Thus, teachers need to provide a variety of examples for children, including having the operation on the right side and having multiple operations, such as $4 + 2 + 1 + 3 + 2 = 12$. In all such work, discuss the nature of addition and subtraction number sentences and the different symbols, the role they play, and their defining and non-defining properties. For example, students might eventually generalize to see not just that $3 + 2 = 5$ and $2 + 3 = 5$, but that $3 + 2 = 2 + 3$. Still, however, they might only see that the order of the numbers "does not matter"—without understanding that this is a property of *addition* (not pairs of numbers in general). Discussions can help them to understand the arithmetic operations as "things to think about" and to discuss their properties (see many examples in Kaput, Carraher, & Blanton, 2008).

Another study of third and fourth graders revealed that teaching the equal sign in equations *contrasted* with the greater than (>) and less than (<) signs helped these students understand the equal sign relational meaning (Hattikudur & Alibali, 2007). The students learned three signs in the same time that the comparison students learned just one.

A final study found that providing second graders with equations such as $2 + 5 + 1 = 3 + \_$ and giving them feedback improved their performance substantially. The type of tasks, non-symbolic, semi-symbolic, or symbolic, did not matter (Sherman, Bisanz, & Popescu, 2007). What probably *does* matter is whether students see such work and *all* arithmetic work as a *sense-making activity*. That is, asked to solve a problem like $8 + 4 = \square + 5$ students often put 12 in the box. Others include the 5 in their total, putting 17 in the box. Others create a running total by putting a 12 in the box and an "= 17" following the 5 (Franke, Carpenter, & Battey, 2008). As discussed, they see the equal sign as an instruction to compute, as "the answer is coming" sign. This is not its mathematical meaning.

Solutions are facilitated when one understands the semantics—the meaning of each symbol. For example, students might think as follows:

What I face is an equation, with a number I don't know. I am supposed to find the number in the box. The two sides of the equation must be equal. I do know how to find the sum on the left-hand side of the equation: $8 + 4 = 12$. So, I can rewrite the equation as

$$12 = \square + 5,$$

or maybe more comfortably as

$$\square + 5 = 12.$$

So, now I'm looking for the number that has the property that when I add 5 to it, I get 12. I know how to do that. The answer is 7, so 7 goes in the box. And, I can check: $8 + 4 = 12$ and $7 + 5 = 12$, so $8 + 4 = 7 + 5$. (Schoenfeld, 2008)

Such solutions depend on knowing the semantics of the equation. If students see these equations in terms of their meaning, they can make sense of them and solve them. Schoenfeld argues that every problem, even $3 + 2 = 5$, is related to meaning (a group of 5 is combined with a group of 2 . . .) and that the more it is explicitly connected to that meaning for students, the stronger will be both their arithmetic and early algebra competence.

This means that teaching computation without attention to relational and algebraic thinking erects a roadblock to students' later progress in math. Students must see all math as a search for patterns, structure, relationships, as a process of making and testing ideas, and, in general, making sense of quantitative and spatial situations (Schoenfeld, 2008). Only if they do so throughout their work with math will they be well prepared for later math, including algebra.

One last project is perhaps the most surprising. The Mathematics Enhancement Project in England has developed algebra activities for preschoolers. Consider the problem of solving two simultaneous linear equations $x + y = 4$ and $x = y$. In this project, 4- to 5-year-old children color in the outlines of snails following two rules: they have to color in four snails, and the number of brown snails must equal the number of yellow snails. The materials were developed by David Burghes based on the Hungary Mathematics Curriculum.

Readers interested in early algebra, especially for students in grades 2 through the intermediate grades, should consult the companion book. There they will find an extended discussion of several other projects with students across those grades.

Learning Trajectory for Pattern and Structure

NCTM's Curriculum Focal Points (NCTM, 2006) identify the following goals as relevant to patterns and algebraic thinking.

Pre-K includes one connection:

- *Algebra:* Children recognize and duplicate simple sequential patterns (e.g., square, circle, square, circle, square, circle, . . .).

K includes one connection:

- *Algebra:* Children identify, duplicate, and extend simple number patterns and sequential and growing patterns (e.g., patterns made with shapes) as preparation for creating rules that describe relationships.

First grade includes one focal point (on addition and subtraction; see Chapter 5) and two connections:

- *Number and Operations and Algebra:* Children use mathematical reasoning, including ideas such as commutativity and associativity and beginning ideas of tens and ones, to solve two-digit addition and subtraction problems with strategies that they understand and can explain. They solve both routine and nonroutine problems.
- *Algebra:* Through identifying, describing, and applying number patterns and properties in developing strategies for basic facts, children learn about other properties of numbers and operations, such as odd and even (e.g., "Even numbers of objects can be paired, with none left over"), and 0 as the identity element for addition.

Second grade includes one focal point (on addition and subtraction; see Chapter 5) and one connection:

- *Algebra:* Children use number patterns to extend their knowledge of properties of numbers and operations. For example, when skip-counting, they build foundations for understanding multiples and factors.

Thus, the early work with sequential patterns soon expands to growing patterns and arithmetical patterns.

A learning trajectory for patterns is presented in Table 12.1. As stated previously, this mostly concerns the simple, typical case of sequential repeated patterns. (Further, the sequence here comes mainly from the few studies on patterning with young children, mostly our *Building Blocks* and TRIAD projects.) This includes but a small portion of the learning about the processes of patterning and the concepts described by "pattern and structure."

Table 12.1 Learning Trajectory for Patterns and Structure.

Age (years)	Developmental Progression	Instructional Tasks
2	**Pre-Explicit Patterner** Detects and uses patterning implicitly, but may not recognize sequential linear patterns explicitly or accurately. Names a striped shirt with no repeating unit a "pattern."	Emphasize the patterns in children's songs, poems, and spontaneous movements, such as dancing. Work with manipulatives such as blocks, puzzles, manipulatives to order (e.g., simple materials such as pencils of different lengths or such commercial materials as those from the Montessori group) and discussions of regularities help children use and eventually recognize patterns.
3	**Pattern Recognizer** Recognizes a simple pattern. "I'm wearing a pattern" about a shirt with black, white, black white . . . stripes.	**Count and Move in Patterns** Spend only a few minutes counting with children in patterns of 2, or another appropriate even number; for example, "one, **two!** . . . three, **four!** . . . five, **six!** . . . ." For more fun, get a drum or use the corners of a wooden block to tap along with the counting, tapping harder for emphasis at each second beat. **Pattern Walk** Read the book, *I See Patterns.* Patterns in the world may be confusing because of all the irrelevant, distracting information available. The book will help explain and distinguish types of patterns. Then go on a pattern walk and find, discuss, photograph, and draw the patterns you see. **Clothes Patterns** Find repeating patterns in children's clothing colors. Encourage them to wear clothes with patterns and to discuss the patterns they wear to school.

Continued Overleaf

Age (years)	Developmental Progression	Instructional Tasks
4	**Pattern Fixer** Fills in missing element of pattern, first with ABAB patterns. Given objects in a row with one missing, ABAB_BAB, identifies and fills in the missing element.	**Pattern Fixer** Show children a geometric pattern and chant it with them (e.g., square, triangle, square, triangle, square, triangle . . . at least three complete units of the pattern). Point to a space later in the pattern where a shape "fell off." Ask children what shape they need to fix the pattern. If children need help, have them chant the pattern as you point to each block, allowing the pattern of words indicate the missing shape.
	Pattern Duplicator AB Duplicates ABABAB pattern. May have to work close to the model pattern. Given objects in a row, ABABAB, makes their own ABABAB row in a different location.	**Pattern Strips** Show children a strip of paper with a geometric pattern pictured on it and have children describe the pattern on the strip (square, circle, square, circle, square, circle . . .). • Have the children help you copy the pattern, if necessary, by placing pattern blocks directly on the pattern strip. • Have them chant the pattern as you point to each block. **Pattern Planes 1: Duplicate AB** Children duplicate a linear AB pattern of flags based on an outline that serves as a guide. When they complete the pattern, they help an airplane land. 
	Pattern Extender AB Extends AB repeating patterns. Given objects in a row, ABABAB, adds ABAB to the end of the row.	**Pattern Strips—Extend** Show children pattern strip with an ABABAB pattern and ask them to use materials to "keep going" with the pattern. Discuss how they knew how to do so. **Marching Patterns 1: Extend AB** Children extend a linear AB pattern of musicians by one full repetition of an entire unit. When they complete the pattern, the musicians march in a parade.
	Pattern Duplicator Duplicates simple patterns (not just alongside the model pattern). Given objects in a row, ABBABBABB, makes their own ABBABBABB row in a different location.	**Dancing Patterns** Tell the children they will be dancing patterns and the first one will be clap ("one"), kick ("one"), kick ("two"); clap ("one"), kick ("one"), kick ("two"); clap ("one"), kick ("one"), kick ("two") . . . . Sing a song along with the pattern. Later, have them describe the pattern. **Pattern Planes 2 (and 3)** Children duplicate a linear AAB or ABB (for 2; ABC for level 3) pattern of flags based on an outline that serves as a guide. When they complete the pattern, they help an airplane land.

Age (years)	Developmental Progression	Instructional Tasks

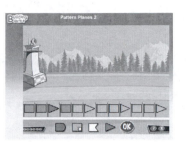

5   **Pattern Extender** Extends simple repeating patterns.

> Given objects in a row, ABBABBABB, adds ABBABB to the end of the row.

Creative Patterns This is a good time to add pattern-creating materials to your creative area. Someone is sure to want to make a pattern they can take home.

Pattern Strips—Extend Show children pattern strip and ask them to use materials to "keep going" with the pattern. Discuss how they knew how to do so.

Stringing Beads Following a "pattern tag" at the end of the string, children place beads on the string to extend the pattern and make a pattern necklace.

Marching Patterns 2 (and 3): Extend Children extend a linear pattern of musicians by one full repetition of an entire unit. When they complete the pattern, the musicians march in a parade. The musicians are in patterns such as AAB and ABB in level 2, ABC in level 3.

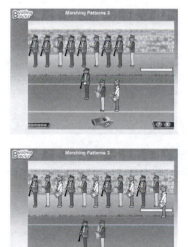

6   **Pattern Unit Recognizer** Identifies the smallest unit of a pattern. Can translate patterns into new media.

> Given objects in a, ABBABBABB pattern, identifies the core unit of the pattern as ABB.

Pattern Strips—The Core Re-introduce Pattern Strips, emphasizing the idea of the core of the pattern.

- Show children a pattern strip and have children describe the pattern on the strip (vertical, vertical, horizontal; vertical, vertical, horizontal; vertical, vertical, horizontal; . . .).
- Ask them what the "core" of this pattern is ("vertical, vertical, horizontal").
- Have the children help you copy the pattern using sticks. Each child should make one copy of the core.
- Ask them to "keep going" by adding additional copies of the core.

Cube Patterns Put a large group of cubes in the middle of the children. Show them a "tower" of cubes of two colors, such as blue, blue, yellow.

Continued Overleaf

Age (years)	Developmental Progression	Instructional Tasks
		• Have each child make a blue, blue, yellow tower. • Have children link them together, making a long cube pattern train! • Chant the colors as you point to each cube in the long pattern train. • Repeat with a different core tower. Scaffolding Strategies • More Help—For children who have difficulty making and extending a pattern, making cube patterns step by step may be useful. Help them to stand up several towers next to each other (e.g., red cube, blue cube), and see they are all the same. "Read" the pattern, chanting each color as you read one tower after another from the bottom up. Finally, link them together and chant the pattern again. • Extra Challenge—Use more complex patterns. Even try ones that end with the same item they begin with, such as a core unit of ABBCA, which produces the confusing pattern: ABBCAABBCAABBCA. **Patterns Free Explore** Students explore patterning by creating rhythmic patterns of their own. The patterns are presented in drum beats (of two pitches), but also visually—emphasizing the *core unit* of the pattern. 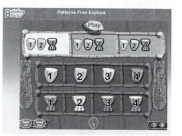
7	**Numeric Patterner** Describes a pattern numerically, can translate between geometric and numeric representation of a series. Given objects in a geometric pattern, describes the numeric progression.	**Growing Patterns** Children observe, copy, and create patterns that grow, especially those such as the square growing pattern and triangular growing pattern, noting the geometric and numerical patterns that they embody. 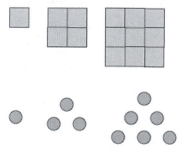 **Arithmetic and Algebraic Thinking** See the many examples in the text.

Data Analysis

The foundations for data analysis, especially for the early years, lie in other areas, such as counting and classification. That is why the Curriculum Focal Points emphasized classification and quantity in its description of data analysis for preschool and kindergarten. And, as "connections" to the focal points, they are always based on analyses of numerical, geometrical, and/or measurement items. Object counting was discussed in Chapter 3. The fundamental competencies in classification will be discussed in Chapter 13.

As a simple example, children initially learn to sort objects *and* quantify their groups. They might sort a collection of buttons into those with one to four holes and count to find out how many they have in each of the four groups. To do this, they focus on and describe the attributes of objects, classifying according to those attributes, and quantify the resulting categories. Children eventually became capable of simultaneously classifying and counting; for example, counting the number of colors in a group of objects, as described previously.

After gathering data to answer questions, children's initial representations often do not use categories. Their interest in data is on the particulars (Russell, 1991). For example, they might simply list each child in their class and each child's response to a question. They then learn to classify these responses and represent data according to category. Finally, young children can use physical objects to make graphs (objects that are the object of attention, such as shows, then manipulatives such as connecting cubes), then picture graphs, then line plots, and, finally, bar graphs that include grid lines to facilitate reading frequencies (Friel, Curcio, & Bright, 2001). By second grade, most children should be able to organize and display data through both simple numerical summaries such as counts, tables, and tallies, and graphical displays, including picture graphs, line plots, and bar graphs (Russell, 1991). They can compare parts of the data, make statements about the data as a whole, and generally determine whether the graphs answer the questions posed initially.

To understand data analysis, students must learn the dual concepts of expectation and variation. Expectation deals with averages and probabilities (such as the mean, one measure of central tendency). Variation deals with uncertainty, "spread" of values (such as the standard deviations), outliers, and anticipated and unanticipated change. Data analysis has been called the search for signals (expectations) within the noise (variation) (Konold & Pollatsek, 2002). This research agrees that children often initially see only the *individuals* in a data display ("That's me. I liked chocolate best"). They do not "pull the pieces together" to think about the data as a whole. Children in the late primary or early intermediate grades can learn to view ranges in data or view the mode (the number or range of numbers that occurs most frequently). Eventually, students can focus on features of the data set as a whole, including the relative frequencies, density ("shape"), and location (centers, such as the mean). Again, more information, especially for older students, is available in the companion book.

A final note connects data representation to the discussion of algebraic thinking. The goal of both should be making sense of quantitative situations and laying the foundation for more complex math to come. At the heart of both is the examination of *quantitative relationships* and representing those relationships to better *make sense* of them.

Experience and Education

NCTM's Curriculum Focal Points (NCTM, 2006) identify the following goals as relevant to data analysis:

Pre-K includes one connection:

- Children learn the foundations of data analysis by using objects' attributes that they have identified in relation to geometry and measurement (e.g., size, quantity, orientation, number of sides or vertices, color) for various purposes, such as describing, sorting, or comparing. For example, children sort geometric figures by shape, compare objects by weight ("heavier," "lighter"), or describe sets of objects by the number of objects in each set.

K includes one connection:

- Children sort objects and use one or more attributes to solve problems. For example, they might sort solids that roll easily from those that do not. Or they might collect data and use counting to answer such questions as, "What is our favorite snack?" They re-sort objects by using new attributes (e.g., after sorting solids according to which ones roll, they might re-sort the solids according to which ones stack easily).

First grade includes one connection:

- Children strengthen their sense of number by solving problems involving measurements and data. Measuring by laying multiple copies of a unit end to end and then counting the units by using groups of tens and ones supports children's understanding of number lines and number relationships. Representing measurements and discrete data in picture and bar graphs involves counting and comparisons that provide another meaningful connection to number relationships.

Second grade includes two connections that are not titled "data analysis" but mention data:

- Children add and subtract to solve a variety of problems, including applications involving measurement, geometry, and data, as well as nonroutine problems.
- Children estimate, measure, and compute lengths as they solve problems involving data, space, and movement through space.

Third grade includes a connection dedicated to data analysis:

- Addition, subtraction, multiplication, and division of whole numbers come into play as students construct and analyze frequency tables, bar graphs, picture graphs, and line plots and use them to solve problems.

Thus, data is seen as an important *context* for solving problems but not as a focal point itself for these age ranges. This is consistent with the consensus of a group attempting to create research-based standards for young children that a main role for data analysis would lie in supporting the development of mathematic processes and the content domains of number, geometry, and spatial sense (Clements & Conference Working Group, 2004). For example, *gathering data to answer a question or make a decision* is potentially an effective means to develop applied problem-solving and number and/or spatial sense, as children simultaneously learn about data analysis.

The educational role of most of the processes has been described in previous chapters as it relates to specific topics (classifying and other processes are discussed in the following chapter, Chapter 13). Here we discuss the role of *graphs*. Preschoolers appear to be able to understand discrete graphs as representations of numerosity based on one-to-one correspondence. Providing them with examples, motivating tasks such as graphing their progress toward gathering items for a scavenger hunt, and feedback, may be helpful.

The instruction in one successful exploratory study used two phases (Schwartz n.d.). Phase 1 consists of group experiences. *Selection of the topics for group graphing* is guided by children's interest and ease of collection of data ("Who are the people that live in their houses?" or "How does each child come to school?" or "What is their favorite home activity?"). *Providing a variety of models for recording data* begins with concrete materials and extends to graphic, alphabetic, and numeric representation. Teachers pose the problem of how the group could save the information, so "we won't forget what we said." Some children suggested using concrete materials for graphing the information. Also, many had little concern for sorting the data as they recorded it. After a plan was agreed upon, children were able to help record the information. *Summarizing and interpreting the data* began with the question, "What did we find out?," which focused attention on sorting the information. If a decision had to be made, such as what kinds of cookies to purchase, children resorted. The second phase was independent data collection for those children who were interested. These experiences build upon those in phase 1, with the teacher providing tools (clipboards were popular), and working with individuals to organize, record, and communicate their findings.

Another study reported success with children working with software that develops foundational skills for data analysis (Hancock, 1995). Using "Tabletop Jr.," children make and arrange objects, such as cartoon characters, pizzas, stick figures, party hats, attribute "blocks," numerals, and abstract designs, which will be used to represent data or be the objects of the exploration. All objects are created by combining simple attributes, just as attribute blocks are structured (such blocks are one of the object sets). Children can choose the attributes for each object produced, or have them generated randomly (Figure 12.2).

Next, they can arrange them in different ways, including using loops (Venn diagrams), bunches, stacks (picture graphs), grids, and chains. Children can make free-form arrangements manually, or they can get the objects to arrange themselves automatically, based on their attributes. The objects are animated and move across the screen to meet whatever rule of arrangement has been defined by the user. Arrangements may be treated as patterns and designs, or as plots and graphs that can help with analyzing data. Figure 12.3 is a computer-generated sort of children's hand sizes.

These tools can be used to play "guess my rule" and others that emphasize attributes, sorting, and arranging data. Anecdotal reports with children as young as 5 years of age are positive (Hancock, 1995).

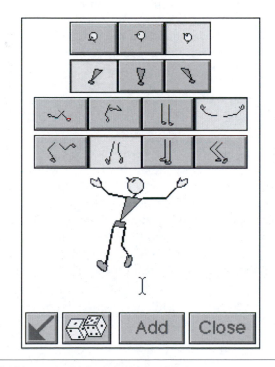

Figure 12.2 Using "Tabletop Jr.," children create stick figures by choosing attributes.

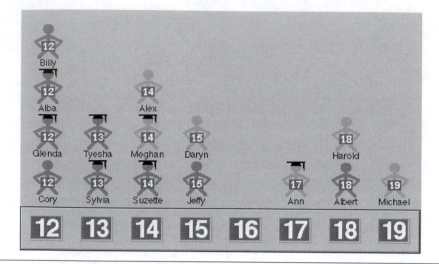

Figure 12.3 Children instruct the computer to sort their data in a pictograph.

Thus, we suggest that curricula and teachers might focus on one big idea: Classifying, organizing, representing, and using information to ask and answer questions. If graphing is to be part of that type of activity, young children might use physical objects to make graphs, such as laying down "shoes or sneakers" in two columns on a square grid laid on the floor. Next, they could use manipulatives, or other discrete, physical objects such as connecting cubes. This could be represented next with picture graphs (Friel et al., 2001) and, in first grade, with simple bar graphs. By third grade, most children should be able to organize and display data through both simple numerical summaries such as counts, frequency tables, and graphical displays, including picture graphs, bar graphs, and line plots, as fits the question and the data (Russell, 1991). Students can compare parts of the data, make statements about the data as a whole, and generally determine whether the graphs address the issue at hand. At all times, emphasis should be on the classifications and the numerical results and how they are used to make decisions or answer the question initially posed.

Final Words

How essential are the topics of this chapter? If viewed as "separate topics"—for example, units of instruction on different types of repeating patterns, or on graphing—they are of secondary importance and may even take too much time away from the core instruction described in previous chapters. However, if they are viewed as fundamental processes and ways of thinking—habits of mind that seek mathematical patterns and structure and classify mathematical objects and ideas—they are an essential component of most all early mathematics education. (The importance of early *graphing* is unknown and we do not emphasize it in our own curriculum development work.) Similar arguments apply to the processes that are the focus of Chapter 13.

13
Mathematical Processes

Carmen had almost filled her pretend pizzas with toppings. As she got ready to roll the number cube, she said, "I'm going to get a high number and win!" "You can't," replied her friend, "You have 4 spaces and the number cube only has 1s, 2s, and 3s on it."

The numbers may be small, but the reasoning is impressive. *Children can reason mathematically.* Indeed, one could argue that mathematics is essential for all thinking. That's a strong statement. How can it be true that all thinking involves mathematics? *Logic (reasoning) is a branch of mathematics, and thinking involves logic at some point.*

Consider the first vignette. Before reading further, ask yourself: What *reasoning* do you think Carmen's friend was using? In our view, Carmen's friend probably intuitively used logic that might be described as the following:

- To win, Carmen must get at least a 4.
- The number cube has only 1, 2, and 3.
- These numbers are less than 4.
- Therefore, Carmen cannot win on her next roll.

Although logic might seem like the most abstract, least likely area of mathematics for young children to learn to use, researchers and other sensitive observers see implicit use of logic in all children. An 18-month-old child pulling a blanket to bring a toy within reach shows the beginnings of "means-end" analysis.

Children appear to be impressive problem-solvers, as we've seen in every previous chapter. Here, we focus on problem-solving, reasoning, and other processes.

Reasoning and Problem-solving

Even though advanced mathematical reasoning would be inappropriate for most young children, you can help them develop mathematical reasoning, along with precision of thinking and definitions, *at their level.* Recall preschoolers arguing about whether a shape is a triangle, *based on its attributes and their definition of a triangle as a (closed) shape with three straight sides* (Chapter 8).

Young children arguing that "we already found 5 + 2 is 7, so we *know* 2 + 5, 'cause you can always add with either number first" shows again their ability to reason from mathematical properties (Chapters 5 and 6).

Of course, children use such reasoning in solving problems. There are also additional strategies possessed by young children. Luke, 3 years old, watched his father unsuccessfully looking under the van for a washer that had fallen and suggested, "Why don't you just roll the car back, so you can find it?" Luke employed means–end analysis better than his father. This strategy involves determining the difference between the current state and the goal, and then taking action that reduces the difference between them, reasoning backward from the goal to set subgoals. Means–end problem-solving may emerge between 6 and 9 months, when, as in the previous example, children learn to pull on a blanket to bring a toy into their reach.

Even young children have multiple problem-solving strategies at their disposal and the ability to choose among them. Means–end analysis is a general strategy, as are several others. Children know and prefer cognitively easier strategies. For example, in hill climbing, children reason forward from the current state in the direction of the desired goal (DeLoache, Miller, & Pierroutsakos, 1998). Trial and error, with light cognitive requirements, begins early, with Piagetian circular reactions trying to make an interesting sight or sound repeat.

These strategies develop throughout the toddler and preschool years, enabling children to address problems of increasing complexity. For example, recall that kindergartners can solve a wide range of addition, subtraction, multiplication, and division problems when they are encouraged to use manipulatives or drawings to model the objects, actions, and relationships in those situations.

In summary, considering their minimal experience, young children are impressive problem-solvers. They are learning to learn and learning the rules of the "reasoning game." Research on problem-solving and reasoning again reveals that children are more skilled, and adults less skilled, than conventionally thought. Finally, although domain-specific knowledge is essential, we should not fail to recognize that reasoning from domain-specific knowledge builds upon the basis of mindful general problem-solving and reasoning abilities that are evident from the earliest years.

Classification and Seriation

Classification

At all ages, children classify intuitively. For example, by 2 weeks of age, infants distinguish between objects they suck and those they do not. By 2 years, toddlers form sets with objects that are similar on some properties, although not necessarily identical.

Not until age 3 can most children follow verbal rules for sorting. In the preschool ages, many children learn to sort objects according to a given attribute, forming categories, although they may switch attributes during the sorting. Not until age 5 or 6 years do children usually sort consistently by a single attribute and re-classify by different attributes.

Seriation

Young children also learn to seriate objects—putting them in order—from early in life. From 18 months of age, they know vocabulary such as "big," "small," and "more." By 2 or 3 years of age, they can compare numbers and number pairs on the basis of a common ordering relation. At 3 years, children can make paired comparisons, and 4-year-olds can make small series, but most do not seriate all objects. At about 5 years, children can put six lengths in order by length. Most 5-year-olds also can insert elements into a series.

Before moving to the next section, we note that *patterning, writ large, is also one of the most important processes and habits of mind for mathematical thinking.* This type of patterning includes but goes far beyond "red, red, blue; red, red, blue . . ." to include the propensity to see relationships, regularities, and structures in every mathematical domain. We discussed this essential process in Chapter 12.

Experience and Education

You present problems, and they figure out what to do. You present problems, and they figure out what to do. Then you ask what process they used. I'm amazed . . . they learn to describe their processes! They'll use this knowledge to answer science questions. They really do critical thinking. Asking, "How do you know?" starting at Pre-K is very powerful.

(Anne, preschool teacher, *Building Blocks* curriculum)

The NCTM, the NAEYC, mathematicians (e.g., Wu, 2007), and research all point to the same educational goal and recommendation: essential processes, especially reasoning and problem-solving, must be central to the mathematical education of students of all ages.

Reasoning

Help children develop pre-mathematical reasoning from the earliest years. Provide an environment that invites exploration and reasoning with objects such as blocks. Encourage language to support the growth of reasoning abilities. For example, labeling situations with both "Daddy/Mommy/ Baby" and "big/little/tiny" led to a 2-year-age gain in reasoning with relations in 3-year-old children. As other chapters have shown, having children explain and justify their solutions to mathematical problems is an effective way to develop mathematical (and general) reasoning.

Problem Solving[1]

Children make progress when they solve many problems over the course of years. Children as young as preschoolers and kindergartners, and perhaps younger, benefit from planned instruction (but not prescribed strategies), from a teacher who believes problem solving is important. They benefit from modeling a wide variety of situations (geometric, and, in arithmetic, varied problem types, including addition, subtraction, and, at least from kindergarten on, multiplication, and division) with concrete objects, and also from drawing a representation to show their thinking, from explaining and discussing their solutions.

Solving more complex word problems remains a challenge for primary grade students. Their conceptions must move from the many messy details of a real-world situation to more abstracted (mathematized) quantitative conceptions (Fuson & Abrahamson, in press). For example, children might read, "Mary bought 8 candies at the store, but she ate 3 on the way home. How many did she still have when she got home?" The children have to see that the store plays little part, but that it's important that there is a group of candies and some got eaten. They might then think, she had 8 but ate 3. Then, I have to find 8 take away 3. Then they might think to model this with fingers, finally putting up 8 fingers and lowering the 3 on one hand.

As an example sequence, start by having as many students as possible solve a problem at the chalkboard, using diagrams, numerals, and so forth, while others solve them at their seats, on student-sized chalk- or whiteboards if available. Then ask two to three to explain their solutions. Have a different group go to the chalkboard to solve the *next* problem. Eventually, all children explain their thinking on at least one problem (and explain to another student on most). English language learners may point to their diagram or co-present a solution with a peer.

Progress from easier to more difficult problem types. For each problem type, move from problems with more familiar situations and language to those that are less familiar. Guide students to use more sophisticated strategies and then to algorithms. Also, introduce problems with extra or missing information, as well as multistep problems. Finally, use larger or more complex numbers (e.g., fractions). Combine new problem types with other problem types and practiced, with feedback. See pp. 62 and 73–80 for problem types.

Research suggests that this process of mathematizing the story situation has a reverse process that is also important. That is, children should also make up word problems that fit number sentences (Fuson & Abrahamson, in press). Problem posing appears to be an effective way for children to express their creativity and integrate their learning (Brown & Walter, 1990; Kilpatrick, 1987; van Oers, 1994). Few empirical studies have been conducted that verify effects of problem-posing, however, and none involved young children.

Classification and Seriation

Provide all young children with opportunities to achieve at least a minimal level of competence with classification and seriation before they reach the primary grades. For classification, they should at the least solve oddity problems—"one of these is not like the others." Even simple teaching strategies—demonstration, practice, and feedback with many varied concrete examples—benefit children, especially those with special needs. Children can be told and shown the rule, but may need help figuring out rules and when to use them. Game-like instruction may help children learn to induce simple rules. Consider alternative, richer, problem-solving approaches that teach these and other competencies (see Clements, 1984; Kamii, Rummelsburg, & Kari, 2005).

When should such instruction begin? Provide informal, child-centered experiences to children younger than 3 years. Many 2.5-year-old children know a rule and have relevant conceptual knowledge but fail to use it to regulate their behavior. Seemingly impervious to efforts to improve their rule use, 32-month-olds could not label pictures in terms of appropriate categories, even with varieties of extra help in sorting, including feedback and reinforcement (Zelazo, Reznick, & Piñon, 1995). Improvements in sorting by rules may require emerging control over actions.

Provide materials to think with, to sort, and to order. The meaningfulness of the representations and tasks are more important than the form of the materials; therefore, well-designed computer materials may be as or more useful than physical materials (Clements, 1999a) for those older than 3 years. In one study, children learning from computer manipulatives learned classification and other topics as well as children learning from physical materials, but only the computer group gained significantly on seriation (Kim, 1994). Further, the computer manipulatives provided children with a more interesting learning environment that generated more time on task.

Challenge older children to label, discuss attributes, and classify objects by more than one attribute. Provide a variety of materials and promote discussion of varied strategies. Similarly, many strategies can be used to teach seriation. As with classification, straightforward teacher-centered activities are among those that are effective. For all such processes, however, there are reasons to believe they should be supplemented with occasions in which the processes are used to solve meaningful everyday problems for the child. As Jean Piaget (1971/1974, p. 17) stated:

> The child may on occasion be interested in seriating for the sake of seriating, in classifying for the sake of classifying, etc., but, in general, it is when events or phenomena must be explained

and goals attained through an organization of causes that operations [logico-mathematical knowledge] will be used [and developed] most.

For example, although many types of activities may support the learning of classification, a guideline of "classify with good causation" (Forman & Hill, 1984) indicates that children will learn from sorting shapes according to teachers' directions, but more from *also* sorting three-dimensional objects to find out which will and will not roll down a ramp . . . and *why*.

Taking a wider Piagetian view, researchers (Kamii et al., 2005) provided low-income first graders a variety of physical knowledge activities, such as bowling, balancing cubes (on a circular plate balanced on a soda bottle), and pick-up sticks, instead of typical mathematics instruction. When they showed "readiness" for arithmetic, they were given arithmetic games and word problems that stimulated the exchange of viewpoints. At the end of the year, the experimental group (who did these activities) was compared with similar groups who received traditional exercises that focused narrowly on number (counting, one-to-one correspondences, and answering questions like 2 + 2). The experimental group was superior in mental arithmetic and logical reasoning as revealed by word problems. The researchers claim that the physical knowledge activities also develop logico-mathematical knowledge, as in classifying the sticks to decide which stick to pick up first and seriating them from easiest to hardest to pick up. Effects of the physical knowledge and arithmetic activities cannot be disaggregated, and there was no random assignment, but the results are suggestive (see also Kamii & Kato, 2005). We need well-designed studies that evaluate these and other approaches, and compare their long-term effects.

Finally, research suggests that the processes of classification and seriation are related to number knowledge—but in surprising ways. Preschoolers were randomly assigned to one of three educational conditions for 8 weeks: classification and seriation, number (subitizing and counting), and control (Clements, 1984). The first two groups improved on what they were taught, but also improved on the *other* topics. Also surprisingly, the number group learned more about classification and seriation than the classification and seriation group learned about number. It may be that all number and counting implies some level of classification. For example, children might count the blue cars, the red cars, and then all the cars.

Final Words

Children can be impressive problem solvers. They are learning to learn and learning the rules of the "reasoning game." Problem posing and problem solving are effective ways for children to express their inventiveness and integrate their learning. They develop mathematics, language, and creativity. And they build *connections* among these—the essence of learning to *think*.

Especially for younger children, mathematical topics should not be treated as isolated topics; rather, they should be connected to each other, often in the context of solving a significant problem or engaging in an interesting project. Thus, this book's main organization based on mathematical content should not be considered a de-emphasis on other aspects of mathematics, including general processes of reasoning, problem solving, representing, communicating, and connecting (NCTM, 2000), which should be interwoven throughout the teaching and learning of content.

This concludes the chapters focused on mathematical goals and specific learning trajectories. This is also the last chapter that is aligned with a corresponding chapter of the companion volume. The next three chapters are unique to this volume, and address issues essential to *implementing* the learning trajectories. Chapter 14 begins with a discussion of cognition (thinking, understanding, and learning), affect (emotions or feelings), and equity (fairness).

14
Cognition, Affect, and Equity

Three teachers are discussing their students who are "good" and "not so good" at math.

Aretha: Some students just are good at math and others aren't. You can't change it. You can tell just by watching them in your classroom.

Brenda: I don't think so. Students get smarter at math by *thinking* about it. Working at it makes them smarter.

Carina: There certainly are a few who seem to find aspects of math particularly challenging and a few who, for whatever reason, can learn new math ideas quickly. But no one's ability is fixed; they all need good experiences to learn more and those experiences make them better at . . . more able to learn more math.

Which teacher do you think is most accurate in her evaluation of the roles of aptitude or ability ("nature") compared to effort and experience ("nurture")? Why?

Thinking, Learning, Feeling, Teaching: The Last Three Chapters

The last three chapters of the book discuss issues that are important for putting learning trajectories into practice. This chapter describes how children think about mathematics and how their feelings are involved, as well as issues of equity. The next one, Chapter 15, discusses the contexts in which early childhood education occurs and the curricula that are used. We conclude with Chapter 16, which describes instructional practices and reviews research on which ones are particularly effective and for whom. The topics of these three chapters are unique to this book. Because there are no corresponding chapters in the companion book, there is more research reviewed. We have marked paragraphs with implications for practitioners with "*Practical implications*," for those who wish to focus only on these.

In this chapter, we discuss issues relevant across various topics of mathematics. Although we have discussed children and their learning throughout the book, there are some general processes that are important to all learning. Every previous chapter has discussed young children's mathematics learning and the ways in which they learn. This chapter discusses, from a more general perspective, the learning processes, achievement, and emotions of these children. This leads to issues of individual differences, cultural differences, and the principle of equity.

Cognitive Science and the Processes of Learning

At the core of our theory of hierarchic interactionalism (see our companion book), and our elaborations of the learning trajectories, are the learning processes of young children. This section "steps back" from the specific mathematics topics to focus on a few important general principles of cognition and learning that you can use to better understand the education of your children. These findings are largely from the field of cognitive science, the study of the processes that underlie cognition and learning (see NMP, 2008, for a more extended discussion).

When children think and learn, they build mental representations (what we call "mental objects"), act on them with cognitive processes ("actions on objects"), and control these actions with executive control ("metacognitive") processes. We will consider each of these categories in turn. First are the cognitive operations, including attention, working memory, long-term memory, and retrieval.

Attention and Self-regulation: Initial Cognitive (Information) Processes

Thinking and problem-solving involve taking in and interpreting information, operating on it, and responding to it. At the beginning of this process is attention—a focusing process that, as most early childhood teachers know, cannot be taken for granted. Good teachers build a repertoire of strategies for capturing and maintaining children's attention.

A broader competence that includes focusing attention is *self-regulation*—the process of intentionally controlling ones impulses, attention, and behavior. It may involve avoiding distractions, and maintaining a focus on setting goals, planning, and monitoring one's attention, actions, and thoughts. *Self-regulation has emerged as a significant influence on certain components of mathematics learning* (Blair & Razza, 2007). Further, the lack of social–emotional self-regulation can stand in the way of a child's ability to have positive teacher child interactions in kindergarten, which, in turn, predicts later poor academic performance and behavior problems (Hamre & Pianta, 2001). Self-regulation and cognitive competencies appear to be related, but develop somewhat independently (T. R. Konold & Pianta, 2005).

Practical implications. Research has also identified certain environments and teaching practices that can help children pay attention, and grow in their ability to do so, as well as to develop general self-regulation competencies (see Chapter 16). Instructional activities in each of this book's learning trajectories have been intentionally designed to help child direct attention. Carefully guiding children to attend to specific mathematical features, such as the number in a collection or the corners of a polygon, is likely to improve their learning. The predisposition to spontaneously recognize number, for example (see Chapter 2), is a skill but also a *habit of mind*, including the ability to *direct attention to number* (Lehtinen & Hannula, 2006). These habits of mind generate further development of specific mathematical knowledge *and* the ability to direct attention to mathematics in situations in which it is relevant; that is, to *generalize* and *transfer* knowledge to new situations.

Working Memory

When children pay attention to something, information can be encoded into their working memories—the amount of mental "space" they have to think about mathematics and solving mathematical problems (indeed, another useful metaphor is that working memory is children's capacity to *attend* to multiple items in memory). This allows children to consciously think about the task or problem. Working memory affects children's ability to solve problems, to learn, and to remember (Ashcraft, 2006). Processes that are slower and more complex put additional demands on working memory. Unsurprisingly, then, limits on working memory may be one cause of learning difficulties or disabilities (Geary, Hoard, & Hamson, 1999; see the section later in this chapter) and a particularly large working memory one cause of superior competence in mathematics.

Practical implications. Children develop greater working memory capacity as they age, probably due to greater self-regulation and executive control and the ability to represent content more efficiently (Cowan, Saults, & Elliott, 2002). At all ages, one way people's minds deal with limits on working memory is to make certain processes *automatic*—fast and easy. Such automatic processes do not take much working memory (Shiffrin & Schneider, 1984). Some automatic processes are "bootstrap" abilities, such as the ability to recognize faces. In mathematics, most must be learned and experienced many times. A familiar example knows arithmetic combinations so well that one "just knows" and does not have to figure them out while performing a more complicated task. Such automaticity requires much practice. Such practice could be "drill," but a broader definition is *repeated experiencing,* which might include drill but also includes use of the skill or knowledge in multiple difference situations, which promotes both automaticity and transfer to new situations.

Long-term Memory and Retrieval

Long-term memory is how people store information. Concepts ("understandings") take effort and time to be built in long-term memory. People have difficulty transferring their knowledge to new situations (different from those in, or about, which they were taught), but without conceptual knowledge, this would be even more difficult.

Practical implications. Helping children build rich representations of concepts (called "Integrated-Concrete Knowledge"; see Chapter 16) and see how something they know can be used to solve new problems helps them remember and transfer what they have learned. Varied situations are not necessarily radically different. In one study, 6- and 7-year-old children practiced using flashcards or worksheets. They had similar performance if tested in the same format, but, if the format was switched, their performance was significantly lower (Nishida & Lillard, 2007a).

Practical implications. Although material that is easy to understand can promote fast initial learning, it does not help store knowledge in long-term memory. *Challenging materials leads to better longer-term memory,* because children have to process it and understand it more thoroughly. Their extra effort translates into more active processing, and thus more likely storage, of information. This helps children remember information longer and retrieve ("remember") it more easily. Thus, they can retrieve the information better and are more likely to transfer its use to new situations.

Executive (Metacognitive) Processes

Executive, or metacognitive, processes control other cognitive processes. For example, they select steps to put together to form a strategy for solving a problem or monitor the overall problem-solving process.

Practical implications. Most students need substantial work in learning these processes, for example, to monitor their reasoning and problem-solving. Helping children *understand* mathematical ideas, and engaging them in conversations about mathematics and how they solved mathematical problems promotes the development of executive processes. The next cognitive category includes the mental objects children build. They include declarative, conceptual, and procedural representations.

Mental Objects—The Mind's Representations

The second category includes the mental objects, or representations, on which processes act. There are different types. *Declarative* knowledge is explicit knowledge of specific information or facts, such as knowing that most people have *two legs. Procedural* knowledge is usually implicit knowledge for sequences of actions or skills, such as turning a puzzle piece into position or moving objects to keep track of which objects have been counted. *Conceptual* knowledge involves understanding ideas, such as the cardinality rule.

As we have seen in previous chapters, all types of knowledge are important and *mutually supportive.* All are best learned when learned together (often simultaneously, but not necessarily). A special type of mental representation is the mental model, a way of building a manipulable mental image or set of images. The "build stairs" series of activities was designed to help children build new mental models for counting, addition (plus 1), and measurement, as well as the connections among them.

Affect (Emotion) and Beliefs (including Aptitude vs. Effort)

Given that mathematical thinking and learning is *cognitive,* what role does emotion play? Even though the processes are cognitive, they are influenced by emotions and beliefs. For example, if people are anxious about mathematics, they may perform poorly, not necessarily because they have limited ability or skills but because nervous thoughts "push" themselves into their minds, limiting the amount of working memory available to work on mathematics (Ashcraft, 2006). In this section, we review key findings about affect (see Malmivuori, 2001, for an elaborate analysis of the dynamic roles of affect, beliefs, and cognition, which is beyond the scope of this section).

As a culture, people in the U.S. have unfortunate emotions (negative) and beliefs about mathematics. Indeed, all it takes to raise math anxiety in the approximately 17% of the population who suffer from this is to show them a number (Ashcraft, 2006)!

One deeply embedded belief is that achievement in mathematics depends mostly on *aptitude* or *ability,* as Aretha illustrated at the beginning of this chapter. In contrast, people from other countries believe that achievement comes from *effort*—Brenda's view. Even more disturbing, *research shows that this U.S. belief hurts children and, further, that it is just not true.* Children who believe—or are helped to understand—that they can learn if they try, work on tasks longer and achieve better throughout their school careers than children who believe you either "have it" (or "get it") or you do not. This latter view often leads to failure and "learned helplessness." Similarly, those who have mastery-oriented goals—who try to learn and see the point of school to develop knowledge and skills, achieve more than children whose goals are directed toward high grades or outperforming others (Middleton & Spanias, 1999; NMP, 2008). They even see failure as an opportunity to learn (cf. Papert, 1980).

As Carina argued, there certainly are differences between children, as will be discussed later in this chapter. However, whether these are due to nature or nurture or an intricate combination is difficult to tell. And all children can develop math competence, and even "intelligence," working in high-quality educational environments.

Fortunately, most young children have positive feelings about math and are motivated to explore numbers and shapes (Middleton & Spanias, 1999). Unfortunately, after only a couple of years in typical schools, they begin to believe that "only some people have the ability to do math." We believe that those who experience math as a *sense-making activity* will build positive feelings about math throughout their school careers.

Practical implications. Provide meaningful tasks that make sense to children and connect with their everyday interests and lives (remember the *Building Blocks* main approach, Chapter 1, p. 18). The right degree of challenge and novelty can promote interest, and facilitating and discussing skill improvement can promote a mastery orientation. Researchers have estimated that children should be successful about 70% of the time to maximize motivation (Middleton & Spanias, 1999).

In summary, many negative beliefs are embedded in our culture. However, you can help children change them. Doing so helps children for a lifetime.

Returning to the emotions, we see that affect plays a significant role in problem solving, involving both joys and frustrations (McLeod & Adams, 1989). Based on Mandler's theory, the source of such emotion is the interruption of a scheme. For example, if a plan is blocked, an emotion is generated, which might be negative or positive.

Practical implications. If children realize they are incorrect, they may believe this warrants embarrassment, but you can change that by directly assuring children that trying and discussing, including making errors and being frustrated, are part of the learning process. Also, discuss how working hard to learn and figure a problem out can make you "feel good" (Cobb, Yackel, & Wood, 1989). Hold such discussions to build positive affect and beliefs about mathematics and mathematical problem solving (an important, interesting activity that is an end in itself), as well as learning (e.g., emphasis on effort, not ability).

Trying hard also requires motivation. Fortunately, most children are motivated to learn. Even better, they are *intrinsically* motivated—they like to learn for the sake of learning. Such intrinsic motivation correlates with and supports academic success. However, children are not motivated equally. Indeed, in one study, children's motivational orientation (e.g., engagement and persistence in tasks) in preschool predicted their mathematics knowledge from kindergarten up into the primary grades (Lepola, Niemi, Kuikka, & Hannula, 2005). Further, those who begin with the lowest mathematics knowledge have the lowest engagement in tasks (Bodovski & Farkas, 2007). Extrinsic motivation is related to performance goals (NMP, 2008). Related to this is children's competence at self-regulation, already discussed. Self-regulation is not just a cognitive process but also has a motivational component.

Practical implications. A final concern is that structured mathematics activities will negatively affect children's motivations or affect. There is no research we know of that supports that concern. Research suggests the opposite (Malofeeva et al., 2004). Educators do have to avoid narrow views of math and learning. Teachers hamper students' learning if they define success only as fast, correct responses and accuracy in following the teacher's example (Middleton & Spanias, 1999).

What Predicts Math Achievement?

Consideration of such general learning and cognitive process, including affect and motivation, raise the question: Do these, or other, competencies or dispositions, *predict* mathematics achievement?

Perhaps most important, the *early learning of mathematics predicts later achievement*. Knowledge of mathematics in preschool correlated 0.46 with *tenth grade math achievement* (Stevenson &

Newman, 1986). Kindergartners' cognitive skills, such as discriminating between same and different visual stimuli and coding visual stimuli, predicted later *interest* in mathematics.

For many topics and abilities, initial knowledge predicts later learning and knowledge (Bransford, Brown, & Cocking, 1999; Jimerson, Egeland, & Teo, 1999; Maier & Greenfield, 2008; Thomson, Rowe, Underwood, & Peck, 2005; Wright et al., 1994). However, *the effect of early knowledge of mathematics is unusually strong and notably persistent* (Duncan, Claessens, & Engel, 2004). Further, the *rate of growth* of mathematical skills is faster among those with higher, rather than lower, initial mathematical skills (Aunola, Leskinen, Lerkkanen, & Nurmi, 2004). Researchers concluded that "by far the most powerful avenue for boosting first grade test scores appears to be improving the basic skills of low-achieving children upon entry into kindergarten." Contrary to the researchers' expectations, "soft" or social–emotional skills, such as being able to sit still in class or make friends upon school entry did *not* predict early achievement (Duncan et al., 2004).

Across six studies the strongest predictors of later achievement were school-entry math and attention skills (Duncan et al., in press). Indeed, early knowledge of reading predicted later success in reading. However, early knowledge of mathematics was a *stronger* predictor of later success in mathematics. Further, early knowledge of mathematics predicted not only success in math, but also *later success in reading.* (All these held children's pre-school cognitive ability, behavior, and other important background characteristics constant.) Other researchers have also found that early reading skill (kindergarten) does not predict either interest or achievement in later (second to third grade) math (McTaggart, Frijters, & Barron, 2005). Other researchers have confirmed that early math predicts reading, but reading does not predict math achievement (Lerkkanen, Rasku-Puttonen, Aunola, & Nurmi, 2005).

To summarize, early math concepts are the most powerful predictors of later learning. They predicted reading achievement as well as early reading skills predicted reading achievement. Language and attention skills were also predictive, but less so (and some, Konold & Pianta, 2005, have found attention alone not strongly predictive). Social–emotional skills such as behavior problems and social skills were insignificant predictors. Of course, we want positive affect, motivation, and social relations. Further, other studies show that, at least for some children with limited cognitive skills, social skills may be important predictors of success (Konold & Pianta, 2005). But it would seem we should develop these *alongside* important knowledge and skills, such as those of mathematics.

Are particular mathematics skills relatively more predictive? Knowing this may be useful for screening, or early identification of those who might have mathematical difficulties (see that section later in this chapter). Some research has found support for specific tasks, such as:

- magnitude discrimination, as in naming the larger of two digits, which may relate to a weakness in spatial representations (Case, Griffin, & Kelly, 1999; Chard et al., 2005; Clarke & Shinn, 2004; Gersten, Jordan, & Flojo, 2005; Jordan, Hanich, & Kaplan, 2003; Lembke & Foegen, 2008; Lembke, Foegen, Whittake, & Hampton, in press).
- numeral identification, such as reading numerals (really a language arts skill) (Chard et al., 2005; Gersten et al., 2005; Lembke & Foegen, 2008; Lembke et al., in press).
- missing number, naming the missing number in a series (Chard et al., 2005; Lembke & Foegen, 2008; Lembke et al., in press).
- spontaneous focusing on number, such as using subitizing independently, which predicts arithmetic but not later reading (see Chapter 2) (Hannula, Lepola, & Lehtinen, 2007).
- object counting and counting strategies, without errors (see Chapters 3 and 5) (Clarke & Shinn, 2004; Gersten et al., 2005).

- fluency in arithmetic combinations, such as addition "facts" (for older children, Geary, Brown, & Smaranayake, 1991; Gersten et al., 2005).

Caution is advised, however, because both the screening measures and the predicted measure often ignore any mathematics outside of routine numerical skills.

Other cognitive measures are also predictive of at least some cases of children with mathematical difficulties or disabilities including working memory (e.g., reverse digit span) (Geary, 2003; Gersten et al., 2005). Others have found working memory not predictive of fact fluency once attention (one of the strongest predictors) was controlled (Fuchs et al., 2005). Attention, working memory, and nonverbal problem-solving predicted conceptual competence. Recall that competence with early counting, including counting confidently and accurate use of counting strategies, and magnitude comparison, appear particularly important (Gersten et al., 2005; Jordan, Hanich, & Kaplan, 2003).

Executive control and the related construct of self-regulation are also predictive of mathematics achievement. Mathematics in one study was correlated with all but one measure of executive function (Bull & Scerif, 2001). The researchers conclude that particular difficulties for children of lower mathematical ability are lack of inhibition and poor working memory, resulting in their having difficulty switching and evaluating new strategies for dealing with a particular task. Persistence was significantly predictive of math achievement for both 3- and 4-year-olds (Maier & Greenfield, 2008).

Both arithmetic combinations and text reading are predicted by the ability to retrieve verbal or visual–verbal associations from long-term memory (Koponen, Aunola, Ahonen, & Nurmi, 2007). This result suggests that, although single-digit calculation is a numerical skill, it is also connected to linguistic abilities; thus, difficulties with language may restrict children's acquisition of calculation skills. Knowledge of algorithms was predicted by knowledge of number concepts and mother's educational level.

Similarly, Blair and colleagues have found that self-regulation, including effortful control and the inhibitory control and attention-shifting aspects of executive function in preschool, were related to measures of math (and literacy) ability in kindergarten (Blair, 2002; Blair & Razza, 2007). These correlations are independent of general intelligence. *Educators need to improve self-regulation skills as well as enhance early academic abilities* to help children succeed in school.

One of the most reliable results (see Chapter 1 and the section on families in Chapter 15) is that children from higher-income families (correlated with higher levels of parental education and use of progressive parenting beliefs) have higher achievement in all subjects, including math (Burchinal, Peisner-Feinberg, Pianta, & Howes, 2002).

In addition, closer relationship with the teacher is positively related to achievement, especially for younger and at-risk children. Finally, children who were more outgoing acquired math (and reading) skills more rapidly (Burchinal et al., 2002). Characteristics of the home and education program also predict math achievement (Pianta et al., 2005), a topic we address in Chapter 15. One study we mention here found that children who were rated highest on social and emotional assets and lowest on behavior concerns by their parents had significantly higher informal mathematics scores (Austin, Blevins-Knabe, & Lindauer, 2008). Best predictors of informal mathematics scores for all children included parents' ratings of behavior concerns, providers' ratings of child assets, and a readiness test.

What predicts engagement? One study of preschool curricula showed no effect for curriculum, gender, or ethnicity, and small effects for entering skill level (the higher the more engaged) and attendance (Bilbrey, Farran, Lipsey, & Hurley, 2007). Importantly, engagement in turn predicted quantitative concepts, as far as into first grade.

These early competencies may interact, some compensating for others. As we saw, cognitive processes, self-regulation, and social skills may develop somewhat independently of each other (Konold & Pianta, 2005). Moreover, skills in one area may help some children compensate for a lack of skills in another. For example, those of average or low cognitive ability had higher grades in first grade if they had good social skills. In comparison, those with high cognitive ability but mild externalizing problems did not suffer from the latter, outperforming all the other groups on achievement.

The classic nature/nurture issue. A long-standing debate is whether nature (genetics), or nurture (the home and school environment) affects children's achievement. A typical answer is that "both do" or that "nature deals the cards but nurture plays them." Both of these hold some truth. Recent research suggests answers that are much more specific. Researchers studying identical twins longitudinally (children were 7 to 10 years of age) concluded that genetics has a large and stable influence (0.48 for mathematics), environment plays a significant but moderate role (0.20 for shared environments, the remainder for unshared environments, as well as errors in measurement). Further, there is lower heritability for general intelligence, or "g" than for learning of subject matter areas. The authors also suggest that genes code for "appetites, not just aptitude." In other words, genetics also affects motivation to engage in learning. They drew three additional conclusions (Kovas, Haworth, Dale, & Plomin, 2007):

1. *The abnormal is normal.* Low performance is the quantitative extreme of the same genetic and environmental influences that operate throughout the normal distribution. The researchers suggest there are no unique "learning disabilities."

2. *Continuity is genetic and change is environmental.* Longitudinal analyses show that age-to-age stability is primarily mediated genetically, whereas the environment contributes to *change* from year to year.

3. *Genes are generalists and environments are specialists.* Genes largely contribute to similarity in performance within and between the three domains of mathematics, English, and science—and with general cognitive ability—whereas environment contributes to differences in performance. About a third of the variance between English and mathematics is common with "g," about a third is general to academic achievement but *not* "g." Non-shared environments have surprising effects. They account for differences between identical twins raised in the same house and school. They account for changes from one age to another. And they account for more variance than the shared environments. Research needs to examine school characteristics to solve the puzzle of what features of these non-shared environments are important.

A caution in drawing implications from all of the studies reviewed in this section is that they are correlational, *not* experimental. We cannot attribute causation to them. However, they are suggestive. Chapter 16 contains evidence from experiments in which we can say something about the effects of providing better early mathematics instruction. For now we simply make several recommendations.

Practical implications. Teach mathematics early. Focus on the key mathematics topics outlined in this book. Also focus on improving self-regulation skills.

Equity: Group and Individual Differences

As stated in Chapter 1, some children come to school far less prepared in mathematics than others. For most, these differences do not disappear, they increase. The "achievement gap" does not close; it widens (Geary, 2006). In this section, we examine differences between groups, such as those from low-resource and higher-resource communities, between individuals, including those with mathematical difficulties and disabilities. The common theme is equity. Both Chapters 15 and 16 discuss how educators can address equity issues in instruction.

Poverty and Minority Status

We advise the editor to reject this article simply because the authors haven't seen the obvious: differences between the low- and higher-income groups stem from IQ. The parents are low-income *because* they are not intelligent enough to get better jobs. They pass their low IQ to their children (from a review of one of the authors' research papers).

As already described in previous chapters, especially Chapter 1 (of this and especially the companion book), children who live in poverty and who are members of linguistic and ethnic minority groups demonstrate significantly lower levels of achievement (Bowman et al., 2001; Brooks-Gunn, Duncan, & Britto, 1999; Campbell & Silver, 1999; Denton & West, 2002; Entwisle & Alexander, 1990; Halle, Kurtz-Costes, & Mahoney, 1997; Mullis et al., 2000; Natriello, McDill, & Pallas, 1990; Rouse, Brooks-Gunn, & McLanahan, 2005; Secada, 1992; Sylva et al., 2005; Thomas & Tagg, 2004). Ethnic gaps widened in the 1990s (Jaekyung Lee, 2002). There is no age so young that equity is not a concern. The achievement gaps have origins in the earliest years, with low-income children possessing less extensive math knowledge than middle-income children of pre-K and kindergarten age (Arnold & Doctoroff, 2003; Denton & West, 2002; Ginsburg & Russell, 1981; Griffin, Case, & Capodilupo, 1995; Jordan, Huttenlocher, & Levine, 1992; Saxe, Guberman, & Gearhart, 1987; Sowder, 1992b). As one example, the ECLS-B (Early Childhood Longitudinal Study) found that the percentage of children demonstrating proficiency in numbers and shapes was 87% in higher socio-economic status (SES) families but only 40% among lower SES families (Chernoff, Flanagan, McPhee, & Park, 2007, but this involved simply reading numerals and so the report does not provide useful details). These differences start early and widen (Alexander & Entwisle, 1988).

Differences in specific aspects of young children's mathematical knowledge have been reported in two types of comparisons. First, there are cross-national differences. As we observed in previous chapters, some mathematical knowledge is more developed in East Asian children than in American children (Geary, Bow-Thomas, Fan, & Siegler, 1993; Ginsburg, Choi, Lopez, Netley, & Chi, 1997; Miller et al., 1995; Starkey et al., 1999). As a caveat, we do not know what mechanisms account for all these cross-national differences. Some factors appear to be nationally situated, such as teachers' knowledge, formal teaching practice, and curriculum standards. Others are transnational, such as language differences, and yet others may be cultural without reflecting national boundaries, such as family values (Wang & Lin, 2005). Japanese kindergartners perform better in mathematics than those from the U.S., but neither families nor schools in Japan emphasize academics for this age group (Bacon & Ichikawa, 1988). Their lower, but perhaps more realistic expectations, reliance on informal instruction at the child's level, including eliciting interest and providing examples rather than direct teaching of procedures, may account for their success.

Second, there are differences related to socioeconomic status. Some mathematical knowledge is more developed in children from middle-income, compared to lower-income, families (Fryer & Levitt, 2004; Griffin & Case, 1997; Jordan et al., 1992; Kilpatrick et al., 2001; NMP, 2008; Sarama & Clements, 2008; Saxe et al., 1987; Starkey & Klein, 1992). The key factors in one study were the educational level attained by the child's mother and the level of poverty in the child's neighborhood (Lara-Cinisomo, Pebley, Vaiana, & Maggio, 2004). These are distinct factors, with income having a direct effect on the child and an effect mediated by the parents' interaction with children (e.g., higher, compared to lower, income parents providing more support for problem-solving; Brooks-Gunn et al., 1999; Duncan, Brooks-Gunn, & Klebanov, 1994). Similarly, an analysis of the

ECLS data shows that SES indicators and the number of books in the home both strongly predict math and reading test scores (Fryer & Levitt, 2004; also controlling for these substantially reduces ethnic differences).

Low-income, compared to middle-income parents, believe that math education is the responsibility of the preschool and that children cannot learn aspects of math that research indicates they can learn (Starkey et al., 1999). Also, low-income families more strongly endorsed a skills perspective than middle-income families, and their "skills" and "entertainment" in perspectives were not predictive of later school achievement, as was the "math in daily living" perspective adopted by more middle-income parents (Sonnenschein, Baker, Moyer, & LeFevre, 2005). These deleterious effects are more prevalent and stronger in the U.S. than other countries and stronger in early childhood than for other age ranges.

Consider these two children. Peter was at the highest levels of competence in number. He could count beyond 120, state the number word before or after any given number word, including those in the hundreds. He could also read those number words. Finally, he could use counting strategies to solve a wide range of addition and subtraction tasks. Tom could not count. The best he could do is say "two" for a pair of objects. Asked for the number after "six," said "horse." After one, he said, comes "bike." He could not read any numerals. *Both Peter and Tom were beginning their kindergarten year* (A. Wright, 1987).

A large-scale study of this gap, a survey of U.S. kindergartners found that 94% of first-time kindergartners passed their Level I test (counting to 10 and recognizing numerals and shapes) and 58% passed their Level 2 test (reading numerals, counting beyond 10, sequencing patterns, and using nonstandard units of length to compare objects). However, 79% of children whose mothers had a bachelor's degree passed the Level 2 test, compared to 32% of those whose mothers had less than a high school degree. Large differences were also found between ethnic groups on the more difficult Level 2 test (NCES, 2000). Differences appear even in the preschool years. The Early Childhood Longitudinal Study (ECLS) showed that, *before entering kindergarten*, low-SES children scored 0.55 standard deviations below middle-SES children on a mathematics assessment; low-SES children scored *1.24 standard deviations below* high-SES children. Being a member of both low SES and minority groups was especially damaging to these children's initial start in school.

Other analyses from the same large ECLS showed that children who begin with the lowest achievement levels show the *lowest* growth in mathematics from kindergarten to the third grade (Bodovski & Farkas, 2007). The authors conclude that more time on mathematics for these children in preschool is essential.

If high-quality mathematics education does not start in preschool and continue through the early years, children are trapped in a trajectory of failure (Rouse et al., 2005). Another study combined the two types of comparisons. Results showed that mathematical knowledge is greater in 3- and 4-year-old Chinese children than in American middle-class children and greater in American middle-class children than in 3- and 4-year-olds from low-income families (Starkey et al., 1999).

Children from low-income families show specific difficulties. They do not understand the relative magnitudes of numbers and how they relate to the counting sequence (Griffin et al., 1994). They have more difficulty solving addition and subtraction problems. Working-class children in the U.K. are a year behind in simple addition and subtraction as early as 3 years of age (Hughes, 1981). Similarly, U.S. low-income children begin kindergarten behind middle-income children and, although they progressed at the same rate on most tasks, they ended behind and made no progress in some tasks. For example, although they performed adequately on nonverbal arithmetic tasks, they made no progress over the entire kindergarten year on arithmetic story problems (Jordan,

Kaplan, Oláh, & Locuniak, 2006). Further, lower-class children were more likely to show a "flat" growth curve for the year.

A recent survey of preschoolers' competencies (Sarama & Clements, 2008) revealed that children from preschools serving middle-SES populations outperformed those serving low-SES populations on the total number score and most individual subtests. The particular subtests that showed significant differences were, with few exceptions, those that measure more sophisticated mathematical concepts and skills. In number, there were no significant differences for simple verbal counting or recognition of small numbers (Clements & Sarama, 2004a, 2007c). There were significant differences on object counting and more sophisticated counting strategies, comparing numbers and sequencing, number composition, arithmetic, and matching numerals to dot cards. In geometry, there were no significant differences on the simple tasks involving shape and comparison of shapes. (The turns subtest was also relatively simple, but because it included only a single task, results should be interpreted with caution.) There were significant differences on representing shapes, composing shapes, and patterning. Measurement was an exception in that sophisticated concepts and skills were involved but no significant difference between the groups was found; development in this domain may be more dependent on school-based teaching.

Regarding individual items, performance of the low-SES group is consistent with these results. In counting, notable differences were on using the cardinality principle, producing a collection of a given number, counting scrambled arrangements, and telling what number comes after another number. The other developmental progressions in number showed a more consistent difference across items; note that both means and differences for Add/Subtract were small. In geometry, items for all three developmental progressions showed the same pattern of consistent differences across items.

The children's levels within various developmental progressions provide another view of these differences. Substantially more children in the middle-SES group were one or two levels above the low-SES group's level of counting, with the former operating at the *Counter (Small Numbers)* or *Counter To (Small Numbers)* level. For comparing number, a majority of the high-SES group succeeded at a *Comparer* task, one level above the level attained by most of the low-SES children. Differences in arithmetic were small, while those in composition were larger, but neither indicated differences in level of thinking. Similarly, differences in patterning and geometry do not indicate distinctions in levels of thinking, but do suggest lower achievement for the lower-SES, compared to the middle-SES group.

Other research confirms the finding that there is greater variation in number knowledge among young children of lower-SES backgrounds (Wright, 1991). This was especially so for beginning kindergartners in the verbal counting and numeral recognition. On the other hand, the most advanced children were the least well served. They were learning nothing throughout the entire kindergarten year. They did not advance in reading multidigit numerals throughout their first grade year.

Similarly, lower-income preschoolers lag behind higher-income peers in the earliest form of subitizing, spontaneous recognition of numerosity (Hannula, 2005). They often lack foundational abilities to classify and seriate (Pasnak, 1987). Older children entering first grade showed a smaller effect of familial factors on computation than on mathematics concepts and reasoning. Majority–minority contrasts were small, but parents' economic and psychological (e.g., high school graduation) resources were strong influences (Entwisle & Alexander, 1990).

Early research indicated that such problems have existed for decades, with serious negative effects (Alexander & Entwisle, 1988). The first year of school has a substantial influence on the trajectories of young children's knowledge of number. Black children gained less than white children in this study, and the gap widened over a 2-year period. Transitions to school, and recovering from initial gaps in learning, may be more problematic for black children than white children.

Into kindergarten and the primary grades, lower-income children use less adaptive and mal-adaptive strategies more than middle-class children, probably revealing a deficit in intuitive knowledge of numbers and different strategies (Griffin et al., 1994; Siegler, 1993). Most 5- and 6-year-old low-income children are unable to answer the simplest arithmetic problems, where most middle-income kindergartners could do so (Griffin et al., 1994). In one study, 75% of children in an upper-middle-class kindergarten were capable of judging the relative magnitude of two different numbers and performing simple mental additions, compared to only 7% of lower-income children from the same community (Case et al., 1999; Griffin et al., 1994). As another example, about 72% of high-, 69% of middle- and 14% of low-SES groups can answer an orally presented problem, "If you had 4 chocolate candies and someone gave you 3 more, how many chocolates would you have altogether?" Low-income children often guess or use other maladaptive strategies such as simple counting (e.g., 3 + 4 = 5). They often do this because they lack knowledge of strategies and understandings of why they work and what goal they achieve (Siegler, 1993). *However, given more experience, lower-income children use multiple strategies, with the same accuracy, speed, and adaptive reasoning as middle-income children.*

Let us return briefly to the question of what predicts mathematics achievement, addressed previously in this chapter. The vignette that opens this section raises an important issue. *What is the role of ability, or IQ, in explaining lower achievement of certain groups?* Genetic factors that in part determine ability, such as IQ, probably influence mathematics achievement. Among middle-class students, such factors, rather than family or neighborhood, correlate with academic performance (Berliner, 2006). *But that is not true for the lowest-income groups. Poverty and lack of opportunities to learn that accompany it are strong predictors.* Even small reductions in poverty lead to increases in positive school behavior and better academic performance (Berliner, 2006). Income, even more than parental education and other indicators of lower SES, is the most powerful predictor (Duncan et al., 1994). Indeed, SES is a better predictor in the U.S. than in other countries. Further, even with IQ controlled, children's cognitive functioning is influenced by their mother's income and the home environment she provides (and, incidentally, her IQ is affected by these same factors). Finally, these effects are strongest in early childhood. This is important, as schools classify children right out of preschool, and being identified as low-achieving affects their entire course of schooling (Brooks-Gunn et al., 1999).

The lack of early learning might even change brain structure—early deficits in opportunities to learn may become biologically embedded (Brooks-Gunn et al., 1999; Case et al., 1999). Children's environments, of course, determine what they have the opportunity to learn. That does not mean these children have no mathematical competencies, far from it. Allowing children to be "off by one" eliminated differences between groups in one study (Ehrlich & Levine, 2007b). They appear to have a grasp of approximate numerosities, but less competence with *exact* numerosities.

The SES gap is broad and encompasses several aspects of mathematical knowledge: numerical, arithmetic, spatial/geometric, patterning, and measurement knowledge (A. Klein & Starkey, 2004; Sarama & Clements, 2008). The reason for this gap appears to be that children from low-income families receive less support for math development in their home and school environments (Blevins-Knabe & Musun-Miller, 1996; Holloway, Rambaud, Fuller, & Eggers-Pierola, 1995; Saxe et al., 1987; Starkey et al., 1999). Public pre-K programs serving low-income, compared to those serving higher-income families provide fewer learning opportunities and supports for mathematical development, including a narrower range of mathematical concepts (Bryant, Burchinal, Lau, & Sparling, 1994; D. C. Farran, Silveri, & Culp, 1991). Lack of resources is the main problem, but research indicates it is not the only explanation. There are also differences in attitudes, motivations, and beliefs that need to be addressed (NMP, 2008). For example, "stereotype threat"—the imposition of societal biases such as the lower-ability mathematics of blacks or women to learn mathematics—can have a negative influence on the performance of the threatened groups (NMP, 2008). We need research on whether this affects young children and how this and other problems can be avoided.

Further, quality is lower in classrooms with more than 60% of the children from homes below the poverty line, when teachers lacked formal training (or a degree) in early childhood education, and held less child-centered beliefs (Pianta et al., 2005). An analysis of the large ECLS data set found that black children had made real gains in mathematics knowledge upon entering kindergarten—*but that over the first two years of school, they lost substantial ground relative to other races* (Fryer & Levitt, 2004). These differences are on arithmetic—addition, subtraction, and even multiplication and division—rather than lower-order skills. There are insufficient resources in these settings to address the needs of the children.

Thus, there is an early developmental basis for later achievement differences in mathematics: Children from different sociocultural backgrounds are provided different foundational experiences (Starkey et al., 1999). Programs need to recognize sociocultural and individual differences in what children know and in what they bring to the educational situation. Knowledge of what children bring should inform planning for programs and instruction. Extra support should be provided those from low-resource communities. We must meet the special needs of all children, especially groups disproportionately under-represented in mathematics, such as children of color and children whose home language is different from that of school. All these children also bring diverse experiences on which to build meaningful mathematical learning (Moll, Amanti, Neff, & Gonzalez, 1992). The younger the child, the more their learning is enhanced by contexts that they find relevant and meaningful. There is no evidence that such children cannot learn the mathematics that other children learn. (If this seems palpable, consider that, historically, it was assumed that children from these groups were less genetically able. And remember the recent comments from the reviewer at the beginning of this section.) Too often, children are not provided with equivalent resources and support (Lee & Burkam, 2002). They have different and inequitable access to foundational experiences, mathematically-structured materials such as unit blocks, technology, and so forth. The settings in which children from different sociocultural backgrounds are served too often have fewer resources and lower levels of high-quality interaction. They also have less to support their physical and mental health (Waber et al., 2007). The needs of children with physical difficulties (e.g., hearing impaired) and learning difficulties (e.g., the mentally retarded) must also be considered. There is a critical need for everyone involved with education to address this problem, so that children at risk receive equitable resources and additional time and support for learning mathematics. This does not mean we should treat children as if they were the same; it means equivalent resources should be available to meet the needs of children who differ in myriad ways, including socioculturally and individually (e.g., developmentally delayed and gifted children). This is important, as knowledge of mathematics in preschool predicts later school success (Jimerson et al., 1999; Stevenson & Newman, 1986; Young-Loveridge, 1989c). Specific quantitative and numerical knowledge is more predictive of later achievement than are tests of intelligence or memory abilities (Krajewski, 2005). Those with low mathematics in the earliest years fall farther behind each year (Arnold & Doctoroff, 2003; Aunola et al., 2004; Wright et al., 1994).

Children who are members of linguistic minority groups also deserve special attention (Nasir & Cobb, 2007). Although teaching specific vocabulary terms ahead of time, emphasizing cognates, is a useful approach, vocabulary alone is insufficient. Teachers need to help students see multiple meanings of terms in both languages (and conflicts between the two languages), and address the *language* of mathematics, not just the "terms" of mathematics. Building on the resources that bilingual children bring to mathematics is also essential. For example, all cultures have "funds of knowledge" that can be used to develop mathematical contexts and understandings (Moll et al., 1992). Further, bilingual children can often see a general mathematical idea more clearly than monolingual children because, after expressing it in two languages, they understand that the abstract mathematical idea is not "tied" to given terms (see Secada, 1992). In general, then, "talking math" is far more than just using math vocabulary.

More children are in deep poverty in the U.S. than other countries. The effects are devastating (Brooks-Gunn et al., 1999).

Practical implications. Children who live in poverty and who are members of linguistic and ethnic minority groups need more math and better math programs (Rouse et al., 2005). They need programs that emphasize the higher-order concepts and skills at each level, as well as base knowledge and skills (Fryer & Levitt, 2004; Sarama & Clements, 2008). What programs address these problems? Several research-based programs are discussed at length in Chapter 15.

Mathematical Learning Difficulties and Disabilities

Similar to those at risk for other reasons, children with special needs often do not fare well in the typical early childhood classroom. Many children show specific learning difficulties in mathematics at young ages. Unfortunately, they are often not identified, or categorized broadly with other children as "developmentally delayed." This is especially unfortunate because focused mathematical interventions at early ages are effective (Berch & Mazzocco, 2007; Dowker, 2004; Lerner, 1997).

Two categories are often used (Berch & Mazzocco, 2007). Children with *mathematical difficulties (MD)* are those who are struggling to learn math for any reason. Sometimes defined as all those below the 35th percentile, estimates can be as high as 40% to 48% of the population. Those with a specific *mathematics learning disability (MLD)* have some form of memory or cognitive deficit that interferes with their ability to learn concepts and/or procedures in one or more domains of math (Geary, 2004). They are, therefore, a small subset of all those with MD, with estimates of 4% to 10% of the population (estimates of 6% to 7% are most common) (Berch & Mazzocco, 2007; Mazzocco & Myers, 2003). Studies have found that such classifications are not stable for many children in the early and primary grades; only 63% of those classified as MLD in kindergarten were still so classified in third grade (Mazzocco & Myers, 2003).

Children with MLD must, by definition, have a genetic basis, but presently must be defined by behaviors. However, what behaviors define MLD—general cognitive, conceptual, skill, or some combination—is still debated (Berch & Mazzocco, 2007). One of the most consistent findings is that children with MLD have difficulty quickly retrieving basic arithmetic facts. This has been hypothesized to be due to an inability to store or retrieve facts, including disruptions in the retrieval process, and to impairments in visuospatial representations. Deficits in working memory and speed of processing have been reported to be important factors as early as kindergarten, especially for those with difficulties in many areas of mathematics (Geary, Hoard, Byrd-Craven, Nugent, & Numtee, 2007).

Others find that the retrieval times of children with MLD can be explained by the same factors that are thought to underlie performance limitations of normally achieving children (Hopkins & Lawson, 2004). So, they may not have an impaired working memory or a special kind of "retrieval deficit," but other difficulties.

Still others have posited that impairments in the executive control of verbal material (Berch & Mazzocco, 2007) may prevent these children from learning basic arithmetic combinations or facts. So, even by second grade, children with MLD may not understand all the counting principles and may have difficulty holding an error violation in working memory.[1] They make more counting errors and persist in using developmentally immature counting strategies. Indeed, they may continue to use immature, "backup" strategies with small variation and limited change throughout elementary school (Ostad, 1998). The immature counting knowledge of MLD children, and their poor skills at detecting counting errors, may underlie their poor computational skills in addition (Geary, Bow-Thomas, & Yao, 1992). Some only abandon finger-counting by the end of the elementary grades. They also have difficulty retrieving arithmetic facts, and, although the other skills develop slowly, retrieval of facts does not improve for most children classified as MLD (Geary et al., 1991). These findings suggest that they have a cognitive disability and not lack of education or experience, poor motivation, or low IQ. These children may also have disrupted functions of the central executive process, including attentional control and poor inhibition of irrelevant associations (e.g., for 5 + 4, saying "6" because it follows 5), and difficulties with information representation and manipulation in the language system (Geary, 2004). However, still other researchers downplay the role of such domain-general cognitive abilities, stating that impairments in specific early numerical systems such as subitizing are more important (Berch & Mazzocco, 2007). There is much that remains to be learned. Here we will examine what early mathematical concepts and skills appear important, and then turn to different types and combinations of disabilities.

Specific mathematical concepts and skills. MLD in the early elementary grades is often characterized by developmental lags in retrieving arithmetic combinations, applying computational strategies, and solving complex story problems (Dowker, 2004; Jordan & Montani, 1997).[2] Representation of numerosity may underlie many such difficulties. "Number sense" measures appear most predictive—kindergartners who perform badly on number comparison, number conservation, and numeral reading are likely to show persistent MLD in grades 2 and 3 (Mazzocco & Thompson, 2005). Another study found that number comparison, nonverbal calculations, story problems, and arithmetic combinations were predictive of first grade math achievement (Jordan, Kaplan, Locuniak, & Ramineni, 2006). Understanding specific deficits can help design programs for individual children. For example, many children with MLD have weak conceptual knowledge and skill in certain areas of counting. These gaps appear to contribute to their difficulties in computational arithmetic. Addressing these early may help.

Thus, children who have MLD or MD may have quite diverse learning needs (Dowker, 2004; Gervasoni, 2005; Gervasoni, Hadden, & Turkenburg, 2007). These findings support the need to understand, assess, and teach these children with topic-specific learning trajectories, as has been the theme of this book. That is, as the *hierarchic interactionalism* tenet of *domain specific progression* would indicate, there are many relatively independent components of arithmetical competence each of which develops along its own learning trajectory. Research on both people with brain injuries and students with mathematical difficulties show that it is possible to have a deficit in any of those areas independent of others (Dowker, 2004, 2005). These include basic fact knowledge, inability to carry out arithmetic procedures, understanding and using arithmetic principles, estimating, possessing other mathematical knowledge, and applying arithmetic in solving problems (Dowker, 2005).

Foundational abilities in subitizing, counting and counting strategies, simple arithmetic, and magnitude comparison are critical for young children with MLD (P. Aunio, Hautamäki, Sajaniemi, & Van Luit, 2008; Aunola et al., 2004; Geary et al., 1999; Gersten et al., 2005). Research has also identified specific difficulties with place value and word problem-solving (Dowker, 2004). Note that these studies often ignore mathematics topics other than number; we will address topics beyond number in a succeeding section.

Math, reading, and language learning disabilities. Further, understanding children's various broad areas of difficulty is important. For example, children with different patterns of achievement in reading and mathematics show different patterns of performance on cognitive measures (Geary et al., 1999). Children with both MLD and reading learning disabilities (RLD) were found to score lower on number production and comprehension tasks, such as number naming, numeral writing, and magnitude comparison. The authors hypothesized that children lacked adequate exposure to Arabic representations of numbers. Children's counting knowledge was assessed with several error recognition tasks. Children with both RLD and MLD were more likely to view counting as a mechanical activity. For example, they believed that counting first one color, then another, of a group of objects was a counting error. They correctly identified the error of counting the last, but not the first, item twice, suggesting that they had difficulties holding information in the phonological loop component of working memory. Perhaps surprisingly, children with only MLD performed less well on actual errors (double counting), perhaps because they have a specific deficit in acting on objects in their working memory (or in the executive control of working memory, Geary et al., 1999). They may not be able to retain information while they act on other information. This is consistent with other research (Rourke & Finlayson, 1978) showing that children who have low achievement in arithmetic but average reading scores often have poor performance on measures of spatial abilities and on timed, but not untimed, arithmetic tests. Children who are low in both reading and arithmetic, in contrast, are poor on verbal and both timed and untimed arithmetic tests. In any case, children with low achievement in arithmetic show many more procedural and retrieval errors (Geary et al., 1999; Jordan & Montani, 1997).

Primary grade students with MLD only have an advantage over their MLD/RLD peers in limited areas (Hanich, Jordan, Kaplan, & Dick, 2001), such as accuracy on exact arithmetic calculations and story problems (and not everyone has found even these differences, Berch & Mazzocco, 2007). They appear to perform similarly in calculation fluency, but the MLD only children used their fingers more accurately, suggesting that they had better facility with counting procedures (N. C. Jordan, Hanich, & Kaplan, 2003). The MLD only and RLD only children performed about the same levels in problem-solving throughout the study, and only slightly below normally-achieving children, suggesting they use different pathways to solving the problems, compensating for their weaknesses with their strengths. The MLD only children may develop math knowledge at a fast rate through the primary grades (Jordan, Kaplan, & Hanich, 2002).

The MLD only and MLD/RLD children did not differ on approximate arithmetic (estimating answers to addition and subtraction problems), suggesting that it is weaknesses in *spatial* representations related to numerical magnitudes (rather than verbal representations) that underpin fact retrieval deficits (Jordan, Hanich, & Kaplan, 2003). Children might have difficulty manipulating visual (nonverbal) representations of a number line—a skill that may be critical for solving addition and subtraction problems. Supporting this, children with poor mastery of number combinations performed worse than children with solid mastery on nonverbal block manipulation and pattern recognition tasks. In contrast, they performed at about the same level on verbal cognitive tasks. Other researchers have also identified a possible spatial component of MLD (Mazzocco & Myers, 2003).

In contrast, another study showed that children with MLD and MLD/RLD could compare the number in *collections* as well as their normal-developing peers, but were impaired when comparing Arabic numerals (Rousselle & Noël, 2007). Importantly, there was no difference between the MLD only and MLD/RLD groups. This suggests that, at least for some children, MLD means having difficulty in accessing number magnitude from *symbols*, rather than in processing numbers. This is significant, as difficulty attaching meaning to numerals could confound children's performance in a wide variety of tasks and be the start of many other related problems with mathematics. Traditional teaching that separates instruction on concepts from procedures would be particularly devastating for these children. Instead, connecting concepts and procedures, concrete/visual representations and abstract symbols, would be more effective.

A recent study confirmed that MLD and MLD/RLD groups display qualitatively distinct mathematical profiles from as young as 5 years of age. Although language appears to facilitate young children's performance on most tasks, its role was secondary in importance to nonverbal mathematics skills (J.-A. Jordan, Wylie, & Mulhern, 2007). They appear to have core deficits in numerical cognition (or "number sense"), including number knowledge, counting, and arithmetic. Those with MLD/RLD are lower on math problem-solving. MLD only children appear to use their verbal strengths to compensate somewhat for their weakness with numbers.

Children with specific language impairments (SLI) may have specific MLD, such as coordinating the items with a structure of correspondences between speech sounds and numerical relations (Donlan, 1998). For example, they may not acquire the quantifiers of their grammatical system, such as "a," "some," "few," or "two" (cf. Carey, 2004). Or, they may have difficulty relating "two, three, four five . . ." to "twenty, thirty, forty, fifty. . . ." Exact arithmetic may depend more heavily on language systems (Berch & Mazzocco, 2007).

Other impairments. Specific disabilities must be considered in a complete picture of infant to adult developmental trajectories (Ansari & Karmiloff-Smith). Different impairments in low-level processes may result in different difficulties in children and adults.

The most prevalent disorder in the U.S. is attention deficit hyperactivity disorder (ADHD, Berch & Mazzocco, 2007). These children habituate to stimuli rapidly and thus have difficulty maintaining attention, spend less time rehearing, and make more errors. Attention to auditory processes is especially problematic. This may account for their difficulty learning basic arithmetic combinations and their difficulty with multistep problems and complex computations. Tutoring and work with computer games have shown some success (Ford, Poe, & Cox, 1993; Shaw, Grayson, & Lewis, 2005). Use of calculators allows some children to succeed (Berch & Mazzocco, 2007).

Most children with Down Syndrome could maintain one-to-one correspondence when counting, but had particular difficulties producing the count words correctly. Their errors were most often skipping words, indicating difficulty with auditory sequential memory. That is, they had inadequate connections between one number word and the next in the sequence. They also lacked approaches to problem-solving or counting strategies (Porter, 1999). Teachers of children with Down Syndrome often neglect number tasks, but this is unwise. Visually presented number sequences may help children learn to count (Porter, 1999).

Physical impairments such as hearing difficulties may be considered risk factors for mathematical difficulties. However, these children seem to learn mathematics the same ways as their peers, and there is not a strong or necessary connection (Nunes & Moreno, 1998). Visually-based interventions may be effective with children who are deaf (Nunes & Moreno, 2002).

An unusual condition is grapheme-color synaesthesia—the involuntary experience of numerals having distinct colors, such as seeing the numeral "5" as blue. Such children may have difficulty in magnitude judgment and often report difficulties with arithmetic (Green & Goswami, 2007).

Blind children cannot rely on visual-spatial strategies for object counting, instead using tactile-motor systems for keeping track of which objects have been counted (Sicilian, 1988). Accurate blind counters used three sets of strategies. Scanning strategies were used to determine the size of the array and any distinctive characteristics, such as linearity or circularity, that could be used to organize counting. Count-organizing strategies capitalized upon these characteristics to create a plan for keeping track. Partitioning strategies selected individual objects and maintained the separation of objects that had and had not yet been counted. The researcher proposed developmental progressions for these, each of which moves from no, to inefficient, to efficient strategies:

- preliminary scanning strategies—no scanning (just started counting); moves the hand across objects unsystematically; moves the hand across all objects in a fixed array systematically, or moves objects during counting.
- organizing strategies—none; follows a row, circle, or array but does not use reference point to mark where started; uses reference point, or moves objects during counting.
- partitioning—no one-to-one correspondence; touches objects but no systematic partitioning, or moves objects but put them back in same group; uses moveable partitioning system or moves objects to new location.

As we have seen, some researchers believe that a deficit in visuospatial strategies is a component of MLD because they may underlie numerical thinking. What about other areas of mathematics, such as geometry, spatial reasoning, and measurement? We know little, possibly due to a bias in researchers. That is, the children are classified as MLD, MD, or normal on the basis of measures that are dominated by numerical and computational items, then their performance compared on computational and numerical word problems. No wonder they are characterized as having "primary impairments" in those areas. We do not know about children's performance in other areas due to such unfortunate, limited, circular thinking. However, we can at least address the needs of children with certain physical disabilities, an issue to which we turn.

Geometry and spatial thinking. Geometry is a more difficult area to address for children who are visually impaired. However, strategies have been proposed for specific skills, such as making distance judgments from a tactile map (Ungar, Blades, & Spencer, 1997). Students were taught to use their fingers to measure relative distances and think in terms of fractions or ratios, or at least in terms of "much longer" or "only a little bit longer." The 30-minute training helped them be as accurate as sighted children.

The discussion of the spatial thinking of blind children in Chapter 7 indicated that all students can build up spatial sense and geometric notions. Spatial knowledge *is* spatial, not "visual." Even children blind from birth are aware of spatial relationships. By age 3, they begin to learn about spatial characteristics of certain visual language (Landau, 1988). They can learn from spatial-kinesthetic (movement) practice (Millar & Ittyerah, 1992). They perform many aspects of spatial tasks similar to blindfolded sighted children (Morrongiello, Timney, Humphrey, Anderson, & Skory, 1995). Second, visual input is important, but spatial relations can be constructed without it (Morrongiello et al., 1995). People who are blind can learn to discriminate the size of objects, or their shape (circle, triangle, and square) with 80% accuracy by distinguishing echoes (Rice, 1967, as cited in Gibson, 1969). They can certainly do so through tactile explorations. For example, students who are blind have been successfully taught to seriate lengths (Lebron-Rodriguez & Pasnak, 1977). Primary grade students can develop the ability to compare rectangular areas by tactile scanning of the two dimensions (Mullet & Miroux, 1996).

However, the more severe the visual impairment, the more you need to make sure that students are given additional activities that build on their experiences with moving their bodies and feeling objects. Students with low vision can follow activities for sighted students, but with enlarged print, visuals, and manipulatives. Sometimes, use of low vision devices facilitates students' geometry learning.

Using real objects and manipulative solids to represent two- and three-dimensional objects is critical for all students with visual impairments. Two-dimensional objects can be represented in tactile form on a two-dimensional plane adequately, but care should be taken that the entire presentation is not too complex. For example, the book *Let's Learn Shapes with Shapely-CAL* presents tactile representations of common shapes (Keller & Goldberg, 1997).

However, two-dimensional tactile representations are *not* adequate for representing three-dimensional objects. Detailed, specific guidance and elaboration of the students' experiences with such objects is important. This is labor-intensive, but an important part of the educational experience for children who are severely visually impaired. Make sure the students explore all components of the object, and reflect on their relationship to each other. Students can explore and describe a three-dimensional solid, reconstruct a solid make of components (such as with Googooplex), and construct a cube given only one edge (e.g., with D-stix).

Research with students who are deaf has indicated that both teachers and students often did not have substantial experience with geometry (Mason, 1995). Language, however, did play an important role. For example, the iconic nature of the American Sign Language (ASL) sign used for triangle is roughly equilateral or isosceles. After an 8-day geometry unit, many students spelled "triangle" instead of using signs, which may indicate a differentiation in their minds between their new definition of the word "triangle" and what they had previously associated with the sign "triangle." When provided with richer learning experiences, a more varied mathematical vocabulary, and exposure to a wide range of geometry concepts, students can experience success and growth in learning geometry (Mason, 1995).

Given the sometimes confusing vocabulary in geometry education, students with limited English proficiency (LEP) require special attention. One study showed that English proficient (EP) and LEP students can work together using computers to construct the concepts of reflection and rotation. Students experiencing the dynamic computer environment significantly outperformed students experiencing a traditional instructional environment on content measures of the concepts of reflection and rotation as well as on measures of two-dimensional visualization ability. LEP students did not perform statistically significantly differently than their EP peers on any of the tests when experiencing the same instructional environments (Dixon, 1995).

Although, as stated, the research has been limited, some children appear to have difficulty with spatial organization across a wide range of tasks. Children with certain mathematics learning difficulties may struggle with spatial relationships, visual-motor and visual-perception, and a poor sense of direction (Lerner, 1997). They may not perceive a shape as a complete and integrated entity as children without learning disabilities do. For example, a triangle may appear to them as 3 separate lines, as a rhombus or even as an undifferentiated closed shape (Lerner, 1997). Children with different brain injuries show different patterns of competence. Those with right hemispheric injuries have difficulty organizing objects into coherent spatial groupings, while those with left hemispheric injuries have difficulty with local relations within spatial arrays (Stiles & Nass, 1991). Teaching with learning trajectories based on the developmental sequences described here is even more important for children with learning disabilities, as well as children with other special needs. Know the developmental sequences through which children pass as they learn geometric ideas.

As noted previously, spatial weakness may underlie children's difficulties with numerical magnitudes (e.g., knowing that 5 is greater than 4, but only by a little, whereas 12 is a lot greater than 4) and rapid retrieval of numeral names and arithmetic combinations (Jordan, Hanich, & Kaplan, 2003). These children may not be able to manipulate visual representations of a number line.

Similarly, due to the difficulties in perceiving shapes and spatial relationships, recognizing spatial relationships, and making spatial judgments, these children are unable to copy geometric forms, shapes, numbers, or letters. They are likely to perform poorly in handwriting as well as in arithmetic. When children cannot write numbers easily, they also cannot read and align their own numbers properly. As a result, they make errors in computation. They must learn to copy and line up numbers accurately to calculate problems in addition and subtraction, in place value, and in multiplication and division (Bley & Thornton, 1981; Thorton, Langrall, & Jones, 1997).

Children diagnosed as autistic need structured interventions from the earliest years. They must be kept engaged with their world, including mathematics. Use intense interests that characterize many children with autism to motivate them to study geometry and spatial structures. For example, if they enjoy construction, they might study how triangles are used in bridges. Many children with autism are visually-oriented. Manipulatives and pictures can aid children's learning of most topics, in geometry, number, and other areas. Children benefit from illustrating even verbs with dramatizations. In a related vein, break down what might have been a long verbal explanation or set of directions. About a tenth of children with autism exhibit savant (exceptional) abilities, often spatial in nature, such as art, geometry, or a particular area of arithmetic. These abilities are probably due not to a mysterious talent, but from massive practice, the reason and motivation for which remains unknown (Ericsson, Krampe, & Tesch-Römer, 1993).

Children who begin kindergarten with the least mathematics knowledge have the most to gain (or to lose) from their engagement with learning (see the previous section in this chapter on affect). It is essential to find ways to keep these children engaged in learning tasks and to increase their initial knowledge (Bodovski & Farkas, 2007).

Summary and policy implications. There are substantial inequities in mathematics experiences in the early years. Some children not only start behind but also begin a negative and immutable trajectory in mathematics (Case et al., 1999). Low mathematical skills in the earliest years are associated with a *slower growth rate*—children without adequate experiences in mathematics start behind and lose ground every year thereafter (Aunola et al., 2004). Interventions should start in pre-K and kindergarten (Gersten et al., 2005). There is substantial evidence that this can be avoided or ameliorated, but also evidence that our society has not taken the necessary steps to do either. Without such interventions, children in special need are often relegated to a path of failure (Baroody, 1999; Clements & Conference Working Group, 2004; Jordan, Hanich, & Uberti, 2003; Wright, 1991; Wright, Stanger, Cowper, & Dyson, 1996).

U.S. children are educationally at risk due to a culture that devalues mathematics, inhospitable schools, bad teaching, and textbooks that make little sense (Ginsburg, 1997). Children are considered learning disabled if they do not learn despite having experienced "conventional instruction." But that instruction is often flawed. This has led some experts to estimate that 80% of children labeled as learning disabled were labeled in error (Ginsburg, 1997, see the footnote on Response-to-Intervention).

We need to determine whether children so labeled benefit from good instruction. For example, some children defined as learning disabled improved after remedial education to the point where they were no longer in remedial education (Geary, 1990). They used cognitive processes that were similar to those of children who were not labeled. Thus, they may have been developmentally delayed but not learning disabled. That is, they were not MLD, but merely miseducated and mislabeled. Better educational experience, including practice, is indicated for such children. The other children did not benefit substantially and appeared to be developmentally different (true MLD children) and in need of specialized instruction.

Children should be *labeled in any way, especially as "MLD," only with great caution* and after good instruction has been provided (see the footnote on Response-to-Intervention). *In the earliest years, such labeling will probably do more harm than good.* Instead, high-quality instruction (preventative education) should be provided to all children.

There is no single cognitive deficit that causes mathematical difficulties (Dowker, 2005; Gervasoni, 2005; Gervasoni et al., 2007; Ginsburg, 1997). This is a problem for children and a problem for research (because of the population on whom they conduct their research). Even more pernicious is that low-income children do not have adequate opportunities to learn mathematics before school, and then attend preschools, childcare, and elementary schools that are themselves low-performing in mathematics. This double dilemma is then compounded as children suffer yet a third assault: Mislabeled as learning disabled, they suffer from lowered expectations from all educators they encounter. This is an educational shame. We must provide complete evaluations of the child's past experiences; present knowledge, skills, and cognitive abilities (e.g., strategic competence, attentional abilities, memorial competencies); and learning potential. If children have difficulties learning, we must determine whether they lack background information and informal knowledge, foundational concepts and procedures, or connections among these. Educative experiences—beyond those regularly provided to children—must be provided over a time frame of months to provide dynamic, formative, assessments of the children's needs (Feuerstein, Rand, & Hoffman, 1979) and the implications for instruction.

Practical implications. Identify children with mathematics difficulties *as early as possible.* Enroll them in research-based mathematical intervention as soon as possible. Identify children who may have been miseducated and mislabeled. Better educational experience, including practice, is indicated for such children. Other children who did not benefit substantially are in need of specialized instruction. Here, drill and practice would not be indicated. Counting on fingers, for example, should be encouraged, not suppressed.

Focus on essential areas such as components of "number sense" and "spatial sense" as described above. Some children with MLD may have difficulty maintaining one-to-one correspondence when counting or matching. They may need to physically grasp and move objects, as grasping is an earlier skill than pointing in development (Lerner, 1997). They often understand counting as a rigid, mechanical activity (Geary, Hamson, & Hoard, 2000). These children also may count objects in small sets one by one for long after their peers are strategically subitizing these amounts. Emphasizing their ability to learn to subitize the smallest number, perhaps representing them on their fingers, may be helpful. (Children who have continued difficulty perceiving and distinguishing even small numbers are at risk of severe general mathematical difficulties, Dowker, 2004.) Other children may have difficulty with subitizing (Landerl, Bevan, & Butterworth, 2004), magnitude comparisons (e.g., knowing which of two digits is larger; Landerl et al., 2004; Wilson, Revkin, Cohen, Cohen, & Dehaene, 2006), and in learning and using more sophisticated counting and arithmetic strategies (Gersten et al., 2005; Wilson, Revkin et al., 2006). Their lack of progress in arithmetic, especially in mastering arithmetic combinations, causes consistent problems; thus, early and intensive intervention is indicated. Young children with MLD are not accurate in evaluating the accuracy of their solutions, which has implications for asking them to "check their work" or "ask for help" (Berch & Mazzocco, 2007).

There are many gaps in resources to help children with special needs. There is no widely-used measure to identify specific learning difficulties or disabilities in mathematics (Geary, 2004). There are too few research-based programs and instructional approaches, but there are some. Those that exist may help these children are discussed in Chapter 15. Finally, however, *the most important implication for early childhood may be to prevent most learning difficulties by providing high-quality early childhood mathematics education to all children* (Bowman et al., 2001). Equity must be complete equity, devoid of labeling, prejudice, and unequal access to opportunities to learn (see Alan J. Bishop & Forgasz, 2007, for a more complete discussion).

Gifted and Talented

Although often perceived by educators as "doing just fine," children with special needs, due to their exceptional abilities, also do not do well in early childhood (and later) programs (NMP, 2008). Teachers sometimes expose gifted and talented children to concepts generally introduced to older students; however, they most frequently teach concepts traditionally found in early childhood programs (Wadlington & Burns, 1993). Even though research shows that these children possess advanced knowledge of measurement, time, and fractions, such topics are rarely explored. Many gifted and talented children may not be identified as such.

One Australian study showed that the kindergarten year mathematics curriculum is most suited to the least advanced children. Talented children learned little or nothing of mathematics throughout an entire kindergarten year (B. Wright, 1991). This is a serious concern because the beginning of preschool and kindergarten can be a critical time for gifted children. They often cannot find peers at their level with similar interests, and become frustrated and bored (Harrison, 2004). Clearly, curricula and educators have to do better to serve the learning needs of all children.

One study showed that parents and teachers can accurately identify gifted children. The children's scores were more than 1 standard deviation above the mean for their age. The children tended to be almost as advanced in verbal and visual-spatial skills on psychometric measures as on measures of mathematical skills. Although boys' level of performance was higher on measures of mathematical skills and visual-spatial working memory span, the underlying relationships among cognitive factors were for the most part similar in girls and boys, with the exception that, for boys, the correlation between verbal and spatial factors was greater than for girls (Robinson, Abbot, Berninger, & Busse, 1996). The highest relationships overall, however, were between visual-spatial and mathematics skills.

Gifted young children show the same characteristics as do older gifted children. They are divergent thinkers, curious, and persistent. They have exceptional memories (one 4-year-old said, "I remember things because I have pictures in my head"). They are able to make abstract connections and engage in independent investigations—formulating, researching, and testing theories. They show advanced thinking, knowledge, visual representations, and creativity. They have advanced awareness of mathematical concepts. At 21 months, they sort out difference between number and letters. One said, "I'll tell you what infinity is. A frog lays eggs, eggs hatch into tadpoles, the tadpole grows back legs and become a frog and then lays eggs again. Now that's a circle. It's infinity. Everything that's alive is infinity . . ." (Harrison, 2004, p. 82).

Practical implications. Identify children with gifts in mathematics *as early as possible.* Make sure they have interesting mathematics to think about and perform. These children are often taught through unstructured activities, discovery learning, centers, and games within small groups, which are supported by research (Wadlington & Burns, 1993). However, they also need to solve engaging, difficult problems using manipulatives, number and spatial sense, and reasoning, including abstract reasoning.

Gender

"My daughter just does not *get* numbers. I told her, 'Don't worry, honey. I was never good at math either.'" "I know," replied her friend. "Only people with special talent can really do math well."

Myths about math abound in our country. You probably recognized two in the above conversation. The first is that only a small number of "talented" people can succeed in mathematics—we discussed that in a previous section in this chapter. The second, just as dangerous, is that women are not usually in that successful group.

Findings and opinions vary widely regarding gender differences in early mathematics. A large meta-analysis of 100 studies found that girls outperformed boys overall a negligible amount (0.05 standard deviations) (Hyde, Fennema, & Lamon, 1990). On computation, 0.14; for understanding 0.03; for complex problem solving, −0.08 (boys were slightly higher). Differences favoring men emerged in high school (−0.29) and college (−0.32). An analysis of the ECLS database showed girls were more likely than males to be proficient in recognizing numbers and shapes, while males were more likely than females to be proficient in addition and subtraction and multiplication and division. All of these differences were small (Coley, 2002). Girls may be better at drawing tasks (Hemphill, 1987). About equal proportions of girls and boys have mathematical difficulties (Dowker, 2004).

One study from the Netherlands found girls having superior numerical skills (Van de Rijt & Van Luit, 1999); another found no differences (Van de Rijt, Van Luit, & Pennings, 1999). Studies of preschoolers from Singapore, Finland, and Hong Kong reported no gender differences (Pirjo Aunio, Ee, Lim, Hautamäki, & Van Luit, 2004), although in another study in Finland, girls performed better on a relational, but not a counting, scale (P. Aunio et al., 2008). Differences were found in mathematics self-concept among young children in Hong Kong (Cheung, Leung, & McBride-Chang, 2007). Mothers' perceived maternal support was correlated to self-concept, but only for girls.

Brain studies show differences, but they tend to be small (Waber et al., 2007). In this study, boys performed slightly better on perceptual analysis, but girls performed a bit better on processing speed and motor dexterity.

Several studies show that boys, more than girls, are likely to be at the low or high end of math achievement (Callahan & Clements, 1984; Hyde et al., 1990; Rathbun & West, 2004; Wright, 1991). This applies even to the gifted young children in the study previously discussed (Robinson et al., 1996), which reflects differences found in gifted adolescents (NMP, 2008).

Some show differences in some number domains but not in geometry and measurement (Horne, 2004). The differences that were significant in one study were not present at the beginning of school, but developed from Kindergarten to grade 4. This finding is consistent with studies showing that boys make slightly greater progress in mathematics than girls (G. Thomas & Tagg, 2004).

One of the most consistent gender differences is in spatial abilities, especially mental rotation. Most research on gender differences in spatial skills has involved older students. Recent research, however, has identified differences in young children (Ehrlich, Levine, & Goldin-Meadow, 2006; M. Johnson, 1987). For example, 4- to 5-year-old males demonstrate a strong advantage on mental rotation, with girls performing at chance levels (Rosser, Ensing, Glider, & Lane, 1984). Similarly, boys showed an advantage by age 4 years 6 months on a spatial transformation task, with the advantage no more robust for rotation than for translation items. A comparable vocabulary task performance indicated that the boys' advantage on the spatial tasks was not attributable to overall intellectual advantage (Levine, Huttenlocher, Taylor, & Langrock, 1999). At least some of this is caused by lack of experience (Ebbeck, 1984). Girls tend to be more social, boys more interested in movement and action, from the first year of life (Lutchmaya & Baron-Cohen, 2002). Boys gesture more and perform better on spatial transformation tasks, providing one way to assess spatial abilities and suggesting that encouraging gesture, especially for girls, may be worthwhile (Ehrlich et al., 2006).

One observational study confirmed that boys' and girls' puzzle play was related to their mental transformation ability (McGuinness & Morley, 1991). However, parents' use of spatial language was only related to girls', not boys', mental transformation skill (controlling for the effects of parents' overall speech to children, SES, and parents' spatial abilities). Parents' spatial language may be more important for girls (Cannon, Levine, & Huttenlocher, 2007).

Similarly, such research suggests that intentional instruction in spatial skills may be especially important for girls. The relationship between spatial skills and mathematics achievement is higher for girls that boys (Battista, 1990; M. B. Casey, Nuttall, & Pezaris, 2001; Friedman, 1995; Kersh et al., in press). Middle school girls who scored high on spatial tests solved mathematics problems as well or better than the boys (Fennema & Tartre, 1985). Those girls with low spatial/high verbal girls performed most poorly. Spatial skills are stronger mediators than even mathematics anxiety or self-confidence (Casey, Nuttall, & Pezaris, 1997). Parents' use of spatial language is related to girls', but not boys' skill at mental transformations. Girls may use more verbal mediation on some tasks (Cannon et al., 2007).

Boys in one study were more confident in mathematics, but they were not accurate, as confidence did not predict math competence (Carr, Steiner, Kyser, & Biddlecomb, 2008). One important difference, however, was that girls preferred using manipulatives to solve problems, but boys preferred more sophisticated strategies. These cognitive strategies may influence their performance and later learning. Such difference in strategy use has been replicated repeatedly and is cause for serious concern (Carr & Alexeev, 2008; Carr & Davis, 2001; Fennema, Carpenter, Franke, & Levi, 1998). The children solved basic arithmetic problems under two conditions: a free-choice condition in which they were allowed to solve the problems any way they preferred and a game condition in which the children's strategy use was constrained so that all children used the same strategies on the same arithmetic problems. Strategy use during the free-choice session replicated the findings of earlier research indicating that girls tend to use strategies utilizing manipulatives and boys tend to use retrieval. During the game condition, when we controlled the types of strategies children used on different problems, we found that boys were as able as girls to calculate solutions using manipulatives. Girls, however, were not as capable as boys in their retrieval of answers to arithmetic problems from memory. No differences were found in error rates or speed of retrieval. Gender differences were found in the variability of correct retrieval, with boys being significantly more variable than girls (Carr & Davis, 2001).

Although the source is unknown, we know that gender differences can be minimized when all children are provided with good education, including encouraging everyone to develop more sophisticated strategies and to take risks. One study suggested that girls' strategy use is guided by classroom norms that do not actively promote the use of more mature strategies. Unfortunately, this pattern resulted in the highest number of failures on the competency test for girls (Carr & Alexeev, 2008). Spatial skills also may promote more mature strategies (Carr, Shing, Janes, & Steiner, 2007).

Practical implications. Teach spatial skills, particularly intentionally to girls, and encourage parents to do so. Encourage girls as well as boys to use sophisticated strategies.

Final Words

To be fully professional and effective, teachers must understand children's cognition and affect, and issues of individual differences and equity. However, this is not sufficient—we also need to understand how to use these understanding to promote thinking, positive dispositions, and fairness. Such is the intent of the next two chapters. Chapter 15 addresses the contexts of instruction—the types of settings in which children are taught, including children's first setting, their families and their homes. It also focuses on specific curricula that are effective in helping young children learn mathematics.

15

Early Childhood Mathematics Education
Contexts and Curricula

> I really enjoy teaching *Building Blocks*. My children have shown *tremendous* growth. One child, who initially could not verbally count at all, is now able to verbally count, use one-to-one correspondence, and make sets up to 20 with confidence.
>
> (Carla F., preschool teacher, 2006)

What makes a good math curriculum for young children? How would you evaluate your own? Previous chapters discussed the roles of experience, education, and teaching for specific topics. This chapter expands that discussion to address the types of settings in which children are taught, including children's first setting—their families and their homes. We then focus on general findings regarding specific curricula that are effective in helping young children learn mathematics. Remember, because there is no corresponding chapter in the companion book, there is more research reviewed in the chapter. We have marked paragraphs with implications for practitioners with "*Practical implications*," for those who wish to focus only on these.

Early Childhood Educational Settings: Past and Present

Let's start by addressing the educational settings of the past and present by eavesdropping on a conversation between two educators, one who is skeptical about mathematics in early childhood.

Skeptic: Organized mathematics experiences are inappropriate for kindergartners.
Math Educator: Well, they certainly can be, if not done well! However, research has indicated that children learn about number and geometry from their first year of life, quite naturally. Further, educational environments can enhance this learning.
Skeptic: Sure, you can always teach them more, but this pressures children and is another modern mistake.
Math Educator: I don't think so. Early childhood educators have always thought about math.

A short historical view of early mathematics confirms this opinion. Frederick Froebel invented kindergarten—originally a multiage early childhood education, so he invented present-day kindergarten *and* preschool. Froebel was a crystallographer. Almost every aspect of his kindergarten crystallized into beautiful mathematical forms—the "universal, perfect, alternative language of geometric form" (Brosterman, 1997). Its ultimate aim was to instill in children an understanding of the mathematically generated logic underlying creation. Froebel used "gifts" to teach children the geometric language of the universe. Cylinders, spheres, cubes, and other materials were arranged and moved to show geometric relationships. For example, Froebel's fundamental gifts were largely manipulatives, moving from solids (spheres, cylinders, cubes) to surfaces, lines, and points, then the reverse. His occupations with such materials included explorations (e.g., spinning the solids in different orientations, showing how, for example, the spun cube can appear as a cylinder), puzzles, paper folding, and constructions. The triangles, well known to children as parts of faces or other pictures, were used to teach concepts in plane geometry. Children covered the faces of cubes with square tiles, and peeled them away to show parts, properties, and congruence. Many blocks and tiles were in carefully planned shapes that fit in the grid in different ways. Shapes and rings and slats were used in plain view on the ever-present grid on the kindergarten table, arranged and rearranged into shifting, symmetric patterns or geometric borders.

Further, structured activities would follow that provided exercises in basic arithmetic, geometry, and the beginning of reading. For example, the cubes that children had made into the chairs and stoves would be made into geometric design on the grid etched into every kindergarten table, and later laid into two rows of four each and expressed as "4 + 4." In this way, connections were key: The "chair" became an aesthetic geometric design, which became a number sentence.

Is it true that the experiences of R. Buckminster Fuller, Frank Lloyd Wright, and Paul Kale in Froebelian kindergartens are the foundation of all their creative work, as claimed (Brosterman, 1997)? Whether you believe that is an overstatement or not, it is clear that mathematics in the early years is not a recent invention.

The pervasiveness of mathematics from the work of Froebel was largely forgotten or diluted. It was often lost in unfortunate conflicts about the type of mathematical experiences that should be provided (Balfanz, 1999). Historically, researchers have repeatedly witnessed children enjoying pre-mathematical activities. However, others expressed fears of the inappropriateness of mathematics for young children, although these opinions were based on broad social theories or trends, not observation or study (Balfanz, 1999). Bureaucratic and commercial imperatives emerging from the institutionalization of early childhood education quashed most of the promising mathematical movements.

One example is stark. Edward Thorndike, who wished to emphasize health, replaced the first gift (small spheres) with a toothbrush and the first mathematical occupation with "sleep" (Brosterman, 1997). Consider another example, the traditional material of kindergarten building blocks. Children create forms and structures that are based on mathematical relationships. For example, children may struggle with length relationships in finding a roof for a building. Length and equivalence are involved in substituting two shorter blocks for one long block. Children also consider height, area, and volume. Recall that the inventor of today's unit blocks, Caroline Pratt (1948), tells of children making enough room for a horse to fit inside a stable. The teacher told Diana that she could have the horse when she had made a stable for it. She and Elizabeth began to build a small construction, but the horse did not fit. Diana had made a large stable with a low roof. After several unsuccessful attempts to get the horse in, she removed the roof, added blocks to the walls to make the roof higher, and replaced the roof. She then tried to put into words what she had done. "Roof too small." The teacher gave her new words, "high" and "low," and she gave a new explanation to the other children. Just building with blocks, children form important ideas. Teachers, such as Diana's, help children explicate and further develop these intuitive ideas by discussing them, giving words to their actions.

For example, children can be helped to distinguish between different quantities such as height, area, and volume. Three preschoolers made towers and argued about whose was the biggest. Their teacher asked them if they meant whose was tallest (gesturing) or widest, or used the most blocks? The children were surprised to find that the tallest tower did not have the most blocks (see Chapter 9 for more on block building).

Unfortunately, the typical kindergarten building blocks have features of the less structured toy design against which Froebel reacted. They do not have the same mathematics modularity. Nevertheless, all these materials were designed with mathematics in mind.

Present Early Childhood Education—Where is the Math?

Generally, children who attend preschool are better prepared for academic work in kindergarten than those who do not (Barnett, Frede, Mobasher, & Mohr, 1987; Lee, Brooks-Gunn, Schnur, & Liaw, 1990). However, these results may differ for different school contexts and for different populations. For example, in one study, Head Start, but not other preschools, raised children's language scores and reduced the frequency that children repeated a grade later in school (Currie & Thomas, 1995). However, benefits dissipated quickly for African-American children, but not for white children. The study did not permit a clear explanation for this, although findings tended to eliminate the effects of the home, thus suggesting that African-American children may be served by lower-quality elementary schools. The lack of effect of other preschools is certainly a concern.

These findings depend on achieving at least *minimal* standards of quality in preschool programs (Barnett et al., 1987). Without a measure of quality, this study would have concluded that preschools were not effective. However, high quality is not always to be found in U.S. early childhood classrooms, especially for children from low-resource communities, and especially regarding the earliest years of mathematics education. In this section, we begin by examining what we know about mathematics in early childhood settings. For example, African American, Asian, and Latino children were more likely than white children to attend a Pre-K class with a high proportion of children from low-income backgrounds. Importantly, poor children are more likely to be taught by teachers with fewer qualifications (Clifford et al., 2005).

Across the board, not much math learning happens in early childhood settings. For example, achievement for children entering first grade is not substantially higher than the mean for those entering kindergarten (Heuvel-Panhuizen, 1996). Kindergarten and first grade curricula may spend too much time teaching children things they already know, and not enough teaching them more challenging mathematics, including problem-solving (Carpenter & Moser, 1984).

Math in kindergarten. How much mathematics is done in early childhood settings? Teacher reports from the large Early Childhood Longitudinal Study (ECLS; Hausken & Rathbun, 2004) indicate that kindergarten teachers spend an average of 39 minutes each session, 4.7 days per week, for a total of 3.1 hours each week of mathematics instruction. This is about half of what they spend on reading. Direct instruction was more commonly used with girls and higher SES, and "constructivist" approaches used more often with children of low ability. Each week teachers engage children in manipulative activities 1–2 times and problem-solving and practice (worksheet) activities 2–3 times. Individual skills were not related to the frequency of exposure to different types of mathematics problems. The authors warn that uniformity of activities across the classrooms may account for these findings. Especially given contrasting data from smaller but more focused studies described later, additional caveats concerning the limitation of post hoc teacher self-report data and the lack of specific information on curricula are warranted.

Math in preschool. Research is beginning to describe corresponding preschool practices. Observations of the full day of 3-year-olds' lives, across all settings, revealed remarkably few mathematics activities, lessons, or episodes of play with mathematical objects, with 60% of the children having no experience across 180 observations (Tudge & Doucet, 2004). Factors such as race-ethnicity, SES, and setting (home or child care) did not significantly affect this low frequency. Another study found that those in child care centers scored significantly higher on formal and informal mathematics skills than those in child care homes (Austin et al., 2008).

A small observational study of four Pre-K teachers from two settings revealed that little mathematics was presented in any of the classrooms, either directly or indirectly (Graham, Nash, & Paul, 1997). Researchers observed only one instance of informal mathematical activity with physical materials and few instances of informal or formal mathematics teaching. Teachers stated that they believed that mathematics was important and that they engaged in mathematical discussions. It appears that selection of materials and activities such as puzzles, blocks, games, songs, and finger plays constituted mathematics for these teachers.

In a similar vein, the large National Center for Early Development and Learning (NCEDL) studies report that children are not engaged in learning or constructive activities during a large proportion of the Pre-K day (Early et al., 2005; Winton et al., 2005). They spent the largest part of their day, up to 44%, in routine maintenance activities (like standing in line) and eating. About 6% to 8% of the day on the average involves mathematics activities in any form. Teachers were observed *not* interacting with child an amazing 73% of the day; 18% was minimal interaction. On average, less than 3% of the time children were engaged in pre-academic experiences, and less than half the children experienced these at all (Winton et al., 2005).

Even in one of the highest-quality programs recently created and run, the Abbott programs, the quality of *mathematics* materials and teaching has been rated as very low (Lamy et al., 2004). This may be one reason that East Asian Countries tend to outperform Western countries—the culture develops mathematical ideas and skills more consistently at earlier ages (Pirjo Aunio et al., 2004; Pirjo Aunio et al., 2006).

Math in preschools using literacy-based curricula. How about the effects of programs that are ostensibly "complete" programs but fundamentally built upon literacy goals? Two curricula, one literacy-oriented (Bright Beginnings), and one developmentally focused (Creative Curriculum), engendered no more math instruction than a control group (Aydogan et al., 2005). However, children in classrooms with stronger emphasis on literacy or math were more likely to be engaged at a higher-quality level during free-choice (play) time. Those in classrooms with an emphasis on both literacy and math were more likely to be engaged at a high-quality level that those in classrooms with only one, or no, such emphasis.

Another study showed that even the OWL (*Opening the World of Learning*) curriculum, which includes mathematics in its all-day, prescribed program, may be woefully inadequate. *In a 360-minute day, only 58 seconds were devoted to math* (Dale C. Farran, Lipsey, Watson, & Hurley, 2007). There was little instruction, few opportunities for children to engage with math materials, and few opportunities for children to talk about math (or anything else, but they talked most in centers, less in small groups, and least in whole-group activities). No children gained math skills, and those beginning with higher scores *lost* math skills over the year. They did gain in literacy skills, but only modestly (Dale C. Farran et al., 2007). *Most children stayed the same or lost mathematics skills during the year.*

Reports from teachers. A survey (Sarama, 2002; Sarama & DiBiase, 2004) asked teachers from a range of preschool settings at what age children should start large-group mathematics instruction. Family and group care providers chose ages 2 or 3 most often, while the other group felt large-group instruction should not start until age 4. Most teachers professed to use manipulatives (95%), number songs (84%), basic counting (74%) and games (71%); few used software (33%) or workbooks (16%). They preferred children to "explore math activities" and engage in "open-ended free play" rather than participate in "large-group lessons" or be "doing math worksheets." When asked about mathematics topics, 67% taught counting, 60%, sorting, 51%, numeral recognition, 46%, patterning, 34%, number concepts, 32%, spatial relations, 16%, making shapes, and 14%, measuring. Geometry and measurement concepts were the least popular. Another survey reported that both public and private preschool teachers *do not think children need specific mathematics teaching* (Starkey, Klein, & Wakeley, 2004). Instead, they believed that children needed "general enrichment."

There are many policy issues that should be considered in addressing these limitations. As we shall see in the next section, family influences are strong. Further, most early childhood teachers are underpaid, and there are large disparities in salaries across settings, with teachers in public schools paid much more than Pre-K teachers in other settings (Early et al., 2005). There is also a wide gap in teachers' education in these settings.

Before we turn to programs and curricula that attempt to address mathematics more adequately, we consider the first and consistently influential setting in which children learn mathematics—the home.

Families

Of course, families also play a major role in young children's development, including their learning of mathematics. There is a relationship between the frequency with which parents use numbers and their children's early mathematical performance (Blevins-Knabe & Musun-Miller, 1996). However, there are several sociocultural barriers. For example, although parents believe that both home and school are important for reading development, they consider the school more important for mathematics development and they provide fewer experiences in mathematics than in reading (Sonnenschein et al., 2005). They believe it is more important to help their children learn literacy than mathematics (Cannon, Fernandez, & Ginsburg, 2005). They prefer teaching language and they believe language is more important to learn than mathematics (Cannon et al., 2005). More for the learning of language than mathematics, parents believe that pedagogy should consist of determination to ensure children acquire specific knowledge, delving deeply into children's understanding, and facilitating children's learning in their everyday lives. These are profound differences that have severe implications.

Further, as with Pre-K teachers, parents have a limited view of the breadth of mathematics appropriate for young children (Sarama, 2002). They know more about what might be taught in language than mathematics (Cannon et al., 2005). This was true regardless of whether parents were Hispanic or not and whether they were low- or middle-SES. However, cultural differences are occasionally relevant. For example, Chinese mothers are more likely than U.S. mothers to teach arithmetic calculation in their everyday involvement with children's learning and maternal instruction was related to Chinese, but not U.S., children's learning of proportional reasoning (Pan, Gauvain, Liu, & Cheng, 2006). Mothers in China rate mathematics as equal in importance to reading, but mothers in the U.S. rate mathematics as of much less importance (Miller, Kelly, & Zhou, 2005).

Let's examine some practices in more detail. The vignette that began the section on gender in the previous chapter, regarding the mother's daughter who "just does not *get* numbers," indicates the effect—sometimes negative—that parents and families can have on children's success in mathematics. Research describes several:

- Prenatal alcohol exposure is associated with poorer calculation abilities. This apparently is mediated entirely by alcohol's effect on children's "number sense"—the basic quantitative bootstrap competence (e.g., Dehaene, 1997; see also Chapters 2 and 4). This competence is associated with activity in the inferior parietal cortex, an area that is disproportionately affected by prenatal alcohol exposure (Burden, Jacobson, Dodge, Dehaene, & Jacobson, 2007).

- Very low birth weight may lead to less mature levels of numerical reasoning on problems with a spatial component and those that required complex problem-solving; however, verbal tasks were affected more strongly by levels of parent education (Wakeley, 2005). Intervention programs can be successful (Liaw, Meisels, & Brooks-Gunn, 1995).
- Poor mother–child engagement related to lower levels of academic success (T. R. Konold & Pianta, 2005).
- Mothers rating themselves as high on affection but also high on psychological control—behaviors that are intrusive and manipulative of children's thoughts, feelings, and attachments to parents (e.g., guilt-inducing)—is predictive of their children's *slow* progress in mathematics. Children may become "enmeshed" in family relations and less independent, or may receive inconsistent messages of their mothers' affection and approval and thus become more anxious about performing well.
- Parents prefer teaching language to teaching mathematics. They are biased towards language and belief there are "universal" grounds for helping children learn language over mathematics. They also have more nuanced beliefs about preschoolers' ability to learn language than mathematics. For language more than mathematics, they believe that teaching should ensure children acquire specific knowledge, that they want to delve deeply into children's understanding, and that they should facilitate children's learning throughout the day (Cannon et al., 2005).
- U.S. parents do not have high expectations. U.S. parents, compared to Chinese parents, set lower standards. The U.S. culture does not value diligent work, as does the Chinese culture. Chinese students' favorite saying was "Genius comes from hard work and knowledge depends on accumulation." U.S. parents said they would be satisfied with 7 points lower than their expectation for their children, but Chinese parents were only satisfied with 10 points higher.
- In many low-income homes, a limited number of mathematical activities are provided (Blevins-Knabe & Musun-Miller, 1996; Ginsburg, Klein, & Starkey, 1998; Thirumurthy, 2003).
- One study reported that U.S. parents work less often and for less time with their children on homework (Chen & Uttal, 1988). However, another found U.S. parents more involved with school activities that Chinese parents, who stressed interest in mathematics and the child's responsibility (Pan & Gauvain, 2007). East Asian parents also provide games, building, and paper-folding activities; U.S. parents allow children's time to be dominated by video games and television.
- Black children may start school with similar competencies, but grow at a slower rate. They are less influenced by parent variables and appear to have a more difficult time transitioning to school. Parent programs that help build bridges and prepare children for school expectations may help alleviate these difficulties (Alexander & Entwisle, 1988).

Several additional "risk factors" for children's homes have been studied, including living below the federal poverty line (set at $16,000), primary home language other than English, mother's highest education less than a high school diploma/GED, and living in a single-parent household The more such factors in a home, the more risk for the child. However, these factors may not be directly responsible for lower learning. For example, being a single parent is not so much the cause as the lack of both resources and high expectations that can accompany it (Entwisle & Alexander, 1997). Other cultural factors must be considered as well. Perhaps the most important is that the achievement gaps between disadvantaged and more advantaged children identified at the beginning of school (West, Denton, & Reaney, 2001) widen over the first 4 years of school attendance (Rathbun & West, 2004).

Children from homes with more risk factors were less likely to have reached each of the highest three levels of math achievement. For example, about 20% of children with no risk factors were proficient by third grade at using rate and measurement knowledge to solve word problems, compared with 11% of children with one family risk factor and 2% with two more.

Of course, parents also are critical in providing positive experiences for their children. The more mathematics activities they engage their children in, the higher the children's achievement (Blevins-Knabe & Musun-Miller, 1996; Blevins-Knabe, Whiteside-Mansell, & Selig, 2007). Programs designed to improve home mathematics learning have been found to be most successful when they had three components: joint and separate sessions for parents and children, a structured numeracy curriculum, and "bridging" activities for parents to develop their child's numeracy at home (Doig, McCrae, & Rowe, 2003).

Parents can provide good materials for play that also will support mathematics learning. Surprisingly, though, one study showed the more the mother "provides behaviors," the lower the child's math ability (Christiansen, Austin, & Roggman, 2005). The researchers found that too many directive behaviors, when the child was not engaged in many math behaviors, might be overstimulating. Introducing formal mathematics also was negatively related to children's informal mathematics knowledge. These relationships, however, appeared to hold only for boys, not girls. The study, like most in this section, is correlational, so we cannot say that parenting behaviors caused higher or lower child knowledge. It does suggest that being responsive to children's actions may be particularly helpful.

Practical implications. Research describes several additional avenues for families to promote positive mathematics learning:

- Discussing mathematical ideas when reading storybooks (A. Anderson, Anderson, & Shapiro, 2004, although the design has limited generalizability).
- Using research-based programs that contain specific suggestions written for parents (Doig et al., 2003).
- Making sure children get sufficient sleep—they usually do not get at least 10 hours per night (Touchette et al., 2007).
- Provision of learning experiences, including sensitivity, quality of assistance in problem-solving, and avoiding of harsh, punitive interactions (all highly related to IQ; Brooks-Gunn et al., 1999).
- Playing math games with children. Parents should ensure they spend some time playing *only* with their young children, as positive interactions and teaching are substantially higher in this case (Benigno & Ellis, 2004).
- Cooking with children, especially using rich vocabulary such as number and measurement words (Young-Loveridge, 1989a). Contingent responses to children are more important than just using the words—giving them feedback and elaborating on their responses is more effective in building their mathematics knowledge.
- Encouraging counting when appropriate, but *also* encouraging a wider range of mathematical experience (Blevins-Knabe & Musun-Miller, 1996).
- Maintaining high to very high expectations for children (Thomson et al., 2005).
- Being willing and able to participate actively in the school's math program and training in how to effectively assist in the classroom (Thomson et al., 2005).
- Supporting and encouraging children, which is associated with children's motivation to learn (Cheung & McBride-Chang, in press). Parents' achievement demands are correlated with actual academic performance. Children's mastery (intrinsic) motivation, not their parents practices or beliefs, explained their perceptions of themselves as competent.

- Using high-quality materials that provide activity ideas and guidance. Perhaps the most useful suggestion for parents is encourage them to get and use books and other resources that provide ideas for activities that will engage their children and their whole family. *Family Math* is a well-established program with books for parents (Stenmark, Thompson, & Cossey, 1986), see http://www.lawrencehallofscience.org/equals/aboutfm.html. NCTM features many resources on their "Figure This! Math Challenges for Familiies" website (see http://www.figurethis.org/fc/family_corner.htm). Searching with the phrase "family math" will yield these and other resources.

Such relationships appear to be reciprocal. For example, in one study the impact of parents' beliefs concerning their primary school children's general school competence was related to children's focusing on school tasks, which in turn was related to children's math performance (Aunola, Nurmi, Lerkkanen, & Rasku-Puttonen, 2003). But parents' beliefs in their children's competence in mathematics contributed directly to their children's high math performance. In the reciprocal relationships, children's high mathematical performance increased parents' subsequent positive beliefs in their children's mathematical competence, and children's task-focusing increased parents' beliefs in their children's overall school competence. Unfortunately, father's beliefs about their sons' math competencies increased over the course of school, but their beliefs decreased for girls (Aunola et al., 2003). This is particularly important because the self-perpetuating, cumulative cycle could be positive or negative.

Parents need mathematics knowledge and skills as well as parenting skills to provide a positive home environment for learning mathematics (Blevins-Knabe et al., 2007). Mothers' attitudes and perceptions about their children's math knowledge appeared to directly affect their children's formal and informal math knowledge, as well as their children's math self-efficacy. These attitudes and perceptions also mediated the effects of the mothers' own mathematics achievement. Parenting behaviors had a direct effect on informal mathematics performance and mediated the effects of the mothers' own mathematics achievement on children's formal mathematics knowledge (Blevins-Knabe et al., 2007). Thus, how much mathematics mothers know matters but is affected by the way they interact with their children. In general, these studies suggest that parents with positive beliefs may encourage or expect their children to engage in mathematical tasks and also provide more challenging tasks.

In working with parents, with policy-makers, and with children, early childhood math educators should be strong advocates for foundational and explicit mathematical experiences for all children, of all ages. In the earliest ages especially, these can often be seamlessly integrated with children's ongoing play and activities ... but this usually requires a knowledgeable adult who creates a supportive environment and provides challenges, suggestions, tasks, and language.

Curricula and Programs—Focusing on Mathematics

Research suggests that children's learning trajectories are influenced by their first educational experiences. Indeed, "the early grades may be precisely the time that schools have their strongest effects" (Alexander & Entwisle, 1988). Early childhood schools and teachers have the power and responsibility to have the strongest positive effect on mathematics learning possible. As we saw, this potential is often left unrealized. Further, those children whose families did not provide strong, positive mathematics experiences are just those who need—but do not receive—those experiences in their early childhood programs. What programs and curriculum provide alternatives that can help meet the needs of these, and all, children? We begin to answer this question by considering those children most in need.

Equity: Children at Risk

As we saw, providing high-quality educational support to children at risk results in greater school readiness upon entry into kindergarten (Bowman et al., 2001; Magnuson & Waldfogel, 2005; Shonkoff & Phillips, 2000), because such support helps young children develop a foundation of informal mathematics knowledge (Clements, 1984). Early knowledge has been shown to support later school mathematics achievement, and lack of it places minorities on a path away from engagement in mathematics and science (Campbell, Pungello, Miller-Johnson, Burchinal, & Ramey, 2001; Oakes, 1990). Longitudinal research indicates that attendance in center-based (but not other types of) care in the Pre-K year is associated with higher mathematics scores in kindergarten and (to a lesser extent) in first grade (Turner & Ritter, 2004), and that achievement in preschool is related to differences in elementary school achievement for Hispanic children (K. Shaw, Nelsen, & Shen, 2001). In another study, African American, Hispanic, and female children who attended an intervention preschool program had a significantly greater probability of achieving high scores in fourth grade than their peers who did not attend school (Roth, Carter, Ariet, Resnick, & Crans, 2000). Child care in general can help, with greater number of hours in child care correlating with greater quantitative skills in low-income children (Votruba-Drzal & Chase, 2004).

High-quality preschool experience is predictive of later school success in mathematics (Broberg, Wessels, Lamb, & Hwang, 1997; F. A. Campbell et al., 2001; Peisner-Feinberg et al., 2001) for many years to come (Brooks-Gunn, 2003). Most important for the effects on mathematics were actual classroom practices—materials, activities, and interactions (Peisner-Feinberg et al., 2001). Although the size of the effects were moderate, they were significant for math (more than other subjects) *for as long as four years* (Peisner-Feinberg et al., 2001).

Unfortunately, children most in need of high-quality environments may not attend high-quality elementary schools, even when their preschools were high in quality. One study revealed very low correlation (0.06 to 0.15) between quality of care in Pre-K and that of the elementary schools (Peisner-Feinberg et al., 2001). In other cases, some effects may even emerge *only* later ("sleeper effects") (Broberg et al., 1997). Thus, for both practice and research, it is critical to evaluate children's entire educational experience.

Other research confirms the importance of high-quality schools. Oklahoma has led the nation in providing preschool education to 70% of its children and maintaining relatively high standards (Barnett, Hustedt, Hawkinson, & Robin, 2006). Two rigorous evaluations indicate substantial positive effects on achievement scores for mathematics and literacy (although smaller effects for mathematics than literacy measures). Children from all ethnic and SES groups benefited (Barnett, Hustedt et al., 2006; Gormley, Gayer, Phillips, & Dawson, 2005). Unfortunately, a commitment to universal Pre-K, high-quality Pre-K, and well-funded Pre-K remain the exception, rather than the norm, in the U.S. (Barnett, Hustedt et al., 2006; Winton et al., 2005).

In a similar vein, state-funded preschool programs in states with high standards have been found to positively affect preschoolers' mathematics achievement (Wong, Cook, Barnett, & Jung, in press), with effects about twice as large as those of Head Start (although the comparison should be made with caution, especially as Head Start results were national, and the five states' preschools did have higher-quality program standards than non-studied states). Further, using randomized assignment, the Head Start Impact Study found no significant impacts for the early mathematics skills for 3- or 4-year-olds (DHHS, 2005). So, such programs may not yet include adequate mathematics.

Practical implications: Interventions focused on math for low-income children—two examples. Most reliably, children living in poverty and those with special needs increase in mathematics achievement after high-quality interventions focused on mathematics (Campbell & Silver, 1999; Fuson, Smith, & Lo Cicero, 1997; Griffin, 2004; Griffin et al., 1995; Ramey & Ramey, 1998), which can be sustained into first (Magnuson, Meyers, Rathbun, & West, 2004) *to* third grade (Gamel-McCormick & Amsden, 2002). As an example, the *Rightstart* (now *Number Worlds*) program (Griffin et al., 1994), featuring games and active experiences with different models of number, led to substantial improvement in children's knowledge of number.[1] Across five studies, almost all children failed the number pre-test, and the majority in the comparison groups failed the post-test as well, whereas the vast majority of those in the program passed the post-test. Children in the program were better able to employ reasonable strategies and also were able to solve arithmetic problems even more difficult than those included in the curriculum. Program children also passed five far-transfer tests that were hypothesized to depend on similar cognitive structures (e.g., balance beam, time, money). The foundation these children received supported their learning of new, more complex, mathematics through first grade. In a 3-year longitudinal study in which children received consistent experiences through the grades from kindergarten through primary, children gained and surpassed both a second low-SES group and a mixed-SES group who showed a higher initial level of performance and attended a magnet school with an enriched mathematics curriculum. The children also compared favorably with high-SES groups from China and Japan (Case et al., 1999). (A caution is that other research indicates that certain components of the curriculum are difficult to implement, Gersten et al., 2008.)

A series of studies have similarly indicated that the *Building Blocks* curriculum (Clements & Sarama, 2007a) significantly and substantially increases the mathematics knowledge of low-SES preschool children. Formative, qualitative research indicated that the curriculum raised achievement in a variety of mathematical topics (Clements & Sarama, 2004a; Sarama & Clements, 2002a). Summative, quantitative research confirmed these findings, with effect sizes ranging from 0.85 (Cohen's *d*) for number to 1.47 for geometry in a small-scale study (Clements & Sarama, 2007c). In a larger study involving random assignment of 36 classrooms, the *Building Blocks* curriculum increased the quantity and quality of the mathematics environment and teaching, and substantially increased scores on a mathematics achievement test. The effect size compared to the control group score was very large ($d = 1.07$) and the effect size compared to a group receiving a different, extensive mathematics curriculum was substantial ($d = .47$). There was no significant interaction by program type (Head Start vs. public preschool).

The *Number Worlds* and *Building Blocks* programs share several characteristics. Both use research to include a comprehensive set of cognitive concepts and processes (albeit *Number Worlds* focuses on the domain of numbers). Both curricula are based on developmentally sequenced activities, and help teachers become aware of, assess, and remediate based on those sequences (projects around the world that use research-based developmental progressions help raise achievement of all children, e.g., Thomas & Ward, 2001; Wright, Martland, Stafford, & Stanger, 2002). Both use a mix of instructional methods.

Alleviating any concern about lack of attention to social-emotional domain, the PCER studies give no indication of negative effects on other measures. Further, another study showed research indicates that mathematics competencies are related to a wide variety of mathematics interventions, with problem behaviors negatively correlated, and self-control, attachment, and especially initiative positively correlated with mathematics skills. Moreover, the intervention increased not only mathematics skills but also these positive social-emotional behaviors (Dobbs, Doctoroff, Fisher, & Arnold, 2006).

Even with few resources, parents can take action to improve their children's school readiness. Parents can read to children themselves or arrange for other adults to do so; provide challenging books, games, and puzzles; help children learn to count and figure out math problems; and participate in reading and other programs at the public library. Providing warm and consistent parenting is also important for school readiness (Lara-Cinisomo et al., 2004).

Children from different income levels receive different types of activities during the early years of school. However, findings are unclear. One large self-report survey indicated that classes with more low-income or minority children were more likely to engage in problem-solving, as well as practice activities (Hausken & Rathbun, 2004). However, other research indicates that, for example, low-income children were more likely to work on drill and less likely to work on problem-solving software (Clements & Nastasi, 1992).

Higher-quality programs result in learning benefits into elementary school, including in mathematics (Fuson, 2004; Griffin, 2004; Karoly et al., 1998). Unfortunately, most American children are not in high-quality programs, much less in programs that use research-based mathematics curricula (Hinkle, 2000). Further, children whose mothers had college degrees were nearly twice as likely to be in higher-quality, center-based care as those whose mothers had not completed high school (Magnuson et al., 2004). As another example, Hispanic children are less likely to be enrolled, even though the benefit they receive from attending is double that for non-Hispanic white children in mathematics and pre-reading (Loeb, Bridges, Bassok, Fuller, & Rumberger, in press). Similarly, children from extremely poor families show a 0.22 *SD* (compared to 0.10 *SD* average for all children) advantage in mathematics concept, compare to peers who remain at home. Further, these average gains would be predictably higher if focused mathematics programs were in place. Thus, children from low-income and minority communities are provided fewer educational opportunities. Implications include providing high-quality programs for all children and their families. Even controlling for parents' occupations and education, family practices such as playing numbers at home have significant impact on children's mathematical development (Sylva, Melhuish, Sammons, Siraj-Blatchford, & Taggart, 2005).

Do children at risk already have substantial math knowledge or not? There appears to be a contradiction between two pictures of the mathematical knowledge and competencies of children of different SES groups. On the one hand, the evidence suggests a substantive and widening gap. On the other hand, there are few, or no, differences between low- and middle-income children in the amount of mathematics they exhibit in their free play (Ginsburg, Ness, & Seo, 2003; Seo & Ginsburg, 2004). The authors often conclude that low-income children are more mathematically competent than expected. This contradiction may have several explanations. Low-income children may not have the same kind of informal opportunities at home (although there is only weak support for this hypothesis; Tudge & Doucet, 2004). Researchers often observe them in a school setting and there is evidence that low-income families provide less support for mathematical thinking (Thirumurthy, 2003). Thus, it may be that they evince mathematics in their play in school, but are still engaged in such play far less than higher-income children. Another explanation is that children have not been provided with the opportunities to reflect on and discuss their pre-mathematical activity. There are huge, meaningful differences in the amount of language in which children from different income levels engage (Hart & Risley, 1995, 1999). Low-income children may engage in pre-mathematical play but be unable to connect this activity to school mathematics because to do so requires the children to bring the ideas to an explicit level of awareness. This is supported by the finding that a main difference between children is not their ability to perform with physical objects but to solve problems verbally (Jordan et al., 1992) or explain their thinking (Sophian, 2002). Consider a child who turned 4 years of age. When asked to solve "how much is ten and one more," she used physical blocks, added 1 to 10, and answered, "eleven." Five minutes later, asked several times using the same wording, "How many is two and one more," the child did not respond, and, asked again, said, "fifteen" . . . in a couldn't-care-less tone of voice (Hughes, 1981, pp. 216–217).

In summary, although there is little direct evidence, we believe the pattern of results suggest that, although low-income children have pre-mathematical knowledge, they do lack important components of mathematical knowledge. They lack the ability—because they have been provided less support to learn—to connect their informal pre-mathematical knowledge to school mathematics. Children must learn to mathematize their informal experiences, abstracting, representing, and elaborating them mathematically, and using mathematical ideas and symbols to create models of their everyday activities. This includes the ability to generalize, connecting the mathematical ideas to different situations and using the ideas and processes adaptively. In all its multifaceted forms, they lack the language of mathematics.

We believe the significance of this conclusion needs to be highlighted. Some authors find that low-income children perform similarly to middle-income children on nonverbal calculation tasks, but significantly worse on verbal calculation tasks (N. C. Jordan, Hanich, & Uberti, 2003), consistent with our review. These authors also state their agreement with others (Ginsburg & Russell, 1981) that the differences are associated with language and approaches to problem-solving rather than "basic mathematical abilities" (p. 366). We prefer to call these *not* "basic *mathematical*," but rather *foundational* abilities. We emphasize that mathematization—including redescribing, reorganizing, abstracting, generalizing, reflecting upon, and giving language to that which is first understood on an intuitive and informal level—*is requisite to basic mathematical ability*. This distinction goes beyond semantics to involve a definition of the construct of mathematics and then to critical ramifications for such practical decisions as allocation of resources based on equity concerns.

Practical implications. Begin with number tasks in which numerosities are represented with objects and model verbal descriptions, facilitating children's receptive and expressive vocabularies. From toddlerhood, naming the number in very small groups supports a variety of number competencies (Hannula, 2005). As another example, the simple task of putting blocks in and out of a box reveals that even 4-year-olds enjoy and can perform arithmetic (Hughes, 1986). (This despite the quoted guidelines of the time that "arithmetic for this age would be ludicrous.") One child, faced with two blocks in the box (which he could not see), was asked to take out three. He replied as follows:

Richard:	You can't, can you?
MH:	Why not?
Richard:	You just have to put one in, don't you?
MH:	Put one in?
Richard:	Yea, and then you can take three out. (p. 27)

Eventually, facilitate children's transition to using more abstract symbols. In general, hold the processes of communication and representation as important, not incidental, goals of mathematics education. These processes are not ways to express mathematics, desirable but secondary accoutrements, but rather essential aspects of mathematical understanding.

Connections between the development of mathematics and literacy are numerous and bidirectional. For example, preschoolers' narrative abilities, particularly their ability to convey all the main events of the story, offer a perspective on the events in the story, and relate the main events of the story through use of conjunctions, predicts mathematics achievement two years later (O'Neill, Pearce, & Pick, 2004). Rich mathematical activities, such as discussing multiple solutions, and posing and solving narrative story problems, helps lay a groundwork for literacy, and rich literacy, that includes but goes beyond phonetic skills, helps lay a groundwork for the development of mathematics.

Gender. Gender equity also remains a concern, as we saw in Chapter 14. Females are socialized to view mathematics as a male domain and themselves as having less ability. Teachers show more concern when boys, rather than girls, struggle. They call on and talk to boys more than girls. Finally, they believe success in mathematics is due to high ability more frequently for boys than girls and view boys as the most successful students in their class. All these unintentionally undermine girls' achievement motivation (Middleton & Spanias, 1999). In more than one study, boys appear more likely than girls to appear in the lowest and highest ranges of scores in mathematics (Callahan & Clements, 1984; Rathbun & West, 2004). In addition, there was evidence of a faster growth rate for high-achieving boys (Aunola et al., 2004). Reasons for this are still unclear, but there are practical ramifications. There are also some indications that boys outperform girls as early as kindergarten on some tasks, such as number sense, estimation, and nonverbal estimation, all of which may have a spatial component (Jordan, Kaplan, Oláh et al., 2006). However, in the U.K., preschool girls scored higher than boys (Sylva et al., 2005).

Practical implications. Thus, the problems are complex, and there are distinct concerns about boys and girls. Educators need to ensure everyone receives complete opportunities to learn.

Children with special needs—MD and MLD. As we saw in Chapter 14, some children show signs of Mathematical Difficulties (MD) and Mathematics Learning Disabilities (MLD) at young ages. Unfortunately, they are often not identified, or categorized broadly with other children as "developmentally delayed." This is especially unfortunate because focused mathematical interventions at early ages are effective (Dowker, 2004; Lerner, 1997). These children often have low skills and concepts in subitizing, counting, fact retrieval, and other aspects of computation. They appear to not use reasoning-based strategies and seem rigid in their use of immature problem-solving, counting, and arithmetic strategies. *Children with special needs require the earliest and most consistent interventions* (Gervasoni, 2005; Gervasoni et al., 2007).

In the primary years, because children with MLD only (not MLD/RLD) performed worse than normally-developing children in timed tests, but performed just as well in untimed tests, children who have MLD only may simply need extra time studying, and extra time to complete, calculation tasks. Probably the use of a calculator and other computation aides would enable these children to concentrate on developing their otherwise good problem-solving skills (Jordan & Montani, 1997). Children with MLD/RLD may need more systematic remedial intervention aimed at problem conceptualization and the development of effective computational strategies as well as efficient fact retrieval (Jordan & Montani, 1997).

Practical implications: Instruction for all *children with special needs.* Many children with special needs have quite *different* learning needs (Gervasoni, 2005; Gervasoni et al., 2007). We *need* to individualize instruction. Moreover, it appears that no particular topic as a whole must precede another topic. For this reason, *teaching with learning trajectories is the best way to address the needs of all children, especially those with special needs.* Using the formative assessment, which has been featured throughout this book but is focused on later in this chapter, is a recommended strategy for putting learning trajectories to work, especially for children with any type of special needs.

A different intervention is important, *but this should not be a replacement but an addition to the mathematics education of these children.* All children learn from good mathematics education. *If we want to close the gap, those with low entering knowledge need more time on better mathematics* (Perry et al., 2008). Full-day kindergarten programs have been shown to produce greater mathematics learning gains than half-day programs, particularly for disadvantaged children (Bodovski & Farkas, 2007). But if other children also participate in full-day programs, the gaps will remain. Children at risk or with special needs need *more* time, *more* mathematics.

As we saw in Chapter 14, affect and motivation are also important. Children who begin kindergarten with the least mathematics knowledge have the most to gain (or to lose) from their engagement with learning (see the previous section in this chapter on affect). The low engagement of these students may be at least partly due to teachers' inability to engage them, or to keep them engaged. Thus, future instructional efforts with these students should focus on innovative attempts to improve their engagement with learning. If low-performing students spent some time daily in small-group instruction that covered the basic number knowledge that they lack, engagement, and hopefully achievement, might be accelerated. Finally, if average beginning achievement of these children can be increased by more intensive preschool interventions, they may be able to also increase their later achievement growth (Bodovski & Farkas, 2007). Interventions that specifically address these needs are discussed in a following section.

Practical implications: Additional resources. There are many resources available to address this country's severe problems with equitable mathematics education. See the bibliography for the following (Nasir & Cobb, 2007).

Other Research-based Early Childhood Mathematics Curricula and Approaches

In Chapter 14, we saw that early knowledge predicted mathematics achievement for years to come. Children with low skills at school entry tend to remain relatively low achievers throughout their education. Many develop math anxiety and never take more advanced courses in mathematics (Wright et al., 1994). However, good programs and good teachers can change that trajectory, putting children on a path to success (Horne, 2005). Several early childhood curricula have been developed recently to serve all children (including, but not limited to, children at risk). Such curricula answer the call from the Psychology in Mathematics Education (PME) group, who reviewed evidence that young children were more capable learners than previously thought and stated that there was a need for integrated curriculum and pedagogy to foster children's mathematical thinking (Hunting & Pearn, 2003).

A Quick Review of Curricula. We have already described several approaches and two example preschool curricula that are based, one way or another, on research. (For a more detailed description of some of these and additional early mathematics curricula, see Ginsburg, 2008.) Here we briefly summarize some of these, before we turn to the major issue—what *is* a truly research-based curriculum?

Early research: Comparing approaches. If we do wish to teach mathematics, how should we do it? One study compared two approaches (Clements, 1984). One took the then popular, and still influential, position that early instruction on number skills is useless (cf. Baroody & Benson, 2001). Based on an interpretation of Piaget, this position held that if a child does not conserve number—that is, believes that changing the arrangement of a collection changes its numbers—instruction may even be harmful. If mathematics was taught at all, it should focus on the logical foundations of classifying, ordering, and conserving. The other approach claimed that children build competency with numbers directly. The position was that number skills, such as counting, are themselves complex cognitive processes that play a critical and constructive role in development number and logical foundations in young children (Clements & Callahan, 1983). Four-year-olds were randomly assigned to one of three groups, a logical foundation group, a number group, and a control group. The group taught classifying and ordering made significant gains on those logical operations. Similarly, the group taught number concepts learned those. This is good news, but not surprising. What's surprising is that the logical foundations group made *small* gains on number concepts, but the number group made *large* gains on classification and orderings—matching the performance of the group taught these specific skills. The control group did not approve on any abilities. So, children benefit by engaging in meaningful number activities, many of which involved classifying and ordering.

Curriculum research in elementary grades. One finding from elementary curriculum that is important to teaching children of any age is that mathematics curricula that teach a combination of skills, concepts, and problem-solving help children learn skills about as well as if they had studied only skills, but also concepts and problem-solving, which children in skills-only curricula do not (e.g., Senk & Thompson, 2003).

Numeracy Recovery. Several intervention programs for young children with MD and MLD have already been described. Another, specially designed for elementary children with weak mathematics abilities, is the *Numeracy Recovery* program. The program focuses on the presumed independent core areas of knowledge children need: counting procedures and principles, written symbolism for numbers, understanding the role of place value in number operations and arithmetic, word problem-solving, number fact retrieval, derived fact strategy use, arithmetical estimation, and translation between arithmetical problems presented in concrete, verbal and numerical formats. Working on those components that children need resulted in significant benefits relative to control children that lasted at least a year (Dowker, 2005).

Math Recovery. Math Recovery is a focused, effective intervention program for at-risk primary school children (Wright, 2003; Wright et al., 1996; Wright et al., 2006). The program for children is based on Steffe's theory of the growth of counting and arithmetic concepts and skills (see Chapters 3 and 5). *Thus, fundamentally, this program is based on the idea of learning trajectories* (we discuss this program more in the early chapters and then later in Chapter 14 of the companion book, dedicated to professional development). Later work has suggested it may be effective for more able children as well (although, as with many others, it *only* addresses number). For example, it is claimed to have affected the group of programs from Australia and New Zealand discussed in the following paragraph (Wright et al., 2002).

Count Me In Too (CMIT), Early Numeracy Research Program (ENRP), and *Early Numeracy Project (ENP).* Several systemic numeracy programs, including the *Count Me In Too* and *Early Numeracy Research Program* in Australia and the *Early Numeracy Project* in New Zealand continue to have a major impact both on the mathematics learning of young children and early childhood mathematics education research in these countries (Perry et al., 2008; Wright et al., 2006; Young-Loveridge, 1989b, 2004). Results are quite positive. These and other effective interventions (e.g., Aubrey, 1997) have been featured throughout this book.

Montessori. An evaluation of the Montessori program, originally created for at-risk children (Montessori, 1964), yielded positive effects on one type of math skills, as well as self-regulation and literacy measures (Lillard & Else-Quest, 2007). Although there was no control for teaching training and the content of the control program, this finding provides potentially important scientific evidence.

A curriculum for Head Start based on the idea of "unit." An experimental mathematics curriculum for Head Start focused on the concept of unit as it applies to enumeration, measurement, and the identification of relations among geometric shapes. Children learned that the numerical result we obtain from counting or other measurement operations will depend on our choice of a unit and that units can be combined to form higher-order units. Results showed significant, but modest, positive effects (Sophian, 2004b).

Round the Rug Math. This supplementary program (Pre-K to grade 2) includes six problem-solving adventure stories. The mathematics concepts are taught to the children through the medium of oral storytelling sagas in an integrated approach that addresses language arts as well as early childhood mathematics competencies, with an emphasis on spatial thinking (B. Casey, Kersh, & Young, 2004).

Project Construct. This process-oriented curriculum had no significant effect compared to a control group. However, neither did teachers implement it with high fidelity. Achieving and assessing fidelity, no matter how difficult, is critical (Mayfield, Morrison, Thornburg, & Scott, 2007).

A synthesized curriculum. A curriculum that synthesized two others was evaluated with a randomized experiment. The experimental group showed enhanced number-sense performance immediately after the instruction ended, but this difference faded after 6 months. There were no statistically significant differences between the groups in general mathematical thinking abilities (transfer tasks) after the intervention (Pirjo Aunio, Hautamäki, & Van Luit, 2005). The researchers suggest that the reason for the limited gains is that teachers were not trained to deliver the intervention. However, the small number of low number-sense children did maintain their relative gain. A similar cognitive acceleration intervention, emphasizing cognitive conflict, social construction, and metacognition, yielded more substantial gains in 5- and 6-year-old children (Adey, Robertson, & Venville, 2002). Teachers worked with small groups on tasks reflecting general cognitive operations, such as classification and seriation. The evaluation using a quasi-experimental design showed significantly greater cognitive gains in the experiment group. Further, these gains included measures of far transfer (to concepts and skills not taught) suggesting that general cognitive development was affected. The success may be attributable to substantial professional development, including 6 inservice days and 3 or 4 coaching visits to each teacher (Adey et al., 2002).

A major conclusion is that *early childhood classrooms underestimate children's ability to learn mathematics and are ill suited to help them learn.* One researcher, noting that children actually *regress* on some math skills during kindergarten, said simply that sorting and classifying, and 1-to-1 correspondence, are just not enough (Wright et al., 1994). *We need more structured, sophisticated, and better-developed and well-sequenced mathematics in early childhood education.* How do we do that well?

A Framework for Research-based Curricula. Although constructivism has been a major force in mathematics education, its influence has decreased. One problem is that researchers have not articulated clear, stable, repeatable products, such as curricula, that can be evaluated in more scaled and systematic ways (Burkhardt, 2006; Confrey & Kazak, 2006). In a similar vein, the (PME) group (Hunting & Pearn, 2003) also called for the development of frameworks to underpin research for children in the early years. We have been working on such a framework for a decade because we too saw a dire need. Government agencies and wider members of the educational research community have also petitioned for research-based curricula. However, the ambiguity of the phrase "research-based" undermines attempts to create a shared research foundation for the development of, and informed choices about, classroom curricula.

Therefore, based on a review of research and expert practice, we constructed and tested a framework for the construct of research-based curricula. Our "Curriculum Research Framework" (CRF, Clements, 2007) rejects the sole use of commercially-oriented "market research" and "research-to-practice" strategies. Although included in the CRF, such strategies are inadequate. For example, because they employ one-way translations of research results, research-to-practice strategies are flawed in their presumptions, insensitive to changing goals in the content area, and unable to contribute to a revision of the theory and knowledge. Such knowledge-building is— alongside the development of a scientifically-based, effective curriculum—a critical goal of a scientific curriculum research program. Indeed, a valid scientific curriculum development program should address two basic issues—effect and conditions—in three domains, practice, policy, and theory, as described in Table 15.1.

To address all these issues, the CRF includes ten phases of the curriculum development research process that warrant the claim that some curriculum is based on research. The ten phases are classified into three categories, reflecting the three categories of knowledge required to meet Table 15.1's goals. These categories include reviewing existing research, building models of children's thinking and learning in a domain, and evaluation. The categories and phases within them are outlined in Table 15.2.

The first curriculum to be developed using the Curriculum Research Framework (CRF) was *Building Blocks*, a NSF-funded Pre-K to grade 2 mathematics research and curriculum development project, one of the first to develop materials that comprehensively address recent standards for early mathematics education for all children (e.g., Clements & Conference Working Group, 2004; NCTM, 2000). We will elaborate the CRF by giving concrete descriptions of how the phases were enacted in the development of the *Building Blocks* preschool curriculum.

The first category, *A Priori Foundations*, includes three variants of the research-to-practice model, in which extant research is reviewed and implications for the nascent curriculum development effort drawn. (1) In *General A Priori Foundation*, developers review broad philosophies, theories, and empirical results on learning and teaching. Based on theory and research on early childhood learning and teaching (Bowman et al., 2001; Clements, 2001), we determined that *Building Blocks'* basic approach would be finding the mathematics in, and developing mathematics from, children's activities, such as "mathematizing" everyday tasks. (2) In *Subject Matter A Priori Foundation*, developers review research and consult with experts to identify mathematics that makes a substantive contribution to students' mathematical development, is generative in students' development of future mathematical understanding, and is interesting to students. We determined subject matter content by considering what mathematics is culturally valued (e.g., NCTM, 2000) and empirical research on what constituted the core ideas and skill areas of mathematics for young children (Baroody, 2004a; Clements & Battista, 1992; Clements & Conference Working Group, 2004; Fuson, 1997), including hypothesized syncretism among domains, especially number and geometry. We revised the subject matter specifications following a content analysis by four mathematicians and mathematics educators, resulting in learning trajectories in the domain of number (counting, subitizing, sequencing, arithmetic), geometry (matching, naming, building and combining shapes), patterning, and measurement. (3) In *Pedagogical A Priori Foundation*, developers review empirical findings on making activities educationally effective—motivating and efficacious—to create general guidelines for the generation of activities. As an example, research using computer software with young children (Clements, Nastasi, & Swaminathan, 1993; Clements & Swaminathan, 1995; Steffe & Wiegel, 1994) showed that preschoolers can use computers effectively and that software can be made more effective by employing animation, children's voices, and clear feedback.

In the second category, *Learning Model*, developers structure activities in accordance with empirically-based models of children's thinking in the targeted subject matter domain. This phase, (4) *Structure According to Specific Learning Model*, involves creation of research-based learning trajectories, which, of course, have been described in detail in this book.

In the third category, *Evaluation*, developers collect empirical evidence to evaluate the appeal, usability, and effectiveness of a version of the curriculum. Past phase (5) *Market Research* is (6) *Formative Research: Small Group*, in which developers conduct pilot tests with individuals or small groups on components (e.g., a particular activity, game, or software environment) or sections of the curriculum. Although teachers are involved in all phases of research and development, the process of curricular enactment is emphasized in the next two phases. Studies with a teacher who participated in the development of the materials in phase (7) *Formative Research: Single Classroom*, and then teachers newly introduced to the materials in phase (8) *Formative Research: Multiple Classrooms*, provide information about the usability of the curriculum and requirements for professional development and support materials. We conducted multiple case studies at each of these three phases (e.g., Clements & Sarama, 2004a; Sarama, 2004), revising the curriculum multiple times, including two distinct published versions (Clements & Sarama, 2003a, 2007a). In the last two phases, (9) *Summative Research: Small Scale* and (10) *Summative Research: Large Scale*, developers evaluate what can actually be achieved with typical teachers under realistic circumstances. An initial phase-9 summary research project (Clements & Sarama, 2007c) yielded effect sizes between 1 and 2 (Cohen's *d*). These effects are illustrated in Figure 15.1. This study only involved four classrooms, however.

Phase 10 also uses randomized trials, which provide the most efficient and least biased designs to assess causal relationships (Cook, 2002), now in a greater number of classrooms, with more diversity, and less ideal conditions. In a larger study (Clements & Sarama, 2008), we randomly assigned 36 classrooms to one of three conditions. The experimental group used *Building Blocks* (Clements & Sarama, 2007b). The comparison group used a different preschool mathematics curriculum—the same as we previously used in the PCER research (mainly Klein, Starkey, & Ramirez, 2002). The control used their schools existing curriculum ("business as usual"). Two observational measures indicated that the curricula were implemented with fidelity and that the experimental condition had significant positive effects on classrooms' mathematics environment and teaching. The experimental group score increased significantly more than the comparison group score (effect size, 0.47) and the control group score (effect size, 1.07); see Figure 15.2. Focused early mathematical interventions, especially those based on a comprehensive model of developing and evaluating research-based curricula, can increase the quality of the mathematics environment and teaching and can help preschoolers develop a foundation of informal mathematics knowledge (Clements & Sarama, 2008).

We believe that these positive effects, even when compared to another curriculum supported equivalently, were due to *Building Blocks' core use of learning trajectories*.

Table 15.1 Goals of Curriculum Research (from Clements, 2007).

	Practice	Policy	Theory
Effects	a. Is the curriculum effective in helping children achieve specific learning goals? Are the intended and unintended consequences positive for children? (What is the quality of the evidence?—Construct an internal validity.) (6–10)* b. Is there credible documentation of both a priori research and research performed on the curriculum indicating the efficacy of the approach as compared to alternative approaches? (all)	c. Are the curriculum goals important? (1, 5, 10) d. What is the effect size for students? (9, 10) e. What effects does it have on teachers? (10)	f. Why is the curriculum effective? (all) g. What were the theoretical bases? (1, 2, 3) h. What cognitive changes occurred and what processes were responsible? That is, what specific components and features (e.g., instructional procedures, materials) account for its impact and why? (4, 6, 7)
Conditions	i. When and where?—Under what conditions is the curriculum effective? (Do findings generalize?—External validity.) (8, 10)	j. What are the support requirements (7) for various contexts? (8–10)	k. Why do certain sets of conditions decrease or increase the curriculum's effectiveness? (6–10) l. How do specific strategies produce previously unattained results and why? (6–10)

Table 15.2 Categories and Phases of the Curriculum Research Framework (CRF).

Categories	Questions Asked	Phases
A Priori Foundations. In variants of the research-to-practice model, extant research is reviewed and implications for the nascent curriculum development effort drawn.	What is already known that can be applied to the anticipated curriculum? <table><tr><td>Goals*</td><td>Phase</td></tr><tr><td>b c f g</td><td>1</td></tr><tr><td>b f g</td><td>2</td></tr><tr><td>b f g</td><td>3</td></tr></table>	Established review procedures (e.g., Light & Pillemer, 1984) and content analyses (NRC, 2004) are employed to garner knowledge concerning the specific subject matter content, including the role it would play in students' development (*phase 1*); general issues concerning psychology, education, and systemic change (*phase 2*); and pedagogy, including the effectiveness of certain types of activities (*phase 3*).
Learning Model. Activities are structured in accordance with empirically-based models of children's thinking and learning in the targeted subject matter domain.	How might the curriculum be constructed to be consistent with models of students' thinking and learning (which are posited to have characteristics and developmental courses that are not arbitrary and therefore not equally amenable to various instructional approaches or curricular routes)? <table><tr><td>Goals</td><td>Phase</td></tr><tr><td>b f h</td><td>4</td></tr></table>	In *phase 4,* the nature and content of activities is based on models of children's mathematical thinking and learning (cf. James, 1892/1958; Tyler, 1949). In addition, a set of activities (the hypothetical mechanism of the research) may be sequenced according to specific learning trajectories (Clements & Sarama, 2004b). What distinguishes phase 4 from phase 3, which concerns pedagogical a priori foundations, is not only the focus on the child's learning, rather than teaching strategies alone, but also the iterative nature of its application. That is, in practice, such models are usually applied and revised (or, not infrequently, created anew) dynamically, simultaneously with the development of instructional tasks, using grounded theory methods, clinical interviews, teaching experiments, and design experiments.
Evaluation. In these phases, empirical evidence is collected to evaluate the curriculum, realized in some form. The goal is to evaluate the appeal, usability, and effectiveness of an instantiation of the curriculum.	How can market share for the curriculum be maximized? <table><tr><td>Goals</td><td>Phase</td></tr><tr><td>b c f</td><td>5</td></tr></table>	*Phase 5* focuses on marketability, using strategies such as gathering information about mandated educational objectives and surveys of consumers.
	Is the curriculum usable by, and effective with, various student groups and teachers? How can it be improved in these areas or adapted to serve diverse situations and needs? <table><tr><td>Goals</td><td>Phase</td></tr><tr><td>a b f h k l</td><td>6</td></tr><tr><td>a b f h j k l</td><td>7</td></tr><tr><td>a b f i j k l</td><td>8</td></tr></table>	Formative *phases 6 to 8* seek to understand the meaning that students and teachers give to the curriculum objects and activities in progressively expanding social contexts; for example, the usability and effectiveness of specific components and characteristics of the curriculum as implemented by a teacher who is familiar with the materials with individuals or small groups (*phase 6*) and whole classes (*phase 7*) and, later, by a diverse group of teachers (*phase 8*). Methods include interpretive work using a mix of model testing and model generation strategies, including design experiments, microgenetic, microethnographic, and phenomenological approaches (*phase 6*), classroom-based teaching experiments and ethnographic participant observation (*phase 7*), and these plus content analyses (*phase 8*). The curriculum is altered based on empirical results, with the focus expanding to include aspects of support for teachers.
	What is the effectiveness (e.g., in affecting teaching practices and ultimately student learning) of the curriculum, now in its complete form, as it is implemented in realistic contexts? <table><tr><td>Goals</td><td>Phase</td></tr><tr><td>a b d f j k l</td><td>9</td></tr><tr><td>a b c d e</td><td>10</td></tr><tr><td>f i j k l</td><td></td></tr></table>	Summative *phases 9 and 10* both use randomized field trials and differ from each other most markedly in the characteristic of scale. That is, *phase 10* examines the fidelity or enactment, and sustainability, of the curriculum when implemented on a large scale, and the critical contextual and implementation variables that influence its effectiveness. Experimental or carefully planned quasi-experimental designs, incorporating observational measures and surveys, are useful for generating political and public support, as well as for their research advantages. In addition, qualitative approaches continue to be useful for dealing with the complexity and indeterminateness of educational activity (Lester & Wiliam, 2002).

* Goals refer to the specific questions in Table 15.1, answers to which are the goals of the CRF.

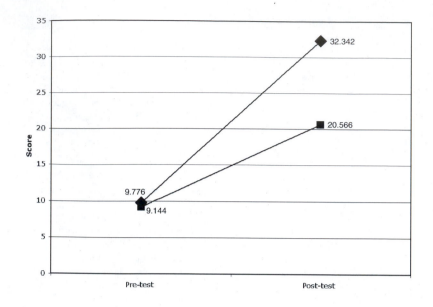

a. Number

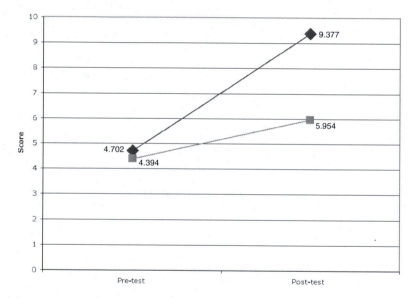

b. Geometry (includes measurement and patterning)

Figure 15.1 Building Blocks compared to a control group.

Are Effects Sustained?

We reviewed multiple studies indicating that mathematics programs for very young children make a meaningful, positive, difference, but, in many longitudinal studies, the effects appear to fade over time. Skeptics have suggested that it is not worth the effort if effects fade. Although we need more research to illuminate this issue, we believe this negative point of view ignores the existing evidence. First, some studies do show lasting effects. Second, programs that are continued into elementary school and that offer substantial exposure to early interventions have the most sustained long-term

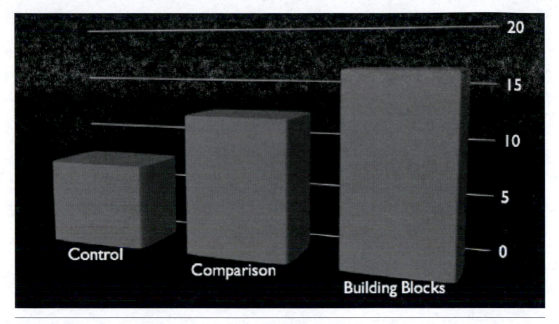

Figure 15.2 Building blocks compared to a control group and to another intensive math curriculum.

effects (Brooks-Gunn, 2003). Third, without such follow-through, it is simply not realistic to expect short-term early interventions to last indefinitely. This is especially so because most children at risk attend the lowest-quality schools. It would be surprising if these children did not gain less than their more advantaged peers year by year (Brooks-Gunn, 2003). Fourth, our TRIAD projects support research already reviewed (and other research reviewed in this chapter) shows that most teachers of young children are not responsive to the needs of those with *high* mathematical knowledge. Thus, the *mathematics-experienced preschoolers who go to kindergarten are given tasks that do not challenge—or teach—them*. Their development is stalled because no new mathematics is offered them. And math is particularly at risk of this tragic phenomenon (Campbell et al., 2001).

Final Words

Understanding the contexts of instruction and curricula used are necessary to be an effective educator. The final area of professionalism deals with specific *instructional strategies*, the topic of Chapter 16.

16
Instructional Practices and Pedagogical Issues

The three friends turn to discussing how they teach math.

Aretha: Math is different. Kids have to memorize specific facts and skills. It's not like language, which you can help kids develop, well, more naturally or informally. Math you have to teach directly.

Brenda: Maybe, but don't you think they have to see math in their world? I mean aren't they doing math when they build with blocks?

Carina: Both of you sound right. Does mixing those types of approaches make sense?

What do you think about instruction? Should you be more teacher-directed or more child-centered? What role is there for play in early math education? What are the best strategies to meet individual children's needs? Are specific manipulatives helpful? Should we emphasize skills or concepts?

Do children have too much technology at home and schools should keep them away from computers, or should we use good environments to show them how to use technology for *learning*? If so, what types, and how much?

This is a long chapter, because it answers these and many other critical questions. In addition to large entities such as a "program" (e.g., Head Start) or a curriculum, there are specific perspectives, approaches, and strategies for teaching math to young children that research indicates are effective. Here, we briefly describe some of the most important. Although there is research evidence for each, this evidence is in most cases qualitative and/or correlational; therefore, unlike the curriculum evaluation described in Chapter 15, we cannot be certain that the specific instructional strategy caused the learning. This is so even when we cite studies that used randomized designs (e.g., Clements & Sarama, 2007c, 2008), because the data on specific *components* of the instruction were not randomly assigned (only the entire curriculum was). Therefore, these results are usually suggestive but not definitive. We note wherever one or more studies did rigorously evaluate a specific approach.

Teaching Beliefs and Basic Pedagogical Strategies

In general, teachers with certain belief systems about early childhood teaching and learning, and those who tend to use a corresponding category of instructional strategies, are more successful at promoting children's learning. For example, observations allowed researchers to reliably categorize teachers into three belief systems: transmission, discovery, and connectionist, or some combination of these (Askew, Brown, Rhodes, Wiliam, & Johnson, 1997). Transmission teachers believe in "teacher telling" and a view of mathematics as a collection of separate skills. They believe in teaching primary grade students mechanical skills with paper and pencil procedures. They view learning as predominantly an individual activity in which one routine at a time is memorized, students' strategies are of little importance, and mistakes are failures to grasp correct methods. They do not expect all students to become fluent (believing that some have more "math ability").

Discovery-oriented teachers believe that children discover mathematics. They believe that children should find answer by any methods, and should learn to apply mathematics to everyday problems. They view learning as an individual activity, often involving manipulatives. They believe that children need to be "ready" to learn.

Finally, connectionist teachers value children's strategies, but also teach strategies in an attempt to establish connections between mathematics ideas, skills, and topics. They believe in efficient methods of calculation, but also an emphasis on mental strategies, on reasoning, and on justifying results. Learning is viewed more as a social activity in which students first develop their own strategies but are helped to refine them by the teacher. Misunderstandings are discussed and worked on. All students are expected to become fluent.

Practical implications. The researchers also classified the teachers' effectiveness, based on their children's actual gain scores in mathematics over the year (Askew et al., 1997). *Those teachers with more connectionist orientations were more likely to be highly effective than teachers with strong discovery or transmission orientations.* These findings are in close agreement with our theory of hierarchic interactionalism and with the content expectations in NCTM's *Curriculum Focal Points.* It is also important that teachers have an *interest* in and *knowledge about* mathematics (Thomson et al., 2005).

Group Size

Our knowledge of what is most effective is limited. The previous study (Askew et al., 1997) did not find that more, compared to less, effective teachers were any more likely to use whole-class, small-group, or individualized approaches (Askew et al., 1997). Small-group work can significantly increase children's scores on tests aligned with that work (Klein & Starkey, 2004; Klein, Starkey, & Wakeley, 1999). Children can also transfer knowledge they learned in small-group activities to tasks that they have not been taught (Clements, 1984).

Practical implications. We suspect that small-group work, individual work at the computer, and perhaps to a lesser extent focused whole-group activities, are the main keys to the success of *Building Blocks.* However, our curriculum also uses centers and everyday activities (Clements & Sarama, 2007c, 2008). All activities are *active*, but we make an extra effort to ensure that the whole-group activities are active—physically ("Counting and Move"), intellectually and individually ("Snapshots" with "bunny ears"—all children are solving problems and showing their solutions individually), or socially ("talk to the person next to you about how you can figure this out")—and usually some combination of these.

Observations in countries that use far more whole-group instruction with young children suggest its advantages may be overlooked in the U.S. For example, the teacher-directed, whole-class

Korean approach provides a positive, nurturing environment that offers children the opportunity to develop essential pre-academic skills (French & Song, 1998).

Intentional, Planned Instruction

Practical implications. Understand the need for planned, intentional, sequenced teaching of mathematics from the earliest years (Thomson et al., 2005). Actively engage with students (Clements & Sarama, 2008; Thomson et al., 2005).

Using Learning Trajectories

A teacher talks about interviewing a child for report cards, and her use of *learning trajectories* to understand the child fully.

> She was able to do verbal counting to 8, and then when she slowed down, she could get to 11. So I said, "Can you make me a group of 6?" And so she did. So then I added . . . I asked her to make a group of 12. She couldn't do it.

> Then I noted that, *so now I'm thinking in the trajectories,* I think she's a "Counter (Small Numbers)," right? She's on her way to being a "Counter (10)." She's in between the two. *I know just what to do to teach her the next level of thinking.* That's what I was thinking of as I did this (Pat, 2004).

Practical implications. Engage in *intentional, planned teaching in relation to learning trajectories* (Carpenter & Moser, 1984; Clarke et al., 2002; Clements & Sarama, 2007c, 2008; Cobb et al., 1991, note that not all projects use that term—the process is the key). *Focus on key ideas* and understand how those key ideas develop in children. Using learning trajectories well, as suggested by Pat's quote above, *implies* a use of the next instructional strategy, formative assessment.

Formative Assessment

Of the ten instructional practices the National Math Panel (NMP) researched, only a few had an adequate number of rigorous studies supporting them. One of the most strongly supported was teachers' use of formative assessment (NMP, 2008). Formative assessment is the ongoing monitoring of student learning *to inform instruction.* One can monitor the class and individuals within it.

Although the NMP's rigorous studies included children only as young as the upper primary grades, other studies confirm that regular assessment and individualization are key to effective early math education (Thomson et al., 2005). Teachers should observe not just answers but *strategies.*

Other syntheses have reported that formative assessment as an intervention has been evaluated to have effect sizes from 0.40 to 0.70, *larger than effects of most instructional programs* (Black & Wiliam, 1998; Shepard, 2005). It helps all children learn, but helps the lower achieving children the most. They gain the higher-order (metacognitive) skills already attained by higher-achieving children.

Again, though, formative assessment is for everyone. In his first year of school, Harry knew all the little mathematics that was presented. Harry did maintain the outward semblance of being interested in the work and, at least, being willing to complete it. However, it seems that the strongest lesson he learned in his kindergarten mathematics experience is that "you do not have to work hard at it" (Perry & Dockett, 2005). Similarly, observations of early childhood teachers show they usually misjudge children's level and give practice ("more of the same") problems *even when they intend to provide learning opportunities* (challenging problems), *especially* to the highest-performing children. This is simply a reminder, discussed in Chapter 14, that it is *just as important to serve the needs of the gifted as those who are struggling* (Bennett, Desforges, Cockburn, & Wilkinson, 1984). Thus, the high-performing children were the least well served—they rarely learned new mathematics. The next most likely mismatched were the lowest performers—teachers rarely move to the lower levels they needed to learn.

Practical implications. Use formative assessment to serve the needs of all children. As with all instructional practices, formative assessment has to be done right. Ask yourself the following questions (Shepard, 2005):

- What is the key error?
- What is the probable reason the child made this error?
- How can I guide the child to avoid this error in the future?

Also, transfer is more likely when you focus your formative assessment on children's understanding of concepts and relationships.

If all this seems obvious and easy, note that an analysis of the ECLS data showed that about half of kindergarten teachers report *never* using such strategies as achievement grouping in mathematics (NRC, in press). Few Pre-K or kindergarten teachers use small groups at all—whole-group instruction dominates.

Interactions, Discussions, and Connecting Mathematics

Effective teachers talk to their children about mathematics. There are dramatic differences between the amounts of math-related talk that preschool teachers provide (Klibanoff, Levine, Huttenlocher, Vasilyeva, & Hedges, 2006). *The more teachers talk about math, the more their children develop mathematical knowledge.* The contexts in which the talk occurred ranged from planned mathematical instruction to everyday activities (e.g., children engaged in an art project that involved constructing a book were asked to put numbered pages in order), to incidental comments about quantity (e.g., "Can you tell me what is different about those two beads?"). A follow-up study showed that it was not the *overall* number of words but the amount of specific *math talk* that is related to children's growth in mathematics (Ehrlich & Levine, 2007a). Further, children in classrooms with low teacher math talk actually *decreased* in mathematics competence.

Practical implications. Talk about math. Effective teachers make greater use of open-ended questions than less effective teachers. Ask children, "Why?" and "How do you know?" Expect children, as young as preschool, to share strategies, explain their thinking, work together to solve problems, and listen to each other (Askew et al., 1997; Carpenter, Fennema, Franke, Levi, & Empson, 1999; Carpenter, Franke, Jacobs, Fennema, & Empson, 1998; Clarke et al., 2002; Clements & Sarama, 2007c, 2008; Cobb et al., 1991; Thomson et al., 2005).

Place a greater emphasis on summarizing key ideas at the end of any activity. Be aware of the properties and relationships of mathematics. Highlight links and connections between mathematical ideas and between mathematics and everyday problems to be solved (Askew et al., 1997; Clarke et al., 2002; Clements & Sarama, 2007c, 2008).

In summary, be actively engaged in discussing mathematics with children around planned activities. Build on and elaborate children's mathematical ideas and strategies and facilitate children's responding (Clements & Sarama, 2008). Although studies that address this specific instructional practice are correlational rather than experimental, the results are promising.

High Expectations

Practical implications. Challenge children. Effective teachers hold higher expectations of children than ineffective teachers (Clarke et al., 2002; Clements & Sarama, 2007c, 2008; Thomson et al., 2005). They hold high expectations of *all* children (Askew et al., 1997).

Developing Positive Mathematics Attitudes

The work of many researchers has identified a common core of characteristics of learning environments that enhance children's early development of a positive mathematical disposition (Anghileri, 2001, 2004; Clements, Sarama, & DiBiase, 2004; Cobb, 1990; Cobb et al., 1991; Cobb et al., 1989; Fennema et al., 1996; Hiebert, 1999; Kutscher et al., 2002; McClain, Cobb, Gravemeijer, & Estes, 1999). Unsurprisingly, most of these simply mirror the pedagogical strategies discussed previously, but the point here is that these have *also* been identified as improving children's attitudes and beliefs about mathematics.

Practical implications. Effective strategies include the following:

- Use problems that have meaning for children (both practical and mathematical).
- Expect that children will invent, explain, and critique their own solution strategies within a social context.
- Provide opportunities for both creative invention and practice.
- Encourage and support children progressing toward increasingly sophisticated and abstract mathematical methods and understandings, and to understand and develop more efficient and elegant solution strategies.
- Help children see connections between various types of knowledge and topics, with the goal of having each child build a well-structured, coherent knowledge of mathematics.

Gifted and Talented

Most children who are gifted and talented are not well served. Many gifted and talented children may not be identified as such, especially the youngest. Teachers sometimes expose gifted and talented children to concepts generally introduced to older students; however, they most frequently teach concepts traditionally found in early childhood programs (Wadlington & Burns, 1993). Even though research shows that these children possess advanced knowledge of measurement, time, and fractions, such topics were rarely explored. Presently, these children are often taught through unstructured activities, discovery learning, centers, and games within small groups, strategies that are supported by research in some contexts. However, these children also need to solve engaging, difficult problems in the domains of number, operations, geometry and spatial sense. They need to be challenged to engaged in high-level mathematical reasoning, including abstract reasoning.

One rigorous study randomly assigned equally able gifted students to a supplemental enrichment mathematics class conducted on Saturdays over two years or to no treatment. The enrichment class, with 28 sessions in all, was constructivist in philosophy, "developmentally appropriate," and adhered to NCTM guidelines. Teachers created social communities that engaged in open-ended problem-solving. At the end of two years, the participants outperformed non-participants (effect size, 0.44, which just missed statistical significance, but is moderately large, and thus remains promising). Children were not accelerated, which is a different strategy frequently used successfully with older students (NMP, 2008).

Primary grade Students with Special Needs—MLD and MD

Practical implications. Several interventions and curricula that can help children with special needs are described in Chapter 15. Research reviews have identified several approaches that helped children at risk, including the following:

- Use information on students' performance, and share this with students (supporting formative assessment, described previously, including differentiated activities).
- Provide clear, specific feedback to parents on their children's mathematics achievement.
- Use peers as tutors (see the next section).
- Encourage students to verbalize their thinking or their strategies, or even the explicit strategies you model.
- Use explicit instruction.
- Target specific areas of need.
- Include individualized work, even for brief periods, as a component of such focused interventions (Dowker, 2004; Gersten et al., 2008).

Interventions are more effective the *earlier* they are started, both in building content knowledge and in preventing negative attitudes and mathematics anxiety (Dowker, 2004). A few additional approaches for primary grade students are described here.

Number and arithmetic. A review of rigorous experiments by the NMP provides guidance regarding effective instruction for students with MD or MLD. A main successful approach was systematic, intentional instruction (often *explicit*, although high-quality implicit instructional approaches were also effective). Such instruction included concrete and visual representations, explanations by teachers, explanations and discussion by children (including having children "think aloud" as they solve problems), collaborative work among students, carefully orchestrated practice with feedback, and high but reasonable expectations (NMP, 2008). Other specific approaches that show promise include teaching *strategies* about computation, mixed with practice (which is usually less interesting and less conceptual) and using visual models and teaching children to analyze the structure of word problems. As an example, one from the NMP studies provided explicit instruction for second grades with MLD who had not learned to "count on from larger" to solve addition problems (Tournaki, 2003):

Teacher: When I get a problem, what do I do?
Student (expected repetition of the rule):   I read the problem: 5 plus 3 equals how many. Then I find the smaller number.
Teacher (points to the number):   3. Now I count the fingers. So how many fingers am I going to count?
Student: 3. [and so forth . . .]

After a few problems, the teacher had students solve problems while thinking aloud, that is, repeating the steps and asking themselves the questions. Teachers always provided clear, immediate feedback when students made errors. The large effect size of this study (1.61) indicates the benefit of teaching a *strategy*, not just providing more practice, especially for MLD students.

Another study included the NMP report, classified as more implicit, examined the effects of 48 small group tutorial sessions, including the use of concrete objects to promote conceptual learning, on low-achieving, at risk, first graders. Those randomly assigned to this intervention, compared to a control group, improved on computation, concepts/applications, and story problems, but not on fact fluency (Fuchs et al., 2005). However, children still did not catch up to their peers who were not at risk. Thus, this appears to be an early intervention for students who exhibit problems in mathematics at the beginning of the first grade, as well as an example of how concepts, procedures and problem-solving can be taught and practiced in an intense, integrated fashion.

A more recent study found that two tutoring conditions, one focused on improving fluency in number combinations, and one designed to teach problem-solving, both improved number combination fluency (Fuchs, Powell, Cirino et al., 2008). Both increased competence in procedural calculations, with the problem-solving condition having the greater effect size. Only the problem-solving condition also developed algebraic thinking and solving word problems. Given these results, the problem-solving condition, which did include one session on counting strategies, as well as work on number combinations in short warm-up and review phases, provided greater benefit.

The NMP report reveals the benefits of several components of the more recent approaches to explicit (or a mixture of explicit and implicit) instruction, which is quite distinct from older models of "direct instruction." Students are explicitly taught *strategies*, building up a repertoire a bit at a time, not just "facts" or "skills." They participate in a considerable amount of small-group interaction where children are encouraged to think aloud as they do mathematics, receiving feedback from peers and the teacher. They are taught to solve problems, using strategies and, often, using concrete objects and visual representations in conjunction with more abstract representations to analyze the problem's structure. The teacher highlights key aspects of each type of problem (*not* "key words") and supports students' ability to discriminate one type from another. At the end of each instructional cycle, they not only practice but also are helped, explicitly, to generalize and transfer their knowledge.

Other interventions have been shown to be effective. For example, tutoring successfully remediated fact retrieval deficits, procedural computation, and computational estimation (Fuchs, Powell, Hamlett et al., 2008). This intervention helped all children equally (e.g., those with MD only or MD and reading difficulties).

Many children with MD or MLD have difficulties related to number "sense." An intervention targeted to exactly that is "The Number Race" computer game (Wilson, Dehaene et al., 2006; Wilson, Revkin et al., 2006). The researchers stated that a basic deficit might be in abilities related to numerical sense, the ability to represent and manipulate numerical quantities nonverbally, emphasizing number comparison and estimation. (The authors call this "number sense," consistent with their previous usage, but to avoid confusion with the much broader mathematics education research use of the term, which they also call number sense, we use "numerical sense" here). The researchers hypothesize that children lack either nonverbal numerical sense or access to it due to dissociation from symbolic representations. As an empirical test, the former, direct impairment of the quantity system should result in failure on both non-symbolic and symbolic numerical tasks, whereas the latter should leave purely non-symbolic tasks intact.

To test their theory and their software intervention, they provided children with adaptive training on numerical comparison for half an hour per day, 4 days per week for 5 weeks. Nine children worked with "The Number Race" software to enhance their numerical sense by providing intensive training on numerical comparison and links between numbers and space. Scaffolding is provided, as is repeated associations in which Arabic, verbal, and quantity codes are presented together, and the role of symbolic information as the basis for decision-making is progressively increased.

Children showed specific increases in performance on core numerical comparison tasks. For example, speed of subitizing and numerical comparison increased by several hundred milliseconds. On numerical comparison, symbolic tasks showed a speed effect, the non-symbolic showed improvements in both accuracy and speed, although the improvements for speed were larger for the symbolic tasks. Subtraction accuracy increased by 23%. Performance in addition and base-ten comprehension tasks did not improve. These results were consistent with theoretical predictions because addition was thought to be frequently solved using a memorized table of facts, compared to subtraction, hypothesized to rely more on numerical sense. Thus, higher-level symptoms such as impairments in subtraction may be a derivative of a dysfunction of the core numerical sense system. Interpretations should be made with caution because their test of transcoding assessed only connections between verbal and symbolic codes, because several findings missed significance, and especially because the number of participants was very low (9) and there was no control group. With those caveats, results suggested that numerical sense might be a core deficit for those with mathematical difficulties and the evidence did not prioritize either nonverbal numerical sense or dissociation from symbolic representations (the authors claim the latter is suggested, but this was based on a single "marginally significant" test).

Other approaches have also shown promise, including those that are more reform-oriented. Even children with mental handicaps are capable of meaningful learning (Baroody, 1986). Teachers must ensure that these children develop basic subitizing and counting skills and concepts. That is, they should avoid a narrow focus on skills when more balanced and comprehensive instruction, using the child's abilities to shore up weaknesses, may provide better long-range results. Visual-spatial training or mass practice should not substitute for experience looking for and using patterns in learning the basic facts or learning arithmetic strategies (Baroody, 1996). Poor instruction may be the reason many children show signs of MD, and even of MLD. Helping these children build on their strengths and informal knowledge, invent counting strategies, connect concepts and procedures, and solve problems may show that many of these children can learn math successfully. Strategies and patterns may need explicit teaching, but should not be neglected (Baroody, 1996).

Teachers need to carefully assess the understanding and skills of children with mental handicaps along the relevant learning trajectories with sensitivity. For example, children with moderate retardation may not count *verbally* up to 5, but may count *collections* of 5 or more. They may just not be motivated to perform oral counting (Baroody, 1999). Training based on these principles showed some success, more on near-transfer tasks (Baroody, 1996). Careful attention to tasks was helpful. For example, helping them master a few $n + 1$ tasks $(4 + 1, 6 + 1)$ helped them discover the number-after-n rule, after which children spontaneously invented counting on (realizing, for example, that if $7 + 1$ is 8, $7 + 2$ is two count words after 7).

Thus, from this perspective, preschoolers with mental retardation typically do not construct the powerful information math knowledge that normally-developing children do. However, many children with mental retardation appear capable of learning the counting, number, and arithmetic concepts and skills that provide the foundation for the meaningful learning of school mathematics (Baroody, 1996). They can be active learners, who, because of developing adaptive expertise, can learn to monitor their own mathematical activity.

Nevertheless, in the context of most curricula, "traditional" or "reform," there are cautions in the research. Teachers should remember that children with MD or MLD might require additional support, so that they are still active and involved (Woodward, 2004).

Spatial thinking and geometry. Although most researchers' intervention programs focus only on number, this is too limited for educators. The link between high-scoring children's numerical ability and their spatial and measurement ability and the lack of any growth on measurement and geometry in lower-scoring children implies that geometry and measurement must also be addressed (Stewart, Leeson, & Wright, 1997). For example, some children have difficulty with spatial organization across a wide range of tasks. Children with certain mathematics learning difficulties may struggle with spatial relationships, visual-motor and visual-perception, and a poor sense of direction (Lerner, 1997). As discussed (p. 227), they may not perceive a shape as a complete and integrated entity as children without learning disabilities do (Lerner, 1997). Children with different brain injuries show different patterns of competence. Those with right hemispheric injuries have difficulty organizing objects into coherent spatial groupings, while those with left hemispheric injuries have difficulty with local relations within spatial arrays (Stiles & Nass, 1991). Teaching with learning trajectories based on the developmental sequences described here is even more important for children with learning disabilities, as well as children with other special needs. Teachers should know the developmental sequences through which children pass as they learn geometric ideas.

Spatial weakness may underlie children's difficulties with numerical magnitudes (e.g., knowing that 5 is a greater than 4, but only by a little, whereas 12 is a lot greater than 4) and rapid retrieval of numeral names and arithmetic combinations (Jordan, Hanich, & Kaplan, 2003). These children may not be able to manipulate visual representations of a number line.

Similarly, due to the difficulties in perceiving shapes and spatial relationships, recognizing spatial relationships, and making spatial judgments, these children are unable to copy geometric forms, shapes, numbers, or letters. They are likely to perform poorly in handwriting as well as in arithmetic. When children cannot write numbers easily, they also cannot read and align their own numbers properly. As a result, they make errors in computation.

Recall the promising results of early emphases on structure and pattern (Chapter 12 and others). The Pattern and Structure Mathematics Awareness Program (PASMAP), focused on improving students' visual memory, the ability to identify and apply patterns, and to seek structure in mathematical ideas and representations, has shown (in very small, non-random studies) to have positive effects on children at risk of later school failure (Fox, 2006).

Children diagnosed as autistic need structured interventions from the earliest years. They must be kept engaged with their world, including mathematics. Use intense interests that characterize many children with autism to motivate them to study geometry and spatial structures. For example, if they enjoy construction, they might study how triangles are used in bridges. Many children with autism are visually-oriented. Manipulatives and pictures can aid children's learning of most topics, in geometry, number, and other areas. Children benefit from illustrating even verbs with dramatizations. In a related vein, teachers might break down what might have been a long verbal explanation or set of directions. About a tenth of children with autism exhibit savant (exceptional) abilities, often spatial in nature, such as art, geometry, or a particular area of arithmetic. These abilities are probably due not to a mysterious talent but from massive practice, the reason and motivation for which remains unknown (Ericsson et al., 1993).

In conclusion, there are substantial inequities in mathematics experiences in the early years. Some children not only start behind but also begin a negative and immutable trajectory in mathematics (Case et al., 1999). Low mathematical skills in the earliest years are associated with a *slower growth rate*—children without adequate experiences in mathematics start behind and lose ground every year thereafter (Aunola et al., 2004). There is substantial evidence that this can be avoided or ameliorated, but also evidence that our society has not taken the necessary steps to do either. Interventions must start in Pre-K and kindergarten (Gersten et al., 2005). Without such interventions, children in special need are often relegated to a path of failure (Baroody, 1999; Clements & Conference Working Group, 2004; Jordan, Hanich, & Uberti, 2003; Wright, 1991; Wright et al., 1996).

Collaborative Learning/Peer Tutoring

The NMP's review of child- and adult-centered instruction in elementary and middle school mathematics concluded that instruction should not be either entirely "child-centered" or "teacher-directed" (NMP, 2008). In the technique *Peer-Assisted Learning Strategies* (PALS) (http://kc.vander bilt.edu/pals/), teachers identify children who require help on specific skills and other who might teach those skills. All pairs then study mathematics. These pairs and the skills change frequently, so that all students have the opportunity to be "coaches" and "players." The teacher circulates, observing and providing individual remedial lessons. Findings regarding this approach were promising, but not definitive. The clearest positive results were for low-achieving students on computational measures. Several studies also used a form of formative assessment, so the relative contributions of these two pedagogical strategies is not known. As an example, kindergartners worked on PALS for 15 weeks (Fuchs, Fuchs, & Karns, 2001). The control group was provided teacher-directed lessons and demonstrations. Positive and practically (but not statistically) significant effects on achievement were detected for special education students (effect size = 0.43), low-achieving students (0.37), and medium-achieving students (0.44).

A similar, class-wide peer tutoring program achieved substantial success (Greenwood, Delquadri, & Hall, 1989). This approach involves weekly pairing of the entire class into tutor-tutee pairs, with rewards for responding to the tasks. When adjustments were made for initial Grade 1 pre-test achievement and measured IQ differences, the low-SES experimental group achieved significantly greater gains in mathematics (and literacy measures) than did the equivalent low- SES control group, which received the standard instructional program, including Chapter 1 services. There were no significant differences between the gains made by the experimental and high-SES comparison group compared with the high-SES comparison group, although the experimental group's effect sizes remained less than those of the high-SES comparison group.

Other cooperative learning strategies have not been evaluated as consistently with rigorous designs (NMP, 2008). However, research provides several guidelines (Nastasi & Clements, 1991, includes elaborate reviews). Children need constructive group discussions, including presentations of different views, group engagement, solicitation and provision of explanations; and shared leadership (Wilkinson, Martino, & Camilli, 1994).

Practical implications. A recommendation for an approach designed to enhance social skills, effectance motivation, and higher-order thinking was based on an integration of the research (Nastasi & Clements, 1991). Groups in this approach have the following characteristics:

- *Positive group interdependence* (i.e., if you do well, I do well). Students in a group share the same goal and resources (e.g., one activity sheet for each pair of students). Each has a specific role to play, and these roles are rotated. Students talk together about the work, encouraging each other to learn.
- *Reciprocal sense-making* (i.e., build upon your partner's ideas). Students strive to understand and elaborate upon the viewpoints of their partners. They engage in a mutual process of constructing ideas.
- *Cognitive conflict, then consensus* (i.e., two heads are better than one—in fact, sometimes two wrongs can make a right!). Students learn by taking the perspective of their partners and trying to synthesize discrepant ideas to produce even better ideas. Individual accountability (i.e., all must learn). Each student is accountable for understanding the concepts.

These lead to the following responsibilities that the teacher must make clear:

- *Work together, explaining fully to each other.*

- *Try to make sense of your partner's explanations.*
- *Ask specific questions when requesting help.* When asked a question by your partner, you have a responsibility to help. Do not just give answers, give explanations. Some teachers also use the "Ask three before me" strategy. Students are not to ask the teacher a question until three other students have been asked and were not able to help.
- *Welcome conflicts of ideas; then work toward consensus.* Partners must agree before writing down the final solution. Of course, they may agree just to "try out" the ideas of one partner!
- *Encourage each other.* When disagreeing, criticize ideas, not people.

As students work together, the teacher's role is to encourage interaction and cooperation, as well as to discuss the children's solutions. For example, if one student does not respond to his or her partner, the teacher would do so to keep the discussion going. The teacher also lets students know that working to understand is more important than getting the single, correct answer. The teacher watches for situations that may be discussed profitably. For example, he/she might tell the whole class that, although a certain pair of students worked on only two problems, they learned a lot from each other by figuring out what the other person was thinking. Sometimes it is also worthwhile to have students discuss social situations that arise. For example, the teacher might ask a pair of students to tell the class how they successfully resolved a conflict over turn-taking. Within a small group, students might be encouraged to discuss and decide how task responsibilities are to be divided.

Suggestions for teachers wishing to promote the development of effective collaborative skills include the following:

- *Emphasize the importance of social support.* Encourage students to provide help for peers. Emphasize that the goal is for all students to learn and be successful.
- *Teach specific communication skills* such as active listening, asking and answering questions, providing explanations, and effective debating techniques.
- *Provide students with informational feedback and social reinforcement regarding their social interactions.* Teach students to give such feedback to each other. In addition, model appropriate interactive behavior.
- *Teach and model conflict resolution skills such as negotiation, compromise, and cooperative problem-solving.*
- *Encourage perspective taking* ("put yourself in the other person's shoes") consistent with the students' developmental levels.

Play

Several findings support the traditional emphasis on play and child-centered experiences. In one study, children made more progress overall and specifically on mathematics when they attended child-initiated, compared to strictly academically-oriented, programs (Marcon, 1992). There was some evidence that these children's grades were higher at the end of elementary school (sixth, but not fifth grade) (Marcon, 2002). This may be consistent with some Asian countries. For example, Japanese Pre-K and kindergarten education places emphasis on social-emotional, rather than academic goals (but "informal" math teaching may be ubiquitous at home and school, as we will describe later in this section). Preschoolers engage in free play most of the day. Parents interact with their children in mathematics, usually in real-life, such as counting down elevator numbers. Few mention workbooks (Murata, 2004). Similarly, Flemish Belgium's pre-primary education is more concerned with overall development and less concerned with teaching specific content areas than education in the Netherlands (Torbeyns et al., 2002). Whereas Dutch children start ahead, they are met and surpassed by Flemish children in the elementary years (but the reasons for this are not clear). Finally, a cross-national study showed that preschools in which free choice activities predominated, compared to those in which personal/social activities (personal care and group social activities) predominated, had higher language scores at age 7 (Montie, Xiang, & Schweinhart, 2006). Whole-group activities in preschool were negatively related to cognitive scores at age 7 (cognition including math-relevant content areas, including quantity, spatial relations, problem-solving, and time). These cognitive scores were positively related to the number and variety of equipment and materials available.

However, there are cautions to those interpreting this literature. Marcon's studies have been criticized on methodological grounds (Lonigan, 2003) and *most of these studies are only correlational*—there is no way to know what caused what effects. Further, exposure to mathematics instruction explained a substantive portion of the greater gains of young Chinese, compared to U.S. children (Geary & Liu, 1996). Perhaps most troubling to a "everyday-" or "play-"oriented approach to mathematics is that many programs stating such a focus frequently show negligible gains. One analysis of the PCER mathematics curriculum showed that teaching math indirectly through everyday activities did not predict achievement gains, whereas group work did. Nevertheless, the importance of well-planned free-choice play should not be underestimated, appropriate to the age of the children.

Perhaps the most important caution is the notion of *what is and is not an academic goal*. Japanese preschool teachers, as stated, distinguish themselves from elementary teachers as enhancing social and emotional growth. However, what they mean is that, instead of direct teaching of numbers, they prepared materials that induced quantitative thinking, such as card games, skipping ropes, score boards on which to write numerals, and so forth (Hatano & Sakakibara, 2004). Further, they enhanced this activity by questioning the children or participating in the activities. They invited children who revealed more advanced understanding to express their ideas to stimulate the thinking of other children (Hatano & Sakakibara, 2004). Given that the boarder Japanese culture put high value on mathematical skills and concepts, such quantitative activities are presented frequently, and attract the children. For example, during free play, a child took a few sheets of newspaper. Other wanted some, and the teacher intervened and gave "one sheet [to] each" (number). She provided two roles of tape on the combined tables of two. Some children started to create origami objects of their own, folding two edges into triangles. One child folded, saying "Fold this into half. Fold this into half" (making fourths, p. 197). The teacher participated by making slightly more advanced paper objects. Children gathered around and conversations developed about geometry and quantity. Children began to make more complex objects of their own. Composition and decompositions of specific shapes were enacted and discussed extensively. Size and measure concepts were threaded throughout the conversations. Thus, these "non-academic" teachers teach mathematics extensively, arranging situations in which children can manipulate materials and discuss ideas; offer increasingly challenging tasks; help children through modeling, participation and provision of guidance; and offer corrective or expanding feedback (Hatano & Sakakibara, 2004). Thus, the ubiquitous occurrence in Japanese children's homes and schools indicates that mathematics education is emphasized, even if contrasted with the elementary schools' "academic" focus on mathematics.

Play has several different faces in mathematics development. "Play creates a zone of proximal development of the child. In play a child always behaves beyond his average age, above his daily behavior; in play it is as though he were a head taller than himself" (Vygotsky, 1978, p. 102). Preschoolers showed at least one sign of math thinking during 43% of the minutes of which they are observed (Ginsburg et al., 1999). Of course, this may have been just a brief episode, but this illustrates that children could be involved in mathematics during a considerable portion of their free play. Six categories of mathematics content emerged from their observations (Seo & Ginsburg, 2004). Classification (2%) includes grouping, sorting, or categorizing by attributes. One girl, Anna, took out all the plastic bugs from the container and sorted them by type of bug and then by color. Magnitude (13%) includes describing or comparing the size of objects. When Brianna brought a newspaper to the art table to cover it, Amy remarked, "This isn't big enough to cover the table." Enumeration (12%) includes saying number words, counting, instantly recognizing a number of objects (subitizing), or reading or writing numbers. Three girls drew pictures of their families and discussed how many brothers and sisters they had and how old their siblings were. Dynamics (5%) includes putting things together, taking them apart, or exploring motions such as flipping. Several girls flatted a ball of clay into a disk, cut it, and made "pizza." Pattern and Shape (21%) includes identifying or creating patterns or shapes, or exploring geometric properties. Jennie made a bead necklace, creating a yellow-red color pattern. Spatial Relations (4%) includes describing or drawing a location or direction. When Teresa put a dollhouse couch beside a window, Katie moved it to the center of the living room, saying, "The couch should be in front of TV" (Seo & Ginsburg, 2004, pp. 93–94). About 88% of children engaged in at least one such activity during their play. In comparison to some preschools in which teachers emphasize only simple verbal counting and shape recognition, this reveals a rich foundation on which to build interesting mathematics. We consider these activities *pre-mathematical*—critically important, but not yet *mathematized* for most children until teachers help children talk about them, reflect on them, and build on them.

Observations also indicate that play can support mathematics learning if it stimulates learning and integrates both children and educators' interests (van Oers, 1994). One observational study found that spontaneous use of mathematics in young children's (4 to 7 years) play was frequent, enough so that there were more teaching opportunities than a teacher could possibly notice, much less seize upon (van Oers, 1996). Although a different categorization scheme was used for categories of mathematics, and just one dramatic play setting, a "shoe store," was observed, some comparisons can be made: classification (5%), counting (5%), 1–1 (4%), measuring (27%), estimating (1%), solving number problems (1%), simple arithmetic (1%), quantitative concepts (20%), number words (11%), space–time (5%), notation (7%), dimensions (5%), money (5%), and seriation and conservation (0%). In another study, young children exposed to a play-based curriculum scored significantly higher than national norms on mathematics. However, the findings are equivocal, as the differences declined from age 5 to 7 to insignificance, and the children scored significantly lower than these norms in literacy (van Oers, 2003, notes that the tests emphasize lower-level content).

There are several types of play, such as sensorimotor/manipulative and symbolic/pretend (Monighan-Nourot, Scales, Van Hoorn, & Almy, 1987; Piaget, 1962). Sensorimotor play might involve rhythmic patterns, correspondences, and exploring materials such as blocks (see the section in geometry).

Symbolic play can be further classified as constructive, dramatic, or rule-governed. In constructive play, children manipulate objects to make something. This constitutes about 40% of the play of 3-year-olds and half of the play of 4- to 6-year-olds. The power lies in children's playing with alternate ways of building something.

Materials such as sand, play dough, and blocks offer many rich opportunities for mathematical thinking and reasoning (Perry & Dockett, 2002). Teachers might provide suggestive materials (cookie cutters), engage in parallel play with children, and raise comments or questions regarding shapes and amount of things; for example, making multiple copies of the same shape in play dough with the cookie cutters or transforming sand or play dough objects into one another. One teacher told two boys she was "going to hide the ball" made of play dough, covered it with a flat piece, and pressed down. The boys said the ball was still there, but when she lifted the piece, the ball was "gone." This delighted them and they copied her actions and discussed that the ball was "in" the "circle" (Forman & Hill, 1984, pp. 31–32).

Such play with materials, when creative use is supported, can help children solve problems. A research review reported that children encouraged to play productively with materials before using them to solve problems were more effective at solving those problems than children who had no such experience or those taught how to use the materials (Holton, Ahmed, Williams, & Hill, 2001).

Dramatic play involves substituting some imaginary situation for the children's immediate environment. Mathematics in constructive play is often enhanced when the dramatic is added. Two children making block buildings in parallel may begin arguing that their skyscraper is the "biggest." Similarly, sociodramatic play can be naturally mathematical with the right setting. One suite of activities in the *Building Blocks* curriculum revolves around a Dinosaur Shop where toys are purchased. Teachers and children put together a shop in the dramatic play area, where the shopkeeper fills orders and asks the customer for money (simply $1 for each dinosaur toy).

In one classroom, Gabi was the shopkeeper. Tamika handed her a 5 card (5 dots and the numeral "5") as her order. Gabi counted out 5 toy dinosaurs:

Teacher (just entering the area): How many did you buy?
Tamika: Five.
Teacher: How do you know?
Tamika: Because Gabi counted.

Tamika was still working on her counting skills, and trusted Gabi's counting more than her own knowledge of five. The play context allowed her to develop her knowledge:

Janelle: I'm getting a big number. She handed Gabi a 2 and a 5 card.
Gabi: I don't have that many.
Teacher: You could give Janelle 2 of one kind and 5 of another.

As Gabi counted out the two separate piles and put them in a basket, Janelle counted out dollars. She miscounted and gave her $6:

Gabi: You need $7.

The sociodramatic play setting, with the teacher's help, was beneficial for children at three levels of mathematical thinking.

Games with rules involve the gradual acceptance of prearranged, often arbitrary rules. Such games are a fertile ground for the growth of mathematical reasoning, especially strategic reasoning, and autonomy, or independence (Griffin, 2004; Kamii, 1985). For example, games with number cards provide experiences with counting and comparison (Kamii & Housman, 1999). Card games can be used or adapted for learning mathematics and reasoning, such as Compare ("War"), Odd Card ("Old Maid"), and Go Fish (Clements & Sarama, 2004a; Kamii & DeVries, 1980). These games are often central inside of a focused, sequential curriculum, which we discuss in a succeeding section.

Teachers support mathematics in play by providing a fertile environment and intervening appropriately. Play in perceptually-oriented toddlers is enhanced with realistic objects. All children should also play with structured, open-ended materials. In both China and America, the use of Legos and blocks is strongly linked with mathematical activity in general and with pattern and shape in particular. However, U.S. preschools have many toys, some of which do not encourage mathematical activity. Chinese preschools have only a few play objects, and blocks and Legos are prominent (Ginsburg et al., 2003). Again, less is more.

In symbolic play, teachers need to structure settings, observe play for its potential, provide materials based on their observations (e.g., if children are comparing sizes, teachers might introduce objects with which to measure), highlight and discuss mathematics as it emerges within play, and ask questions such as "How do you know?" and "Are you sure?" (about your answer or solution) (van Oers, 1996).

These examples bring us another type, *mathematical play, or play with mathematics itself* (cf. Steffe & Wiegel, 1994). For example, recall Abby playing with three of the five identical toy train engines her father had brought home. Abby said, "I have 1, 2, 3. So [pointing in the air] foooour, fiiiive . . . two are missing, four and five. [pause] No! I want these to be [pointing at the three engines] one, three, and five. So, two and four are missing. Still two missing, but they're numbers two and four." Abby transformed her symbolic play into playing with the idea that counting words themselves could be counted.

The following features of mathematical play have been suggested: (a) it is a solver-centered activity with the solver in charge of the process; (b) it uses the solver's current knowledge; (c) it develops links between the solver's current schemes while the play is occurring; (d) it will, via "c," reinforce current knowledge; (e) as well as assist future problem-solving/mathematical activity as it enhances future access to knowledge; and (f) these behaviors and advantages are irrespective of the solver's age (Holton et al., 2001).

Teachable Moments

If play has so much potential to elicit mathematical thinking, should educators simply use "teaching moments"? A old and honored tradition capitalizing on teachable moments is an important pedagogical strategy. The teacher carefully observes children and identifies elements in the spontaneously-emerging situations that can be used to promote learning of mathematics (Ginsburg, 2008). However, there are serious problems with *depending* on this approach. For example, most teachers spend little time in careful observation necessary to find such moments (Ginsburg, 2008; J. Lee, 2004). They spend little time with them during their free play (Seo & Ginsburg, 2004). As we have seen, many teachers have a difficult time engaging children in tasks at their mathematical level (Bennett et al., 1984). Most teachers do not have the mathematics language and concepts at their command. For example, they do not tend to think about relational terms in mathematics. According to researchers, their language in general may influence their ability to see opportunities for teaching mathematics throughout the curriculum (Ginsburg, 2008; Moseley, 2005). Finally, it is unrealistic for them to see opportunities for multiple children to build multiple concepts (Ginsburg, 2008).

Practical implications. Seek and exploit teachable moments. However, recognize that in most situations, they will constitute only a small portion of the mathematics activities children need.

Direct Instruction, Child-centered Approaches, and Play—How to Develop Math Knowledge *and* Self-regulation Skills

We have seen research supporting explicit instruction (for low achievers), *and* some evidence for child-centered curricula. Other studies have indicated that direct instruction techniques may affect achievement, especially in the short term, but more child-centered techniques favor overall intelligence in the long term (Schweinhart & Weikart, 1988, 1997). What are educators to conclude? In this section, we synthesize research to provide clear (if still tentative) recommendations.

Unfortunately, the term child-centered approaches has been the catch-all for everything from a laissez-faire classroom where teachers do not teach anything to well-planned teacher–child interactions that lead the child toward the development of more mature levels of underlying skills such as self-regulation. No wonder many conclude that child-centered approaches are not effective. Child-centered activities, such as play, *when planned and implemented carefully*, can support the development of underlying cognitive and social emotional skills necessary for school readiness and performance on academic tasks.

Specific child-centered pedagogical strategies can build the essential competence of self-regulation. Young children have limited ability to pay attention, and minimizing distractions is helpful. Building their positive self-regulation skills is also possible, with multiple benefits. Encouraging children to talk to each other in solving a problem in small-group or large-group settings ("turn to your partner and figure out what you think the number will be") facilitates its development. Promoting high-level sociodramatic play is a key way to develop self-regulation, as children have to negotiate roles and rules—and keep to them, if they want to be included. Just as important is eliminating the dead times, dull routines, and overly authoritarian environments that do not develop children's self-regulation. Such strategies have been proven successful in improving young children's self-regulation competencies and academic achievement (e.g., Bodrova & Leong, 2005). Used as a part of a comprehensive preschool curriculum as well as a part of an early literacy intervention, these strategies have been proven successful in improving young children's self-regulation and academic achievement (Barnett, Yarosz, Thomas, & Hornbeck, 2006; Bodrova & Leong, 2001, 2003; Bodrova, Leong, Norford, & Paynter, 2003; Diamond, Barnett, Thomas, & Munro, 2007).

Also, unfortunately, much of the research against direct instruction (Schweinhart & Weikart, 1988, 1997) may not be reliable. Results are mostly non-significant, the approaches used in different groups were not as different as one might suppose, numbers are very small, and so forth (Bereiter, 1986; Gersten, 1986; Gersten & White, 1986). Finally, research supports *certain types* of explicit instruction, as we saw previously.

Research indicates that curricula designed to improve self-regulation skills *and* enhance early academic abilities are most effective in helping children succeed in school (e.g., Blair & Razza, 2007). Further, research has shown that children in classrooms with intentional focus on mathematics do better in mathematics . . . but that is not all. *Children in classrooms with math content are more likely to engage at high-quality level during free play* (Dale C. Farran, Kang, Aydogan, & Lipsey, 2005).

Practical implications. Our conclusions from these diverse bodies of research are as follows:

- When explicit content-oriented instruction is mistakenly implemented as (only) teacher-led activities at the expense of engaging children in activities of their choice, children practice being "teacher-regulated" and are not given an opportunity to develop self-regulated behaviors which affect their ability to later engage in learning behaviors of their own accord. *The dichotomy between explicit instruction and child-centered approach is a false one and high-quality early math programs combine an explicit focus on content with equally explicit focus on promoting play and self-regulatory behaviors.*
- Child-centered approaches, such as the implementation of dramatic, make-believe play, and the use of small-group discussions (including pairs of children discussing solutions during whole-group time) make a valuable contribution to a child's development, *when well structured and mediated by the teacher.*
- Curricula designed *both* to improve self-regulation skills and to enhance early academic abilities are most effective in helping children succeed in school.

- Recall (see Chapter 15) that mathematics curricula that teach a combination of skills, concepts, and problem-solving help children learn skills about as well as if they had studied only skills, but also concepts and problem-solving, which children in skills-only curricula do not (e.g., Senk & Thompson, 2003).

Projects

Mathematics should be gleaned from myriad everyday situations, including play, but going beyond it as well. For example, a group of young children investigated many measurement ideas as they attempted to draw plans for a carpenter, so that he could build them a new table (Malaguzzi, 1997). However, the PCER studies found no differences in children's development of mathematics in project approach, compared to control, classrooms. We do not yet know whether these teachers did not implement the project well, or whether project-based, or other child-centered, programs are not effective in supporting long-term, comprehensive growth of mathematical skills and ideas. Research is still needed to ascertain if rich environments such as Reggio Emelia and project-based programs can be implemented well at scale and what the benefits are.

Time

The more time they spend learning, the more children learn. This applies to full-day compared to half-day programs (Lee, Burkam, Ready, Honigman, & Meisels, 2006; Walston & West, 2004). Children spent more time on mathematics (although the effects may not persist to grade 3; Walston, West, & Rathbun, 2005). For preschoolers in the average-quality preschooler, see Loeb et al., in press. Further, average-quality centers may have negative impact on social-emotional development. Attending more than 15–30 hours may benefit children from low-resource communities, but not those from higher-resource communities. Children gained the most if they entered centers between the ages of 2 and 3 years (Loeb et al., in press). Remember that these studies involve large numbers of children, but are correlational only.

Similarly, the more time in the school day children spent on mathematics, and the more math activities in which they engaged (up to about 20–30 minutes per day in Pre-K), the more they learn—without harming their development in other areas (Clements & Sarama, 2008).

Multiage Grouping

One study indicated that multiage grouping alone did not support learning (Wood & Frid, 2005). Rather, effective learning was dependent upon the teacher's capacities to develop productive discussions among children, as well as implement developmentally appropriate curricula that addressed the needs of the different children. Teacher planning, teacher "assisted performance," peer sharing and tutoring, and peer regulation were identified as important aspects. That is, teachers used direct instruction when they needed to explain activities and set parameters for completion of these activities. However, when monitoring students' progress in activities, or when students sought assistance with their learning, the teachers used questioning, paraphrasing, and suggestions as alternative strategies to guide the children to solve the problems by themselves. No measure of the *effectiveness* of each technique was provided, but the constellation of strategies is consistent with findings on those strategies.

Class Size and Teachers' Aides

A meta-analysis found that small class size might have the greatest positive effects on reading and mathematics achievement and on students in grades K-3, when class size was 22 or fewer students, and when students were economically disadvantaged or belonged to a racial/ethnic minority group (Robinson, 1990). The Project STAR studies, large-scale randomized experiments (Finn & Achilles, 1990; Finn, Gerber, Achilles, & Boyd-Zaharias, 2001; Finn, Pannozzo, & Achilles, 2003), indicated that at every grade, K-3 students who attended smaller classes outperformed students who attended regular-size classrooms or regular-size classrooms with aides on every academic measure (Finn & Achilles, 1990; Finn et al., 2001). Students who started attending small classes in the earliest grades, and who attended small classes for more years benefitted most.

Less attention has been given to *why* small classes are helpful. Some studies suggest that teacher morale is improved, teachers spend more time in direction instruction and less on mere management, there are fewer discipline problems, students' engaging in learning is increased, and in-grade retentions and drop-outs are reduced (Finn, 2002). Thus, teachers may teach more effectively. In addition, students may become better students. They may be more engaged, exhibiting more pro-learning and pro-social behaviors and fewer anti-social behaviors (Finn et al., 2003).

There are at least two policy pitfalls, or "how to do small classes the wrong way" (Finn, 2002). First, administrators might overlook the need for expert teachers (California reduced class sizes so quickly that it accepted many low-quality teachers who lacked credentials—STAR had all credentialed teachers). Second, they might confuse student-teacher ratios (two adults in a classroom with 30 children has a small ratio but a large class size—and the research is on *class size*). Just reducing class size without planning will likely make no difference (Milesi & Gamoran, 2006).

Practical implications. In summary, there are benefits of smaller classes, *especially* for younger students, and especially for children at risk for school failure (Finn, 2002; Finn et al., 2001). They are not a "cause" of better teaching and learning but an opportunity for both to be more effective. Project STAR had no additional intervention. One could hope for larger-effect sizes of teachers engaged in professional development specifically designed to show them how to use innovative curriculum and formative assessment effectively in the context of the smaller classes.

Another surprising result from these studies is that the presence of teacher aides makes little difference in learning (Finn, 2002 see also NMP, 2008). Funding might be better spent on additional teachers and/or additional professional development (see Chapter 14 of the companion book).

Practice, or Repeated Experiencing

For young children learning knowledge that needs to be practiced, such as subitizing, counting, comparing number, shape naming, or arithmetic combinations, research has some clear guidelines. *Substantial practice is required.* We prefer the term *repeated experience* because it suggests many contexts and different types of activities, none of which has to be "drill" for young children and because varying contexts support generalization and transfer. Also, *distributed, spaced practice is better than massed* (all in one session, repetition of the same item over and over) practice (Cepeda, Pashler, Vul, Wixted, & Rohrer, 2006). Because we want such knowledge available quickly throughout the student's life, short, frequent practice sessions of facts and skills *whose conceptual foundations have been well learned and understood* are recommended.

Manipulatives and "Concrete" Representations

The notion of "concrete," from concrete manipulatives to pedagogical sequences such as "concrete to abstract," is embedded in educational theories, research, and practice, especially in mathematics education. Although widely accepted notions often have a good deal of truth behind them, they can also become immune from critical reflection.

Generally, students who use manipulatives in their mathematics classes outperform those who do not (Driscoll, 1983; Greabell, 1978; Johnson, 2000; Lamon & Huber, 1971; Raphael & Wahlstrom, 1989; Sowell, 1989; Suydam, 1986), although the benefits may be slight (Anderson, 1957). These benefits hold across grade level, ability level, and topic, given that use of a manipulative "makes sense" for that topic. Manipulative use also increases scores on retention and problem-solving tests. Attitudes toward mathematics are improved when students have instruction with concrete materials provided by teachers knowledgeable about their use (Sowell, 1989).

However, manipulatives do not guarantee success (Baroody, 1989). One study showed that classes not using manipulatives outperformed classes using manipulatives on a test of transfer (Fennema, 1972). Second graders were taught multiplication as repeated addition with manipulatives (colored rods) or symbolically (e.g., 2 + 2 + 2). Both groups learned multiplication but the symbolic group scored higher on a transfer test. All teachers in this study emphasized learning with understanding whether using manipulatives, mental math, or paper and pencil.

Another study revealed that there is often a lack of connection between children's representations, such as with manipulatives or paper and pencil. For example, they found that some students who performed subtraction best with manipulatives were the worst with paper and pencil, and vice versa (Resnick & Omanson, 1987). The researchers explored the benefit of "mapping instruction," designed to help children link their "concrete" knowledge shown by their use of manipulatives to symbolic work with numerals. Although this sounded reasonable, it had limited benefit. The only children who benefitted were those who received extensive instruction and used that time to make more correct verbalizations of the *quantities* involved in renaming. Thus, it was not simple "concrete" experience that helped but rather attention to *quantities*. Concrete objects may be a role but they need to be used carefully to create a strong understanding and justification for each step of a procedure (Resnick & Omanson, 1987). Students sometimes learn to use manipulatives only in a rote manner. They perform the correct steps but have learned little more. For example, a student working on place value with beans and beansticks used the (one) bean as ten and the beanstick (with ten beans on it) as one (Hiebert & Wearne, 1992).

These and other studies support an essential point: Manipulatives do not "carry" mathematical ideas. As a final example, educators commonly have children measure a length with concrete materials using different unit sizes to teach measurement concepts. However, children gain knowledge that the number of units measured is inversely related to the size of the unit *before* they recognize the importance of maintaining a standard unit of measure, even though experience with the latter is assumed to build knowledge of the former (Carpenter & Lewis, 1976).

Given these cautions and nuances, a final concern is that teachers often use manipulatives as a way to reform their mathematics teaching, without reflecting on their use of representations of mathematical ideas or on the other aspects of their instruction that must be changed (Grant, Peterson, & Shojgreen-Downer, 1996). Both teachers and parents often believe that reform in mathematics education indicates that "concrete" is good and "abstract" is bad.

In summary, although research might suggest that instruction begin "concretely," it also warns that manipulatives are not sufficient to guarantee meaningful learning. To understand the role of concrete manipulatives and any concrete-to-abstract pedagogical sequence, we must further define what we mean by "concrete."

Most practitioners and researchers argue that manipulatives are effective because they are concrete. By "concrete," most mean physical objects that students can grasp with their hands. This sensory nature ostensibly makes manipulatives "real," connected with one's intuitively meaningful personal self, and therefore helpful. There are, however, problems with this view (cf. Metz, 1995). First, it cannot be assumed that concepts can be "read off" manipulatives. That is, the physical objects may be manipulated meaningfully without the concepts being illuminated. Working with Cuisenaire rods, John Holt said that he and his fellow teacher "were excited about the rods because we could see strong connections between the world of rods and the world of numbers. We therefore assumed that children, looking at the rods and doing things with them, could *see* how the world of numbers and numerical operations worked. The trouble with this theory is that [my colleague] and I *already* knew how the numbers worked. We could say, 'Oh, the rods behaved just the way numbers do.' But if we *hadn't* known how numbers behaved, would looking at the rods enable us to find out? Maybe so, maybe not" (Holt, 1982, pp. 138–139).

Second, even if children begin to make connections between manipulatives and nascent ideas, physical actions with certain manipulatives may suggest different mental actions than those we wish students to learn. For example, researchers found a mismatch among students using the number line to perform addition. When adding 6 + 3, the students located 6, counted "one, two, three" and read the answer at "9." This did not help them solve the problem mentally, for to do so they have to count "seven, eight, nine" and at the same time *count the counts*—7 is 1, 8 is 2, and so on. These actions are quite different (Gravemeijer, 1991). These researchers also found that students' external actions on an abacus do not always match the mental activity intended by the teacher. Indeed, some authors believe that the number line model does not help young children learn addition and subtraction, and that, certainly, using the number line model to assess children's knowledge of arithmetic makes several important assumptions about what *else* they know (Ernest, 1985). In any case, the number line cannot be viewed as a "transparent" model; if used, it must be *taught*.

Similarly, second graders did not learn more sophisticated strategies (e.g., adding 34 and 52 by counting by tens: "34, 44, 54 . . .") using a hundreds board, because it did not correspond to students' activity or help them to build useful figural imagery that supported creation of abstract composite units of ten (Cobb, 1995).

Therefore, although manipulatives have an important place in learning, their physicality does not carry—and may not even be essential in supporting—the meaning of the mathematical idea. They can even be used in a rote manner, as did the student who used the bean as ten and the beanstick as one. Students may require concrete materials to build meaning initially, but they must *reflect on their actions* with manipulatives to do so. They need teachers who can reflect on their students' representations for mathematical ideas and help them develop increasing sophisticated and mathematical representations. "Although kinesthetic experience can enhance perception and thinking, understanding does not travel through the fingertips and up the arm" (Ball, 1992, p. 47).

Further, when we speak of concrete understanding, we are not always referring to physical objects. Teachers of later grades expect students to have a concrete understanding that goes beyond manipulatives. For example, we like to see that numbers—as mental objects ("I can think of 43 + 26")—are "concrete" for older students. It appears that there are different ways to think about "concrete."

We have *Sensory-Concrete* knowledge when we need to *use* sensory material to make sense of an idea. For example, at early stages, children cannot count, add, or subtract meaningfully unless they have actual things. Consider Brenda, a primary grade student. The interviewer had covered four of seven squares with a cloth, told Brenda that four were covered, and asked how many in all. Brenda tried to raise the cloth but was thwarted by the interviewer. She then counted the three visible squares.

B: 1, 2, 3 (touches each visible item in turn).

I: There's four here (taps the cloth).

B: (Lifts the cloth, revealing two squares) 4, 5. (touches each and puts cloth back).

I: Ok, I'll show you two of them (shows two). There's four here, you count them.

B: 1, 2 (then counts each visible): 3, 4, 5.

I: There's two more here (taps the cloth).

B: (Attempts to lift the cloth.)

I: (Pulls back the cloth.)

B: 6, 7 (touches the last two squares). (Steffe & Cobb, 1988)

Brenda's attempt to lift the cloth indicates that she was aware of the hidden squares and wanted to count the collection. This did not lead to counting because she could not yet coordinate saying the number word sequence with items that she only imagined. She needed physically present items to count. Note that this does not mean that manipulatives were the original root of the idea. Research tends to indicate that is not the case (Gelman & Williams, 1997). However, there appears to be a level of thinking when children can solve tasks with physical objects that they cannot solve without such objects. For example, consider asking a girl who just turned 4 years of age to add small numbers with and without blocks ("bricks") (Hughes, 1981).

(1)   E: Let's just put one more in (does so). Ten and one more, how many's that?

C: Err . . .(thinks) . . . eleven!

E: Yes, very good. Let's just put one more in (does so). Eleven and one more, how many's that?

C: Twelve!

Five minutes later, with the bricks put away:

(2)   E: I'm just going to ask you some questions, OK? How many is two and one more?

C: (No response.)

E: Two and one more, how many's that?

C: Err . . . makes . . .

E   Makes . . . how many?

C: Err . . . fifteen (in couldn't-care-less tone of voice). (pp. 216–217)

The following involved a slightly older boy.

E: What's three and one more? How many is three and one more?

C: Three and what? One what? Letter—I mean number?

(We had earlier been playing a game with magnetic numbers, and he is presumably referring to them here.)

E: How many is three and one more?

C: One more what?

E: Just one more, you know?

C: I *don't* know (disgruntled). (p. 218)

This is consistent with research showing that most children do not solve larger-number problems without the support of concrete objects until 5.5 years of age (Levine, Jordan, & Huttenlocher,

1992). They have, apparently, not only learned the counting sequence and the cardinal principle (usually about 3.5 years), but have also developed the ability to convert verbal number words to quantitative meaning (cf. the ordinal-to-cardinal shift in Fuson, 1992a). Preschoolers are more successful solving arithmetic problems when they have blocks available (Carpenter & Moser, 1982) and may not be able to solve even the simplest of problems without such physical, concrete support (Baroody, Eiland, Su, & Thompson, 2007).

At an even younger age, researchers argue that children have a relatively concrete understanding of number until they learn number words. At that point, they gain a more abstract understanding (Spelke, 2003).

In summary, those with *Sensory-Concrete* knowledge need to *use* or at least *refer directly to* sensory material to make sense of a concept or procedure (Jordan, Huttenlocher, & Levine, 1994). Such material often facilitates children's development of mathematical operations by serving as material support for children's action schemes (Correa, Nunes, & Bryant, 1998). This does not mean that their understanding is only concrete; even infants make and use abstractions in thinking (Gelman, 1994). As another example, preschoolers understand—at least as "theories-in-action"— principles of geometric distance and do not need to depend on concrete, perceptual experience to judge distances (Bartsch & Wellman, 1988).

Concrete "versus" abstract? Then what of abstraction? Some decry limited abstract knowledge. This can occur: "Direct teaching of concepts is impossible and fruitless. A teacher who tries to do this usually accomplishes nothing but empty verbalism, a parrot-like repetition of words by the child, simulating a knowledge of the corresponding concepts but actually covering up a vacuum" (Vygotsky, 1934/1986, p. 150). This is *abstract-only* knowledge.

However, abstraction is not to be avoided, at any age. Mathematics is *about* abstraction and generalization. "Two"—as a concept—is an abstraction. Further, even infants use conceptual categories that are abstract as they classify things (Lehtinen & Hannula, 2006; Mandler, 2004), including by quantity. These are enabled by innately specified knowledge-rich predispositions that give children a head start in constructing knowledge. These are "abstractions-in-action," not represented explicitly by the child but used to build knowledge (Karmiloff-Smith, 1992). When an infant says "two doggies," she is using abstraction structures of numerosity to label a concrete situation. Thus, the situation is analogical to Vygotsky's (1934/1986) formulation of spontaneous ("concrete") vs. scientific ("abstract") concepts in that abstractions-in-action guide the development of concrete knowledge and eventually, depending largely on social mediation, become explicated as linguistic abstractions. What of this type of knowledge, a synthesis of concrete and abstract understandings?

Integrated-Concrete knowledge is knowledge that is *connected* in special ways. This is the root of the word concrete—"to grow together." What gives sidewalk concrete its strength is the combination of separate particles in an interconnected mass. What gives Integrated-Concrete thinking its strength is the combination of many separate ideas in an interconnected structure of knowledge. For students with this type of interconnected knowledge, physical objects, actions performed on them, and abstractions are all interrelated in a strong mental structure. Ideas such as "75," "3/4," and "rectangle" become as real, tangible, and strong as a concrete sidewalk. Each idea is as concrete as a wrench is to a plumber—an accessible and useful tool. Knowledge of money was in the process of becoming such a tool for him.

Therefore, an idea is not simply concrete or not concrete. Depending on what kind of *relationship* you have with the knowledge (Wilensky, 1991), it might be Sensory-Concrete, abstract-only, or Integrated-Concrete. Further, we as educators can not engineer mathematics into Sensory-Concrete materials because ideas such as number are not "out there." As Piaget has shown us, they are constructions—reinventions—of each human mind. "Fourness" is no more "in" four blocks than it is "in" a picture of four blocks. The child creates "four" by building a representation of number and connecting it with either physical or pictured blocks (Clements, 1989; Clements & Battista, 1990; Kamii, 1973, 1985, 1986). As Piaget's collaborator Hermine Sinclair says, ". . . numbers are *made* by children, not *found* (as they may find some pretty rocks, for example) or *accepted* from adults (as they may accept and use a toy)" (Sinclair, Forward, in Steffe & Cobb, 1988, p. v).

What ultimately makes mathematical ideas Integrated-Concrete is not their physical characteristics. Indeed, physical knowledge is a different kind of knowledge than logical/mathematical knowledge, according to Piaget (Kamii, 1973). Also, some research indicates that pictures are as effective for learning as physical manipulatives (Scott & Neufeld, 1976). What makes ideas Integrated-Concrete is how "meaning-full"—connected to other ideas and situations—they are. John Holt reported that children who already understood numbers could perform the tasks with or without the blocks. "But children who could not do these problems without the blocks didn't have a clue about how to do them with the blocks . . . . They found the blocks . . . as abstract, as disconnected from reality, mysterious, arbitrary, and capricious as the numbers that these blocks were supposed to bring to life" (Holt, 1982, p. 219). *Good uses of manipulatives are those that aid students in building, strengthening, and connecting various representations of mathematical ideas.* Indeed, we often assume that more able or older students' greater facility with mathematics stems from their greater knowledge or mathematical procedures or strategies. However, it is more often true that younger children possess the relevant knowledge but cannot effectively create a mental representation of the necessary information (Greeno & Riley, 1987). This is where good manipulatives can play a role.

Comparing the two levels of concrete knowledge, we see a shift in what the adjective "concrete" describes. *Sensory-Concrete* refers to knowledge that demands the support of concrete objects and children's knowledge of manipulating these objects. *Integrated-Concrete* refers to knowledge that is "concrete" at a higher level because they are connected to other knowledge, both physical knowledge that has been abstracted and thus distanced from concrete objects and abstract knowledge of a variety of types. Such knowledge consists of units that "are primarily *concrete*, embodied, incorporated, lived" (Varela, 1999, p. 7). Ultimately, these are descriptions of changes in the configuration of knowledge as children develop. Consistent with other theoreticians (J. R. Anderson, 1993), we do not believe there are fundamentally different, incommensurable types of knowledge, such as "concrete" versus "abstract" or "concrete" versus "symbolic."

Practical implications: Instructional use of manipulatives. Too often, manipulatives are used to "make math fun," where "manipulative math" and "real math" are seen as difference enterprises (Moyer, 2000). Manipulatives are used as a diversion, frequently because teachers do not understand their role as representations of mathematical ideas. Justification for their *instructional* role is often that they are "concrete" and thus "understandable." We have seen, however, that—like beauty—"concrete" is, quite literally, in the mind of the beholder.

What role should manipulatives play? Research offers some guidelines:

- *Model with manipulatives.* We noted that young children can solve problems and, at the earliest ages, appear to need concrete manipulatives—or, more precisely, sensory-concrete support—to do so. However, the key is that they are successful because they can model the situation (Carpenter, Ansell, Franke, Fennema, & Weisbeck, 1993; Outhred & Sardelich, 1997). Nevertheless, early number recognition, counting, and arithmetic may require (recall Brenda), or benefit from, the use of sensory-concrete support, *if they help children investigate and understand the mathematical structures and processes.* For example, children benefitted more from using pipe cleaners than pictures to make non-triangles into triangles (Martin, Lukong, & Reaves, 2007). They merely drew on top of the pictures but they transformed the pipe cleaners. Further, even subtle changes in such support can make a difference at certain developmental levels. One study showed that 3-year-olds who used more "interesting" manipulatives (fruit instead of plain blocks) were more likely to accurately identify numbers in a recall task and answer subtraction questions correctly (Nishida & Lillard, 2007b). There was no difference in children's attentiveness to the lesson (Nishida & Lillard, 2007b). The authors give no further hypotheses, but connections to children's existing experiences, perhaps building more elaborated mental models, may have accounted for the difference.

- *Ensure manipulatives serve as symbols.* Recall the work on models and maps (DeLoache, 1987). Multiple studies such as this (Munn, 1998; Uttal, Scudder, & DeLoache, 1997) support this guideline: Physical "concreteness" is not necessarily an instruction advantage. This can physically make it difficult for children to use a manipulative as a symbol. To be useful, children must interpret the manipulative as representing a mathematical idea. A second example comes from early introduction of algebraic thinking. When the goal is abstraction, concrete materials may not be particularly helpful. For example, working with differences in children's heights (e.g., Mary is 4 inches taller than Tom), agreeing that Tom's height would be T, children resisted representing Mary's height as "T + 4," preferring "M" (Schliemann, Carraher, & Brizuela, 2007). Others solved some problems but still said "T" stood for "tall" or "ten." Also, students tended to think of the differences in height as the (absolute) heights. Part of their difficulty was thinking of any letter as a variable amount when the concrete situations used in the instruction implied that there was a particular quantity—unknown, perhaps, but not one that varies. That is, children could think of the value of a height, or the amount of money in a wallet as unknown, or a "surprise," but had difficulty thinking of it as a range of values. In contrast, they learned more playing activities such as "guess my rule," in which the context was simply mathematics, not with physical manipulatives, objects, or settings. The pure number activities were meaningful and had advantages in helping children from a low-performing school to think about numerical relationships and to use algebraic notations. In summary, the relationship of manipulatives to the concepts they are to represent is not transparent to children (Uttal, Marzolf et al., 1997). Children must be able to see the manipulative as a symbol for a mathematical idea. In addition, in some contexts the physicality of a manipulative may interfere with students' mathematical development, and other representations may be more effective for learning. Further, active teaching must guide children to make, maintain, and use manipulatives as symbols or tools for doing mathematics. As we describe in more detail in a subsequent section, *connecting* manipulative work (e.g., place value blocks) with verbal and representations can build both concepts and skills successfully (Brownell & Moser, 1949; Fuson & Briars, 1990; Hiebert & Wearne, 1993).

In summary, children must construct, understand, and use the structural similarities between any representation and the problem situation to use objects as tools for thinking. When children do not see those similarities, manipulatives may fail to help, and many even hinder, problem-solving and learning (Outhred & Sardelich, 1997). As we saw in the previous section, if they do not mirror the mental actions we wish children to develop, their use could be a waste of time or even counterproductive. Manipulatives, drawings, and other representations should as far as possible, be used instructionally in ways consistent with the mental actions on objects that students are to develop:

- *Encourage appropriate play with manipulatives.* Is it good to let children play with manipulatives? Usually yes, sometimes no. Most teachers recognize that if young children have not explored a manipulative on their own (say, toy dinosaurs), getting them to address the teachers agenda (say, counting) can be at best inefficient, and at worst, near impossible.

Further, children can and do learn pre-mathematical foundations through their self-directed play, especially with structured manipulatives, such as pattern blocks or building blocks (Seo & Ginsburg, 2004). However, these experiences are rarely mathematical without teacher guidance. Counterintuitively, play can sometimes be counterproductive. When a physical object is intended to serve as a symbol, playing with the object can interfere with understanding. For example, having these children play with a model of a room decreased young children's success in using it as a symbol in a map search task, and eliminating any interaction increased their success (DeLoache, Miller, Rosengren, & Bryant, 1997). Thus, the purpose and intended learning with the manipulatives must be considered carefully.

- *Use few manipulatives well.* Some research indicates the more manipulatives, the better. However, U.S. teachers tend to use different manipulatives to increase "motivation" and "make math more fun" (Moyer, 2000; Uttal, Marzolf et al., 1997). Further, Dienes "multiple embodiment" theory suggests that to truly abstract a mathematical concept, students need to experience it in more than one context. However, there are opposing practices and evidence. Successful teachers in Japan tend to reuse the same manipulatives repeatedly (Uttal, Marzolf et al., 1997). Research indicates that, indeed, deeper experience with one manipulative is more productive than equivalent experiences using various manipulatives (Hiebert & Wearne, 1996). A synthesis seems to indicate that multiple representations are useful (e.g., a manipulative, drawings, verbalizations, symbols), but many different manipulatives may be less useful. These manipulatives should be used for multiple tasks, so children do not view them as objects to play with but tools for thinking (Sowell, 1989).

- *Use caution in beginning with "prestructured" manipulatives.* We must be wary of using "prestructured" manipulatives—ones where the mathematics is built in by the manufacturer, such as base-ten blocks (as opposed to interlocking cubes). They can be as colored rods for John Holt's students—"another kind of numeral, symbols made of colored wood rather than marks on paper" (Holt, 1982). Sometimes the simpler the better. For example, educators from the Netherlands found students did not learn well using base-ten blocks and other structured base-ten materials. There may have been a mismatch between trading one base-ten block for another and the actions of mentally separating a ten into ten ones or thinking of the same quantity simultaneously as "one ten" and "ten ones." The Netherlands' students were more successful hearing a story of a sultan who often wants to count his gold. The setting of the story gave students a reason for counting and grouping: The gold had to be counted, packed, and sometimes unwrapped—and an inventory constantly maintained (Gravemeijer, 1991). So, students might best start using manipulatives with which they create and break up groups of tens into ones (e.g., interlocking cubes) rather than base-ten blocks (Baroody, 1990). Settings that provide reasons for grouping are ideal.

- *Use drawings and symbols—move away from manipulatives as soon as possible.* Children using manipulatives in second grade to do arithmetic tend to do so even in fourth grade (Carr & Alexeev, 2008). That is a failure to move along the learning trajectory. Although modeling necessitates manipulatives at some early levels of thinking, even preschoolers and kindergartners can use other representations, such as drawings and symbols, with, or instead of, physical manipulatives (Carpenter et al., 1993; Outhred & Sardelich, 1997; van Oers, 1994). Even for children as young as 5 years of age, *physical* manipulatives may play a surprisingly small role. For example, in one study there was no significant difference between kindergartners given and not given manipulatives accuracy or in the discovery of arithmetic strategies (Grupe & Bray, 1999). The similarities go on: Children without manipulatives used their fingers on 30% of all trials, while children with manipulatives used the bears on 9% of the trials but used their fingers on 19% of trials for a combined total of 28%. Finally, children stopped using external aids approximately halfway through the 12-week study. Physical objects can make an important contribution, but are not guaranteed to help (Baroody, 1989; Clements, 1999a). Drawings can include models, such as the "empty number line" approach (Klein, Beishuizen, & Treffers, 1998; see Chapter 5). Another consideration here is children's use of images. High-achieving children build images that have a spectrum of quality and a more conceptual and relational core. They are able to link different experiences and abstract similarities. Low-achieving children's images tended to be dominated by surface features. Instruction might help them develop more sophisticated images (Gray & Pitta, 1999).

With both physical and computer manipulatives, we should choose *meaningful* representations in which the objects and actions available to the student parallel the mathematical objects (ideas) and actions (processes or algorithms) we wish the students to learn. We then need to guide students to make connections between these representations (Fuson & Briars, 1990; Lesh, 1990).

Technology—Computers and TV

Kindergartner Chris is making shapes with a simplified version of Logo (Clements et al., 2001). He has been typing "R" (for rectangle) and then two numbers for the side lengths. This time he chooses 9 and 9. He sees a square and laughs.

Adult: Now, what do the two nines mean for the rectangle?
Chris: I don't know, now! Maybe I'll name this a square rectangle!
Chris uses his invented terminology repeatedly on succeeding days.

Computer Technology. At what age will computers support children's development, both of mathematics and of the "whole child?" In 1995, we argued that "we no longer need to ask whether the use of technology is 'appropriate' " in early childhood education (Clements & Swaminathan, 1995). The research supporting that statement was, and remains, convincing. However, misunderstandings and unfounded criticisms of computers in early childhood continue to be published (e.g., Cordes & Miller, 2000). This is important, because some teachers retain a bias against computers that contradicts research evidence. Especially those teaching in middle-SES schools believe it is "inappropriate" to have computers in classrooms for young children (Lee & Ginsburg, 2007):

I just hate computers for children this age. . . . It's just too removed, too far removed from the senses. . . . There's no thought involved. It's totally just pressing buttons. If this doesn't work right with one button, they just randomly press another button. There's no thinking, there's no process involved. There's no logical analysis of anything going on there.

I think that computers tend to just block in one child at a time. I mean, maybe it'll take in two or three, doing group activity. But it kind of isolates the child. I really don't think that computers have a place in early childhood (Lee & Ginsburg, 2007, p. 15).

We have countered such criticisms elsewhere (Clements & Sarama, 2003b). Here, we simply summarize some basic findings from research on young children and computers:

- Children overwhelmingly display positive emotions when using computers (Ishigaki, Chiba, & Matsuda, 1996; Shade, 1994). They show higher positive affect and interest when they use the computer together (Shade, 1994) and prefer to work with a peer rather than alone

(Lipinski, Nida, Shade, & Watson, 1986; Rosengren, Gross, Abrams, & Perlmutter, 1985; Swigger & Swigger, 1984). Further, working on the computer can instigate new instances and forms of collaborative work such as helping or instructing, and discussing and building upon each others' ideas (Clements, 1994).

- Children who had access to a computer at home performed better on measures of school readiness and cognitive development, controlling for children's developmental stage and family socioeconomic status (Li & Atkins, 2004).
- The addition of a computer center does not disrupt ongoing play or social interaction but does facilitate extensive positive social interaction, cooperation, and helping behaviors (Binder & Ledger, 1985; King & Alloway, 1992; Rhee & Chavnagri, 1991; Rosengren et al., 1985). Even in the preschool classroom, a computer center fosters a positive climate characterized by praise and encouragement of peers (Klinzing & Hall, 1985).
- Computers may represent an environment in which both cognitive and social interactions simultaneously are encouraged, each to the benefit of the other (Clements, 1986; Clements & Nastasi, 1985).
- Computers can motivate academic work (see the many references in Clements & Sarama, 2003b). Children are energized. They are active and took charge of their learning processes. Those behind in other areas excelled (Primavera, Wiederlight, & DiGiacomo, 2001).
- Computers can engender creativity, including creative mathematical thinking (Clements, 1986, 1995; Clements & Sarama, 2003b).
- Computers can facilitate young children's mathematical thinking.

This last point is most directly relevant to this book, so we will elaborate on it especially. To begin, we provide the NMP's summary of rigorous studies, most of which were conducted with older elementary students. Those reviews indicated that computer-assisted instruction (CAI) practice programs, as well as tutorial programs (often combined with drill and practice), that are well designed and implemented, could have a positive impact on mathematics performance. Also, learning to write computer programs improves students' performance compared to conventional instruction, with the greatest effects on understanding of concepts and applications, especially geometric concepts (NMP, 2008). Next, we consider a wider variety of studies, including, but not limited to, those with rigorous designs but involving very young children.

Computer-assisted instruction (CAI). Children can use CAI to practice arithmetic processes and to foster deeper conceptual thinking. Practice software can help young children develop competence in such skills as counting and sorting (Clements & Nastasi, 1993) as well as addition combinations (Fuchs et al., 2006). Indeed, some reviewers claim that the largest gains in the use of CAI have been in mathematics for preschool (Fletcher-Flinn & Gravatt, 1995) or primary grade children, especially in compensatory education (Lavin & Sanders, 1983; Niemiec & Walberg, 1984; Ragosta, Holland, & Jamison, 1981). About 10 minutes per day proved sufficient for significant gains; 20 minutes was even better. This CAI approach may be as—or more—cost-effective as traditional instruction (Fletcher, Hawley, & Piele, 1990) and as other instructional interventions, such as peer tutoring and reducing class size (Niemiec & Walberg, 1987). Such an approach is successful with all children, with substantial gains reported for children from low-resource communities (Primavera et al., 2001).

Computer drill and practice can be helpful for all children who need to develop automaticity but especially for those who have MD or MLD. However, this must come at the right point in the learning trajectory. Drill does *not* help children who are at the level of more immature counting strategies; they must understand the concepts and even know the arithmetic fact (although they may remember it slowly) before drill is useful (Hasselbring, Goin, & Bransford, 1988).

Computer management. Many of these systems employ computer-managed instruction (CMI), in which computers keep track of children's progress and help individualize the instruction they receive. For example, *Building Blocks* software stores records of how children are doing on every activity. It assigns them to just the right difficulty level according to children's performance, using the research-based learning trajectories for each topic. Teachers can view records of how the whole group or any individual is doing at any time. The management system automatically adjusts the activity for difficulty and provides appropriate feedback and help.

A related type of CMI system does not present the instruction, but stores and analyzes results of assessments to help teachers differentiate instruction, make instructional adaptations for students of all ability levels, and provide students with relevant practice and immediate feedback. That is, they help teachers implement formative assessment (see that section in this chapter). Some provide testing and worksheet generators. Such programs have been shown to increase math achievement of low-, middle- and high-performing students (Ysseldyke et al., 2003).

Computer games. Properly chosen, computer games may also be effective. Kraus (1981) reported that second graders with an average of one hour of interaction with a computer game over a 2-week period responded correctly to twice as many items on an addition facts speed test as did students in a control group. Preschoolers benefit from a wide variety of on-, as well as off-computer games (Clements & Sarama, 2008).

How young? How young can children be and still obtain such benefits? Three-year-olds learned sorting from a computer task as easily as from a concrete doll task (Brinkley & Watson, 1987–88a). Reports of gains in such skills as counting have also been reported for kindergartners (Hungate, 1982). However, the nature of such programs should be evaluation; there are possibilities that primary students will be less motivated to perform academic work following *drill* (Clements & Nastasi, 1985) and that their creativity may be harmed by a consistent diet of drill (Haugland, 1992).

Logo and turtle geometry. Another approach, for primary studies, is turtle geometry. Seymour Papert (1980) invented the turtle because it was "body syntonic." A large research corpus on Logo and mathematics learning is based on the position that students construct initial spatial notions not from passive viewing but from actions, both perceptual[1] and imagined, and from reflections on these actions (Piaget & Inhelder, 1967). These are valuable active experiences for students; however, unless these experiences are mathematized[2] they remain only intuitions. There are several ways to help students reflect on and represent these experiences; research indicates that Logo's turtle geometry is one potent way (Clements & Sarama, 1997).

Logo environments are in fact action-based. By first having children form paths and shapes by walking, then using Logo, children can learn to think of the turtle's actions as ones that they can perform; that is the turtle's actions become "body syntonic." But why not just draw it without a computer? There are at least two reasons. First, drawing a geometric figure on paper, for example, is for most people a proceduralized process. This is especially true for young children, who have not re-represented the sequential instructions that they implicitly follow. Then, they cannot alter the drawing procedure in any substantive manner (Karmiloff-Smith, 1990), much less consciously reflect on it. In creating a Logo procedure to draw the figure, however, students must analyze the visual aspects of the figure and their movements in drawing it, thus requiring them to reflect on how the components are put together. Writing a sequence of Logo commands, or a procedure, to draw a figure ". . . allows, or obliges, the student to externalize intuitive expectations. When the intuition is translated into a program it becomes more obtrusive and more accessible to reflection" (Papert, 1980, p. 145). That is, students must analyze the spatial aspects of the shape and reflect on how they can build it from components. Primary grade children have shown greater explicit awareness of the properties of shapes and the meaning of measurements after working with the turtle

(Clements & Nastasi, 1993). They learn about measurement of length (Campbell, 1987; Clements, Battista, Sarama, Swaminathan et al., 1997; Sarama, 1995) and angle (Browning, 1991; Clements & Battista, 1989; du Boulay, 1986; Frazier, 1987; Kieran, 1986; Kieran & Hillel, 1990; Olive, Lankenau, & Scally, 1986). One microgenetic study confirmed that students transform physical and mental action into concepts of turn and angle in combined off- and on-computer experiences (Clements & Burns, 2000). Students synthesized and integrated two schemes, turn as body movement and turn as number, as originally found (Clements, Battista, Sarama, & Swaminathan, 1996). They used a process of psychological curtailment in which students gradually replace full rotations of their bodies with smaller rotations of an arm, hand, or finger, and eventually internalized these actions as mental imagery.

Logo is not easy to learn. However, as one primary grade student declared, "This picture was very hard and it took me 1 hour and 20 minutes to do it, but it had to be done. I liked doing it" (Carmichael, Burnett, Higginson, Moore, & Pollard, 1985, p. 90). Moreover, when the environment is gradually and systematically introduced to the children and when the interface is age-appropriate, even young children learn to control the turtle and benefit cognitively (Allen, Watson, & Howard, 1993; Brinkley & Watson, 1987–88b; Clements, 1983–84; R. Cohen & Geva, 1989; Howard, Watson, & Allen, 1993; Stone, 1996; Watson, Lange, & Brinkley, 1992). Thus, there is substantial evidence that young children can learn Logo and can transfer their knowledge to other areas, such as map-reading tasks and interpreting right and left rotation of objects. They reflect on mathematics and their own problem-solving. For example, first grader Ryan wanted to turn the turtle to point into his rectangle. He asked the teacher, "What's half of 90?" After she responded, he typed RT 45. "Oh, I went the wrong way." He said nothing, keeping his eyes on the screen. "Try LEFT 90," he said at last. This inverse operation produced exactly the desired effect (Kull, 1986).

These effects are not limited to small studies. A major evaluation of a Logo-based geometry curriculum included 1,624 students and their teachers and a wide assortment of research techniques, pre- and post-paper-and-pencil-testing, interviews, classroom observations, and case studies (Clements et al., 2001). Across grades K-6, Logo students scored significantly higher than control students on a general geometry achievement test, making about double the gains of the control groups. These are especially significant because the test was paper-and-pencil, not allowing access to the computer environments in which the experimental group had learned and because the curriculum is a relatively short intervention, lasting only 6 weeks. Other assessments confirmed these results, and indicated that Logo was a particularly felicitous environment for learning mathematics, reasoning, and problem-solving.

These studies and hundreds of others (Clements & Sarama, 1997) indicate that Logo, used thoughtfully, can provide an additional evocative context for young children's explorations of mathematical ideas. Such "thoughtful use" includes structuring and guiding Logo work to help children form strong, valid mathematical ideas (Clements et al., 2001). Children often do not appreciate the mathematics in Logo work unless someone helps them see the work mathematically. Effective teachers raise questions about "surprises" or conflicts between children's intuitions and computer feedback to promote reflection. They pose challenges and tasks designed to make the mathematical ideas explicit for children. They help children build bridges between the Logo experience and their regular mathematics work (Clements, 1987; Watson & Brinkley, 1990/91). This is a general implication that should be emphasized. Research indicates that working with appropriate computers can help children learn mathematics. *Not always*, however. Effects are more consistently positive in some situations. What can teachers do?

Computer manipulatives. Alternatives include the use of activity tutorials and problem-solving-oriented practice, as well as computer manipulatives such as provided in the *Building Blocks* software. The uses and advantages of these software programs have been described throughout the book. Evaluations indicate that large increases in achievement caused by the *Building Blocks* Pre-K curriculum are in part attributable to children's use of this software (Clements & Sarama, 2008).

Let us return to the topic of manipulatives. Even if we agree that "concrete" cannot simply be equated with physical manipulatives, we might have difficulty accepting objects on the computer screen as valid manipulatives. However, computers might provide representations that are just as personally meaningful to students as physical objects. Paradoxically, research indicates that computer representations may even be more manageable, "clean," flexible, and extensible than their physical counterparts. For example, one group of young students learned number concepts with a computer environment. They constructed "bean-stick pictures" by selecting and arranging beans, sticks, and number symbols. Compared to a physical bean-stick environment, this computer environment offered equal, and sometimes greater control and flexibility to students (Char, 1989). The computer manipulatives were just as meaningful and easier to use for learning. Both computer and physical beansticks were worthwhile. However, addressing the issues of pedagogical sequencing work with one did not need to precede work with the other. In a similar vein, students who used physical and software manipulatives demonstrated a much greater sophistication in classification and logical thinking than did a control group that used physical manipulatives only (Olson, 1988). The reason partially lies in the ways computer manipulatives can follow the guidelines described in the previous section. These and other potential advantages of using computer manipulatives are summarized in two broad categories: those that offer mathematical or psychological benefits to the student and teacher, and those that offer practical and pedagogical benefits.

Mathematical/Psychological Benefits. Perhaps the most powerful feature of the software is that the actions possible with the software embody the processes we want children to develop and internalize as mental actions:

- *Bringing mathematical ideas and processes to conscious awareness.* Most students can use physical manipulatives to perform motions such as slides, flips, and turns; however, they make intuitive movements and corrections without being aware of these geometric motions. Even young children can move puzzle pieces into place without conscious awareness of the geometric motions that can describe these physical movements. Our research has shown that using computer tools to manipulate shapes brings those geometric motions to an explicit level of awareness (Sarama et al., 1996). For example, Pre-K children working on pattern block puzzles off-computer were unable to explain the motions needed to make the pieces fit. On computer, the children were quickly able to adapt to the tools and were able to explain to peers what they needed to do: "You need to click there. You need to turn it."
- *Encouraging and facilitating complete, precise, explanations.* Compared to students using paper and pencil, students using computers work with more precision and exactness (Clements et al., 2001; Gallou-Dumiel, 1989; Johnson-Gentile, Clements, & Battista, 1994).
- *Supporting mental "actions on objects."* The flexibility of computer manipulatives allows them to mirror mental "actions on objects" better than physical manipulatives. For example, physical base-ten blocks can be so clumsy and the manipulations so disconnected one from the other that students see only the trees—manipulations of many pieces—and miss the forest—place value ideas. In addition, students can break computer base-ten blocks into ones, or glue ones together to form tens. Such actions are more in line with the *mental actions* that we want students to learn. Geometric tools can encourage composition and decomposition of shapes (Clements & Sarama, 2007c; Sarama et al., 1996). As an example, Mitchell started making a hexagon out of triangles (Sarama et al., 1996). After placing two, he counted with his finger on the screen around the center of the incomplete hexagon, imaging the other triangles. He announced that he would need four more. After placing the next one, he said,

"Whoa! Now, three more!" Whereas off-computer, Mitchell had to check each placement with a physical hexagon, the intentional and deliberate actions on the computer lead him to form mental images (decomposing the hexagon imagistically) and predict each succeeding placement. Further, compositions of shapes allow the construction of units of units in children's tilings and patterning. Identify the unit of units that forms the core. Show how the glue tool in the software can be used to actually make such a unit and then slide, turn, and flip it as a unit. It also makes building such patterns much easier (and more elegant). Sets of grouped shapes turn, flip, and otherwise act *as a unit*. Thus, the actions children perform on the computer are a reflection of the mental operations we wish to help children develop. Actions on computer manipulatives can include precise decompositions that cannot easily be duplicated with manipulatives; for example, cutting a shape (e.g., a regular hexagon) into other shapes (e.g., not only into two trapezoids but also two pentagons and variety of other combinations). Computer manipulatives have supported dramatic gains in this competency (Clements, Battista, Sarama, & Swaminathan, 1997; Clements & Sarama, 2007c; Sarama et al., 1996).

- *Changing the very nature of the manipulative.* In a similar vein, computer manipulatives' flexibility allows children to explore geometric figures in ways not available with physical shape sets. For example, children can change the size of the computer shapes, altering all shapes or only some. Matthew wanted to make an all blue man and recognized that he could overlap the computer rhombuses and to exactly cover a triangle space. In a study of patterning, researchers stated that the computer manipulative's flexibility had several positive effects on kindergartners' patterning (Moyer, Niezgoda, & Stanley, 2005). They made a greater number of patterns and used more elements in their patterns, with computer manipulatives than with physical manipulatives or drawing. Finally, only when working on computer did they create new shapes (by partial occlusion).

- *Symbolizing and making connections.* Computer manipulatives can also serve as symbols for mathematical ideas, often better than physical manipulatives. For example, the manipulative can have just the mathematical features that we wish it to have, and just the actions on it that we wish to promote, and not additional properties that may be distracting.

- *Linking the concrete and the symbolic with feedback.* Closely related, the computer can link manipulative to symbols—the notion of multiple linked representations. For example, the number represented by the base-ten blocks is dynamically linked to the students' actions on the blocks, so that when the student changes the blocks the number displayed is automatically changed as well. This can help students make sense of their activity and the numbers. Is it too restrictive or too hard to have to operate on symbols rather than directly on the manipulatives? Ironically, less "freedom" might be *more* helpful. In a study of place value, one group of students worked with a computer base-ten manipulative. The students could not move the computer blocks directly. Instead, they had to operate on symbols (Thompson, 1992; Thompson & Thompson, 1990). Another group of students used physical base-ten blocks. Although teachers frequently guided students to see the connection between what they did with the blocks and what they wrote on paper, the physical blocks group did not feel constrained to write something that represented what they did with blocks. Instead, they appeared to look at the two as separate activities. In comparison, the computer group used symbols more meaningfully, tending to connect them to the base-ten blocks. In computer environments such as computer base-ten blocks or computer programming, students cannot overlook the consequences of their actions, whereas that is possible to do with physical manipulatives. So, computer manipulatives can help students build on their physical experiences, tying them tightly to symbolic representations. In this way, computers help students link Sensory-Concrete and abstract knowledge so they can build Integrated-Concrete knowledge.

- *Recording and replaying students' actions.* Computers allow us to store more than static configurations. Once we finish a series of actions, it's often difficult to reflect on them. But computers have the power to record and replay *sequences* of our actions on manipulatives. We can record our actions and later replay, change, and view them. This encourages real mathematical exploration. Computer games such as "Tetris" allow students to replay the same game. In one version, *Tumbling Tetrominoes* (Clements, Russell, Tierney, Battista, & Meredith, 1995), students try to cover a region with a random sequence of tetrominoes. If students believe they could improve their strategy, they can elect to receive the same tetrominoes in the same order and try a new approach.

Practical/pedagogical benefits. This group includes advantages that help students in a practical manner or provide pedagogical opportunities for the teacher:

- *Providing another medium, one that can store and retrieve configurations. Shapes* serves as another medium for building, especially one in which careful development can take place day after day (i.e., physical blocks have to be put away most of the time—on the computer, they can be saved and worked on again and again, and there's an infinite supply for all children). We observed this advantage when a group of children were working on a pattern with physical manipulatives. They wanted to move it slightly on the rug. Two girls (four hands) tried to keep the design together, but they were unsuccessful. Marisssa told Leah to fix the design. Leah tried, but in re-creating the design, she inserted two extra shapes and the pattern wasn't the same. The girls experienced considerable frustration at their inability to get their "old" design back. Had the children been able to save their design, or had they been able to move their design and keep the pieces together, their group project would have continued.
- *Providing a manageable, clean, flexible manipulative. Shapes* manipulatives are more manageable and clean than their physical counterparts. For example, they always snap into correct position even when filling an outline and—also unlike physical manipulatives—they stay where they are put. If children want them to stay where they're put no matter what, they can "freeze" them into position. We observed that while working on the *Shapes* software, children quickly learned to glue the shapes together and move them as a group when they needed more space to continue their designs.
- *Providing an extensible manipulative.* Certain constructions are easier to make with the software than with physical manipulatives. For example, trying to build triangles from different classes. That is, we have observed children making non-equilateral triangles by partially occluding shapes with other shapes, creating many different types of triangle. Making right angles by combining and occluding various shapes is a similar example.
- *Recording and extending work.* The printouts make instant record-your-work, take-it-home, post-it paper copies. (Although we are also in favor of kids recording their work with templates and/or cutouts, but this is time-consuming and should not be required all the time.)

Computers encourage students to make their knowledge explicit, which helps them build Integrated-Concrete knowledge.

Computers and play. Research shows that the dynamic aspects of the computer often engage children in mathematical play more so than do physical manipulatives or paper media (Steffe & Wiegel, 1994). For example, two preschoolers were playing with the free explore level of a set of activities called "Party Time" from the *Building Blocks* project (Clements & Sarama, 2004a) in which they could put out any number of items, with the computer counting and labeling for them. "I have an idea!" said one girl, clearing off all the items and dragging placemats to every chair. "You have to put out cups for everybody. But first you have to tell me how many cups that'll be." Before her friend could start counting, she interrupted—"And everyone needs one cup for milk and one for juice!" The girls worked hard cooperatively, at first trying to find cups in the house center, but finally counting two times on each placemat on the screen. Their answer—initially 19—wasn't exact, but they were not upset to be corrected when they actually placed the cups and found they needed 20. These children played with the mathematics in the situation, with solutions, as they played with each other.

Mathematics can be intrinsically interesting to children if they are building ideas while engaged in mathematical play (Steffe & Wiegel, 1994). To do so, the materials, physical, on a computer, or just verbal, must be of high quality.

Practical implications: Effective teaching with computers.[3] Initial adult support helps young children use computers to learn (Rosengren et al., 1985; Shade, Nida, Lipinski, & Watson, 1986). With such help, they can often use computers independently. Still, children are more attentive, more engaged, and less frustrated when an adult is nearby (Binder & Ledger, 1985). One implication of research, therefore, is that teachers make the computer one of many choices, placed where they or other adults can supervise and assist children (Sarama & Clements, 2002b). In this section, we provide more details on research implications regarding arranging and managing the classroom, choosing software, strategies for interacting with children in computer environments, and supporting children with special needs:

- *Arranging the classroom.* The physical arrangement of the computers in the classroom can enhance their social use (Davidson & Wright, 1994; Shade, 1994). The parts of the computer with which the children interact, the keyboard, mouse, monitor, and microphone, should be at the children's eye level, on a low table or even on the floor. If children are changing CD-ROMs, they can be placed so that children can see and change them easily. Software might be changed, along with other centers, to match educational themes. The other parts should be out of children's reach. All parts can be stabilized and locked down as necessary. If computers are to be shared, rolling carts might be used.
- *Placing two seats in front of the computer and one at the side for the teacher encourages positive social interaction.* If more than two children work with a computer, they assert the right to control the keyboard frequently (Shrock, Matthias, Anastasoff, Vensel, & Shaw, 1985). Placing computers close to each other can facilitate the sharing of ideas among children. Computers that are centrally located in the classroom invite other children to pause and participate in the computer activity. Such an arrangement also helps keep teacher participation at an optimum level. They are nearby to provide supervision and assistance as needed (Clements, 1991). Other factors, such as the ratio of computers to children, may also influence social behaviors. Less than a 10:1 ratio of children to computers might ideally encourage computer use, cooperation, and equal access to girls and boys (Lipinski et al., 1986; Yost, 1998). Cooperative use of computers raises achievement (Xin, 1999); a mixture of use in pairs and individual work may be ideal (Shade, 1994).
- *To encourage children to connect off- and on-computer experiences, place print materials, manipulatives, and real objects next to the computer* (Hutinger & Johanson, 2000). This also provides good activities for children who are observing or waiting for their turn.
- *Managing the computer center.* As you might with any center, teach children proper computer use and care, and post signs to remind them of the rules (e.g., no liquids, sand, food, or magnets near computers pays dividends). Using a child-oriented utility that helps children find and use the programs they want and prevents them from inadvertently harming other programs or files makes everyone's life easier.

- *Monitoring the time children spend on computers and giving everyone fair access is, of course, important.* However, at least one study has found that rigid time limits generated hostility and isolation instead of social communication (Hutinger & Johanson, 2000). A better idea is flexible time with sign-up lists that encourage children to manage themselves. The sign-up list itself can have a positive effect on preschoolers' emergent literacy (Hutinger & Johanson, 2000).

- *Introduce computer work gradually.* Provide substantial support and guidance initially, even sitting with children at the computer to encourage turn-taking. Then gradually foster self-directed and cooperative learning. When necessary, teach children effective collaboration; for example, communication and negotiation skills. For young children, this might include such matters as what constitutes a "turn" in a particular game or free explore environment. However, do not mandate sharing the computer all the time. Especially with construction-oriented programs such as manipulatives, free explore environments, or Logo, children sometimes need to work alone. If possible, make at least two computers available so that peer teaching and other kinds of interaction can take place, even if children are working on one computer.

- *Once children are working independently, provide enough guidance, but not too much.* Intervening too much or at the wrong times can decrease peer tutoring and collaboration (Bergin, Ford, & Mayer-Gaub, 1986; Emihovich & Miller, 1988; Riel, 1985). On the other hand, without any teacher guidance, children tend to "jockey" for position at the computer and use the computer in the turn-taking, competitive manner of video games (Lipinski et al., 1986; Silvern, Countermine, & Williamson, 1988).

- Research shows that the introduction of a microcomputer often places many additional demands on the teacher (Shrock et al., 1985). Plan carefully the use only of computer programs that will substantially benefit your children. The computer should not be simply an end unto itself. Computers can help children learn and should be used reflectively by both children and their teachers. Children should learn to understand how and why the programs they use work the way they do (Turkle, 1997).

- *Use effective teaching strategies.* Critical to effective use of computers is teacher planning, participation, and support. Optimally, the teacher's role should be that of a facilitator of children's learning. Such facilitation includes not only physical structuring of the environment but also establishing standards for and supporting specific types of learning environments. When using open-ended programs, for example, considerable support may need to precede independent use. Other important aspects of support include structuring and discussing computer work to help children form viable concepts and strategies, posing questions to help children reflect on these concepts and strategies, and "building bridges" to help children connect their computer and non-computer experiences. Ideally, the computer software should be closely aligned with the rest of the curriculum.

- *Be actively involved.* Across the educational goals, we find that teachers whose children benefit significantly from using computers are always active. Such active mentoring has significant positive effects on children's learning with computers (Primavera et al., 2001). They closely guide children's learning of basic tasks, and then encourage experimentation with open-ended problems. They are frequently encouraging, questioning, prompting, and demonstrating, without offering unnecessary help or limiting children's opportunity to explore (Hutinger & Johanson, 2000). They redirect inappropriate behaviors, model strategies, and give children choices (Hutinger et al., 1998). Such scaffolding leads children to reflect on their own thinking behaviors and brings higher-order thinking processes to the fore. Such metacognitively-oriented instruction includes strategies of identifying goals, active monitoring, modeling, questioning, reflecting, peer tutoring, discussion, and reasoning (Elliott & Hall, 1997).

- *Make the subject matter to be learned clear and extend the ideas children encounter.* They focus attention on critical aspects and ideas of the activities. When appropriate, they facilitate disequilibrium by using the computer feedback to help children reflect on and question their ideas and eventually strengthen their concepts. They also help children build links between computer and non-computer work. Whole-group discussions that help children communicate about their solution strategies and reflect on what they've learned are also essential components of good teaching with computers (Galen & Buter, 1997). Effective teachers avoid overly directive teaching behaviors (except as necessary for some populations and on topics such as using the computer equipment), and, as has been stated, strict time limits (which generate hostility and isolation instead of social communication), and offering unnecessary help without allowing children the opportunity to explore (Hutinger et al., 1998). Instead, prompt children to teach each other by physically placing one child in a teaching role or verbally reminding a child to explain his or her actions and respond to specific requests for help (Paris & Morris, 1985).
- *Remember that preparation and follow-up are as necessary for computer activities as they are for any other.* Do not omit critical whole-group discussion sessions following computer work. Consider using a single computer with a large screen or with overhead projector equipment.
- *Support children with special needs.* Even critics of technology support its use in supporting young children with special needs. Used well, technology can increase children's ability to function in diverse and less restrictive settings. Computers' unique advantages include (Schery & O'Connor, 1997): being patient and non-judgmental, providing undivided attention, proceeding at the child's pace, and providing immediate reinforcement. These advantages lead to significant improvements for children with special needs. Teachers should attempt to ensure that they select such software and guide children with special needs to use it successfully. However, we should be careful not to limit children with special needs to "compensatory" software. They also can benefit from exploratory and problem-solving software. For example, several studies reveal that Logo is a particularly engaging activity to young children, fostering higher-order thinking in children from preschool through the primary grades, including special needs students (Clements & Nastasi, 1988; Degelman, Free, Scarlato, Blackburn, & Golden, 1986; Lehrer, Harckham, Archer, & Pruzek, 1986; Nastasi, Clements, & Battista, 1990).

Software can help, but we could do better. Few software programs are designed based on explicit (i.e., published) theoretical and empirical research foundations (but see Clements, 2007; Clements & Sarama, 2007c; Ritter, Anderson, Koedinger, & Corbett, 2007). More continuous, committed, iterative research and development projects are needed in this area. Research-based iterative cycles of evaluation and development, fine-tuning software's mathematics and pedagogy within each cycle, can make a substantial differences in learning (e.g., see Aleven & Koedinger, 2002; Clements & Battista, 2000; Clements et al., 2001; Laurillard & Taylor, 1994; Steffe & Olive, 2002). Such research could identify how and why software designs could be improved (NMP, 2008).

TV. There is even more debate in the early childhood field about the influences—positive and especially negative—of television. There is an extensive literature (see Clements & Nastasi, 1993). The following summarize key findings:

- Content matters—violent TV can lead to aggressiveness, but educational programming can lead to prosocial behaviors.

- Many experts advise no TV for children less than 3 years of age (and some advise none until the primary school years).
- Educational TV such as *Sesame Street, Blue's Clues*, and *Peep and the Big Wide World* have positive effects on learning, and continue to be updated in content and pedagogy. *Watching educational programs predicts school readiness at age 5.*
- Longitudinal studies show that *high school students who watched educational television have higher grades* than those who did not. This is probably due to the *early learning model—* learning leads to success in the first grades of school, which leads to positive motivation, perceptions of teachers of competence, placement in higher-ability groups, receiving more attention, and thus continuous success in school.
- Children's learning is increased when adults mediate the children's use of TV (as well as other media). Parents might watch educational TV with their children and discuss what is viewed. They might involve the child in active engagement with the material, following suggestions from the show or creating their own. Interactive books can actually increase the time parents read with their children.
- Providing parents with print materials or in-person workshops on how to follow up on media is necessary and helpful.

One disturbing result is that high-SES preschoolers understand the mathematical ideas presented on *Sesame Street* better than their low-SES counterparts. Also, the better the vocabulary and math understanding the child has, the better that child can comprehend the mathematics presented on the screen (Morgenlander, 2005). Another finding that "the rich get richer" presents a challenge to educators and the society as a whole.

Integrate Teaching of Concepts, Skills, and Problem-solving

The National Panel concluded, "The curriculum must simultaneously develop conceptual understanding, computational fluency, and problem-solving skills". The debate about whether teachers should concentrate on "skills" or "ideas" should end—both are needed, and both should be developed at the same time, in an integrated fashion. As just one example, second grade classes were randomly assigned to one of two instructional programs. The first was a reformed-based program based on Realistic Mathematics Education, in which students create and discuss their solution procedure. From the beginning of instruction, this program emphasized developing both conceptual understanding simultaneously with procedural skill, and flexible application of multiple strategies. These students outperformed those in a traditional textbook program that focused on mastery of procedures initially, and varied application of strategies only toward the end of instruction. The reform group children more often selected strategies related to the number properties of the problems and used strategies more adaptively, such as solving problems with an integer ending with the digit 8 with compensation strategies. That is, flexible problem-solvers are those who can adapt their strategies to the number characteristics of the problem at hand; for example, solving $62 - 49$ as $62 - 50 = 12$, $12 + 1 = 13$, but solving $62 - 44$ as $44 + 6 = 50$, $50 + 10 = 60$, $60 + 2 = 62$, and $6 + 10 + 2 = 18$. Such flexible use indicates both conceptual understanding and procedural skill. The traditional group did not use the procedures flexibly, even after months of instruction in that program emphasized such flexible use. The reform group scored higher on three measures, showing superior conceptual understanding. Children in both groups developed conceptual understanding before achieving procedural skill, but the two domains were more interconnected for the reform group (Blöte, Van der Burg, & Klein, 2001).

Other studies send the same message. For example, low-SES, urban first and second graders learned to use the standard arithmetic algorithms skillfully and to understand them conceptually, when taught conceptually, by connecting place value block and written representations (Fuson & Briars, 1990). A far older study had similar conclusions. Second graders taught mechanically were faster and more accurate on an immediate post-test, but those taught meaningfully were better able to explain why the algorithm worked, scored better on the retention test, and transferred their knowledge more successfully (Brownell & Moser, 1949). A third study similarly showed the benefits of conceptual instruction (Hiebert & Wearne, 1993), bringing low-achieving children up to the level of their high-achieving peers. Each of these has limitations but the pattern is clear: Good conceptual and procedural instruction is superior to mechanical instruction in helping children achieve today's mathematical goals (Hiebert & Grouws, 2007).

A final study found that, unlike the usual "skills" approach (Stipek & Ryan, 1997), poor children benefit more from a greater emphasis on meaning, understanding, and problem-solving (Knapp, Shields, & Turnbull, 1992). Such an approach is more effective at building advanced skills and is more—or at least as—effective at teaching basic skills. Further it engages children more extensively in academic learning.

For the least to the most able children, studies show that the foundation of flexible and creative use of mathematical procedures is *conceptual understanding*. Children's knowledge must connect procedures to ideas, to everyday experiences, to analogies, and to other skills and concepts (Baroody & Dowker, 2003).

Practical implications. Teach students conceptually to help them build skills *and* ideas, helping them use skills *adaptively*. Students then have *fluent* and *adaptive* expertise rather than mere efficiency (Baroody, 2003). Pose problems, make connections, and then work out these problems in ways that make the connections visible, playing both more and less active roles.

Final Words

Teaching techniques are tools, and as such, must be used carefully, thoughtfully, and appropriately. Every strategy, from play to direct instruction, can be educative or mis-educative. "Any experience is mis-educative that has the effect of arresting or distorting the growth of further experience" (Dewey, 1938/1997, p. 25). For example, mis-educative experiences resulting from inappropriate direct teaching may decrease sensitivity to the wide range of applications of mathematical ideas, or develop automatic skill but narrow the range of further experience with the idea underlying the skill. Conversely, child-centered education that totally rejects the structures or sequencing of subject matter content may be motivating to children at the time, yet be so disconnected as to limit later integrative experiences. "High-quality learning results from formal and informal experiences during the preschool years. 'Informal' does not mean unplanned or haphazard" (NCTM, 2000, p. 75). As Dewey said, "Just because traditional education was a matter of routine in which the plans and programs were handed down from the past, it does not follow that progressive education is a matter of planless improvisation" (p. 28). Such everyday activities have been shown to effectively raise mathematics knowledge in Head Start classrooms (Arnold, Fisher, Doctoroff, & Dobbs, 2002).

In summary, in this new educational arena, we know mainly that several approaches, if performed in high-quality settings, can be effective. Most successful pedagogical strategies, even those with focused goals, include play or play-like activities. All approaches have a shared core of concern for children's interest and engagement and content matched to children's cognitive level. Although some studies support general, play-oriented approaches, learning mathematics seems to be a distinct process, even in preschool (Day, Engelhardt, Maxwell, & Bolig, 1997), and approaches focused on mathematics have been successful.

Regardless of instructional approach or strategy, educators must remember that the ideas young children construct can be uniquely different from those of adults (e.g., Piaget & Inhelder, 1967; Steffe & Cobb, 1988). Early childhood teachers must be particularly careful not to assume that children "see" situations, problems, or solutions as adults do. Successful teachers interpret what the child is doing and thinking and attempt to see the situation from the child's point of view. Based on their interpretations, they conjecture what the child might be able to learn or abstract from his or her experiences. Similarly, when they interact with the child, they also consider their own actions from the child's point of view. This makes early childhood teaching both demanding and rewarding.

Not only are children's conceptions uniquely different from those of adults, they are the best foundation on which to build subsequent learning. Research and expert practice agree that children should learn skills in conjunction with learning the corresponding concepts—indeed, learning skills before developing understanding can lead to learning difficulties (Baroody, 2004a, 2004b; Fuson, 2004; Kilpatrick et al., 2001; Sophian, 2004a; Steffe, 2004). Successful innovative curricula and teaching build directly on students' thinking (the understandings and skills they possess), provide opportunities for both invention and practice, and ask children to explain their various strategies (Hiebert, 1999). Such programs facilitate conceptual growth and higher-order thinking without sacrificing the learning of skills.

In all their interactions with children, teachers should help children develop strong relationships between concepts and skills because skill development is promoted by a strong conceptual foundation. They should encourage children to create and describe their own solution methods and should encourage methods found to be effective, introducing them when appropriate, and should encourage children to describe and compare different solution methods. Research indicates that instruction that views children as active learners with relevant initial knowledge and that provides substantial support during learning is superior to traditional instruction that lacks these characteristics (Fuson, 2004). Teachers need to consistently integrate real-world situations, problem-solving, and mathematical content (Fuson, 2004). This integration is more than a pedagogical strategy; it is necessary to achieve both sense-making and the development of skills such as computational fluency. It supports transfer to future learning and out-of-school contexts. Mathematics itself involves a vast web of connections among concepts and topics (NCTM, 2000). Programs for prekindergarten through the primary grades should interweave real-world, meaningful contexts; problem-solving; and mathematical concepts and skills. Such programs have a good chance of countering the unfortunate pattern in U.S. mathematics education, in which young children who are initially motivated to explore mathematics (Perlmutter, Bloom, Rose, & Rogers, 1997) come to "learn" that effort does not matter and that only a select few are "talented" at mathematics (Middleton & Spanias, 1999). Teachers should use inquiry-based and discourse-rich approaches, emphasize working hard to understand mathematics (rather than "finishing" or "correctness"), and focus on intrinsic motivation. Making connections to real-life situations may also enhance children's knowledge and beliefs about mathematics (Perlmutter et al., 1997).

Nevertheless, early competence still reflects limited understanding. Varied reasons account for this. Expectations have risen. Only a few hundred years ago, college-level work in mathematics involved simple arithmetic. Cultural tools for mathematics have multiplied. Most instruction in the U.S. is not based on awareness of these tools and/or of the power of children's thinking and the necessity of plumbing the depths of that thinking, engendering children's inventions. We believe that the knowledge we have tried to help you develop through this book will empower you to be a truly effective, professional educator.

Notes

Preface

1   Like most acronyms, TRIAD "almost" works; we jokingly ask people to accept the "silent p" in Professional Development.

1 Young Children and Mathematics Learning

1   As stated in the Preface, an elaborate review of the research supporting *this and all other statements* in this book can be found in the companion book, *Early Childhood Mathematics Education Research: Learning Trajectories for Young Children* (Sarama & Clements, 2009).

2   One of the authors, Douglas Clements, was a member of the National Math Panel and co-author of the report, which can be found at http://www.ed.gov/about/bdscomm/list/mathpanel/.

3   *Building Blocks—Foundations for Mathematical Thinking, Pre-Kindergarten to Grade 2: Research-based Materials Development* was funded by NSF to create and evaluate mathematics curricula for young children based on a theoretically sound research and development framework. We describe the framework and research in detail in Chapter 15. (National Science Foundation Grant No. ESI-9730804 to D. H. Clements and J. Sarama "Building Blocks—Foundations for Mathematical Thinking, Pre-Kindergarten to Grade 2: Research-based Materials Development.") For the purposes of full disclosure, note that we have subsequently made this curriculum available through a publisher, and thus receive royalties. All research was conducted with independent assessors and evaluators.

2 Quantity, Number, and Subitizing

1   Later grades use subitizing in various ways, such as in supporting the development of counting concepts and skills and solving arithmetic problems. These goals will be highlighted in later chapters.

3 Verbal and Object Counting

1   Later grades contain significant counting. Because such counting melds with counting, number relationships, and place value (Chapter 4), as well as counting *strategies* for arithmetic (Chapter 5), we will focus on these aspects of counting in those chapters.

5 Arithmetic: Early Addition and Subtraction and Counting Strategies

1   Several important and complex issues regarding manipulatives are discussed at length in Chapter 16.

13 Mathematical Processes

1   Most of the information regarding teaching problem-solving is integrated within the content chapters.

14 Cognition, Affect, and Equity

1   Another study showed that children with MLD understood the counting principles and what counting was for. However, their fluency and control of counting operations were lower than normal children, even in such simple tasks as verbal counting to 20, on which they were very slow (Hitch & McAuley, 1991). They may have lacked practice, possibly due to avoidance of those tasks, or have basic cognitive deficits such as impaired verbal working memory or executive control (e.g., monitoring the counting process).

2   Children, who can catch up, especially with high-quality instruction, may be developmentally delayed, but not disabled. The Response-to-Intervention (RTI) model includes this basic idea—if children are behind because of a lack of high-quality experiences and education, *they* have no "mathematical difficulties"—their environment is to blame and must be improved.

15 Early Childhood Mathematics Education: Contexts and Curricula

1   We have made the point previously that we receive royalties from the sale of *Building Blocks*, but, for full disclosure, note also that the *Building Blocks* software is a (very small) component of the *Number Worlds* curriculum as well. However, we had no connection to the research, which, in addition, was conducted before the addition of the software to the curriculum.

16 Instructional Practices and Pedagogical Issues

1   Perceptual is used here, consistent with Piaget's original formulation, as meaning phenomena or experiences that depend on sensory input, in contrast to those that are represented mentally (and thus can be "re-presented" imagistically without sensory support). Thus, perceptual should not be confused with the notion that we, with Piaget, reject—that of "immaculate perception" in which perceived objects are immediately registered in the brain.

2   Mathematization emphasizes representing and elaborating mathematically—creating models of an everyday activity with mathematical objects, such as numbers and shapes; mathematical actions, such as counting or transforming shapes; and their structural relationships. Mathematizing involves reinventing, redescribing, reorganizing, quantifying, structuring, abstracting, and generalizing that which is first understood on an intuitive and informal level in the context of everyday activity.

3   This section is adapted from Clements & Sarama (2002).

References

Adey, P., Robertson, A., & Venville, G. (2002). Effects of a cognitive acceleration programme on Year 1 pupils. *British Journal of Educational Psychology, 72,* 1–5.

Aleven, V. A. W. M. M., & Koedinger, K. R. (2002). An effective metacognitive strategy: Learning by doing and explaining with a computer-based Cognitive Tutor. *Cognitive Science, 26*(2).

Alexander, K. L., & Entwisle, D. R. (1988). Achievement in the first 2 years of school: Patterns and processes. *Monographs of the Society for Research in Child Development, 53*(2, Serial No. 157).

Allen, J., Watson, J. A., & Howard, J. R. (1993). The impact of cognitive styles on the problem solving strategies used by preschool minority children in Logo microworlds. *Journal of Computing in Childhood Education, 4,* 203–217.

Anderson, A., Anderson, J., & Shapiro, J. (2004). Mathematical discourse in shared storybook reading. *Journal for Research in Mathematics Education, 35,* 5–33.

Anderson, G. R. (1957). Visual-tactual devices and their efficacy: An experiment in grade eight. *Arithmetic Teacher, 4,* 196–203.

Anderson, J. R. (Ed.). (1993). *Rules of the mind.* Hillsdale, NJ: Lawrence Erlbaum Associates.

Anghileri, J. (2001). What are we trying to achieve in teaching standard calculating procedures? In M. v. d. Heuvel-Panhuizen (Ed.), *Proceedings of the 25th Conference of the International Group for the Psychology in Mathematics Education* (Vol. 2, pp. 41–48). Utrecht, the Netherlands: Freudenthal Institute.

Anghileri, J. (2004). Disciplined calculators or flexible problem solvers? In M. J. Høines & A. B. Fuglestad (Eds.), *Proceedings of the 28th Conference of the International Group for the Psychology in Mathematics Education* (Vol. 1, pp. 41–46). Bergen, Norway: Bergen University College.

Ansari, D., & Karmiloff-Smith, A. (2002). Atypical trajectories of number development: A neuroconstructivist perspective. *Trends in Cognitive Sciences, 6*(12), 511–516.

Arditi, A., Holtzman, J. D., & Kosslyn, S. M. (1988). Mental imagery and sensory experience in congenital blindness. *Neuropsychologia, 26,* 1–12.

Arnold, D. H., & Doctoroff, G. L. (2003). Early education of socioeconomically disadvantaged children. *Annual Review of Psychology, 54,* 517–545.

Arnold, D. H., Fisher, P. H., Doctoroff, G. L., & Dobbs, J. (2002). Accelerating math development in Head Start classrooms: Outcomes and gender differences. *Journal of Educational Psychology, 94,* 762–770.

Ashcraft, M. H. (2006, November). *Math performance, working memory, and math anxiety: Some possible directions for neural functioning work.* Paper presented at The Neural Basis of Mathematical Development, Nashville, TN.

Askew, M., Brown, M., Rhodes, V., Wiliam, D., & Johnson, D. (1997). Effective teachers of numeracy in UK primary schools: Teachers' beliefs, practices, and children's learning. In M. v. d. Heuvel-Panhuizen (Ed.), *Proceedings of the 21st Conference of the International Group for the Psychology of Mathematics Education* (Vol. 2, pp. 25–32). Utrecht, the Netherlands: Freudenthal Institute.

Aubrey, C. (1997). Children's early learning of number in school and out. In I. Thompson (Ed.), *Teaching and learning early number* (pp. 20–29). Philadelphia, PA: Open University Press.

Aunio, P., Ee, J., Lim, S. E. A., Hautamäki, J., & Van Luit, J. E. H. (2004). Young children's number sense in Finland, Hong Kong and Singapore. *International Journal of Early Years Education, 12,* 195–216.

Aunio, P., Hautamäki, J., Sajaniemi, N., & Van Luit, J. E. H. (2008). Early numeracy in low-performing young children. *British Educational Research Journal.*

Aunio, P., Hautamäki, J., & Van Luit, J. E. H. (2005). Mathematical thinking intervention programmes for preschool children with normal and low number sense. *European Journal of Special Needs Education, 20,* 131–146.

Aunio, P., Niemivirta, M., Hautamäki, J., Van Luit, J. E. H., Shi, J., & Zhang, M. (2006). Young children's number sense in China and Finland. *Scandinavian Journal of Psychology, 50,* 483–502.

Aunola, K., Leskinen, E., Lerkkanen, M.-K., & Nurmi, J.-E. (2004). Developmental dynamics of math performance from pre-school to grade 2. *Journal of Educational Psychology, 96,* 699–713.

Aunola, K., Nurmi, J.-E., Lerkkanen, M.-K., & Rasku-Puttonen, H. (2003). The roles of achievement-related behaviours and parental beliefs in children's mathematical performance. *Educational Psychology, 23,* 403–421.

Austin, A. M. B., Blevins-Knabe, B., & Lindauer, S. L. K. (2008). Informal and formal mathematics concepts: Of children in center and family child care. *Unpublished manuscript.*

Aydogan, C., Plummer, C., Kang, S. J., Bilbrey, C., Farran, D. C., & Lipsey, M. W. (2005). *An investigation of prekindergarten curricula: Influences on classroom characteristics and child engagement.* Paper presented at the NAEYC.

Bacon, W. F., & Ichikawa, V. (1988). Maternal expectations, classroom experiences, and achievement among kindergartners in the United States and Japan. *Human Development, 31*, 378–383.

Balfanz, R. (1999). Why do we teach young children so little mathematics? Some historical considerations. In J. V. Copley (Ed.), *Mathematics in the early years* (pp. 3–10). Reston, VA: National Council of Teachers of Mathematics.

Ball, D. L. (1992). Magical hopes: Manipulatives and the reform of math education. *American Educator, 16*(2), 14; 16–18; 46–47.

Baratta-Lorton, M. (1976). *Mathematics their way.* Menlo Park, CA: Addison-Wesley.

Barnett, W. S., Frede, E. C., Mobasher, H., & Mohr, P. (1987). The efficacy of public preschool programs and the relationship of program quality to efficacy. *Educational Evaluation and Policy Analysis, 10*, 37–49.

Barnett, W. S., Hustedt, J. T., Hawkinson, L. E., & Robin, K. B. (2006). *The state of preschool 2006.* New Brunswick, NJ: National Institute for for Early Education Research (NIEER).

Barnett, W. S., Yarosz, D. J., Thomas, J., & Hornbeck, A. (2006). *Educational effectiveness of a Vygotskian approach to preschool education: A randomized trial:* National Institute of Early Education Research.

Baroody, A. J. (1986, December). Counting ability of moderately and mildly handicapped children. *Education and Training of the Mentally Retarded, 21*, 289–300.

Baroody, A. J. (1987). *Children's mathematical thinking.* New York: Teachers College.

Baroody, A. J. (1989). Manipulatives don't come with guarantees. *Arithmetic Teacher, 37*(2), 4–5.

Baroody, A. J. (1990). How and when should place value concepts and skills be taught? *Journal for Research in Mathematics Education, 21*, 281–286.

Baroody, A. J. (1996). An investigative approach to the mathematics instruction of children classified as learning disabled. In D. K. Reid, W. P. Hresko & H. L. Swanson (Eds.), *Cognitive approaches to learning disabilities* (pp. 547–615). Austin, TX: Pro-ed.

Baroody, A. J. (1999). The development of basic counting, number, and arithmetic knowledge among children classified as mentally handicapped. In L. M. Glidden (Ed.), *International review of research in mental retardation* (Vol. 22, pp. 51–103). New York: Academic Press.

Baroody, A. J. (2003). The development of adaptive expertise and flexibility: The integration of conceptual and procedural knowledge. In A. J. Baroody & A. Dowker (Eds.), *The development of arithmetic concepts and skills: Constructing adaptive expertise* (pp. 1–33). Mahwah, NJ: Lawrence Erlbaum Associates.

Baroody, A. J. (2004a). The developmental bases for early childhood number and operations standards. In D. H. Clements, J. Sarama & A.-M. DiBiase (Eds.), *Engaging young children in mathematics: Standards for early childhood mathematics education* (pp. 173–219). Mahwah, NJ: Lawrence Erlbaum Associates.

Baroody, A. J. (2004b). The role of psychological research in the development of early childhood mathematics standards. In D. H. Clements, J. Sarama & A.-M. DiBiase (Eds.), *Engaging young children in mathematics: Standards for early childhood mathematics education* (pp. 149–172). Mahwah, NJ: Lawrence Erlbaum Associates.

Baroody, A. J., & Benson, A. P. (2001). Early number instruction. *Teaching Children Mathematics, 8*, 154–158.

Baroody, A. J., & Dowker, A. (2003). *The development of arithmetic concepts and skills: Constructing adaptive expertise.* Mahwah, NJ: Lawrence Erlbaum Associates.

Baroody, A. J., Eiland, M., Su, Y., & Thompson, B. (2007). *Fostering at-risk preschoolers' number sense.* Paper presented at the American Educational Research Association.

Baroody, A. J., Lai, M.-L., & Mix, K. S. (2005, December). *Changing views of young children's numerical and arithmetic competencies.* Paper presented at the National Association for the Education of Young Children, Washington, DC.

Baroody, A. J., Lai, M.-l., & Mix, K. S. (2006). The development of young children's number and operation sense and its implications for early childhood education. In B. Spodek & O. N. Saracho (Eds.), *Handbook of research on the education of young children* (pp. 187–221). Mahwah, NJ: Lawrence Erlbaum Associates.

Baroody, A. J., & Tiilikainen, S. H. (2003). Two perspectives on addition development. In A. J. Baroody & A. Dowker (Eds.), *The development of arithmetic concepts and skills: Constructing adaptive expertise* (pp. 75–125). Mahwah, NJ: Lawrence Erlbaum Associates.

Bartsch, K., & Wellman, H. M. (1988). Young children's conception of distance. *Developmental Psychology, 24*(4), 532–541.

Battista, M. T. (1990). Spatial visualization and gender differences in high school geometry. *Journal for Research in Mathematics Education, 21*, 47–60.

Beilin, H. (1984). Cognitive theory and mathematical cognition: Geometry and space. In B. Gholson & T. L. Rosenthanl (Eds.), *Applications of cognitive-developmental theory* (pp. 49–93). New York: Academic Press.

Beilin, H., Klein, A., & Whitehurst, B. (1982). *Strategies and structures in understanding geometry.* New York: City University of New York.

Benigno, J. P., & Ellis, S. (2004). Two is greater than three: Effects of older siblings on parental support of preschoolers' counting in middle-income families. *Early Childhood Research Quarterly, 19*, 4–20.

Bennett, N., Desforges, C., Cockburn, A., & Wilkinson, B. (1984). *The quality of pupil learning experiences.* Hillsdale, NJ: Lawrence Erlbaum Associates.

Berch, D. B., & Mazzocco, M. M. M. (Eds.). (2007). *Why is math so hard for some children? The nature and origins of mathematical learning difficulties and disabilities.* Baltimore, MD: Paul H. Brooks.

Bereiter, C. (1986). Does direct instruction cause delinquency? Response to Schweinhart and Weikart. *Educational Leadership,* 20–21.

Bergin, D. A., Ford, M. E., & Mayer-Gaub, G. (1986). Social and motivational consequences of microcomputer use in kindergarten. San Francisco, CA: American Educational Research Association.

Berliner, D. C. (2006). Our impoverished view of educational research. *Teachers College Record, 108*, 949–995.

Bilbrey, C., Farran, D. C., Lipsey, M. W., & Hurley, S. (2007, April). *Active involvement by rural children from low income families in prekindergarten classrooms: Predictors and consequences.* Paper presented at the Biennial Meeting of the Society for Research in Child Development, Boston, MA.

Binder, S. L., & Ledger, B. (1985). *Preschool computer project report.* Oakville, Ontario, Canada: Sheridan College.

Bishop, A. J. (1980). Spatial abilities and mathematics achievement—A review. *Educational Studies in Mathematics, 11*, 257–269.

Bishop, A. J. (1983). Space and geometry. In R. A. Lesh & M. S. Landau (Eds.), *Acquisition of mathematics concepts and processes* (pp. 7–44). New York: Academic Press.

Bishop, A. J., & Forgasz, H. J. (2007). Issues in access and equity in mathematics education. In F. K. Lester, Jr. (Ed.), *Second Handbook of research on mathematics teaching and learning* (pp. 1145–1167). New York: Information Age Publishing.

Black, P., & Wiliam, D. (1998). Assessment and classroom learning. *Assessment in Education: Principles, Policy & Practice, 5*(1), 7–76.

Blair, C. (2002). School readiness: Integrating cognition and emotion in a neurobiological conceptualization of children's functioning at school entry. *American Psychologist, 57*(2), 111–127.

Blair, C., & Razza, R. P. (2007). Relating effortful control, executive function, and false belief understanding to emerging math and literacy ability in kindergarten. *Child Development, 78*, 647–663.

Blevins-Knabe, B., & Musun-Miller, L. (1996). Number use at home by children and their parents and its relationship to early mathematical performance. *Early Development and Parenting, 5*, 35–45.

Blevins-Knabe, B., Whiteside-Mansell, L., & Selig, J. (2007). Parenting and mathematical development. *Academic Exchange Quarterly, 11*, 76–80.

Bley, N. S., & Thornton, C. A. (1981). *Teaching mathematics to the learning disabled*. Rockville, MD: Aspen Systems Corportation.

Blöte, A. W., Van der Burg, E., & Klein, A. S. (2001). Students' flexibility in solving two-digit addition and subtraction problems: Instruction effects. *Journal of Educational Psychology, 93*, 627–638.

Bodovski, K., & Farkas, G. (2007). Mathematics growth in early elementary school: The roles of beginning knowledge, student engagement, and instruction. *The Elementary School Journal, 108*(2), 115–130.

Bodrova, E., & Leong, D. J. (2001). *The tools of the mind: A case study of implementing the Vygotskian approach in American early childhood and primary classrooms*. Geneva, Switzerland: International Bureau of Education.

Bodrova, E., & Leong, D. J. (2003). Self-regulation as a key to school readiness: How can early childhood teachers promote this critical competency? In M. Zaslow & I. Martinez-Beck (Eds.), *Critical issues in early childhood professional development* (pp. 203–224). Baltimore, MD: Brookes Publishing.

Bodrova, E., & Leong, D. J. (2005). Self-Regulation as a key to school readiness: How can early childhood teachers promote this critical competency? In M. Zaslow & I. Martinez-Beck (Eds.), *Critical issues in early childhood professional development*. Baltimore, MD: Brookes Publishing.

Bodrova, E., Leong, D. J., Norford, J., & Paynter, D. (2003). It only looks like child's play. *Journal of Staff Development, 24*(2), 47–51.

Bowman, B. T., Donovan, M. S., & Burns, M. S. (Eds.). (2001). *Eager to learn: Educating our preschoolers*. Washington, DC: National Academy Press.

Bransford, J. D., Brown, A. L., & Cocking, R. R. (Eds.). (1999). *How people learn*. Washington, DC: National Academy Press.

Brinkley, V. M., & Watson, J. A. (1987–88a). Effects of microworld training experience on sorting tasks by young children. *Journal of Educational Technology Systems, 16*, 349–364.

Brinkley, V. M., & Watson, J. A. (1987–88b). Logo and young children: Are quadrant effects part of initial Logo mastery? *Journal of Educational Technology Systems, 19*, 75–86.

Broberg, A. G., Wessels, H., Lamb, M. E., & Hwang, C. P. (1997). Effects of day care on the development of cognitive abilities in 8-year-olds: A longitudinal study. *Developmental Psychology, 33*, 62–69.

Brooks-Gunn, J. (2003). Do you believe in magic? What we can expect from early childhood intervention programs. *Social Policy Report, 17*(1), 1, 3–14.

Brooks-Gunn, J., Duncan, G. J., & Britto, P. R. (1999). Are socioeconomic gradients for children similar to those for adults? In D. P. Keating & C. Hertzman (Eds.), *Developmental health and the wealth of nations* (pp. 94–124). New York: Guilford.

Brosterman, N. (1997). *Inventing kindergarten*. New York: Harry N. Abrams.

Brown, S. I., & Walter, M. I. (1990). *The art of problem posing*. Mahwah, NJ: Lawrence Erlbaum Associates.

Brownell, W. A., & Moser, H. E. (1949). *Meaningful vs. mechanical learning: A study in grade III subtraction*. Durham, NC: Duke University Press.

Browning, C. A. (1991). Reflections on using LegofiTC Logo in an elementary classroom. In E. Calabrese (Ed.), *Proceedings of the Third European Logo Conference* (pp. 173–185). Parma, Italy: Associazione Scuola e Informatica.

Bryant, D. M., Burchinal, M. R., Lau, L. B., & Sparling, J. J. (1994). Family and classroom correlates of Head Start children's developmental outcomes. *Early Childhood Research Quarterly, 9*, 289–309.

Bull, R., & Scerif, G. (2001). Executive functioning as a predictor of children's mathematics ability: Inhibition, switching, and working memory. *Developmental Neuropsychology, 19*, 273–293.

Burchinal, M. R., Peisner-Feinberg, E., Pianta, R., & Howes, C. (2002). Development of academic skills from preschool through second grade: Family and classroom predictors of developmental trajectories. *Developmental Psychology, 40*, 415–436.

Burden, M. J., Jacobson, S. W., Dodge, N. C., Dehaene, S., & Jacobson, J. L. (2007). *Effects of prenatal alcohol and cocaine exposure on arithmetic and "number sense"*. Paper presented at the Society for Research in Child Development.

Burger, W. F., & Shaughnessy, J. M. (1986). Characterizing the van Hiele levels of development in geometry. *Journal for Research in Mathematics Education, 17*, 31–48.

Burkhardt, H. (2006). From design research to large-scale impact: Engineering research in education. In J. V. d. Akker, K. P. E. Gravemeijer, S. McKenney & N. Nieveen (Eds.), *Educational design research* (pp. 133–162). London: Routledge.

Callahan, L. G., & Clements, D. H. (1984). Sex differences in rote counting ability on entry to first grade: Some observations. *Journal for Research in Mathematics Education, 15*, 378–382.

Campbell, F. A., Pungello, E. P., Miller-Johnson, S., Burchinal, M., & Ramey, C. T. (2001). The development of cognitive and academic abilities: Growth curves from an early childhood educational experiment. *Developmental Psychology, 37*, 231–242.

Campbell, P. F. (1987). *Measuring distance: Children's use of number and unit. Final report submitted to the National Institute of Mental Health Under the ADAMHA Small Grant Award Program. Grant No. MSMA 1 R03 MH423435–01*, University of Maryland, College Park.

Campbell, P. F., & Silver, E. A. (1999). *Teaching and learning mathematics in poor communities*. Reston, VA: National Council of Teachers of Mathematics.

Cannon, J., Fernandez, C., & Ginsburg, H. P. (2005, April). *Parents' preference for supporting preschoolers' language over mathematics learning: A difference that runs deep.* Paper presented at the Biennial Meeting of the Society for Research in Child Development, Atlanta, GA.

Cannon, J., Levine, S. C., & Huttenlocher, J. (2007, Marach). *Sex differences in the relation between early puzzle play and mental transformation skill.* Paper presented at the Biennial Meeting of the Society of Research in Child Development, Boston, MA.

Canobi, K. H., Reeve, R. A., & Pattison, P. E. (1998). The role of conceptual understanding in children's addition problem solving. *Developmental Psychology, 34*, 882–891.

Carey, S. (2004). Bootstrapping and the origin of concepts. *Daedulus.*

Carmichael, H. W., Burnett, J. D., Higginson, W. C., Moore, B. G., & Pollard, P. J. (1985). *Computers, children and classrooms: A multisite evaluation of the creative use of microcomputers by elementary school children.* Toronto, Ontario, Canada: Ministry of Education.

Carnegie Corporation. (1998). Years of promise: A comprehensive learning strategy for America's children [Electronic Version]. Retrieved June 13, 1998, from http://www.carnegie.org/sub/pubs/execsum.html.

Carpenter, T. P., Ansell, E., Franke, M. L., Fennema, E. H., & Weisbeck, L. (1993). Models of problem solving: A study of kindergarten children's problem-solving processes. *Journal for Research in Mathematics Education, 24*, 428–441.

Carpenter, T. P., Coburn, T., Reys, R. E., & Wilson, J. (1975). Notes from National Assessment: Basic concepts of area and volume. *Arithmetic Teacher, 22*, 501–507.

Carpenter, T. P., Fennema, E. H., Franke, M. L., Levi, L., & Empson, S. B. (1999). *Children's mathematics: Cognitively guided instruction.* Portsmouth, NH: Heinemann.

Carpenter, T. P., Franke, M. L., Jacobs, V. R., Fennema, E. H., & Empson, S. B. (1998). A longitudinal study of invention and understanding in children's multidigit addition and subtraction. *Journal for Research in Mathematics Education, 29*, 3–20.

Carpenter, T. P., Franke, M. L., & Levi, L. (2003). *Thinking mathematically: Integrating arithmetic and algebra in elementary school.* Portsmouth, NH: Heinemann.

Carpenter, T. P., & Levi, L. (1999). *Developing conceptions of algebraic reasoning in the primary grades.* Montreal, Canada: American Educational Research Association.

Carpenter, T. P., & Lewis, R. (1976). The development of the concept of a standard unit of measure in young children. *Journal for Research in Mathematics Education, 7*, 53–58.

Carpenter, T. P., & Moser, J. M. (1982). The development of addition and subtraction problem solving. In T. P. Carpenter, J. M. Moser & T. A. Romberg (Eds.), *Rational numbers: An integration of research.* Hillsdale, NJ: Lawrence Erlbaum Associates.

Carpenter, T. P., & Moser, J. M. (1984). The acquisition of addition and subtraction concepts in grades one through three. *Journal for Research in Mathematics Education, 15*, 179–202.

Carper, D. V. (1942). Seeing numbers as groups in primary-grade arithmetic. *The Elementary School Journal, 43*, 166–170.

Carr, M., & Alexeev, N. (2008). Developmental trajectories of mathematic strategies: Influence of fluency, accuracy and gender. *Submittted for publication.*

Carr, M., & Davis, H. (2001). Gender differences in arithmetic strategy use: A function of skill and preference. *Contemporary Educational Psychology, 26*, 330–347.

Carr, M., Shing, Y. L., Janes, P., & Steiner, H. H. (2007). *Early gender differences in strategy use and fluency: Implications for the emergence of gender differences in mathematics.* Paper presented at the Society for Research in Child Development.

Carr, M., Steiner, H. H., Kyser, B., & Biddlecomb, B. (2008). A comparison of predictors of early emerging gender differences in mathematics competence. *Learning and Individual Differences, 18*, 61–75.

Case, R., Griffin, S., & Kelly, W. M. (1999). Socieconomic gradients in mathematical ability and their responsiveness to intervention during early childhood. In D. P. Keating & C. Hertzman (Eds.), *Developmental health and the wealth of nations* (pp. 125–149). New York: Guilford.

Casey, B., Kersh, J. E., & Young, J. M. (2004). Storytelling sagas: An effective medium for teaching early childhood mathematics. *Early Childhood Research Quarterly, 19*, 167–172.

Casey, M. B., Nuttall, R. L., & Pezaris, E. (1997). Mediators of gender differences in mathematics college entrance test scores: A comparison of spatial skills with internalized beliefs and anxieties. *Developmental Psychology, 33*, 669–680.

Casey, M. B., Nuttall, R. L., & Pezaris, E. (2001). Spatial-mechanical reasoning skills versus mathematics self-confidence as mediators of gender differences on mathematics subtests using cross-national gender-based items. *Journal for Research in Mathematics Education, 32*, 28–57.

Cepeda, N. J., Pashler, H., Vul, E., Wixted, J. T., & Rohrer, D. (2006). Distributed practice in verbal recall tasks: A review and quantitative synthesis. *Psychological Bulletin, 132*, 354–380.

Char, C. A. (1989). *Computer graphic feltboards: New software approaches for young children's mathematical exploration.* San Francisco: American Educational Research Association.

Chard, D. J., Clarke, B., Baker, S., Otterstedt, J., Braun, D., & Katz, R. (2005). Using measures of number sense to screen for difficulties in mathematics: Preliminary findings. *Assessment for Effective Intervention, 30*(2), 3–14.

Chen, C., & Uttal, D. H. (1988). Cultural values, parents' beliefs, and children's achievement in the United States and China. *Human Development, 31*, 351–358.

Chernoff, J. J., Flanagan, K. D., McPhee, C., & Park, J. (2007). *Preschool: First findings from the third follow-up of the early childhood longitudinal study, birth cohort (ECLS-B) (NCES 2008–025).* Washington, DC.: National Center for Education Statistics, Institute of Education Sciences, U.S. Department of Education.

Cheung, C., Leung, A., & McBride-Chang, C. (2007). *Gender differences in mathematics self concept in Hong Kong children: A function of perceived maternal academic support.* Paper presented at the Society for Research in Child Development.

Cheung, C., & McBride-Chang, C. (in press). Relations of perceived maternal parenting style, practices, and learning motivation to academic competence in Chinese children. *Merrill-Palmer Quarterly.*

Christiansen, K., Austin, A., & Roggman, L. (2005, April). *Math interactions in the context of play: Relations to child math ability.* Paper presented at the Biennial Meeting of the Society for Research in Child Development, Atlanta, GA.

Clarke, B., & Shinn, M. R. (2004). A preliminary investigation into the identification and development of early mathematics curriculum-based measurement. *School Psychology Review, 33*(2), 234–248.

Clarke, B. A., Clarke, D. M., & Horne, M. (2006). A longitudinal study of children's mental computation strategies. In J. Novotná, H. Moraová, M. Krátká & N. a. Stehlíková (Eds.), *Proceedings of the 30th Conference of the International Group for the Psychology in Mathematics Education* (Vol. 2, pp. 329–336). Prague, Czecho: Charles University.

Clarke, D. M., Cheeseman, J., Gervasoni, A., Gronn, D., Horne, M., McDonough, A., et al. (2002). *Early Numeracy Research Project Final Report*: Department of Education, Employment and Training, the Catholic Education Office (Melbourne), and the Association of Independent Schools Victoria.

Clements, D. H. (1983–84). Supporting young children's Logo programming. *The Computing Teacher, 11* (5), 24–30.

Clements, D. H. (1984). Training effects on the development and generalization of Piagetian logical operations and knowledge of number. *Journal of Educational Psychology, 76*, 766–776.

Clements, D. H. (1986). Effects of Logo and CAI environments on cognition and creativity. *Journal of Educational Psychology, 78*, 309–318.

Clements, D. H. (1987). Longitudinal study of the effects of Logo programming on cognitive abilities and achievement. *Journal of Educational Computing Research, 3*, 73–94.

Clements, D. H. (1989). *Computers in elementary mathematics education.* Englewood Cliffs, NJ: Prentice-Hall.

Clements, D. H. (1991). Current technology and the early childhood curriculum. In B. Spodek & O. N. Saracho (Eds.), *Yearbook in early childhood education, Volume 2: Issues in early childhood curriculum* (pp. 106–131). New York: Teachers College Press.

Clements, D. H. (1994). The uniqueness of the computer as a learning tool: Insights from research and practice. In J. L. Wright & D. D. Shade (Eds.), *Young children: Active learners in a technological age* (pp. 31–50). Washington, D.C.: National Association for the Education of Young Children.

Clements, D. H. (1995). Teaching creativity with computers. *Educational Psychology Review, 7*(2), 141–161.

Clements, D. H. (1999a). "Concrete" manipulatives, concrete ideas. *Contemporary Issues in Early Childhood, 1*(1), 45–60.

Clements, D. H. (1999b). Subitizing: What is it? Why teach it? *Teaching Children Mathematics, 5*, 400–405.

Clements, D. H. (1999c). Teaching length measurement: Research challenges. *School Science and Mathematics, 99*(1), 5–11.

Clements, D. H. (2001). Mathematics in the preschool. *Teaching Children Mathematics, 7*, 270–275.

Clements, D. H. (2007). Curriculum research: Toward a framework for "research-based curricula". *Journal for Research in Mathematics Education, 38*, 35–70.

Clements, D. H., & Battista, M. T. (1989). Learning of geometric concepts in a Logo environment. *Journal for Research in Mathematics Education, 20*, 450–467.

Clements, D. H., & Battista, M. T. (1990). Constructivist learning and teaching. *Arithmetic Teacher, 38*(1), 34–35.

Clements, D. H., & Battista, M. T. (Artist). (1991). *Logo geometry*

Clements, D. H., & Battista, M. T. (1992). Geometry and spatial reasoning. In D. A. Grouws (Ed.), *Handbook of research on mathematics teaching and learning* (pp. 420–464). New York: Macmillan.

Clements, D. H., & Battista, M. T. (2000). Designing effective software. In A. E. Kelly & R. A. Lesh (Eds.), *Handbook of research design in mathematics and science education* (pp. 761–776). Mahwah, NJ: Lawrence Erlbaum Associates.

Clements, D. H., Battista, M. T., & Sarama, J. (1998). Students' development of geometric and measurement ideas. In R. Lehrer & D. Chazan (Eds.), *Designing learning environments for developing understanding of geometry and space* (pp. 201–225). Mahwah, NJ: Lawrence Erlbaum Associates.

Clements, D. H., Battista, M. T., & Sarama, J. (2001). Logo and geometry. *Journal for Research in Mathematics Education Monograph Series, 10*.

Clements, D. H., Battista, M. T., Sarama, J., & Swaminathan, S. (1996). Development of turn and turn measurement concepts in a computer-based instructional unit. *Educational Studies in Mathematics, 30*, 313–337.

Clements, D. H., Battista, M. T., Sarama, J., & Swaminathan, S. (1997). Development of students' spatial thinking in a unit on geometric motions and area. *The Elementary School Journal, 98*, 171–186.

Clements, D. H., Battista, M. T., Sarama, J., Swaminathan, S., & McMillen, S. (1997). Students' development of length measurement concepts in a Logo-based unit on geometric paths. *Journal for Research in Mathematics Education, 28*(1), 70–95.

Clements, D. H., & Burns, B. A. (2000). Students' development of strategies for turn and angle measure. *Educational Studies in Mathematics, 41*, 31–45.

Clements, D. H., & Callahan, L. G. (1983). Number or prenumber experiences for young children: Must we choose? *The Arithmetic Teacher, 31*(3), 34–37.

Clements, D. H., & Callahan, L. G. (1986). Cards: A good deal to offer. *The Arithmetic Teacher, 34*(1), 14–17.

Clements, D. H., & Conference Working Group. (2004). Part one: Major themes and recommendations. In D. H. Clements, J. Sarama & A.-M. DiBiase (Eds.), *Engaging young children in mathematics: Standards for early childhood mathematics education* (pp. 1–72). Mahwah, NJ: Lawrence Erlbaum Associates.

Clements, D. H., & Meredith, J. S. (1993). Research on Logo: Effects and efficacy. *Journal of Computing in Childhood Education, 4*, 263–290.

Clements, D. H., & Meredith, J. S. (1994). Turtle math [Computer software]. Montreal, Quebec: Logo Computer Systems, Inc. (LCSI).

Clements, D. H., & Nastasi, B. K. (1985). Effects of computer environments on social-emotional development: Logo and computer-assisted instruction. *Computers in the Schools, 2*(2–3), 11–31.

Clements, D. H., & Nastasi, B. K. (1988). Social and cognitive interactions in educational computer environments. *American Educational Research Journal, 25*, 87–106.

Clements, D. H., & Nastasi, B. K. (1992). Computers and early childhood education. In M. Gettinger, S. N. Elliott & T. R. Kratochwill (Eds.), *Advances in school psychology: Preschool and early childhood treatment directions* (pp. 187–246). Mahwah, NJ: Lawrence Erlbaum Associates.

Clements, D. H., & Nastasi, B. K. (1993). Electronic media and early childhood education. In B. Spodek (Ed.), *Handbook of research on the education of young children* (pp. 251–275). New York: Macmillan.

Clements, D. H., Nastasi, B. K., & Swaminathan, S. (1993). Young children and computers: Crossroads and directions from research. *Young Children, 48*(2), 56–64.

Clements, D. H., Russell, S. J., Tierney, C., Battista, M. T., & Meredith, J. S. (1995). *Flips, turns, and area.* Cambridge, MA: Dale Seymour Publications.

Clements, D. H., & Sarama, J. (1996). Turtle Math: Redesigning Logo for elementary mathematics. *Learning and Leading with Technology, 23*(7), 10–15.

Clements, D. H., & Sarama, J. (1997). Research on Logo: A decade of progress. *Computers in the Schools, 14*(1–2), 9–46.

Clements, D. H., & Sarama, J. (2002). Teaching with computers in early childhood education: Strategies and professional development. *Journal of Early Childhood Teacher Education, 23*, 215–226.

Clements, D. H., & Sarama, J. (2003a). *DLM Early Childhood Express Math Resource Guide.* Columbus, OH: SRA/McGraw-Hill.

Clements, D. H., & Sarama, J. (2003b). Strip mining for gold: Research and policy in educational technology—A response to "Fool's Gold". *Educational Technology Review, 11*(1), 7–69.

Clements, D. H., & Sarama, J. (2003c). Young children and technology: What does the research say? *Young Children, 58*(6), 34–40.

Clements, D. H., & Sarama, J. (2004a). *Building Blocks* for early childhood mathematics. *Early Childhood Research Quarterly, 19*, 181–189.

Clements, D. H., & Sarama, J. (2004b). Learning trajectories in mathematics education. *Mathematical Thinking and Learning, 6*, 81–89.

Clements, D. H., & Sarama, J. (2007a). *Building Blocks—SRA Real Math Teacher's Edition, Grade PreK.* Columbus, OH: SRA/McGraw-Hill.

Clements, D. H., & Sarama, J. (2007b). *Building Blocks—SRA Real Math, Grade PreK.* Columbus, OH: SRA/McGraw-Hill.

Clements, D. H., & Sarama, J. (2007c). Effects of a preschool mathematics curriculum: Summative research on the *Building Blocks* project. *Journal for Research in Mathematics Education, 38*, 136–163.

Clements, D. H., & Sarama, J. (2008). Experimental evaluation of the effects of a research-based preschool mathematics curriculum. *American Educational Research Journal, 45*, 443–494.

Clements, D. H., Sarama, J., & DiBiase, A.-M. (2004). *Engaging young children in mathematics: Standards for early childhood mathematics education.* Mahwah, NJ: Lawrence Erlbaum Associates.

Clements, D. H., & Stephan, M. (2004). Measurement in preK-2 mathematics. In D. H. Clements, J. Sarama & A.-M. DiBiase (Eds.), *Engaging young children in mathematics: Standards for early childhood mathematics education* (pp. 299–317). Mahwah, NJ: Lawrence Erlbaum Associates.

Clements, D. H., & Swaminathan, S. (1995). Technology and school change: New lamps for old? *Childhood Education, 71*, 275–281.

Clements, D. H., Swaminathan, S., Hannibal, M. A. Z., & Sarama, J. (1999). Young children's concepts of shape. *Journal for Research in Mathematics Education, 30*, 192–212.

Clifford, R., Barbarin, O., Chang, F., Early, D., Bryant, D., Howes, C., et al. (2005). What is pre-kindergarten? Characteristics of public pre-kindergarten programs. *Applied Developmental Science, 9*, 126–143.

Cobb, P. (1990). A constructivist perspective on information-processing theories of mathematical activity. *International Journal of Educational Research, 14*, 67–92.

Cobb, P. (1995). Cultural tools and mathematical learning: A case study. *Journal for Research in Mathematics Education, 26*, 362–385.

Cobb, P., Wood, T., Yackel, E., Nicholls, J., Wheatley, G., Trigatti, B., et al. (1991). Assessment of a problem-centered second-grade mathematics project. *Journal for Research in Mathematics Education, 22*(1), 3–29.

Cobb, P., Yackel, E., & Wood, T. (1989). Young children's emotional acts during mathematical problem solving. In D. B. McLeod & V. M. Admas (Eds.), *Affect and mathematical problem solving: A new perspective* (pp. 117–148). New York: Springer-Verlag.

Cohen, J. (1977). *Statistical power analysis for the behavioral sciences (rev. ed.).* New York: Academic Press.

Cohen, R., & Geva, E. (1989). Designing Logo-like environments for young children: The interaction between theory and practice. *Journal of Educational Computing Research, 5*, 349–377.

Coley, R. J. (2002). *An unequal start: Indicators of inequality in school readiness.* Princeton, NJ: Educational Testing Service.

Confrey, J., & Kazak, S. (2006). A thirty-year reflection on constructivism in mathematics education in PME. In A. Gutiérrez & P. Boero (Eds.), *Handbook of research on the psychology of mathematics education: Past, present, and future* (pp. 305–345). Rotterdam, the Netherlands: Sense Publishers.

Cook, T. D. (2002). Randomized experiments in educational policy research: A critical examination of the reasons the educational evaluation community has offered for not doing them. *Educational Evaluation and Policy Analysis, 24*, 175–199.

Cooper, R. G., Jr. (1984). Early number development: Discovering number space with addition and subtraction. In C. Sophian (Ed.), *Origins of cognitive skills* (pp. 157–192). Mahwah, NJ: Lawrence Erlbaum Associates.

Cordes, C., & Miller, E. (2000). Fool's gold: A critical look at computers in childhood. Retrieved November 7, 2000, from http://www.allianceforchildhood.net/projects/computers/computers_reports.htm.

Correa, J., Nunes, T., & Bryant, P. (1998). Young children's understanding of division: The relationship between division terms in a noncomputational task. *Journal of Educational Psychology, 90*, 321–329.

Cowan, N., Saults, J. S., & Elliott, E. M. (2002). The search for what is fundamental in the development of working memory. *Advances in Child Development and Behavior, 29*, 1–49.

Currie, J., & Thomas, D. (1995). Does Head Start make a difference? *American Economic Review, 85*, 341–364.

Curtis, R. P. (2005). *Preschoolers' counting in peer interacction.* Paper presented at the American Educational Research Association, New Orleans, LA.

Davidson, J., & Wright, J. L. (1994). The potential of the microcomputer in the early childhood classroom. In J. L. Wright & D. D. Shade (Eds.), *Young children: Active learners in a technological age* (pp. 77–91). Washington, DC: National Association for the Education of Young Children.

Davis, R. B. (1984). *Learning mathematics: The cognitive science approach to mathematics education.* Norwood, NJ: Ablex.

Davydov, V. V. (1975). On the formation of an elementary concept of number by the child. In J. Kilpatrick & I. Wirszup (Eds.), *Soviet studies in the psychology of learning and teaching mathematics* (Vol. 13). Stanford, CA: School Mathematics Study Group, Stanford, University.

Dawson, D. T. (1953). Number grouping as a function of complexity. *The Elementary School Journal, 54,* 35–42.

Day, J. D., Engelhardt, J. L., Maxwell, S. E., & Bolig, E. E. (1997). Comparison of static and dynamic assessment procedures and their relation to independent performance. *Journal of Educational Psychology, 89*(2), 358–368.

Degelman, D., Free, J. U., Scarlato, M., Blackburn, J. M., & Golden, T. (1986). Concept learning in preschool children: Effects of a short-term Logo experience. *Journal of Educational Computing Research, 2*(2), 199–205.

Dehaene, S. (1997). *The number sense: How the mind creates mathematics.* New York: Oxford University Press.

DeLoache, J. S. (1987). Rapid change in the symbolic functioning of young children. *Science, 238,* 1556–1557.

DeLoache, J. S., Miller, K. F., & Pierroutsakos, S. L. (1998). Reasoning and problem solving. In D. Kuhn & R. S. Siegler (Eds.), *Handbook of child psychology (5th Ed.): Vol. 2. Cognition, perception, & language* (pp. 801–850). New York: Wiley.

DeLoache, J. S., Miller, K. F., Rosengren, K., & Bryant, N. (1997). The credible shrinking room: Very young children's performance with symbolic and nonsymbolic relations. *Psychological Science, 8,* 308–313.

Denton, K., & West, J. (2002). Children's reading and mathematics achievement in kindergarten and first grade. 2002, from http://nces.ed.gov/pubsearch/pubsinfo.asp?pubid=2002125.

Dewey, J. (1938/1997). *Experience and education.* New York: Simon & Schuster.

DHHS. (2005). *Head Start impact study: First year findings.* Washington, DC.: U.S. Department of Health and Human Services; Administration for Children and Families.

Diamond, A., Barnett, W. S., Thomas, J., & Munro, S. (2007). Preschool program improves cognitive control. *Science, 318,* 1387–1388.

Dixon, J. K. (1995). Limited English proficiency and spatial visualization in middle school students' construction of the concepts of reflection and rotation. *The Bilingual Research Journal, 19*(2), 221–247.

Dobbs, J., Doctoroff, G. L., Fisher, P. H., & Arnold, D. H. (2006). The association between preschool children's socio-emotional functioning and their mathematical skill. *Journal of Applied Developmental Psychology, 27,* 97–108.

Doig, B., McCrae, B., & Rowe, K. (2003). *A good start to numeracy: Effective numeracy strategies from research and practice in early childhood.* Canberra ACT, Australia: Australian Council for Educational Research.

Donlan, C. (1998). Number without language? Studies of children with specific language impairments. In C. Donlan (Ed.), *The development of mathematical skills* (pp. 255–274). East Sussex, UK: Psychology Press.

Dowker, A. (2004). *What works for children with mathematical difficulties? (Research Report No. 554).* Nottingham, UK: University of Oxford/DfES Publications.

Dowker, A. (2005). Early identification and intervention for students with mathematics difficulties. *Journal of Learning Disabilities, 38,* 324–332.

Downs, R. M., & Liben, L. S. (1988). Through the map darkly: Understanding maps as representations. *The Genetic Epistemologist, 16,* 11–18.

Downs, R. M., Liben, L. S., & Daggs, D. G. (1988). On education and geographers: The role of cognitive developmental theory in geographic education. *Annals of the Association of American Geographers, 78,* 680–700.

Draisma, J. (2000). Gesture and oral computation as resources in the early learning of mathematics. In T. Nakahara & M. Koyama (Eds.), *Proceedings of the 24th Conference of the International Group for the Psychology in Mathematics Education* (Vol. 2, pp. 257–264).

Driscoll, M. J. (1983). *Research within reach: Elementary school mathematics and reading.* St. Louis: CEMREL, Inc.

du Boulay, B. (1986). Part II: Logo confessions. In R. Lawler, B. du Boulay, M. Hughes & H. Macleod (Eds.), *Cognition and computers: Studies in learning* (pp. 81–178). Chichester, England: Ellis Horwood Limited.

Duncan, G. J., Brooks-Gunn, J., & Klebanov, P. K. (1994). Economic deprivation and early childhood development. *Child Development, 65,* 296–318.

Duncan, G. J., Claessens, A., & Engel, M. (2004). *The contributions of hard skills and socio-emotional behavior to school readiness* Evanston, IL: Northwestern University.

Duncan, G. J., Dowsett, C. J., Claessens, A., Magnuson, K., Huston, A. C., Klebanov, P., et al. (in press). School readiness and later achievement. *Developmental Psychology.*

Early, D., Barbarin, O., Burchinal, M. R., Chang, F., Clifford, R., Crawford, G., et al. (2005). *Pre-Kindergarten in Eleven States: NCEDL's Multi-State Study of Pre-Kindergarten & Study of State-Wide Early Education Programs (SWEEP).* Chapel Hill, NC: University of North Carolina.

Ebbeck. M. (1984). Equity for boys and girls: Some important issues. *Early Child Development and Care, 18,* 119–131.

Edwards, C., Gandini, L., & Forman, G. E. (1993). *The hundred languages of children: The Reggio Emilia approach to early childhood education.* Norwood, N.J.: Ablex Publishing Corp.

Ehrlich, S. B., & Levine, S. C. (2007a, April). *The impact of teacher "number talk" in low- and middle-SES preschool classrooms.* Paper presented at the American Educational Research Association, Chicago, IL.

Ehrlich, S. B., & Levine, S. C. (2007b, Marach). *What low-SES children DO know about number: A comparison of Head Start and tuition-based preschool children's number knowledge.* Paper presented at the Biennial Meeting of the Society of Research in Child Development, Boston, MA.

Ehrlich, S. B., Levine, S. C., & Goldin-Meadow, S. (2006). The importance of gesture in children's spatial reasoning. *Developmental Psychology, 42,* 1259–1268.

Eimeren, L. v., MacMillan, K. D., & Ansari, D. (2007, April). *The role of subitizing in children's development of verbal counting.* Paper presented at the Society for Research in Child Development, Boston, MA.

Elliott, A., & Hall, N. (1997). The impact of self-regulatory teaching strategies on "at-risk" preschoolers' mathematical learning in a computer-mediated environment. *Journal of Computing in Childhood Education, 8*(2/3), 187–198.

Emihovich, C., & Miller, G. E. (1988). Talking to the turtle: A discourse analysis of Logo instruction. *Discourse Processes, 11,* 183–201.

Entwisle, D. R., & Alexander, K. L. (1990). Beginning school math competence: Minority and majority comparisons. *Child Development, 61,* 454–471.

Entwisle, D. R., & Alexander, K. L. (1997). Family type and children's growth in reading and math over the primary grades. *Journal of Marriage and the Family, 58*, 341–355.

Ericsson, K. A., Krampe, R. T., & Tesch-Römer, C. (1993). The role of deliberate practice in the acquisition of expert performance. *Psychological Review, 100*, 363–406.

Ernest, P. (1985). The number line as a teaching aid. *Educational Studies in Mathematics, 16*, 411–424.

Evans, D. W. (1983). *Understanding infinity and zero in the early school years.* Unpublished doctoral dissertation, University of Pennsylvania.

Farran, D. C., Kang, S. J., Aydogan, C., & Lipsey, M. (2005). Preschool classroom environments and the quantity and quality of children's literacy and language behaviors. In D. Dickinson & S. Neuman (Eds.), *Handbook of early literacy research, Vol. 2.* New York: Guilford Publications.

Farran, D. C., Lipsey, M. W., Watson, B., & Hurley, S. (2007). *Balance of content emphasis and child content engagement in an early reading first program.* Paper presented at the American Educational Research Association.

Farran, D. C., Silveri, B., & Culp, A. (1991). Public preschools and the disadvantaged. In L. Rescorla, M. C. Hyson & K. Hirsh-Pase (Eds.), *Academic instruction in early childhood: Challenge or pressure? New directions for child development* (pp. 65–73). San. Francisco: Jossey-Bass.

Fennema, E. H. (1972). The relative effectiveness of a symbolic and a concrete model in learning a selected mathematics principle. *Journal for Research in Mathematics Education, 3*, 233–238.

Fennema, E. H., Carpenter, T. P., Frank, M. L., Levi, L., Jacobs, V. R., & Empson, S. B. (1996). A longitudinal study of learning to use children's thinking in mathematics instruction. *Journal for Research in Mathematics Education, 27*, 403–434.

Fennema, E. H., Carpenter, T. P., Franke, M. L., & Levi, L. (1998). A longitudinal study of gender differences in young children's mathematical thinking. *Educational Researcher, 27*, 6–11.

Fennema, E. H., & Tartre, L. A. (1985). The use of spatial visualization in mathematics by girls and boys. *Journal for Research in Mathematics Education, 16*, 184–206.

Feuerstein, R., Rand, Y. a., & Hoffman, M. B. (1979). *The dynamic assessment of retarded performers: The Learning Potential Assessment Device, theory, instruments, and techniques.* Baltimore, MD: University Park Press.

Finn, J. D. (2002). Small classes in American schools: Research, practice, and politics. *Phi Delta Kappan, 83*, 551–560.

Finn, J. D., & Achilles, C. M. (1990). Answers and questions about class size. *American Educational Research Journal, 27*(3), 557–577.

Finn, J. D., Gerber, S. B., Achilles, C. M., & Boyd-Zaharias, J. (2001). The enduring effects of small classes. *Teachers College Record, 103*(2), 145–183.

Finn, J. D., Pannozzo, G. M., & Achilles, C. M. (2003). The "why's" of class size: Student behavior in small classes. *Review of Educational Research, 73*, 321–368.

Fletcher, J. D., Hawley, D. E., & Piele, P. K. (1990). Costs, effects, and utility of microcomputer assisted instruction in the classroom. *American Educational Research Journal, 27*, 783–806.

Fletcher-Flinn, C. M., & Gravatt, B. (1995). The efficacy of computer assisted instruction (CAI): A meta-analysis. *Journal of Educational Computing Research, 12*, 219–242.

Flexer, R. J. (1989). Conceptualizing addition. *Teaching Exceptional Children, 21*(4), 21–25.

Fluck, M. (1995). Counting on the right number: Maternal support for the development of cardinality. *Irish Journal of Psychology, 16*, 133–149.

Fluck, M., & Henderson, L. (1996). Counting and cardinality in English nursery pupils. *British Journal of Educational Psychology, 66*, 501–517.

Ford, M. J., Poe, V., & Cox, J. (1993). Attending behaviors of ADHD children in math and reading using various types of software. *Journal of Computing in Childhood Education, 4*, 183–196.

Forman, G. E., & Hill, F. (1984). *Constructive play: Applying Piaget in the preschool (revised edition).* Menlo Park, CA: Addison Wesley.

Fox, J. (2005). Child-initiated mathematical patterning in the pre-compulsory years. In H. L. Chick & J. L. Vincent (Eds.), *Proceedings of the 29th Conference of the International Group for the Psychology in Mathematics Education* (Vol. 2, pp. 313–320). Melbourne, AU: PME.

Fox, J. (2006). A justification for mathematical modelling experiences in the preparatory classroom. In P. Grootenboer, R. Zevenbergen & M. Chinnappan (Eds.), *Proceedings of the 29th annual conference of the Mathematics Education Research Group of Australia* (pp. 221–228). Canberra, Australia.: MERGA.

Franke, M. L., Carpenter, T. P., & Battey, D. (2008). Algebra in the early grades. In J. J. Kaput, D. W. Carraher & M. L. Blanton (Eds.), (pp. 333–359). Mahwah, NJ: Lawrence Erlbaum Associates.

Frazier, M. K. (1987). *The effects of Logo on angle estimation skills of 7th graders.* Unpublished master's thesis, Wichita State University.

French, L., & Song, M.-J. (1998). Developmentally appropriate teacher-directed approaches: Images from Korean kindergartens. *Journal of Curriculum Studies, 30*, 409–430.

Friedman, L. (1995). The space factor in mathematics: Gender differences. *Review of Educational Research, 65*(1), 22–50.

Friel, S. N., Curcio, F. R., & Bright, G. W. (2001). Making sense of graphs: Critical factors influencing comprehension and instructional implications. *Journal for Research in Mathematics Education, 32*, 124–158.

Frontera, M. (1994). On the initial learning of mathematics: Does schooling really help? In J. E. H. Van Luit (Ed.), *Research on learning and instruction of mathematics in kindergarten and primary school* (pp. 42–59). Doetinchem, the Netherlands: Graviant.

Fryer, J., Roland G., & Levitt, S. D. (2004). Understanding the black-white test score gap in the first two years of school. *The Review of Economics and Statistics, 86*, 447–464.

Fuchs, L. S., Compton, D. L., Fuchs, D., Paulson, K., Bryant, J. D., & Hamlett, C. L. (2005). The prevention, identification, and cognitive determinants of math difficulty. *Journal of Educational Psychology, 97*, 493–513.

Fuchs, L. S., Fuchs, D., & Karns, K. (2001). Enhancing kindergartners' mathematical development: Effects of peer-assisted learning strategies. *Elementary School Journal, 101*, 495–510.

Fuchs, L. S., Fuchs, D., Hamlett, C. L., Powell, S. R., Capizzi, A. M., & Seethaler, P. M. (2006). The effects of computer-assisted instruction on number combination skill in at-risk first graders. *Journal of Learning Disabilities, 39,* 467–475.

Fuchs, L. S., Powell, S. R., Cirino, P. T., Fletcher, J. M., Fuchs, D., & Zumeta, R. O. (2008). *Enhancing number combinations fluency and math problem-solving skills in third-grade students with math difficulties: A field-based randomized control trial.* Paper presented at the Institute of Education Science 2007 Research Conference.

Fuchs, L. S., Powell, S. R., Hamlett, C. L., Fuchs, D., Cirino, P. T., & Fletcher, J. M. (2008). Remediating computational deficits at third grade: A randomized field trial. *Journal of Research on Educational Effectiveness, 1,* 2–32.

Fuson, K. C. (1988). *Children's counting and concepts of number.* New York: Springer-Verlag.

Fuson, K. C. (1992a). Research on learning and teaching addition and subtraction of whole numbers. In G. Leinhardt, R. Putman & R. A. Hattrup (Eds.), *Handbook of research on mathematics teaching and learning* (pp. 53–187). Mahwah, NJ: Lawrence Erlbaum Associates.

Fuson, K. C. (1992b). Research on whole number addition and subtraction. In D. A. Grouws (Ed.), *Handbook of research on mathematics teaching and learning* (pp. 243–275). New York: Macmillan.

Fuson, K. C. (1997). Research-based mathematics curricula: New educational goals require programs of four interacting levels of research. *Issues in Education, 3*(1), 67–79.

Fuson, K. C. (2004). Pre-K to grade 2 goals and standards: Achieving 21st century mastery for all. In D. H. Clements, J. Sarama & A.-M. DiBiase (Eds.), *Engaging young children in mathematics: Standards for early childhood mathematics education* (pp. 105–148). Mahwah, NJ: Lawrence Erlbaum Associates.

Fuson, K. C. (in press). Mathematically-desirable and accessible whole-number algorithms: Achieving understanding and fluency for all students.

Fuson, K. C., & Abrahamson, D. (in press). Word problem types, numerical situation drawings, and a conceptual phase model to implement an algebraic approach to problem-solving in elementary classrooms.

Fuson, K. C., & Briars, D. J. (1990). Using a base-ten blocks learning/teaching approach for first- and second-grade place-value and multidigit addition and subtraction. *Journal for Research in Mathematics Education, 21,* 180–206.

Fuson, K. C., Perry, T., & Kwon, Y. (1994). Latino, Anglo, and Korean children's finger addition methods. In J. E. H. Van Luit (Ed.), *Research on learning and instruction of mathematics in kindergarten and primary school* (pp. 220–228). Doetinchem, the Netherlands: Graviant.

Fuson, K. C., Smith, S. T., & Lo Cicero, A. (1997). Supporting Latino first graders' ten-structured thinking in urban classrooms. *Journal for Research in Mathematics Education, 28,* 738–760.

Gadanidis, G., Hoogland, C., Jarvis, D., & Scheffel, T.-L. (2003). Mathematics as an aesthetic experience. In *Proceedings of the 27th Conference of the International Group for the Psychology in Mathematics Education* (Vol. 1, pp. 250). Honolulu, HI: University of Hawai'i.

Gagatsis, A., & Elia, I. (2004). The effects of different modes of representation on mathematical problem solving. In M. J. Høines & A. B. Fuglestad (Eds.), *Proceedings of the 28th Conference of the International Group for the Psychology in Mathematics Education* (Vol. 2, pp. 447–454). Bergen, Norway: Bergen University College.

Galen, F. H. J. v., & Buter, A. (1997). De rol van interactie bij leren rekenen met de computer (Computer tasks and classroom discussions in mathematics). *Panama-Post. Tijdschrift voor nascholing en onderzoek van het reken-wiskundeonderwijs, 16*(1), 11–18.

Gallou-Dumiel, E. (1989). Reflections, point symmetry and Logo. In C. A. Maher, G. A. Goldin & R. B. Davis (Eds.), *Proceedings of the eleventh annual meeting, North American Chapter of the International Group for the Psychology of Mathematics Education* (pp. 149–157). New Brunswick, NJ: Rutgers University.

Gamel-McCormick, M., & Amsden, D. (2002). *Investing in better outcomes: The Delaware early childhood longitudinal study.* Delaware Interagency Resource Management Committee and the Department of Education.

Geary, D. C. (1990). A componential analysis of an early learning deficit in mathematics. *Journal of Experimental Child Psychology, 49,* 363–383.

Geary, D. C. (1994). *Children's mathematical development: Research and practical applications.* Washington, DC: American Psychological Association.

Geary, D. C. (2003). Learning disabilities in arithmetic: Problem solving differences and cognitive deficits. In H. L. Swanson, K. Harris & S. Graham (Eds.), *Handbook of learning disabilities.* New York: Guilford.

Geary, D. C. (2004). Mathematics and learning disabilities. *Journal of Learning Disabilities, 37,* 4–15.

Geary, D. C. (2006). Development of mathematical understanding. In D. Kuhn, R. S. Siegler, W. Damon & R. M. Lerner (Eds.), *Handbook of child psychology: Volume 2: Cognition, perception, and language (6th ed.)* (pp. 777–810). Hoboken, NJ: Wiley.

Geary, D. C., Bow-Thomas, C. C., Fan, L., & Siegler, R. S. (1993). Even before formal instruction, Chinese children outperform American children in mental addition. *Cognitive Development, 8,* 517–529.

Geary, D. C., Bow-Thomas, C. C., & Yao, Y. (1992). Counting knowledge and skill in cognitive addition: A comparison of normal and mathematically disabled children. *Journal of Experimental Child Psychology, 54,* 372–391.

Geary, D. C., Brown, S. C., & Smaranayake, V. A. (1991). Cognitive addition: A short longitudinal study of strategy choice and speed-of-processing differences in normal and mathematically disabled children. *Developmental Psychology, 27,* 787–797.

Geary, D. C., Hamson, C. O., & Hoard, M. K. (2000). Numerical and arithmetical cognition: A longitudinal study of process and concept deficits in children with learning disability. *Journal of Experimental Child Psychology, 77,* 236–263.

Geary, D. C., Hoard, M. K., Byrd-Craven, J., Nugent, L., & Numtee, C. (2007). Cognitive mechanisms underlying achievement deficits in children with mathematical learning disability. *Child Development, 78,* 1343–1359.

Geary, D. C., Hoard, M. K., & Hamson, C. O. (1999). Numerical and arithmetical cognition: Patterns of functions and deficits in children at risk for a mathematical disability. *Journal of Experimental Child Psychology, 74,* 213–239.

Geary, D. C., & Liu, F. (1996). Development of arithmetical competence in Chinese and American children: Influence of age, language, and schooling. *Child Development, 67*(5), 2022–2044.

Gelman, R. (1994). Constructivism and supporting environments. In D. Tirosh (Ed.), *Implicit and explicit knowledge: An educational approach* (Vol. 6, pp. 55–82). Norwood, NJ: Ablex.

Gelman, R., & Williams, E. M. (1997). Enabling constraints for cognitive development and learning: Domain specificity and epigenesis. In D. Kuhn & R. Siegler (Eds.), *Cognition, perception, and language. Volume 2: Handbook of Child Psychology* (5th ed., pp. 575–630). New York: John Wiley & Sons.

Gersten, R. (1986). Response to "consquences of three preschool curriculum models through age 15". *Early Childhood Research Quarterly, 1*, 293–302.

Gersten, R., Chard, D. J., Jayanthi, M., Baker, M. S., Morpy, S. K., & Flojo, J. R. (2008). *Teaching mathematics to students with learning disabilities: A meta-analysis of the intervention research.* Portsmouth, NH: RMC Research Corporation, Center on Instruction.

Gersten, R., Jordan, N. C., & Flojo, J. R. (2005). Early identification and interventions for students with mathematical difficulties. *Journal of Learning Disabilities, 38*, 293–304.

Gersten, R., & White, W. A. T. (1986). Castles in the sand: Response to Schweinhart and Weikart. *Educational Leadership*, 19–20.

Gervasoni, A. (2005). The diverse learning needs of children who were selected for an intervention program. In H. L. Chick & J. L. Vincent (Eds.), *Proceedings of the 29th Conference of the International Group for the Psychology in Mathematics Education* (Vol. 3, pp. 33–40). Melbourne, AU: PME.

Gervasoni, A., Hadden, T., & Turkenburg, K. (2007). Exploring the number knowledge of children to inform the development of a professional learning plan for teachers in the Ballarat Diocese as a means of building community capacity. In J. Watson & K. Beswick (Eds.), *Mathematics: Essential research, essential practice (Proceedings of the 30th annual conference of the Mathematics Education Research Group of Australasia)* (Vol. 3, pp. 305–314). Hobart, Australia: MERGA.

Gibson, E. J. (1969). *Principles of perceptual learning and development.* New York: Appleton-Century-Crofts, Meredith Corporation.

Ginsburg, H. P. (1977). *Children's arithmetic.* Austin, TX: Pro-ed.

Ginsburg, H. P. (1997). Mathematics learning disabilities: A view from developmental psychology. *Journal of Learning Disabilities, 30*, 20–33.

Ginsburg, H. P. (2008). Mathematics education for young children: What it is and how to promote it. *Social Policy Report, 22*(1), 1–24.

Ginsburg, H. P., Choi, Y. E., Lopez, L. S., Netley, R., & Chi, C.-Y. (1997). Happy birthday to you: The early mathematical thinking of Asian, South American, and U.S. children. In T. Nunes & P. Bryant (Eds.), *Learning and teaching mathematics: An international perspective* (pp. 163–207). East Sussex, England: Psychology Press.

Ginsburg, H. P., Inoue, N., & Seo, K.-H. (1999). Young children doing mathematics: Observations of everyday activities. In J. V. Copley (Ed.), *Mathematics in the early years* (pp. 88–99). Reston, VA: National Council of Teachers of Mathematics.

Ginsburg, H. P., Klein, A., & Starkey, P. (1998). The development of children's mathematical thinking: Connecting research with practice. In W. Damon, I. E. Sigel & K. A. Renninger (Eds.), *Handbook of child psychology. Volume 4: Child psychology in practice* (pp. 401–476). New York: John Wiley & Sons.

Ginsburg, H. P., Ness, D., & Seo, K.-H. (2003). Young American and Chinese children's everyday mathematical activity. *Mathematical Thinking and Learning, 5*, 235–258.

Ginsburg, H. P., & Russell, R. L. (1981). Social class and racial influences on early mathematical thinking. *Monographs of the Society for Research in Child Development, 46*(6, Serial No. 193).

Gormley, W. T., Jr., Gayer, T., Phillips, D., & Dawson, B. (2005). The effects of universal pre-K on cognitive development. *Developmental Psychology, 41*, 872–884.

Graham, T. A., Nash, C., & Paul, K. (1997). Young children's exposure to mathematics: The child care context. *Early Childhood Education Journal, 25*, 31–38.

Grant, S. G., Peterson, P. L., & Shojgreen-Downer, A. (1996). Learning to teach mathematics in the context of system reform. *American Educational Research Journal, 33*(2), 509–541.

Gravemeijer, K. P. E. (1990). Realistic geometry instruction. In K. P. E. Gravemeijer, M. van den Heuvel & L. Streefland (Eds.), *Contexts free productions tests and geometry in realistic mathematics education* (pp. 79–91). Utrecht, the Netherlands: OW&OC.

Gravemeijer, K. P. E. (1991). An instruction-theoretical reflection on the use of manipulatives. In L. Streefland (Ed.), *Realistic mathematics education in primary school* (pp. 57–76). Utrecht, the Netherlands: Freudenthal Institute, Utrecht University.

Gray, E. M., & Pitta, D. (1997). Number processing: Qualitative differences in thinking and the role of imagery. In L. Puig & A. Gutiérrez (Eds.), *Proceedings of the 20th Annual Conference of the Mathematics Education Research Group of Australasia* (Vol. 3, pp. 35–42).

Gray, E. M., & Pitta, D. (1999). Images and their frames of reference: A perspective on cognitive development in elementary arithmetic. In O. Zaslavsky (Ed.), *Proceedings of the 23rd Conference of the International Group for the Psychology of Mathematics Education* (Vol. 3, pp. 49–56). Haifa, Israel: Technion.

Greabell, L. C. (1978). The effect of stimuli input on the acquisition of introductory geometric concepts by elementary school children. *School Science and Mathematics, 78*(4), 320–326.

Green, J. A. K., & Goswami, U. (2007). *Synaesthesia and number cognition in children.* Paper presented at the Society for Research in Child Development.

Greeno, J. G., & Riley, M. S. (1987). Processes and development of understanding. In R. E. Weinert & R. H. Kluwe (Eds.), *Metacognition, motivation, and understanding* (pp. 289–313): Lawrence Erlbaum Associates.

Greenwood, C. R., Delquadri, J. C., & Hall, R. V. (1989). Longitudinal effects of classwide peer tutoring. *Journal of Educational Psychology, 81*, 371–383.

Griffin, S. (2004). Number Worlds: A research-based mathematics program for young children. In D. H. Clements, J. Sarama & A.-M. DiBiase (Eds.), *Engaging young children in mathematics: Standards for early childhood mathematics education* (pp. 325–342). Mahwah, NJ: Lawrence Erlbaum Associates.

Griffin, S., & Case, R. (1997). Re-thinking the primary school math curriculum: An approach based on cognitive science. *Issues in Education, 3*(1), 1–49.

Griffin, S., Case, R., & Capodilupo, A. (1995). Teaching for understanding: The importance of the Central Conceptual Structures in the elementary mathematics curriculum. In A. McKeough, J. Lupart & A. Marini (Eds.), *Teaching for transfer: Fostering generalization in learning* (pp. 121–151). Mahwah, NJ: Lawrence Erlbaum Associates.

Griffin, S., Case, R., & Siegler, R. S. (1994). Rightstart: Providing the central conceptual prerequisites for first formal learning of arithmetic to students at risk for school failure. In K. McGilly (Ed.), *Classroom lessons: Integrating cognitive theory and classroom practice* (pp. 25–49). Cambridge, MA: MIT Press.

Grupe, L. A., & Bray, N. W. (1999). What role do manipulatives play in kindergartners' accuracy and strategy use when solving simple addition problems? Albuquerque, NM: Society for Research in Child Development.

Halle, T. G., Kurtz-Costes, B., & Mahoney, J. L. (1997). Family influences on school achievement in low-income, African American children. *Journal of Educational Psychology, 89*, 527–537.

Hamre, B. K., & Pianta, R. C. (2001). Early teacher-child relationships and the trajectory of children's school outcomes through eighth grade. *Child Development, 72*, 625–638.

Hancock, C. M. (1995). Das Erlernen der Datenanalyse durch anderweitige Beschäftigungen: Grundlagen von Datencompetenz bei Schülerinnen und Schülern in den klassen 1 bis 7. [Learning data analysis by doing something else: Foundations of data literacy in grades 1–7]. *Computer und Unterricht, 17*(1).

Hanich, L. B., Jordan, N. C., Kaplan, D., & Dick, J. (2001). Performance across different areas of mathematical cognition in children with learning difficulties. *Journal of Educational Psychology, 93*, 615–626.

Hannula, M. M. (2005). *Spontaneous focusing on numerosity in the development of early mathematical skills.* Turku, Finland: University of Turku.

Hannula, M. M., Lepola, J., & Lehtinen, E. (2007). *Spontaneous focusing on numerosity at Kindergarten predicts arithmetical but not reading skills at grade 2.* Paper presented at the Society for Research in Child Development.

Harris, L. J. (1981). Sex-related variations in spatial skill. In L. S. Liben, A. H. Patterson, & N. Newcombe (Eds.), *Spatial representation and behavior across the life span* (pp. 83–125). New York: Academic Press.

Harrison, C. (2004). Giftedness in early childhood: The search for complexity and connection. *Roeper Review, 26*(2), 78–84.

Hart, B., & Risley, T. R. (1995). *Meaningful differences in the everyday experience of young American children.* Baltimore, MD: Paul H. Brookes.

Hart, B., & Risley, T. R. (1999). *The social world of children: Learning to talk.* Baltimore, MD: Paul H. Brookes.

Hasselbring, T. S., Goin, L. I., & Bransford, J. (1988). Developing math automaticity in learning handicapped children: The role of computerized drill and practice. *Focus on Exceptional Children, 20*(6), 1–7.

Hatano, G., & Sakakibara, T. (2004). Commentary: Toward a cognitive-sociocultural psychology of mathematical and analogical development. In L. D. English (Ed.), *Mathematical and analogical reasoning of young learners* (pp. 187–200). Mahwah, NJ: Lawrence Erlbaum Associates.

Hattikudur, S., & Alibali, M. (2007). *Learning about the equal sign: Does contrasting with inequalities help?* Paper presented at the Society for Research in Child Development.

Haugland, S. W. (1992). Effects of computer software on preschool children's developmental gains. *Journal of Computing in Childhood Education, 3*(1), 15–30.

Hausken, E. G., & Rathbun, A. (2004). *Mathematics instruction in kindergarten: Classroom practices and outcomes.* Paper presented at the American Educational Research Association.

Hegarty, M., & Kozhevnikov, M. (1999). Types of visual-spatial representations and mathematical problems-solving. *Journal of Educational Psychology, 91*, 684–689.

Hemphill, J. A. R. (1987). *The effects of meaning and labeling on four-year-olds' ability to copy triangles.* Columbus, OH: The Ohio State University.

Heuvel-Panhuizen, M. v. d. (1996). *Assessment and realistic mathematics education.* Utrecht, the Netherlands: Freudenthal Institute, Utrecht University.

Hiebert, J. C. (1999). Relationships between research and the NCTM Standards. *Journal for Research in Mathematics Education, 30*, 3–19.

Hiebert, J. C., & Grouws, D. A. (2007). The effects of classroom mathematics teaching on students' learning. In F. K. Lester, Jr. (Ed.), *Second Handbook of Research on Mathematics Teaching and Learning* (pp. 371–404). New York: Information Age Publishing.

Hiebert, J. C., & Wearne, D. (1992). Links between teaching and learning place value with understanding in first grade. *Journal for Research in Mathematics Education, 23*, 98–122.

Hiebert, J. C., & Wearne, D. (1993). Instructional tasks, classroom discourse, and student learning in second-grade classrooms. *American Educational Research Journal, 30*, 393–425.

Hiebert, J. C., & Wearne, D. (1996). Instruction, understanding, and skill in multidigit addition and subtraction. *Cognition and Instruction, 14*, 251–283.

Hinkle, D. (2000). *School involvement in early childhood.* Washington, DC: National Institute on Early Childhood Development and Education, U.S. Department of Education, Office of Educational Research and Improvement.

Hitch, G. J., & McAuley, E. (1991). Working memory in children with specific arithmetical learning disabilities. *British Journal of Psychology, 82*, 375–386.

Holloway, S. D., Rambaud, M. F., Fuller, B., & Eggers-Pierola, C. (1995). What is "appropriate practice" at home and in child care?: Low-income mothers' views on preparing their children for school. *Early Childhood Research Quarterly, 10*, 451–473.

Holt, J. (1982). *How children fail.* New York: Dell.

Holton, D., Ahmed, A., Williams, H., & Hill, C. (2001). On the importance of mathematical play. *International Journal of Mathematical Education in Science and Technology, 32*, 401–415.

Hopkins, S. L., & Lawson, M. J. (2004). Explaining variability in retrieval times for addition produced by students with mathematical learning difficulties. In M. J. Høines & A. B. Fuglestad (Eds.), *Proceedings of the 28th Conference of the International Group for the Psychology in Mathematics Education* (Vol. 3, pp. 57–64). Bergen, Norway: Bergen University College.

Horne, M. (2004). Early gender differences. In M. J. Høines & A. B. Fuglestad (Eds.), *Proceedings of the 28th Conference of the International Group for the Psychology in Mathematics Education* (Vol. 3, pp. 65–72). Bergen, Norway: Bergen University College.

Horne, M. (2005). The effects of number knowledge at school entry on subsequent number development: A five-year longitudinal study. In P. Clarkson, A. Downtown, D. Gronn, M. Horne, A. McDonough, R. Pierce & A. Roche (Eds.), *Building connections: Research, theory and practice (Proceedings of the 28th annual conference of the Mathematics Education Research Group of Australasia)* (pp. 443–450). Melbourne, Australia: MERGA.

Howard, J. R., Watson, J. A., & Allen, J. (1993). Cognitive style and the selection of Logo problem-solving strategies by young black children. *Journal of Educational Computing Research, 9*, 339–354.

Hudson, T. (1983). Correspondences and numerical differences between disjoint sets. *Child Development, 54*, 84–90.

Hughes, M. (1981). Can preschool children add and subtract? *Educational Psychology, 1*, 207–219.

Hughes, M. (1986). *Children and number: Difficulties in learning mathematics.* Oxford, U.K.: Basil Blackwell.

Hungate, H. (1982, January). Computers in the kindergarten. *The Computing Teacher, 9*, 15–18.

Hunting, R., & Pearn, C. (2003). The mathematical thinking of young children: Pre-K-2. In N. S. Pateman, B. J. Dougherty & J. Zilliox (Eds.), *Proceedings of the 27th Conference of the International Group for the Psychology in Mathematics Education* (Vol. 1, pp. 187). Honolulu, HI: University of Hawai'i.

Hutinger, P. L., Bell, C., Beard, M., Bond, J., Johanson, J., & Terry, C. (1998). *The early childhood emergent literacy technology research study. Final report.* Macomb, IL: Western Illinois University.

Hutinger, P. L., & Johanson, J. (2000). Implementing and maintaining an effective early childhood comprehensive technology system. *Topics in Early Childhood Special Education, 20*(3), 159–173.

Huttenlocher, J., Jordan, N. C., & Levine, S. C. (1994). A mental model for early arithmetic. *Journal of Experimental Psychology: General, 123*, 284–296.

Hyde, J. S., Fennema, E. H., & Lamon, S. J. (1990). Gender differences in mathematics performance: A meta-analysis. *Psychological Bulletin, 107*, 139–155.

Irwin, K. C., Vistro-Yu, C. P., & Ell, F. R. (2004). Understanding linear measurement: A comparison of Filipino and New Zealand children. *Mathematics Education Research Journal, 16*(2), 3–24.

Ishigaki, E. H., Chiba, T., & Matsuda, S. (1996). Young children's communication and self expression in the technological era. *Early Childhood Development and Care, 119*, 101–117.

James, W. (1892/1958). *Talks to teachers on psychology: And to students on some of life's ideas.* New York: Norton.

Jimerson, S., Egeland, B., & Teo, A. (1999). A longitudinal study of achievement trajectories: Factors associated with change. *Journal of Educational Psychology, 91*, 116–126.

Johnson, M. (1987). *The body in the mind.* Chicago: The University of Chicago Press.

Johnson, V. M. (2000). *An investigation of the effects of instructional strategies on conceptual understanding of young children in mathematics.* New Orleans, LA: American Educational Research Association.

Johnson-Gentile, K., Clements, D. H., & Battista, M. T. (1994). The effects of computer and noncomputer environments on students' conceptualizations of geometric motions. *Journal of Educational Computing Research, 11*, 121–140.

Jordan, J.-A., Wylie, J., & Mulhern, G. (2007). *Ability profiles of five to six-year-olds with mathematical learning difficulties.* Paper presented at the Society for Research in Child Development.

Jordan, N. C., Hanich, L. B., & Kaplan, D. (2003). A longitudinal study of mathematical competencies in children with specific mathematics difficulties versus children with comorbid mathematics and reading difficulties. *Child Development, 74*, 834–850.

Jordan, N. C., Hanich, L. B., & Ubèrti, H. Z. (2003). Mathematical thinking and learning difficulties. In A. J. Baroody & A. Dowker (Eds.), *The development of arithmetic concepts and skills: Constructing adaptive expertise* (pp. 359–383). Mahwah, NJ: Lawrence Erlbaum Associates.

Jordan, N. C., Huttenlocher, J., & Levine, S. C. (1992). Differential calculation abilities in young children from middle- and low-income families. *Developmental Psychology, 28*, 644–653.

Jordan, N. C., Huttenlocher, J., & Levine, S. C. (1994). Assessing early arithmetic abilities: Effects of verbal and nonverbal response types on the calculation performance of middle-and low-income children. *Learning and Individual Differences, 6*, 413–432.

Jordan, N. C., Kaplan, D., & Hanich, L. B. (2002). Achievement growth in children with learning difficulties in mathematics: Findings of a two-year longitudinal study. *Journal of Educational Psychology, 94*, 586–597.

Jordan, N. C., Kaplan, D., Locuniak, M. N., & Ramineni, C. (2006). Predicting first-grade math achievement from developmental number sense trajectories. *Learning Disabilities Research and Practice, 22*(1), 36–46.

Jordan, N. C., Kaplan, D., Oláh, L. N., & Locuniak, M. N. (2006). Number sense growth in kindergarten: A longitudinal investigation of children at risk for mathematics difficulties. *Child Development, 77*, 153–175.

Jordan, N. C., & Montani, T. O. (1997). Cognitive arithmetic and problem solving: A comparison of children with specific and general mathematics difficulties. *Journal of Learning Disabilities, 30*, 624–634.

Kamii, C. (1973). Pedagogical principles derived from Piaget's theory: Relevance for educational practice. In M. Schwebel & J. Raph (Eds.), *Piaget in the classroom* (pp. 199–215). New York: Basic Books.

Kamii, C. (1985). *Young children reinvent arithmetic: Implications of Piaget's theory.* New York: Teaching College Press.

Kamii, C. (1986). Place value: An explanation of its difficulty and educational implications for the primary grades. *Journal of Research in Childhood Education, 1*, 75–86.

Kamii, C. (1989). *Young children continue to reinvent arithmetic: 2nd grade. Implications of Piaget's theory.* New York: Teaching College Press.

Kamii, C., & DeVries, R. (1980). *Group games in early education: Implications of Piaget's theory.* Washington, DC: National Association for the Education of Young Children.

Kamii, C., & Dominick, A. (1997). To teach or not to teach algorithms. *Journal of Mathematical Behavior, 16*, 51–61.

Kamii, C., & Dominick, A. (1998). The harmful effects of algorithms in grades 1–4. In L. J. Morrow & M. J. Kenney (Eds.), *The teaching and learning of algorithms in school mathematics* (pp. 130–140). Reston, VA: National Council of Teachers of Mathematics.

Kamii, C., & Housman, L. B. (1999). *Young children reinvent arithmetic: Implications of Piaget's theory* (2nd ed.). New York: Teachers College Press.

Kamii, C., & Kato, Y. (2005). Fostering the development of logico-mathematical knowledge in a card game at ages 5–6. *Early Education & Development, 16*, 367–383.

Kamii, C., Rummelsburg, J., & Kari, A. R. (2005). Teaching arithmetic to low-performing, low-SES first graders. *Journal of Mathematical Behavior, 24*, 39–50.

Kaput, J. J., Carraher, D. W., & Blanton, M. L. (Eds.). (2008). *Algebra in the early grades.* Mahwah, NJ: Lawrence Erlbaum Associates.

Karmiloff-Smith, A. (1990). Constraints on representational change: Evidence from children's drawing. *Cognition, 34*, 57–83.

Karmiloff-Smith, A. (1992). *Beyond modularity: A developmental perspective on cognitive science.* Cambridge, MA: MIT Press.

Karoly, L. A., Greenwood, P. W., Everingham, S. S., Houbé, J., Kilburn, M. R., Rydell, C. P., et al. (1998). *Investing in our children: What we know and don't know about the costs and benefits of early childhood interventions.* Santa Monica, CA: Rand Education.

Kawai, N., & Matsuzawa, T. (2000). Numerical memory span in a chimpanzee. *Nature, 403*, 39–40.

Keller, S., & Goldberg, I. (1997). *Let's Learn Shapes with Shapely-CAL.* Great Neck, NY: Creative Adaptations for Learning, Inc.

Kersh, J., Casey, B., & Young, J. M. (in press). Research on spatial skills and block building in girls and boys: The relationship to later mathematics learning. In B. Spodek & O. N. Saracho (Eds.), *Mathematics, science, and technology in early childhood education.*

Kieran, C. (1986). Logo and the notion of angle among fourth and sixth grade children. In C. Hoyles & L. Burton (Eds.), *Proceedings of the tenth annual meeting of the International Group for the Psychology in Mathematics Education* (pp. 99–104). London: City University.

Kieran, C., & Hillel, J. (1990). "It's tough when you have to make the triangles angles": Insights from a computer-based geometry environment. *Journal of Mathematical Behavior, 9*, 99–127.

Kilpatrick, J. (1987). Problem formulating: Where do good problems come from? In A. H. Schoenfeld (Ed.), *Cognitive science and mathematics education* (pp. 123–147). Hillsdale, NJ: Lawrence Erlbaum Associates.

Kilpatrick, J., Swafford, J., & Findell, B. (2001). *Adding it up: Helping children learn mathematics.* Washington, DC: National Academy Press.

Kim, S.-Y. (1994). The relative effectiveness of hands-on and computer-simulated manipulatives in teaching seriation, classification, geometric, and arithmetic concepts to kindergarten children. *Dissertation Abstracts International, 54/09*, 3319.

King, J. A., & Alloway, N. (1992). Preschooler's use of microcomputers and input devices. *Journal of Educational Computing Research, 8*, 451–468.

Klein, A., & Starkey, P. (2004). Fostering preschool children's mathematical development: Findings from the Berkeley Math Readiness Project. In D. H. Clements, J. Sarama & A.-M. DiBiase (Eds.), *Engaging young children in mathematics: Standards for early childhood mathematics education* (pp. 343–360). Mahwah, NJ: Lawrence Erlbaum Associates.

Klein, A., Starkey, P., & Ramirez, A. B. (2002). *Pre-K mathematics curriculum.* Glenview, IL: Scott Foresman.

Klein, A., Starkey, P., & Wakeley, A. (1999). *Enhancing pre-kindergarten children's readiness for school mathematics.* Paper presented at the American Educational Research Association.

Klein, A. S., Beishuizen, M., & Treffers, A. (1998). The empty number line in Dutch second grades: Realistic versus gradual program design. *Journal for Research in Mathematics Education, 29*, 443–464.

Klibanoff, R. S., Levine, S. C., Huttenlocher, J., Vasilyeva, M., & Hedges, L. V. (2006). Preschool children's mathematical knowledge: The effect of teacher "math talk". *Developmental Psychology, 42*, 59–69.

Klinzing, D. G., & Hall, A. (1985). *A study of the behavior of children in a preschool equipped with computers.* Chicago: American Educational Research Association.

Knapp, M. S., Shields, P. M., & Turnbull, B. J. (1992). *Academic challenge for the children of poverty.* Washington, DC: U.S. Department of Education.

Konold, C., & Pollatsek, A. (2002). Data analysis as the search for signals in noisy processes. *Journal for Research in Mathematics Education, 33*, 259–289.

Konold, T. R., & Pianta, R. C. (2005). Empirically-derived, person-oriented patterns of school readiness in typically-developing children: Description and prediction to first-grade achievement. *Applied Developmental Science, 9*, 174–187.

Koponen, T., Aunola, K., Ahonen, T., & Nurmi, J.-E. (2007). Cognitive predictors of single-digit and procedural calculation and their covariation with reading skill. *Journal of Experimental Child Psychology, 97*, 220–241.

Kovas, Y., Haworth, C. M. A., Dale, P. S., & Plomin, R. (2007). The genetic and environmental origins of learning abilities and disabilities in the early school years. *Monographs of the Society for Research in Child Development, 72*, whole number 3, Serial No. 188, 1–144.

Krajewski, Kristin. "Prediction of Mathematical (Dis-)Abilities in Primary School: A 4-Year German Longitudinal Study from Kindergarten to Grade 4" Paper presented at the Biennial Meeting of the Society for Research in Child Development, Atlanta, GA, April 2005.

Kull, J. A. (1986). Learning and Logo. In P. F. Campbell & G. G. Fein (Eds.), *Young children and microcomputers* (pp. 103–130). Englewood Cliffs, NJ: Prentice-Hall.

Kutscher, B., Linchevski, L., & Eisenman, T. (2002). From the Lotto game to subtracting two-digit numbers in first-graders. In A. D. Cockburn & E. Nardi (Eds.), *Proceedings of the 26th Conference of the International Group for the Psychology in Mathematics Education* (Vol. 3, pp. 249–256).

Lamon, W. E., & Huber, L. E. (1971). The learning of the vector space structure by sixth grade students. *Educational Studies in Mathematics, 4*, 166–181.

Lamy, C. E., Frede, E., Seplocha, H., Strasser, J., Jambunathan, S., Juncker, J. A., et al. (2004). Inch by inch, row by row, gonna make this garden grow: Classroom quality and language skills in the Abbott Preschool Program (Publication. Retrieved September 29, 2007: from http://nieer.org/docs/?DocID=94.

Landau, B. (1988). The construction and use of spatial knowledge in blind and sighted children. In J. Stiles-Davis, M. Kritchevsky & U. Bellugi (Eds.), *Spatial cognition: Brain bases and development* (pp. 343–371). Mahwah, NJ: Lawrence Erlbaum Associates.

Landerl, K., Bevan, A., & Butterworth, B. (2004). Developmental dyscalculia and basic numerical capacities: A study of 8–9-year-old children. *Cognition, 93*(99–125).

Lansdell, J. M. (1999). Introducing young children to mathematical concepts: Problems with "new" terminology. *Educational Studies, 25*, 327–333.

Lara-Cinisomo, S., Pebley, A. R., Vaiana, M. E., & Maggio, E. (2004). *Are L.A.'s children ready for school?* Santa Monica, CA: RAND Corporation.

Laurillard, D., & Taylor, J. (1994). Designing the Stepping Stones: An evaluation of interactive media in the classroom. *Journal of Educational Television, 20,* 169–184.

Lavin, R. J., & Sanders, J. E. (1983). *Longitudinal evaluation of the C/A/I Computer Assisted Instruction Title 1 Project: 1979–82*: Chelmsford, MA: Merrimack Education Center.

Lebron-Rodriguez, D. E., & Pasnak, R. (1977). Induction of intellectual gains in blind children. *Journal of Experimental Child Psychology, 24,* 505–515.

Lee, J. (2002). Racial and ethnic achievement gap trends: Reversing the progress toward equity? *Educational Researcher, 31,* 3–12.

Lee, J. (2004). Correlations between kindergarten teachers' attitudes toward mathematics and teaching practice. *Journal of Early Childhood Teacher Education, 25*(2), 173–184.

Lee, J. S., & Ginsburg, H. P. (2007). What is appropriate mathematics education for four-year-olds? *Journal of Early Childhood Research, 5*(1), 2–31.

Lee, V. E., Brooks-Gunn, J., Schnur, E., & Liaw, F.-R. (1990). Are Head Start effects sustained? A longitudinal follow-up comparison of disadvantaged children attending Head Start, no preschool, and other preschool programs. *Child Development, 61,* 495–507.

Lee, V. E., & Burkam, D. T. (2002). *Inequality at the starting gate.* Washington, DC: Economic Policy Institute.

Lee, V. E., Burkam, D. T., Ready, D. D., Honigman, J. J., & Meisels, S. J. (2006). Full-day vs. half-day kindergarten: In which program do children learn more?. *American Journal of Education, 112,* 163–208.

Leeson, N. (1995). Investigations of kindergarten students' spatial constructions. In B. Atweh & S. Flavel (Eds.), *Proceedings of 18th Annual Conference of Mathematics Education Research Group of Australasia* (pp. 384–389). Darwin, AU: Mathematics Education Research Group of Australasia.

Leeson, N., Stewart, R., & Wright, R. J. (1997). Young children's knowledge of three-dimensional shapes: Four case studies. In F. Biddulph & K. Carr (Eds.), *Proceedings of the 20th Annual Conference of the Mathematics Education Research Group of Australasia* (Vol. 1, pp. 310–317). Hamilton, New Zealand: MERGA.

Lehrer, R. (2003). Developing understanding of measurement. In J. Kilpatrick, W. G. Martin & D. Schifter (Eds.), *A research companion to Principles and Standards for School Mathematics* (pp. 179–192). Reston, VA: National Council of Teachers of Mathematics.

Lehrer, R., Harckham, L. D., Archer, P., & Pruzek, R. M. (1986). Microcomputer-based instruction in special education. *Journal of Educational Computing Research, 2,* 337–355.

Lehrer, R., Jacobson, C., Thoyre, G., Kemeny, V., Strom, D., Horvarth, J., et al. (1998). Developing understanding of geometry and space in the primary grades. In R. Lehrer & D. Chazan (Eds.), *Designing learning environments for developing understanding of geometry and space* (pp. 169–200). Mahwah, NJ: Lawrence Erlbaum Associates.

Lehrer, R., Jenkins, M., & Osana, H. (1998). Longitudinal study of children's reasoning about space and geometry. In R. Lehrer & D. Chazan (Eds.), *Designing learning environments for developing understanding of geometry and space* (pp. 137–167). Mahwah, NJ: Lawrence Erlbaum Associates.

Lehrer, R., & Pritchard, C. (2002). Symbolizing space into being. In K. P. E. Gravemeijer, R. Lehrer, B. Van Oers & L. Verschaffel (Eds.), *Symbolizing, modeling and tool use in mathematics education* (pp. 59–86). Dordrecht: Kluwer Academic Publishers.

Lehrer, R., Strom, D., & Confrey, J. (2002). Grounding metaphors and inscriptional resonance: Children's emerging understandings of mathematical similarity. *Cognition and Instruction, 20*(3), 359–398.

Lehtinen, E., & Hannula, M. M. (2006). Attentional processes, abstraction and transfer in early mathematical development. In L. Verschaffel, F. Dochy, M. Boekaerts & S. Vosniadou (Eds.), *Instructional psychology: Past, present and future trends. Fifteen essays in honour of Erik De Corte* (Vol. 49, pp. 39–55). Amsterdam: Elsevier.

Lembke, E. S., & Foegen, A. (2008). Identifying indicators of performance in early mathematics for kindergarten and grade 1 students. *Submitted for publication.*

Lembke, E. S., Foegen, A., Whittake, T. A., & Hampton, D. (in press). Establishing technically adequate measures of progress in early numeracy. *Assessment for Effective Intervention.*

Lepola, J., Niemi, P., Kuikka, M., & Hannula, M. M. (2005). Cognitive-linguistic skills and motivation as longitudinal predictors of reading and arithmetic achievement: A follow-up study from kindergarten to grade 2. *International Journal of Educational Research, 43,* 250–271.

Lerkkanen, M.-K., Rasku-Puttonen, H., Aunola, K., & Nurmi, J.-E. (2005). Mathematical performance predicts progress in reading comprehension among 7-year-olds. *European Journal of Psychology of Education, 20*(2), 121–137.

Lerner, J. (1997). *Learning disabilities.* Boston: Houghton Mifflin Company.

Lesh, R. A. (1990). Computer-based assessment of higher order understandings and processes in elementary mathematics. In G. Kulm (Ed.), *Assessing higher order thinking in mathematics* (pp. 81–110). Washington, DC: American Association for the Advancement of Science.

Lester, F. K., Jr., & Wiliam, D. (2002). On the purpose of mathematics education research: Making productive contributions to policy and practice. In L. D. English (Ed.), *Handbook of international research in mathematics education* (pp. 489–506). Mahwah, NJ: Lawrence Erlbaum Associates.

Levine, S. C., Huttenlocher, J., Taylor, A., & Langrock, A. (1999). Early sex differences in spatial skill. *Developmental Psychology, 35*(4), 940–949.

Levine, S. C., Jordan, N. C., & Huttenlocher, J. (1992). Development of calculation abilities in young children. *Journal of Experimental Child Psychology, 53,* 72–103.

Li, Z., & Atkins, M. (2004). Early childhood computer experience and cognitive and motor development. *Pediatrics, 113,* 1715–1722.

Liaw, F.-r., Meisels, S. J., & Brooks-Gunn, J. (1995). The effects of experience of early intervention on low birth weight, premature children: The Infant Health and Development Program. *Early Childhood Research Quarterly, 10,* 405–431.

Liben, L. S. (2008). Understanding maps: Is the purple country on the map really purple? *Knowledge Question, 36,* 20–30.

Light, R. J., & Pillemer, D. B. (1984). *Summing up: The science of reviewing research.* Cambridge, MA: Harvard University Press.

Lillard, A. S., & Else-Quest, N. (2007). Evaluating Montessori education. *Science, 313*, 1893–1894.

Linnell, M., & Fluck, M. (2001). The effect of maternal support for counting and cardinal understanding in pre-school children. *Social Development, 10*, 202–220.

Lipinski, J. M., Nida, R. E., Shade, D. D., & Watson, J. A. (1986). The effects of microcomputers on young children: An examination of free-play choices, sex differences, and social interactions. *Journal of Educational Computing Research, 2*, 147–168.

Loeb, S., Bridges, M., Bassok, D., Fuller, B., & Rumberger, R. (2007). How much is too much? The influence of preschool centers on children's development nationwide. *Economics of Education Review 26*, 52–56.

Lonigan, C. J. (2003). Comment on Marcon (ECRP, Vol. 4, No. 1, Spring 2002): "Moving up the grades: Relationship between preschool model and later school success". *Early Childhood Research & Practice, 5*(1).

Lutchmaya, S., & Baron-Cohen, S. (2002). Human sex differences in social and non-social looking preferences, at 12 months of age. *Infant Behavior and Development, 25*, 319–325.

Magnuson, K. A., Meyers, M. K., Rathbun, A., & West, J. (2004). Inequality in preschool education and school readiness. *American Educational Research Journal, 41*, 115–157.

Magnuson, K. A., & Waldfogel, J. (2005). Early childhood care and education: Effects on ethnic and racial gaps in school readiness. *The Future of Children, 15*, 169–196.

Maier, M. F., & Greenfield, D. B. (2008). *The differential role of initiative and persistence in early childhood*. Paper presented at the Institute of Education Science 2007 Research Conference.

Malaguzzi, L. (1997). *Shoe and meter*. Reggio Emilia, Italy: Reggio Children.

Malmivuori, M.-L. (2001). *The dynamics of affect, cognition, and social environment in the regulation of personal learning processes: The case of mathematics*. University of Helsinki, Helsinki.

Malofeeva, E., Day, J., Saco, X., Young, L., & Ciancio, D. (2004). Construction and evaluation of a number sense test with Head Start children. *Journal of Education Psychology, 96*, 648–659.

Mandler, J. M. (2004). *The foundations of mind: Origins of conceptual thought*. New York: Oxford University Press.

Marcon, R. A. (1992). Differential effects of three preschool models on inner-city 4-year-olds. *Early Childhood Research Quarterly, 7*, 517–530.

Marcon, R. A. (2002). Moving up the grades: Relationship between preschool model and later school success. *Early Childhood Research & Practice* Retrieved 1, 4, from http://ecrp.uiuc.edu/v4n1/marcon.html.

Markovits, Z., & Hershkowitz, R. (1997). Relative and absolute thinking in visual estimation processes. *Educational Studies in Mathematics, 32*, 29–47.

Martin, T., Lukong, A., & Reaves, R. (2007). The role of manipulatives in arithmetic and geometry tasks. *Journal of Education and Human Development, 1*(1).

Mason, M. M. (1995). Geometric knowledge in a deaf classroom: An exploratory study. *Focus on Learning Problems in Mathematics, 17*(3), 57–69.

Mayfield, W. A., Morrison, J. W., Thornburg, K. R., & Scott, J. L. (2007). *Project Construct: Child outcomes based on curriculum fidelity*. Paper presented at the Society for Research in Child Development.

Mazzocco, M. M. M., & Myers, G. F. (2003). Complexities in identifying and defining mathematics learning disability in the primary school-age years. *Annals of Dyslexia, 53*, 218–253.

Mazzocco, M. M. M., & Thompson, R. E. (2005). Kindergarten predictors of math learning disability. *Quarterly Research and Practice, 20*, 142–155.

McClain, K., Cobb, P., Gravemeijer, K. P. E., & Estes, B. (1999). Developing mathematical reasoning within the context of measurement. In L. V. Stiff & F. R. Curcio (Eds.), *Developing mathematical reasoning in grades K-12* (pp. 93–106). Reston, VA: National Council of Teachers of Mathematics.

McGee, M. G. (1979). Human spatial abilities: Psychometric studies and environmental, genetic, hormonal, and neurological influences. *Psychological Bulletin, 86*, 889–918.

McGuinness, D., & Morley, C. (1991). Gender differences in the development of visuo-spatial ability in pre-school children. *Journal of Mental Imagery, 15*, 143–150.

McLeod, D. B., & Adams, V. M. (Eds.). (1989). *Affect and mathematical problem solving*. New York: Springer-Verlag.

McTaggart, J., Frijters, J., & Barron, R. (2005, April). *Children's interest in reading and math: A longitudinal study of motivational stability and influence on early academic skills*. Paper presented at the Biennial Meeting of the Society for Research in Child Development, Atlanta, GA.

Metz, K. E. (1995). Reassessment of developmental constraints on children's science instruction. *Review of Educational Research, 65*, 93–127.

Middleton, J. A., & Spanias, P. (1999). Motivation for achievement in mathematics: Findings, generalizations, and criticisms of the research. *Journal for Research in Mathematics Education, 30*, 65–88.

Milesi, C., & Gamoran, A. (2006). Effects of class size and instruction on kindergarten achievement. *Education Evaluation and Policy Analysis, 28*(4), 287–313.

Millar, S., & Ittyerah, M. (1992). Movement imagery in young and congenitally blind children: Mental practice without visuo-spatial information. *International Journal of Behavioral Development, 15*, 125–146.

Miller, K. F. (1984). Child as the measurer of all things: Measurement procedures and the development of quantitative concepts. In C. Sophian (Ed.), *Origins of cognitive skills: The eighteenth annual Carnegie symposium on cognition* (pp. 193–228). Hillsdale, NJ: Lawrence Erlbaum Associates.

Miller, K. F. (1989). Measurement as a tool of thought: The role of measuring procedures in children's understanding of quantitative invariance. *Developmental Psychology, 25*, 589–600.

Miller, K. F., Kelly, M., & Zhou, X. (2005). Learning mathematics in China and the United States: Cross-cultural insights into the nature and course of preschool mathematical development. In J. I. D. Campbell (Ed.), *Handbook of mathematical cognition* (pp. 163–178). New York: Psychology Press.

Miller, K. F., Smith, C. M., Zhu, J., & Zhang, H. (1995). Preschool origins of cross-national differences in mathematical competence: The role of number-naming systems. *Psychological Science, 6*, 56–60.

Mitchelmore, M. C. (1989). The development of children's concepts of angle. In G. Vergnaud, J. Rogalski & M. Artique (Eds.),

Proceedings of the 13th Conference of the International Group for the Psychology of Mathematics Education (pp. 304–311). Paris: City University.

Mitchelmore, M. C. (1992). Children's concepts of perpendiculars. In W. Geeslin & K. Graham (Eds.), *Proceedings of the 16th Conference of the International Group for the Psychology in Mathematics Education* (Vol. 2, pp. 120–127). Durham, NH: Program Committee of the 16th PME Conference.

Moll, L. C., Amanti, C., Neff, D., & Gonzalez, N. (1992). Funds of knowledge for teaching: Using a qualitative approach to connect homes and classrooms. *Theory into Practice, 31*, 132–141.

Monighan-Nourot, P., Scales, B., Van Hoorn, J., & Almy, M. (1987). *Looking at children's play: A bridge between theory and practice.* New York: Teachers College.

Montessori, M. (1964). *The Montessori method.* New York: Schocken Books.

Montie, J. E., Xiang, Z., & Schweinhart, L. J. (2006). Preschool experience in 10 countries: Cognitive and language performance at age 7. *Early Childhood Research Quarterly, 21*, 313–331.

Morgenlander, M. (2005). *Preschoolers' understanding of mathematics presented on Sesame Street.* Paper presented at the American Educational Research Association, New Orleans, LA.

Morrongiello, B. A., Timney, B., Humphrey, G. K., Anderson, S., & Skory, C. (1995). Spatial knowledge in blind and sighted children. *Journal of Experimental Child Psychology, 59*, 211–233.

Moseley, B. (2005). Pre-service early childhood educators' perceptions of math-mediated language. *Early Education & Development, 16*(3), 385–396.

Moyer, P. S. (2000). Are we having fun yet? Using manipulatives to teach "real math".

Moyer, P. S., Niezgoda, D., & Stanley, J. (2005). Young children's use of virtual manipulatives and other forms of mathematical representations. In W. Masalski & P. C. Elliott (Eds.), *Technology-supported mathematics learning environments: 67th Yearbook* (pp. 17–34). Reston, VA: National Council of Teachers of Mathematics.

Mullet, E., & Miroux, R. (1996). Judgment of rectangular areas in children blind from birth. *Cognitive Development, 11*, 123–139.

Mulligan, J., Prescott, A., Mitchelmore, M. C., & Outhred, L. (2005). Taking a closer look at young students' images of area measurement. *Australian Primary Mathematics Classroom, 10*(2), 4–8.

Mullis, I. V. S., Martin, M. O., Gonzalez, E. J., Gregory, K. D., Garden, R. A., O'Connor, K. M., et al. (2000). *TIMSS 1999 international mathematics report.* Boston: The International Study Center, Boston College, Lynch School of Education.

Munn, P. (1998). Symbolic function in pre-schoolers. In C. Donlan (Ed.), *The development of mathematical skills* (pp. 47–71). East Sussex, UK: Psychology Press.

Murata, A. (2004). Paths to learning ten-structured understanding of teen sums: Addition solution methods of Japanese Grade 1 students. *Cognition and Instruction, 22*, 185–218.

Nasir, N. i. S., & Cobb, P. (2007). *Improving access to mathematics: Diversity and equity in the classroom.* New York: Teachers College Press.

Nastasi, B. K., & Clements, D. H. (1991). Research on cooperative learning: Implications for practice. *School Psychology Review, 20*, 110–131.

Nastasi, B. K., Clements, D. H., & Battista, M. T. (1990). Social-cognitive interactions, motivation, and cognitive growth in Logo programming and CAI problem-solving environments. *Journal of Educational Psychology, 82*, 150–158.

Natriello, G., McDill, E. L., & Pallas, A. M. (1990). *Schooling disadvantaged children: Racing against catastrophe.* New York: Teachers College Press.

NCES. (2000). *America's kindergartners (NCES 2000070).* Washington, DC: National Center for Education Statistics, U.S. Government Printing Office.

NCTM. (2000). *Principles and standards for school mathematics.* Reston, VA: National Council of Teachers of Mathematics.

NCTM. (2006). *Curriculum focal points for prekindergarten through grade 8 mathematics: A quest for coherence.* Reston, VA: National Council of Teachers of Mathematics.

Niemiec, R. P., & Walberg, H. J. (1984). Computers and achievement in the elementary schools. *Journal of Educational Computing Research, 1*, 435–440.

Niemiec, R. P., & Walberg, H. J. (1987). Comparative effects of computer-assisted instruction: A synthesis of reviews. *Journal of Educational Computing Research, 3*, 19–37.

Nishida, T. K., & Lillard, A. S. (2007a, April). *From flashcard to worksheet: Children's inability to transfer across different formats.* Paper presented at the Society for Research in Child Development, Boston, MA.

Nishida, T. K., & Lillard, A. S. (2007b, April). *Fun toy or learning tool?: Young children's use of concrete manipulatives to learn about simple math concepts.* Paper presented at the Society for Research in Child Development, Boston, MA.

NMP. (2008). *Foundations for Success: The Final Report of the National Mathematics Advisory Panel.* Washington D.C.: U.S. Department of Education, Office of Planning, Evaluation and Policy Development.

NRC. (2004). *On evaluating curricular effectiveness: Judging the quality of K-12 mathematics evaluations.* Washington, D.C.: Mathematical Sciences Education Board, Center for Education, Division of Behavioral and Social Sciences and Education, The National Academies Press.

Nührenbörger, M. (2001). Insights into children's ruler concepts—Grade-2 students' conceptions and knowledge of length measurement and paths of development. In M. v. d. Heuvel-Panhuizen (Ed.), *Proceedings of the 25th Conference of the International Group for the Psychology in Mathematics Education* (Vol. 3, pp. 447–454). Utrecht, the Netherlands: Freudenthal Institute.

Nunes, T., & Moreno, C. (1998). Is hearing impairment a cause of difficulties in learning mathematics? In C. Donlan (Ed.), *The development of mathematical skills* (Vol. 7, pp. 227–254). Hove, UK: Psychology Press.

Nunes, T., & Moreno, C. (2002). An intervention programme for promoting deaf pupils' achievement in mathematics. *Journal of Deaf Studies and Deaf Education*, 120–133.

O'Neill, D. K., Pearce, M. J., & Pick, J. L. (2004). Preschool children's narratives and performance on the Peabody Individualized Achievement Test Revised: Evidence of a relation between early narrative and later mathematical ability. *First Language.*

Oakes, J. (1990). Opportunities, achievement, and choice: Women and minority students in science and mathematics. In C. B. Cazden (Ed.), *Review of research in education* (Vol. 16, pp. 153–222). Washington, DC: American Educational Research Association.

Olive, J., Lankenau, C. A., & Scally, S. P. (1986). *Teaching and understanding geometric relationships through Logo: Phase II. Interim Report: The Atlanta–Emory Logo Project.* Altanta, GA: Emory University.

Olson, J. K. (1988). Microcomputers make manipulatives meaningful. Budapest, Hungary: International Congress of Mathematics Education.

Ostad, S. A. (1998). Subtraction strategies in developmental perspective: A comparison of mathematically normal and mathematically disabled children. In A. Olivier & K. Newstead (Eds.), *Proceedings of the 22nd Conference for the International Group for the Psychology of Mathematics Education* (Vol. 3, pp. 311–318). Stellenbosch, South Africa: University of Stellenbosch.

Outhred, L. N., & Sardelich, S. (1997). Problem solving in kindergarten: The development of representations. In F. Biddulph & K. Carr (Eds.), *People in Mathematics Education. Proceedings of the 20th Annual Conference of the Mathematics Education Research Group of Australasia* (Vol. 2, pp. 376–383). Rotorua, New Zealand: Mathematics Education Research Group of Australasia.

Owens, K. (1992). Spatial thinking takes shape through primary-school experiences. In W. Geeslin & K. Graham (Eds.), *Proceedings of the 16th Conference of the International Group for the Psychology in Mathematics Education* (Vol. 2, pp. 202–209). Durham, NH: Program Committee of the 16th PME Conference.

Pan, Y., & Gauvain, M. (2007). *Parental involvement in children's mathematics learning in American and Chinese families during two school transitions.* Paper presented at the Society for Research in Child Development.

Pan, Y., Gauvain, M., Liu, Z., & Cheng, L. (2006). American and Chinese parental involvement in young children's mathematics learning. *Cognitive Development, 21,* 17–35.

Papert, S. (1980). *Mindstorms: Children, computers, and powerful ideas.* New York: Basic Books.

Paris, C. L., & Morris, S. K. (1985). *The computer in the early childhood classroom: Peer helping and peer teaching.* Cleege Park, MD: Microworld for Young Children Conference.

Parker, T. H., & Baldridge, S. J. (2004). *Elementary mathematics for teachers.* Quebecor World, MI: Sefton-Ash Publishing.

Pasnak, R. (1987). Accelerated cognitive development of kindergartners. *Psychology in the Schools, 28,* 358–363.

Peisner-Feinberg, E. S., Burchinal, M. R., Clifford, R. M., Culkins, M. L., Howes, C., Kagan, S. L., et al. (2001). The relation of preschool child-care quality to children's cognitive and social developmental trajectories through second grade. *Child Development, 72,* 1534–1553.

Perlmutter, J., Bloom, L., Rose, T., & Rogers, A. (1997). Who uses math? Primary children's perceptions of the uses of mathematics. *Journal of Research in Childhood Education, 12*(1), 58–70.

Perry, B., & Dockett, S. (2002). Young children's access to powerful mathematical ideas. In L. D. English (Ed.), *Handbook of International Research in Mathematics Education* (pp. 81–111). Mahwah, NJ: Lawrence Erlbaum Associates.

Perry, B., & Dockett, S. (2005). "I know that you don't have to work hard": Mathematics learning in the first year of primary school. In H. L. Chick & J. L. Vincent (Eds.), *Proceedings of the 29th Conference of the International Group for the Psychology in Mathematics Education* (Vol. 4, pp. 65–72). Melbourne, AU: PME.

Perry, B., Young-Loveridge, J. M., Dockett, S., & Doig, B. (2008). The development of young children's mathematical understanding. In H. Forgasz, A. Barkatsas, A. Bishop, B. A. Clarke, S. Keast, W. T. Seah & P. Sullivan (Eds.), *Research in mathematics education in Australasia 2004–2007* (pp. 17–40). Rotterdam/Taipei: Sense Publishers.

Piaget, J. (1962). *Play, dreams and imitation in childhood.* New York: W. W. Norton.

Piaget, J. (1971/1974). *Understanding causality.* New York: Norton.

Piaget, J., & Inhelder, B. (1967). *The child's conception of space.* New York: W. W. Norton.

Pianta, R. C., Howes, C., Burchinal, M. R., Bryant, D., Clifford, R., Early, D., et al. (2005). Features of pre-kindergarten programs, classrooms, and teachers: Do they predict observed classroom quality and child–teacher interactions? *Applied Developmental Science, 9,* 144–159.

Pollio, H. R., & Whitacre, J. D. (1970). Some observations on the use of natural numbers by preschool children. *Perceptual and Motor Skills, 30,* 167–174.

Porter, J. (1999). Learning to count: A difficult task? *Down Syndrome Research and Practice, 6*(2), 85–94.

Pratt, C. (1948). *I learn from children.* New York: Simon and Schuster.

Primavera, J., Wiederlight, P. P., & DiGiacomo, T. M. (2001, August). *Technology access for low-income preschoolers: Bridging the digital divide.* Paper presented at the American Psychological Association, San Francisco, CA.

Ragosta, M., Holland, P., & Jamison, D. T. (1981). *Computer-assisted instruction and compensatory education: The ETS/LAUSD study.* Princeton, NJ: Educational Testing Service.

Ramey, C. T., & Ramey, S. L. (1998). Early intervention and early experience. *American Psychologist, 53,* 109–120.

Raphael, D., & Wahlstrom, M. (1989). The influence of instructional aids on mathematics achievement. *Journal for Research in Mathematics Education, 20,* 173–190.

Rathbun, A., & West, J. (2004). *From kindergarten through third grade: Children's beginning school experiences.* Washington, DC: U.S. Department of Education, National Center for Education Statistics.

Razel, M., & Eylon, B.-S. (1986). Developing visual language skills: The Agam Program. *Journal of Visual Verbal Languaging, 6*(1), 49–54.

Razel, M., & Eylon, B.-S. (1990). Development of visual cognition: Transfer effects of the Agam program. *Journal of Applied Developmental Psychology, 11,* 459–485.

Razel, M., & Eylon, B.-S. (1991, July). *Developing mathematics readiness in young children with the Agam Program,* Genova, Italy.

Resnick, L. B., & Omanson, S. (1987). Learning to understand arithmetic. In R. Glaser (Ed.), *Advances in instructional psychology* (pp. 41–95). Hillsdale, NJ: Lawrence Erlbaum Associates.

Rhee, M. C., & Chavnagri, N. (Cartographer). (1991). *Four-year-old children's peer interactions when playing with a computer.* ERIC Document No. ED342466.

Richardson, K. (2004). Making sense. In D. H. Clements, J. Sarama & A.-M. DiBiase (Eds.), *Engaging young children in mathematics: Standards for early childhood mathematics education* (pp. 321–324). Mahwah, NJ: Lawrence Erlbaum Associates.

Riel, M. (1985). The Computer Chronicles Newswire: A functional learning enviornment for acquiring literacy skills. *Journal of Educational Computing Research, 1,* 317–337.

Ritter, S., Anderson, J. R., Koedinger, K. R., & Corbett, A. (2007). Cognitive Tutor: Applied research in mathematics education. *Psychonomics Bulletin & Review, 14*(2), 249–255.

Robinson, G. E. (1990). Synthesis of research on effects of class size. *Educational Leadership, 47*(7), 80–90.

Robinson, N. M., Abbot, R. D., Berninger, V. W., & Busse, J. (1996). The structure of abilities in math-precocious young children: Gender similarities and differences. *Journal of Educational Psychology, 88*(2), 341–352.

Rosengren, K. S., Gross, D., Abrams, A. F., & Perlmutter, M. (1985). An observational study of preschool children's computing activity. Austin, TX: "Perspectives on the Young Child and the Computer" conference, University of Texas at Austin.

Rosser, R. A. (1994). The developmental course of spatial cognition: Evidence for domain multidimensionality. *Child Study Journal, 24*, 255–280.

Rosser, R. A., Ensing, S. S., Glider, P. J., & Lane, S. (1984). An information-processing analysis of children's accuracy in predicting the appearance of rotated stimuli. *Child Development, 55*, 2204–2211.

Rosser, R. A., Horan, P. F., Mattson, S. L., & Mazzeo, J. (1984). Comprehension of Euclidean space in young children: The early emergence of understanding and its limits. *Genetic Psychology Monographs, 110*, 21–41.

Roth, J., Carter, R., Ariet, M., Resnick, M. B., & Crans, G. (2000, April). *Comparing fourth-grade math and reading achievement of children who did and did not participate in Florida's statewide Prekindergarten Early Intervention Program.* Paper presented at the American Educational Research Association, New Orleans, LA.

Rourke, B. P., & Finlayson, M. A. J. (1978). Neuropsychological significance of variations in patterns of academic performance: Verbal and visual-spatial abilities. *Journal of Abnormal Child Psychology, 6*(121–133).

Rouse, C., Brooks-Gunn, J., & McLanahan, S. (2005). Introducing the issue. *The Future of Children, 15*, 5–14.

Rousselle, L., & Noël, M.-P. (2007). Basic numerical skills in children with mathematics learning disabilities: A comparison of symbolic vs non-symbolic number magnitude processing. *Cognition, 102*, 361–395.

Russell, S. J. (1991). Counting noses and scary things: Children construct their ideas about data. In D. Vere-Jones (Ed.), *Proceedings of the Third International Conference on Teaching Statistics.* Voorburg, the Netherlands: International Statistical Institute.

Sandhofer, C. M., & Smith, L. B. (1999). Learning color words involves learning a system of mappings. *Developmental Psychology, 35*, 668–679.

Sarama, J. (1995). *Redesigning Logo: The turtle metaphor in mathematics education.* Unpublished doctoral dissertation, State University of New York at Buffalo.

Sarama, J. (2002). Listening to teachers: Planning for professional development. *Teaching Children Mathematics, 9*, 36–39.

Sarama, J. (2004). Technology in early childhood mathematics: Building Blocks™ as an innovative technology-based curriculum. In D. H. Clements, J. Sarama & A.-M. DiBiase (Eds.), *Engaging young children in mathematics: Standards for early childhood mathematics education* (pp. 361–375). Mahwah, NJ: Lawrence Erlbaum Associates.

Sarama, J., & Clements, D. H. (2002a). *Building Blocks for young children's mathematical development. Journal of Educational Computing Research, 27*(1&2), 93–110.

Sarama, J., & Clements, D. H. (2002b). Learning and teaching with computers in early childhood education. In O. N. Saracho & B. Spodek (Eds.), *Contemporary Perspectives on Science and Technology in Early Childhood Education* (pp. 171–219). Greenwich, CT: Information Age Publishing, Inc.

Sarama, J., & Clements, D. H. (2008). Mathematics knowledge of low-income entering preschoolers. *Manuscript submitted for publication.*

Sarama, J., & Clements, D. H. (2009). *Early childhood mathematics education research: Learning trajectories for young children.* New York: Taylor & Francis.

Sarama, J., Clements, D. H., Swaminathan, S., McMillen, S., & González Gómez, R. M. (2003). Development of mathematical concepts of two-dimensional space in grid environments: An exploratory study. *Cognition and Instruction, 21*, 285–324.

Sarama, J., Clements, D. H., & Vukelic, E. B. (1996). The role of a computer manipulative in fostering specific psychological/mathematical processes. In E. Jakubowski, D. Watkins & H. Biske (Eds.), *Proceedings of the 18th annual meeting of the North America Chapter of the International Group for the Psychology of Mathematics Education* (Vol. 2, pp. 567–572). Columbus, OH: ERIC Clearinghouse for Science, Mathematics, and Environmental Education.

Sarama, J., & DiBiase, A.-M. (2004). The professional development challenge in preschool mathematics. In D. H. Clements, J. Sarama & A.-M. DiBiase (Eds.), *Engaging young children in mathematics: Standards for early childhood mathematics education* (pp. 415–446). Mahwah, NJ: Lawrence Erlbaum Associates.

Saxe, G. B., Guberman, S. R., & Gearhart, M. (1987). Social processes in early number development. *Monographs of the Society for Research in Child Development, 52*(2, Serial #216).

Schery, T. K., & O'Connor, L. C. (1997). Language intervention: Computer training for young children with special needs. *British Journal of Educational Technology, 28*, 271–279.

Schliemann, A. c. D., Carraher, D. W., & Brizuela, B. M. (2007). *Bringing out the algebraic character of arithmetic.* Mahwah, NJ: Lawrence Erlbaum Associates.

Schoenfeld, A. H. (2008). Algebra in the early grades. In J. J. Kaput, D. W. Carraher & M. L. Blanton (Eds.), (pp. 479–510). Mahwah, NJ: Lawrence Erlbaum Associates.

Schwartz, S. (2004). Explorations in graphing with prekindergarten children. In B. Clarke, D. Clark et al. (Eds.), *International perspectives on learning and teaching mathematics* (pp. 83–97). Goteborg, Sweden: National Centre for Mathematics Education.

Schweinhart, L. J., & Weikart, D. P. (1988). Education for young children living in poverty: Child-initiated learning or teacher-directed instruction? *The Elementary School Journal, 89*, 212–225.

Schweinhart, L. J., & Weikart, D. P. (1997). The High/Scope curriculum comparison study through age 23. *Early Childhood Research Quarterly, 12*, 117–143.

Scott, L. F., & Neufeld, H. (1976). Concrete instruction in elementary school mathematics: Pictorial vs. manipulative. *School Science and Mathematics, 76*, 68–72.

Secada, W. G. (1992). Race, ethnicity, social class, language, and achievement in mathematics. In D. A. Grouws (Ed.), *Handbook of research on mathematics teaching and learning* (pp. 623–660). New York: Macmillan.

Senk, S. L., & Thompson, D. R. (2003). *Standards-based school mathematics curricula. What are they? What do students learn?* Mahwah, NJ: Lawrence Erlbaum Associates.

Seo, K.-H., & Ginsburg, H. P. (2004). What is developmentally appropriate in early childhood mathematics education? In D. H. Clements, J. Sarama & A.-M. DiBiase (Eds.), *Engaging young children in mathematics: Standards for early childhood mathematics education* (pp. 91–104). Mahwah, NJ: Lawrence Erlbaum Associates.

Shade, D. D. (1994). Computers and young children: Software types, social contexts, gender, age, and emotional responses. *Journal of Computing in Childhood Education, 5*(2), 177–209.

Shade, D. D., Nida, R. E., Lipinski, J. M., & Watson, J. A. (1986). Microcomputers and preschoolers: Working together in a classroom setting. *Computers in the Schools, 3*, 53–61.

Shaw, K., Nelsen, E., & Shen, Y.-L. (2001, April). *Preschool development and subsequent school achievement among Spanish-speaking children from low-income families.* Paper presented at the American Educational Research Association, Seattle, WA.

Shaw, R., Grayson, A., & Lewis, V. (2005). Inhibition, ADHD, and comptuer games: The inhibitory performance of children with ADHD on computerized tasks and games. *Journal of Attention Disorders, 8*, 160–168.

Shepard, L. (2005). Assessment. In L. Darling-Hammond & J. Bransford (Eds.), *Preparing teachers for a changing world* (pp. 275–326). San Francisco: Jossey-Bass.

Sherman, J., Bisanz, J., & Popescu, A. (2007, April). *Tracking the path of change: Failure to success on equivalence problems.* Paper presented at the Society for Research in Child Development, Boston, MA.

Shiffrin, R. M., & Schneider, W. (1984). Controlled and automatic human information processing: II. Perceptual learning, automatic attending, and a general theory. *Psychological Review, 84*, 127–190.

Shonkoff, J. P., & Phillips, D. A. (Eds.). (2000). *From neurons to neighborhoods: The science of early childhood development.* Washington, DC: National Academy Press.

Shrock, S. A., Matthias, M., Anastasoff, J., Vensel, C., & Shaw, S. (1985). Examining the effects of the microcomputer on a real world class: A naturalistic study. Anaheim, CA: Association for Educational Communications and Technology.

Sicilian, S. P. (1988). Development of counting strategies in congenitally blind children. *Journal of Visual Impairment & Blindness*, 331–335.

Siegler, R. S. (1993). Adaptive and non-adaptive characteristics of low income children's strategy use. In L. A. Penner, G. M. Batsche, H. M. Knoff & D. L. Nelson (Eds.), *Contributions of psychology to science and mathematics education* (pp. 341–366). Washington, DC: American Psychological Association.

Siegler, R. S. (1995). How does change occur: A microgenetic study of number conservation. *Cognitive Psychology, 28*, 255–273.

Siegler, R. S., & Booth, J. L. (2004). Development of numerical estimation in young children. *Child Development, 75*, 428–444.

Silverman, I. W., York, K., & Zuidema, N. (1984). Area-matching strategies used by young children. *Journal of Experimental Child Psychology, 38*, 464–474.

Silvern, S. B., Countermine, T. A., & Williamson, P. A. (1988). Young children's interaction with a microcomputer. *Early Child Development and Care, 32*, 23–35.

Slovin, H. (2007, April). *Revelations from counting: A window to conceptual understanding.* Paper presented at the Research Presession of the 85th Annual Meeting of the National Council of Teachers of Mathematics, Atlanta, GA.

Sonnenschein, S., Baker, L., Moyer, A., & LeFevre, S. (2005, April). *Parental beliefs about children's reading and math development and relations with subsequent achievement.* Paper presented at the Biennial Meeting of the Society for Research in Child Development, Atlanta, GA.

Sophian, C. (2002). Learning about what fits: Preschool children's reasoning about effects of object size. *Journal for Research in Mathematics Education, 33*, 290–302.

Sophian, C. (2004a). A prospective developmental perspective on early mathematics instruction. In D. H. Clements, J. Sarama & A.-M. DiBiase (Eds.), *Engaging young children in mathematics: Standards for early childhood mathematics education* (pp. 253–266). Mahwah, NJ: Lawrence Erlbaum Associates.

Sophian, C. (2004b). Mathematics for the future: Developing a Head Start curriculum to support mathematics learning. *Early Childhood Research Quarterly, 19*, 59–81.

Sophian, C., & Adams, N. (1987). Infants' understanding of numerical transformations. *British Journal of Educational Psychology, 5*, 257–264.

Sowder, J. T. (1992a). Estimation and number sense. In D. A. Grouws (Ed.), *Handbook of research on mathematics teaching and learning* (pp. 371–389). New York: Macmillan.

Sowder, J. T. (1992b). Making sense of numbers in school mathematics. In G. Leinhardt, R. Putman & R. A. Hattrup (Eds.), *Analysis of arithmetic for mathematics teaching.* Mahwah, NJ: Lawrence Erlbaum Associates.

Sowell, E. J. (1989). Effects of manipulative materials in mathematics instruction. *Journal for Research in Mathematics Education, 20*, 498–505.

Spelke, E. S. (2003). What makes us smart? Core knowledge and natural language. In D. Genter & S. Goldin-Meadow (Eds.), *Language in mind* (pp. 277–311). Cambridge, MA: MIT Press.

Spitler, M. E., Sarama, J., & Clements, D. H. (2003). *A preschooler's understanding of "Triangle:" A case study.* Paper presented at the 81st Annual Meeting of the National Council of Teachers of Mathematics.

Starkey, P., & Klein, A. (1992). Economic and cultural influence on early mathematical development. In F. L. Parker, R. Robinson, S. Sombrano, C. Piotrowski, J. Hagen, S. Randoph & A. Baker (Eds.), *New directions in child and family research: Shaping Head Start in the 90s* (pp. 440). New York: National Council of Jewish Women.

Starkey, P., Klein, A., Chang, I., Qi, D., Lijuan, P., & Yang, Z. (1999, April). *Environmental supports for young children's mathematical development in China and the United States.* Paper presented at the Society for Research in Child Development, Albuquerque, NM.

Starkey, P., Klein, A., & Wakeley, A. (2004). Enhancing young children's mathematical knowledge through a pre-kindergarten mathematics intervention. *Early Childhood Research Quarterly, 19*, 99–120.

Steen, L. A. (1988). The science of patterns. *Science, 240*, 611–616.

Steffe, L. P. (1991). Operations that generate quantity. *Learning and Individual Differences, 3*, 61–82.

Steffe, L. P. (2004). *PSSM* from a constructivist perspective. In D. H. Clements, J. Sarama & A.-M. DiBiase (Eds.), *Engaging young children in mathematics: Standards for early childhood mathematics education* (pp. 221–251). Mahwah, NJ: Lawrence Erlbaum Associates.

Steffe, L. P., & Cobb, P. (1988). *Construction of arithmetical meanings and strategies.* New York: Springer-Verlag.

Steffe, L. P., & Olive, J. (2002). Design and use of computer tools for interactive mathematical activity (TIMA). *Journal of Educational Computing Research, 27*(1&2), 55–76.

Steffe, L. P., Thompson, P. W., & Richards, J. (1982). Children's counting in arithmetical problem solving. In T. P. Carpenter, J. M. Moser & T. A. Romberg (Eds.), *Addition and subtraction: A cognitive perspective.* Mahwah, NJ: Lawrence Erlbaum Associates.

Steffe, L. P., & Wiegel, H. G. (1994). Cognitive play and mathematical learning in computer microworlds. *Journal of Research in Childhood Education, 8*(2), 117–131.

Stenmark, J. K., Thompson, V., & Cossey, R. (1986). *Family math.* Berkeley, CA: Lawrence Hall of Science, University of California.

Stephan, M., & Clements, D. H. (2003). Linear, area, and time measurement in prekindergarten to grade 2. In D. H. Clements (Ed.), *Learning and teaching measurement: 65th Yearbook* (pp. 3–16). Reston, VA: National Council of Teachers of Mathematics.

Stevenson, H. W., & Newman, R. S. (1986). Long-term prediction of achievement and attitudes in mathematics and reading. *Child Development, 57*, 646–659.

Stewart, R., Leeson, N., & Wright, R. J. (1997). Links between early arithmetical knowledge and early space and measurement knowledge: An exploratory study. In F. Biddulph & K. Carr (Eds.), *Proceedings of the Twentieth Annual Conference of the Mathematics Education Research Group of Australasia* (Vol. 2, pp. 477–484). Hamilton, New Zealand: MERGA.

Stigler, J. W., Fuson, K. C., Ham, M., & Kim, M. S. (1986). An analysis of addition and subtraction word problems in American and Soviet elementary mathematics textbooks. *Cognition and Instruction, 3*, 153–171.

Stiles, J., & Nass, R. (1991). Spatial grouping activity in young children with congenital right or left hemisphere brain injury. *Brain and Cognition, 15*, 201–222.

Stipek, D. J., & Ryan, R. H. (1997). Economically disadvantaged preschoolers: Ready to learn but further to go. *Developmental Psychology, 33*, 711–723.

Stone, T. T., III. (1996). The academic impact of classroom computer usage upon middle-class primary grade level elementary school children. *Dissertation Abstracts International, 57–06*, 2450.

Suydam, M. N. (1986). Manipulative materials and achievement. *Arithmetic Teacher, 33*(6), 10, 32.

Swigger, K. M., & Swigger, B. K. (1984). Social patterns and computer use among preschool children. *AEDS Journal, 17*, 35–41.

Sylva, K., Melhuish, E., Sammons, P., Siraj-Blatchford, I., & Taggart, B. (2005). *The effective provision of pre-school education [EPPE] project: A longitudinal study funded by the DfEE (1997–2003).* London: EPPE Project, Institute of Education, University of London.

Tharp, R. G., & Gallimore, R. (1988). *Rousing minds to life: Teaching, learning, and schooling in social contexts.* New York: Cambridge University Press.

Thirumurthy, V. (2003). *Children's cognition of geometry and spatial thinking—A cultural process.* Unpublished doctoral dissertation, University of Buffalo, State University of New York.

Thomas, B. (1982). *An abstract of kindergarten teachers' elicitation and utilization of children's prior knowledge in the teaching of shape concepts:* Unpublished manuscript, School of Education, Health, Nursing, and Arts Professions, New York University.

Thomas, G., & Tagg, A. (2004). *An evaluation of the Early Numeracy Project 2003.* Wellington, Australia: Ministry of Education.

Thomas, G., & Ward, J. (2001). *An evaluation of the Count Me In Too pilot project.* Wellington, New Zealand: Ministry of Education.

Thompson, P. W. (1992). Notations, conventions, and constraints: Contributions to effective use of concrete materials in elementary mathematics. *Journal for Research in Mathematics Education, 23*, 123–147.

Thompson, P. W., & Thompson, A. G. (1990). Salient aspects of experience with concrete manipulatives. In F. Hitt (Ed.), *Proceedings of the 14th Annual Meeting of the International Group for the Psychology of Mathematics* (Vol. 3, pp. 337–343). Mexico City: International Group for the Psychology of Mathematics Education.

Thomson, S., Rowe, K., Underwood, C., & Peck, R. (2005). *Numeracy in the early years: Project Good Start.* Camberwell, Victoria, Australia: Australian Council for Educational Research.

Thorton, C. A., Langrall, C. W., & Jones, G. A. (1997). Mathematics instruction for elementary students with learning disabilities. *Journal of Learning Disabilities, 30*, 142–150.

Torbeyns, J., van den Noortgate, W., Ghesquière, P., Verschaffel, L., Van de Rijt, B. A. M., & van Luit, J. E. H. (2002). Development of early numeracy in 5- to 7-year-old children: A comparison between Flanders and the Netherlands. *Educational Research and Evaluation. An International Journal on Theory and Practice, 8*, 249–275.

Touchette, E., Petit, D., Séguin, J. R., Boivin, M., Tremblay, R. E., & Jacques Y. Montplaisir. (2007). Associations between sleep duration patterns and behavioral/cognitive functioning at school entry. *Sleep, 30*, 1213–1219.

Tournaki, N. (2003). The differential effects of teaching addition through strategy instruction versus drill and practice to students with and without learning disabilities. *Journal of Learning Disabilities, 36*(5), 449–458.

Tudge, J. R. H., & Doucet, F. (2004). Early mathematical experiences: Observing young Black and White children's everyday activities. *Early Childhood Research Quarterly, 19*, 21–39.

Turkle, S. (1997). Seeing through computers: Education in a culture of simulation. *The American Prospect, 31*, 76–82.

Turner, R. C., & Ritter, G. W. (2004, April). *Does the impact of preschool childcare on cognition and behavior persist throughout the elementary years?* Paper presented at the American Educational Research Association, San Diego, CA.

Tyler, R. W. (1949). *Basic principles of curriculum and instruction.* Chicago: University of Chicago Press.

Ungar, S., Blades, M., & Spencer, C. (1997). Teaching visually impaired children to make distance judgments from a tactile map. *Journal of Visual Impairment and Blindness, 91*, 163–174.

Uttal, D. H., Marzolf, D. P., Pierroutsakos, S. L., Smith, C. M., Troseth, G. L., Scudder, K. V., et al. (1997). Seeing through symbols: The development of children's understanding of symbolic relations. In O. N. Saracho & B. Spodek (Eds.), *Multiple perspectives on play in early childhood education* (pp. 59–79). Albany, NY: State University of New York Press.

Uttal, D. H., Scudder, K. V., & DeLoache, J. S. (1997). Manipulatives as symbols: A new perspective on the use of concrete objects to teach mathematics. *Journal of Applied Developmental Psychology, 18*, 37–54.

Van de Rijt, B. A. M., & Van Luit, J. E. H. (1999). Milestones in the development of infant numeracy. *Scandinavian Journal of Psychology, 40*, 65–71.

Van de Rijt, B. A. M., Van Luit, J. E. H., & Pennings, A. H. (1999). The construction of the Utrecht early mathematical competence scales. *Educational and Psychological Measurement, 59*, 289–309.

van Oers, B. (1994). Semiotic activity of young children in play: The construction and use of schematic representations. *European Early Childhood Education Research Journal, 2*, 19–33.

van Oers, B. (1996). Are you sure? Stimulating mathematical thinking during young children's play. *European Early Childhood Education Research Journal, 4*, 71–87.

van Oers, B. (2003). Learning resources in the context of play. Promoting effective learning in early childhood. *European Early Childhood Education Research Journal, 11*, 7–25.

Varela, F. J. (1999). *Ethical know-how: Action, wisdom, and cognition.* Stanford, CA: Stanford University Press.

Vergnaud, G. (1978). The acquisition of arithmetical concepts. In E. Cohors-Fresenborg & I. Wachsmuth (Eds.), *Proceedings of the 2nd Conference of the International Group for the Psychology of Mathematics Education* (pp. 344–355). Osnabruck, Germany.

Verschaffel, L., Greer, B., & De Corte, E. (2007). Whole number concepts and operations. In F. K. Lester, Jr. (Ed.), *Second handbook of research on mathematics teaching and learning* (pp. 557–628). New York: Information Age Publishing.

Votruba-Drzal, E., & Chase, L. (2004). Child care and low-income children's development: Direct and moderated effects. *Child Development, 75*, 296–312.

Vurpillot, E. (1976). *The visual world of the child.* New York: International Universities Press.

Vygotsky, L. S. (1934/1986). *Thought and language.* Cambridge, MA: MIT Press.

Vygotsky, L. S. (1978). Internalization of higher psychological functions. In M. Cole, V. John-Steiner, S. Scribner & E. Souberman (Eds.), *Mind in society* (pp. 52–57). Cambridge, MA: Harvard University Press.

Waber, D. P., de Moor, C., Forbes, P., Almli, C. R., Botteron, K., Leonard, G., et al. (2007?). The NIH MRI study of normal brain development: Performance of a population based sample of healthy children aged 6 to 18 years on a neuropsychological battery. *Journal of the International Neuropsychological Society, 18.*

Wadlington, E., & Burns, J. M. (1993). Instructional practices within preschool/kindergarten gifted programs. *Journal for the Education of the Gifted, 17*(1), 41–52.

Wagner, S. W., & Walters, J. (1982). A longitudinal analysis of early number concepts: From numbers to number. In G. E. Forman (Ed.), *Action and Thought* (pp. 137–161). New York: Academic Press.

Wakeley, A. (2005, April). *Mathematical knowledge of very low birth weight pre-kindergarten children.* Paper presented at the Biennial Meeting of the Society for Research in Child Development, Atlanta, GA.

Walston, J. T., & West, J. (2004). Full-day and half-day kindergarten in the United States: Findings from the Early Childhood Longitudinal Study, Kindergarten Class 1998–99. (NCES 2004–078).

Walston, J. T., West, J., & Rathbun, A. H. (2005). *Do the greater academic gains made by full-day kindergarten children persist through third grade?.* Paper presented at the Annual Meeting of the American Educational Research Association, Montreal, Canada.

Wang, J., & Lin, E. (2005). Comparative studies on U.S. and Chinese mathematics learning and the implications for standards-based mathematics teaching reform. *Educational Researcher, 34*(5), 3–13.

Watson, J. A., & Brinkley, V. M. (1990/91). Space and premathematic strategies young children adopt in initial Logo problem solving. *Journal of Computing in Childhood Education, 2*, 17–29.

Watson, J. A., Lange, G., & Brinkley, V. M. (1992). Logo mastery and spatial problem-solving by young children: Effects of Logo language training, route-strategy training, and learning styles on immediate learning and transfer. *Journal of Educational Computing Research, 8*, 521–540.

Wellman, H. M., & Miller, K. F. (1986). Thinking about nothing: Development of concepts of zero. *British Journal of Developmental Psychology, 4*, 31–42.

West, J., Denton, K., & Reaney, L. (2001). The kindergarten year: Findings from the Early Childhood Longitudinal Study, kindergarten class of 1998–1999. 2004, from http://nces.ed.gov/pubsearch/pubsinfo.asp?pubid=2002125.

Wheatley, G. (1996). *Quick draw: Developing spatial sense in mathematics.* Tallahassee, FL: Mathematics Learning.

Wiegel, H. G. (1998). Kindergarten students' organizations of counting in joint counting tasks and the emergence of cooperation. *Journal for Research in Mathematics Education, 29*, 202–224.

Wilensky, U. (1991). Abstract mediations on the concrete and concrete implications for mathematics education. In I. Harel & S. Papert (Eds.), *Constructionism* (pp. 193–199). Norwood, NJ: Ablex.

Wilkinson, L. A., Martino, A., & Camilli, G. (1994). Groups that work: Social factors in elementary students mathematics problem solving. In J. E. H. Van Luit (Ed.), *Research on learning and instruction of mathematics in kindergarten and primary school* (pp. 75–105). Doetinchem, the Netherlands: Graviant.

Wilson, A. J., Dehaene, S., Pinel, P., Revkin, S. K., Cohen, L., & Cohen, D. K. (2006). Principles underlying the design of "The Number Race", an adaptive computer game for remediation of dyscalculia. *Behavioral and Brain Functions, 2:19.*

Wilson, A. J., Revkin, S. K., Cohen, D. K., Cohen, L., & Dehaene, S. (2006). An open trial assessment of "The Number Race", an adaptive computer game for remediation of dyscalculia. *Behavioral and Brain Functions, 2:20.*

Winton, P., Buysse, V., Bryant, D., Clifford, D., Early, D., & Little, L. (2005, Spring). NCEDL Pre-kindergarten study. *Early Developments, 9.*

Wong, V. C., Cook, T. D., Barnett, W. S., & Jung, K. (in press). An effectiveness-based evaluation of five state pre-kindergarten programs. *Journal of Policy Anlaysis and Management.*

Wood, K., & Frid, S. (2005). Early childhood numeracy in a multiage setting. *Mathematics Education Research Journal, 16*(3), 80–99.

Woodward, J. (2004). Mathematics education in the United States: Past to present. *Journal of Learning Disabilities, 37*, 16–31.

Wright, A. (1987). The process of microtechnological innovation in two primary schools: A case study of teachers' thinking. *Educational Review, 39*(2), 107–115.

Wright, B. (1991). What number knowledge is possessed by children beginning the kindergarten year of school? *Mathematics Education Research Journal, 3*(1), 1–16.

Wright, R. J. (2003). A mathematics recovery: Program of intervention in early number learning. *Australian Journal of Learning Disabilities, 8*(4), 6–11.

Wright, R. J., Martland, J., Stafford, A. K., & Stanger, G. (2002). *Teaching number: Advancing children's skills and strategies.* London: Paul Chapman Publications/Sage.

Wright, R. J., Stanger, G., Cowper, M., & Dyson, R. (1994). A study of the numerical development of 5-year-olds and 6-year-olds. *Educational Studies in Mathematics, 26,* 25–44.

Wright, R. J., Stanger, G., Cowper, M., & Dyson, R. (1996). First-graders' progress in an experimental mathematics recovery program. In J. Mulligan & M. Mitchelmore (Eds.), *Research in early number learning* (pp. 55–72). Adelaide, Australia: AAMT.

Wright, R. J., Stanger, G., Stafford, A. K., & Martland, J. (2006). *Teaching number in the classroom with 4–8 year olds.* London: Paul Chapman Publications/Sage.

Wu, H. (2007). *Whole numbers, fractions, and rational numbers.* Berkeley, CA: University of California.

Wynn, K. (1992). Addition and subtraction by human infants. *Nature, 358,* 749–750.

Xin, J. F. (1999). Computer-assisted cooperative learning in integrated classrooms for students with and without disabilities. *Information Technology in Childhood Education Annual, 1*(1), 61–78.

Yackel, E., & Wheatley, G. H. (1990). Promoting visual imagery in young pupils. *Arithmetic Teacher, 37*(6), 52–58.

Yost, N. J. M. (1998). Computers, kids, and crayons: A comparative study of one kindergarten's emergent literacy behaviors. *Dissertation Abstracts International, 59–08,* 2847.

Young-Loveridge, J. M. (1989a). The development of children's number concepts: The first year of school. *Australian Journal of Early Childhood, 21,* 16–20.

Young-Loveridge, J. M. (1989b). The development of children's number concepts: The first year of school. *New Zealand Journal of Educational Studies, 24*(1), 47–64.

Young-Loveridge, J. M. (1989c). The relationship between children's home experiences and their mathematical skills on entry to school. *Early Child Development and Care, 43,* 43–59.

Young-Loveridge, J. M. (2004). Effects on early numeracy of a program using number books and games. *Early Childhood Research Quarterly, 19,* 82–98.

Ysseldyke, J., Spicuzza, R., Kosciolek, S., Teelucksingh, E., Boys, C., & Lemkuil, A. (2003). Using a curriculum-based instructional management system to enhance math achievement in urban schools. *Journal of Education for Students Placed at Risk, 8*(2), 247–265.

Zelazo, P. D., Reznick, J. S., & Piñon, D. E. (1995). Response control and the execution of verbal rules. *Developmental Psychology, 31,* 508–517.

Zur, O., & Gelman, R. (2004). Young children can add and subtract by predicting and checking. *Early Childhood Research Quarterly, 19,* 121–137.

Index